# Germany
## IN THE
## TWENTIETH
## CENTURY

# Germany
# IN THE
# TWENTIETH
# CENTURY

# DAVID CHILDS

ICON EDITIONS
*An Imprint of* HarperCollins *Publishers*

# Acknowledgement

I want to express my thanks to Mrs Helga Tallon, MA, of the Nottingham University of for helping me correct the manuscript for this book. Obviously, any errors, omissions or shortcomings which remain, are entirely the author's responsibility.

ISBN: 0–06–430862–6 (Hardcover)
      0–06–430221–0 (Paperback)

Library of Congress Catalog No. 91–58394

# Contents

# Preface to the third edition

I was very pleased when Batsford asked me to prepare a third edition of *Germany Since 1918*. However, after considering all that had happened in Germany since the appearance of the second edition in 1980 we decided something more was needed than just another chapter. In addition, as the century is drawing to a close, it seemed appropriate to sketch the developments over the whole 90 years or so. *Germany Since 1918* has been transformed therefore into the present volume. In it I have tried to break new ground and give both the academic and the general reader as much information as possible in what is, considering the dramatic nine decades it covers, a relatively small book. I hope that chapter 1 goes some way to revising the widely held, wholly negative, view of pre-1914 Germany and will promote a more balanced image of a time when Germany and Britain (and the USA) were friends as well as rivals.

One innovation is a statistical section at the end of the book and brief biographies of 152 Germans. I have tried to make this biographical list representative both of the different periods and, although this is primarily a political book, of Germans other than politicians who have become public figures. The limitations of space have forced me to leave out many other Germans equally deserving of attention. No doubt some of those included will lose their present significance with the passage of time.

Because *Germany Since 1918* was so well received I have left much of the original material intact. However, I have made some amendments where new information has come to light and added new material where I felt there were gaps. Given the astonishing changes since 1989 and given Germany's growing role, it is natural that the book gives much attention to these last few years and to the contemporary situation. In a book like this errors are bound to creep in and, as in the past, I would be glad to hear from any reader who discovers any. Equally, I would be most pleased to hear from readers who have found the book useful.

I hope the book makes a small contribution to our understanding of the Germans, their achievements, trials and tragedies and to their successes over the past 45 years in building a democratic state in the new Europe.

*David Childs*
*Nottingham, February 1991*

# Abbreviations

| | | | |
|---|---|---|---|
| ADF | Action for Democratic Freedom | EC | European Community |
| BFD | League of Free Democrats | EEC | European Economic Community (forerunner of EC) |
| BHE | League of Expellees and those without Rights | FDGB | Free German Trade Union Federation (of DDR) |
| BfV | Federal Office for the Protection of the Constitution (similar to US FBI or British MI5) | FDJ | Free German Youth |
| | | FDP | Free Democratic Party |
| | | Gestapo | Secret State Police |
| | | HJ | Hitler Youth |
| BND | Federal Intelligence Service | KPD | Communist Party of Germany |
| BP | Bavarian Party | LDPD | Liberal Democratic Party of Germany |
| BUU | Citizens' Initiative for Lower Elbe Environmental Protection | INF | Intermediate-Range Nuclear Forces |
| BVP | Bavarian People's Party | NATO | North Atlantic Treaty Organisation |
| CDU | Christian Democratic Union | NDPD | National Democratic Party of Germany (DDR) |
| CPSU | Communist Party of the Soviet Union | NPD | National Democratic Party of Germany (West Germany) |
| CSCE | Conference on Security and Co-operation in Europe | NSDAP | National Socialist German Workers' Party |
| CSU | Christian Social Union | NVA | National People's Army (armed forces of the DDR) |
| DA | Democratic Awakening | |
| DBD | Democratic Farmers (Peasants') Party of Germany | PDS | Party of Democratic Socialism |
| DDR | German Democratic Republic | REP | The Republicans |
| | | SA | Storm Detachment (of NSDAP) |
| DFD | Democratic Women's Federation of Germany | SDAP | Social Democratic Workers' Party |
| DFU | German Peace Union | SDP | Social Democratic Party (in the DDR) |
| DGB | German Trade Union Federation | SED | Socialist Unity Party of Germany |
| DKP | German Communist Party | |
| DKP | German Conservative Party | SPD | Social Democratic Party of Germany |
| DNVP | German National People's Party | SRP | Socialist Reich Party |
| DP | German Party | SSD | State Security Service (of the DDR) |
| DRP | German Reich Party | |
| DSU | German Social Union | SS | Defence Squadron (of NSDAP) |
| DVP | German People's Party | | |

German Empire
1871-1918

Boundary of German
Confederation (1815–1866)

RUSSIA

DENMARK

NETHERLANDS

BELGIUM

FRANCE

SWITZERLAND

AUSTRIA-HUNGARY

Memel
Königsberg
Danzig
Thorn
Bialystok
Warsaw
Vistula
Kalisch
Posen
Breslau
Kattowitz
Cracow
Kolberg
Stettin
Küstrin
Frankfurt
Oder
Neiße
Görlitz
Prague
Rostock
Berlin
Magdeburg
Dresden
Eger
Copenhagen
Ribe
Flensburg
Lübeck
Lüneburg
Elbe
Leipzig
Erfurt
Hamburg
Bremen
Hannover
Braunschwg.
Cassel
Oldenbg.
Groningen
Amsterd.
Münster
Düsseldrf.
Köln
Aachen
Brussels
Liège
Meuse
Verdun
Lux.
Luxembg.
Mainz
Frankfurt
Main
Würzburg
Nürnberg
Rhön
Saarbrücken
1871
Strasbourg
Stuttgart
Toul
Regensbg.
Donau
Passau
München
Konstanz
Innsbruck
Besançon
Bern
Basel
Salzburg
Vienna
Buda
Graz
Klagenfurt

**Germany within the borders of 1937**

*Map of Germany showing the Länder, with the old frontier of 1949–90*

# — 1 —

# Germany before 1918

The spy thriller *The Riddle of the Sands*, by the Anglo-Irish writer Erskine Childers, was first published in 1903. It was the story of two Englishmen who used a yachting holiday off the northwest coast of Germany to engage in espionage. They discover the Germans rehearsing an invasion of England. The book has remained popular up to the 1990s and, for many of its post-1945 readers, it represents one of the few glimpses they are likely to have of the forgotten world of the Kaiser's Germany. It must have contributed greatly to the negative image, in so far as any image of it exists at all in the English-speaking world, of the German Reich between 1871 and 1918. That image is usually one of marching, robot-like soldiers wearing spiked helmets and commanded by arrogant and often sadistic officers.

The growing German fleet was a cause for concern in Britain but Germany had no plans to invade the British Isles. It had built up the most efficient army in Europe, an army which had a great influence on German society, and was regarded by many in Britain, the USA and elsewhere as, in most respects, the leading European state.

## The German contribution to the U S A and Britain

Before 1914 British and American reformers often referred to the German example when they sought to initiate improvements in their own societies. Between 1820 and 1979 more immigrants arrived in the U S A from Germany than from any other country. Other German-speakers arrived from Austria. Some of them were political refugees who fled the repression which followed the failed 1848 revolution or Bismarck's anti-Socialist laws (in force 1878–90). Some emigrated as a result of the *Kulturkampf* against the Catholic church. Many others simply went in search of a better standard of living as well as a little more freedom. They built up flourishing German-speaking communities as far apart as the cities of New Braunfels and Fredericksburg in

Texas and those like Cincinnati, Chicago and Milwaukee in the Mid-West. In such places German was taught in the schools and German-style institutions were proudly developed and preserved. They gave the U S A much, from beer brewing, Levi Jeans and Heinz '57 varieties' to great orchestras, opera, and libraries. Some of the U S A's most prestigious universities such as Johns Hopkins, Cornell and Chicago were established following the German model, as were the graduate schools of Yale and Harvard.

Britain had no such large German communities but German academics, scientists and businessmen played an important part in the development of education, trade and industry in Britain before 1914. At the top of British society the royal family was intimately connected with Germany. Between 1714 and 1901 the House of Hanover provided the British monarchs. The last of them, Queen Victoria, married Prince Albert, of the house of Saxe-Coburg and Gotha, a very minor German state. Wilhelm II, German emperor 1888–1918, was her grandson and nephew of Edward VII, British monarch, 1901–10.

The pages of *Hansard*, the official report of the proceedings in the British parliament, reveal the great interest in Germany before 1914. While the German fleet bulked large, much was also said about German education, social welfare, railways, local government, industry and technology. In 1901 Sir Charles Dilke raised his voice to deplore the lack of progress made in reducing plumbism (lead poisoning) in the British china and earthenware industry compared with Germany. In that same year a number of Irish and other MPs compared the sorry state of higher education in British-ruled Ireland with the situation in Germany. They attacked the lack of opportunities for Catholics to study in Ireland compared with those for Catholics in Protestant-led Germany. The Liberal, R. B. Haldane, commented in the same debate:

> The success of the industries of large towns depends upon the application of skill, knowledge and science. Any of the small insignificant German towns would put Belfast in the shade in this respect.

Belfast was then even more important as the key industrial city of Ireland than it is today. Haldane's remarks applied equally to the poor situation in England and Wales, compared with Germany. Fear of German competition was already leading to some improvements. In 1901 some MPs criticised the fact that the British army used German artillery and the navy had bought Duerr water-tube boilers for some of its ships. These purchases were just two of many signs that

Britain had lost its place as the world's leading industrial state and had been overtaken, in many fields, by Germany. The Reich was second only to the United States.

## German industrial growth

From being backward in industrial terms in the first half of the nineteenth century, Germany swept ahead in the second half and especially after 1871. Germany had overcome a number of handicaps to achieve this. Except for potash it lacked raw material reserves. Its iron ore was poor, and inferior brown coal had to be used because of the limited amount of hard coal.

Many of its industrial centres were far from the sea. But the removal of internal barriers within Germany and the building of external ones helped to stimulate and protect home industries. The indemnity paid by France after its defeat in the war of 1870–1 helped, and the enthusiasm caused by the creation of the Reich in 1871 was an important psychological factor. The movement of population from the land to the towns was both a result of the industrial upsurge and helped to cause it. The same was true of technical innovation. Finally, Germany, through its extremely well-developed education system was able to provide a skilled labour force and to initiate change based on new technologies.

Fear of German competition had led Britain in 1887 to impose a 'Made in Germany' stamp on German goods imported into Britain. This gradually became an advantage to German exporters as their goods, from toys to musical instruments, cutlery to furniture, motor cars to machines, became recognised for their high quality. Among the inventions Germany gave the world before 1914 were: modern printing and paperback books, fluorescent lighting, refrigeration, synthetic rubber, artificial fertilisers, the concept of vitamins, the x-ray machine, precision optics, the Geiger counter, the Diesel engine, and the motor cars of Daimler and Benz. The engineer Werner von Siemens built the first electric train and electric dynamo and founded the company which still bears his name. The photographer Josef Albert developed the practical foundations of photographic printing and Johann Christian Eberle, Mayor of Nossen, started the first giro bank in 1909.

## German education

Between 1901 and 1919 Germans were awarded 18 Nobel Prizes in science—more than those awarded to scientists of any other nation. This was no accident nor was it the result of native German brilliance. It was the outcome of Germany's investment in education over a long period. Britain's lack of such investment was undoubtedly an important factor in its industrial decline.

Influenced by the German example the M P H. H. Mundella attempted in 1870 to have compulsory education introduced in Britain. He failed, Conservative critics claiming such a move would be un-British. Ten years later, as Vice-President of the Board of Education (forerunner of the Ministry of Education), he persuaded a majority to vote for such a measure. Prussia, the main German state, proclaimed compulsory school attendance by royal decrees in 1716 and 1717. The small state of Weimar introduced it in 1619. No doubt these, and similar decrees were not fully implemented until some time later, no doubt the teaching was not always very effective, but there can be no doubt either that most Germans were receiving some kind of meaningful instruction long before the bulk of the population in England, Wales and Ireland.

Germany's system of technical education came to be admired even more than its elementary schools and its long-established universities. At the top of this system was the Technical University at Charlottenburg in Berlin. The T U Charlottenburg was proclaimed a full university by the Kaiser in 1899. There were ten other such technical universities most of them founded in the first half of the nineteenth century as vocational schools. Below them was a vast network of lesser institutions which produced the managers, supervisors, foremen and skilled workers. Finally, there were the continuation schools of more recent origin. They were under local control. In many parts of the country evening attendance was compulsory for two or three years after completion of the *Volksschule* (elementary school). The pupils were in the 14 to 18 age group and the subjects closely related to the needs of industry. In Britain and America attempts were made to imitate these developments on a very limited scale.

German education faced a variety of critics, both at home and abroad. Some criticised the patriotic indoctrination, others claimed there was too much learning by rote. But such criticisms could have been made about all educational systems at the time. H. M. Felkin, a Nottingham man whose business was in Chemnitz, observed in his pioneering *Technical Education In A Saxon Town* (1881): 'Everything is taught ... in such a manner, that it is mentally grasped by the pupil, and there is a minimum of learning by rote.' He urged his native city to emulate Chemnitz and helped to create the climate of opinion there which led to the setting up of a university college in 1881. Imperial College in London was also an attempt to imitate the technical universities of Germany.

The Kaiser's Germany was widely admired for its successful encouraging of the arts. The Labour M P John Burn commented in the British House of Commons in 1901 that the Kaiser 'spent an enormous proportion of his salary in art patronage ... a practice that might well be followed by those in high places here'. Every German state prided itself on its opera, theatre and orchestral concerts. Richard Wagner until his death in 1883, Johannes Brahms and Richard Strauss, were the great cultural ambassadors of the Reich. The Silesian playwright Gerhart Hauptmann gained the Nobel Prize in 1912 for his contribution to literature, the fourth German to do so since its inception in 1901. Far more significant internationally, however, was to be Thomas Mann whose epic family chronicle *Buddenbrooks* appeared in 1901. His Nobel Prize came in 1929. The major intellectual and philosophical presence brooding over the period was however that of Friedrich Nietzsche, who went mad in 1889 and died of syphilis in Weimar in 1900. The son of a pastor, he became a self-proclaimed anti-Christ, atheist and nihilist. Appointed professor of classical philology at Basel University at the age of 24, he never liked the job. Influenced by Friedrich Albert Lange's *History of Materialism* he took up Darwinian ideas, ethical materialism and the free market economics of the Manchester School. He favoured an intellectual hierarchy but was neither anti-semitic nor a German nationalist. His 'superman' was a European intellectual rather than a German warrior. His ideas appealed to the educated liberal bourgeoisie who resented church and aristocracy but feared the rise of the mob, represented in their eyes by the Social Democratic Party of Germany (S P D).

## The first welfare state and the S P D

Otto von Bismarck, Chancellor of the German Reich 1871–90, and before that Chancellor of Prussia, also feared the S P D. Bismarck sought to halt the rise of Social Democracy by introducing welfare measures which, he hoped, would take the wind out of the S P D's sails. During his chancellorship four main laws were introduced, setting up factory inspection (1878); sickness insurance (1883); accident insurance (1884); and old age pensions and pensions for the disabled (1889). The

British Liberal government studied the German example when it passed laws in 1905, 1909 and 1911 covering the same areas. Under successive chancellors these measures were extended before 1914 to include regulation of child and female labour and the recognition of Sunday as a rest day.

The S P D rejected these measures on the grounds that they were an attempt to lure the workers into accepting a crust when they could have the whole loaf which, the S P D believed, they had baked anyway. Founded in 1875 at Gotha, the Socialist Workers' Party of Germany (S A P D) represented the coming together of two earlier socialist parties. In the new party the followers of Marx and Engels got the upper hand over those of Ferdinand Lassalle. The S A P D preached the inevitability of Socialism and its unalterable opposition to the Kaiser and the German state. It thrived on the problems of the growing working class as Germany industrialised. Bismarck's anti-socialist laws restricted the S A P D's activities but they did not entirely rule out Social Democrats being elected to the parliament, the Reichstag. The party grew nevertheless. The S A P D changed its name to Social Democratic Party of Germany (S P D) in 1890, the year the anti-socialist laws expired: it emerged from the elections as the biggest single party, and came to attract over one third of the voters. In the last elections of the Kaiser's Germany, in 1912, it gained 34.8 per cent of the votes and 110 seats out of 397. Although it had adopted a Marxist programme at Erfurt in 1891 it was essentially a pacifist parliamentary party. Eduard Bernstein became known as a revisionist because he wanted the S P D to admit its true nature and admit that Marx was wrong in certain essentials. However, S P D leader August Bebel felt that such an admission could undermine the morale of the party faithful in this, the first mass political party in history.

## Catholics and Jews

The final quarter of the nineteenth century saw the triumph of liberal secularism in many European states and a consequent hardening of opposition to the Catholic church. This happened in Germany as well as France and Italy. The Catholics had not opposed German unity as such but would have liked the inclusion of Catholic Austria rather than a 'small' Germany under the hegemony of Protestant Prussia. The proclamation of the dogma of Papal infallibility in 1870 helped to sharpen suspicion of the Catholic church. A number of laws were passed aimed at reducing Catholic influence in Prussia and, where possible, throughout the Reich. The Jesuit Order was banned in 1872, obligatory civil marriage was introduced first in Prussia and then, in 1875, throughout Germany, and control of education was tightened up. These and other measures and press campaigns against the Catholic church became known as the *Kulturkampf* or cultural struggle. Part of the Catholic response was the setting up of a political party to represent their interests—*das Zentrum* or the Centre Party, so-called because it took its seats in the centre of the parliament. In its early days it was led by a Hanoverian aristocrat and former minister of Hanover, Ludwig Windthorst. In 1887 Bismarck reached a compromise with Pope Leo XIII but within Germany the *Kulturkampf* continued in a milder form. The Centre Party's vote reveals to a degree the changing strength of feeling in Catholic circles: 18.6 per cent in 1871; 23.2 in 1881; 18.6 in 1890; 19.7 in 1903; and 16.4 in 1912. In the 1912 election it is believed to have lost votes to the S P D and the Liberals. It had developed a comprehensive social reform programme and its own trade unions in an effort to counter the S P D influence among Catholic workers. It vigorously defended the rights of the German states against the centralising influences of Prussia and Berlin. It attempted to defend the interests of Polish Catholics within the Reich. It also attacked the excesses of German colonialism.

In 1791 revolutionary France was the first European state to emancipate the Jews, granting them all the rights and duties of other citizens. This became a disadvantage for German and other Jews after the defeat of revolutionary/Napoleonic France in 1815. While continuing to be persecuted as the slayers of Christ, they were now linked also with the terror and disorder of the French revolution. Jewish emancipation was adopted by the North German Federation in 1869 and was extended to the German Reich as a whole on its foundation in 1871. Because of the earlier restrictions placed on them the Jews were heavily concentrated in certain trades and professions. In rural areas they were often horse traders, corn merchants, travelling traders and money lenders—all activities which could cause resentment against them from time to time. In the cities they became heavily involved with the stock exchange, retail trade, the theatre, the textile trade and the liberal press and publishing. The crash of the stock market in 1873 exposed them to the anger of many small investors who lost their money. In anti-S P D circles the Jews were regarded with suspicion, since Karl Marx and Lassalle were of Jewish origin as were a number of prominent Social Democrats. At a political level anti-Semitism was organised by Adolf Stöcker in his Christian Social movement. Stöcker was elected to the Reichstag in 1881 and joined the Conservatives, but his movement failed. However, the German Conservatives adopted an anti-Jewish plank as part of their Tivoli Programme in 1892. This was later abandoned. At the intellectual level Heinrich von Treitschke, professor of history and National Liberal member of the Reichstag, 1871–1884, was probably more effective in pressing the anti-Semitic message. Anti-Semitism existed throughout Europe at the time. In Russia and Hungary there were pogroms. In France the Dreyfus affair revealed the strength of anti-Jewish sentiment. In Britain the first immigration control measures were introduced before 1914 to control the flow of Jews from eastern Europe. Anti-Semitism was also widespread in the U S A. On the other hand, Jews did reach the highest levels of society in Germany as well as in France, Britain and elsewhere despite much unofficial discrimination. Albert Ballin, an unbaptised Jew, rose to be head of the great Hamburg-Amerika shipping line and a friend of the Kaiser. Albert Einstein became the symbol of Jewish intellectual achievement, but there were many others in science and the arts such as Max Liebermann, the painter, and Max Reinhardt, the theatre director. If anti-Semitism was alive and well in the Kaiser's Germany, it failed to succeed in an organised political form while Jewish organisations flourished and individual Jews climbed the ladder to success.

## Universal suffrage but unrepresentative government

Election to the parliament of the Reich, the Reichstag, was by secret ballot and universal, male adult suffrage. On the face of it this made the German parliament the most democratic in 1871. Yet the reality was somewhat different. Firstly, the constituencies became more and more unrepresentative, not taking account of the population drift from the conservative rural areas to the more radical towns. Secondly, parliament had only restricted competence. The individual German states retained limited powers and some matters, defence for instance, were only put before the Reichstag at seven yearly intervals. A contemporary American writer, Robert Herndon Fife Jr, in his *The German Empire Between Two Wars*, explained:

> As compared with the American system of parliamentary government with an executive veto, the German government is a dynastic government with a parliamentary veto; as compared with the British system of parliamentary rule through a responsible ministry, the German system provides for parliamentary acquiescence in legislation prepared by ministers responsible to the sovereign alone.

In addition to the Reichstag, there was the Bundesrat (Federal Council) of 58 members consisting of representatives of both the dynasties of the 22 German states and the 3 city states: Bremen, Hamburg and Lübeck. In the Federal Council Prussia held 17 votes, Bavaria 6, Saxony 4, Würrttemberg 4, Baden 3, Hesse 3, Mecklenburg-Schwerin 2, Brunswick 2 and the other 17 states one each. It prepared legislation under the guidance of a ministry appointed by the Kaiser. This was then presented to the Reichstag for acceptance or rejection. To ensure acceptance the Kaiser's Chancellor, who was also Prime Minister of Prussia, built an alliance of the Conservatives with the National Liberals and later, of the Conservatives with the Centre Party, a 'blue-black' alliance. This existed from 1877 to 1906 and again from 1909 to 1912. The Conservatives were divided into two parties: the German Conservative Party (D K P), supported by many of the Protestant upper class in the aristocracy, military, state service, church and big landed interest; and the German Reich Party or 'Free Conservatives' who were more closely associated with the industrial interest. The National Liberals were the more nationalist wing of the Protestant middle class and the left Liberals were drawn from the professions, handicrafts and retail trade. The left Liberals wanted a British-style constitutional monarchy.

## Colonial and naval expansion

In 1906 the government of Chancellor von Bülow failed to get the support of the Centre Party for its repressive measures against the Herero revolt in South-West Africa, a German colony. The S P D, which was regarded as subversive, was also opposed to government colonial policy. The revolt was, nevertheless, crushed by shooting, burning and hanging. Under orders German troops revealed some of the ruthlessness the S S were to display in the Second World War. But Germany was probably no more ruthless than the Belgians, the British, the French, the Portuguese and all the other European states engaged in colonial 'police' actions during these years and later. *Hansard* reveals that 20,000 or more Boer civilians, mainly women and children, died in British-run concentration camps where they were confined after the British had deliberately burned down their homes towards the end of the South African War. During the crushing of the Boxer rebellion in China in 1900 these and other European states were joined by contingents from the U S A and Japan, and exhibited a brutality which no doubt the Chinese have embedded in their collective memory. Compared with the great British or French empires the German was tiny, but it took in bits of China, South-West Africa, East Africa, Togo, the Cameroons, and the South Sea Islands in the south-west Pacific. Like their European rivals, the Germans were imperialists because of their sense of racial superiority, their desire to bring *Kultur* to lesser breeds and their belief that they needed to control sources of raw materials and provide land for their surplus people.

The German search for colonies was an important element in their determination to become a top naval power. Another factor was the protection of their growing overseas trade, while a third was undoubtedly the desire for prestige. The navy, built up by Grand Admiral Alfred von Tirpitz, also provided jobs for middle-class sons who would not readily have been commissioned in the still aristocrat-dominated army. In 1898 the Reichstag passed the first naval bill, another following in 1900. Despite a frantic building programme the German fleet never reached the size of the British or French fleets. Writing in 1912, a British expert on German politics, Dr J. Holland Rose, found it natural for Germany to build up its fleet for defensive purposes for Germany's

> oceanic commerce has to pass through the Straits of Dover and down the English Channel, within easy striking distance of the French and British fleets at Brest, Plymouth, Cherbourg, Portsmouth, and Dover. This is what makes her nervous about her mercantile marine. This is what makes her build a great fleet; and again, I say, were we in her situation we should do the same.

He saw no danger in this. Yet many have argued that the failure of Britain and Germany to reach a naval agreement in that year made war inevitable. Lord Haldane, Liberal Minister of War (a great admirer of Germany, Hegel scholar and fluent German speaker), went to Germany in 1912 in search of an agreement. He failed.

## Growing militarisation

Because of German military successes before 1871, the Prussian-German army was feared and admired throughout the world. At home many Germans regarded it with pride as the vehicle which had brought about German unity, and the protector of German achievements. This view was fostered in the schools, in much of the press and among the recruits who had to do their compulsory military service. The German army had proved itself to be technically efficient and innovative at a time when weapons were getting more sophisticated and military organisation more complex. Its officers and regular soldiers prided themselves on their professionalism. Professionalism was a concept in tune with the times and this enhanced the military's 'image'. The army was also protected by laws against ridicule and criticism. The percentage of officers who were aristocrats was falling, by 1913 it was only 30 per cent. It was as high as 80 per cent in the cavalry and as low as 41 per cent in field artillery and much lower still in other, more technical branches. But at the top most officers were still aristocrats and the anti-democratic and feudalistic ideas of the Prussian military had a negative influence on society. Uniforms were popular, with those of officers being the most popular. To be a lieutenant of the reserve was regarded as very chic. At official functions officers were placed before mere civilians even if the civilians held important offices of state. Within the army duelling was still regarded as the honorable way to settle disputes between officers. Germany probably had more in common with Austria, Spain and Russia in this respect than with Britain or the United States. France probably came in between since there too the officer corps was powerful and reactionary, but the civilian leadership controlled the state.

## The road to war

The failure to conclude an Anglo-German naval agreement was just one factor which led to war in the summer of 1914, colonial and trade rivalry were others. Certainly many in Britain resented Germany's success in trade, while many in France were incensed by Germany's challenge to France's authority in Morocco. In 1905 the Kaiser, Wilhelm II, urged on by Chancellor von Bülow, landed at Tangier to visit the Sultan and announce German support for Moroccan independence. This attempted diplomatic coup merely pushed Britain and France closer together. The two states had agreed an *entente cordiale* in 1904, with Britain recognising Morocco as France's sphere of influence and France recognising Egypt as Britain's. Britain also overcame its earlier suspicion of Russia and agreed spheres of influence—in Iran, Afghanistan and Tibet—with the Czarist empire in 1907. The British were worried that Germany's growing influence in Turkey, including the proposal to build a railway to Baghdad, could be a threat to their empire. Since 1894 Russia had been allied with France, and Germany felt increasingly encircled. In 1909 France and Germany came to an understanding over Morocco, but this broke down in 1911 when French troops occupied Rabat and Fez. The German response was to send the gun boat *Panther* to the Moroccan port of Agadir. The Germans proposed French hegemony in Morocco in exchange for Germany taking over the French Congo. Supported by Britain France resisted and Germany had to be content with just small concessions.

The European powers kept out of the Balkan Wars (1912–13), a nationalist revolt against Turkish (Ottoman) rule. When the Austrian Archduke Franz Ferdinand was assassinated in Sarajevo, Bosnia, on 28 June 1914, Germany encouraged its ally (since 1879 in the Triple Alliance with Italy) Austria-Hungary to get tough with Serbia, which was allegedly involved in the assassination. Unexpectedly, an over-confident Czar backed Serbia, resulting in Russia being at war with Austria-Hungary. Germany and France then went to the aid of their respective allies. On 1 August Germany declared war on Russia and, on 3 August, on France. Britain joined in on 4 August by declaring war on Germany after German troops had invaded Belgium, whose neutrality had been guaranteed by Britain (and Germany and France). Italy kept out only to join Britain and France in 1915 but Germany and Austria-Hungary, 'the Central Powers', were joined by Turkey on 30 October, and Bulgaria a year later.

Was war inevitable? Given the perceived needs of the various states, the massive arms build up, the system of alliances, the imperialist and militarist values which gripped influential sections of all the countries involved, war seemed very likely. However, over the previous 40-odd years there had been any number of crises which had not led to a major war. A. J. P. Taylor, in his *War by Time Table*, argues that there was an element of miscalculation and that war became inevitable because military strategists foresaw a quick victory going to the power which completed its mobilisation first. Diplomacy functioned until the German demand that France and Russia should not mobilise. The Germans, he believes, had no plan to subvert the liberties of Europe. The leaders had little time to think and were trapped by the ingenuity of their military strategies. There were those, both inside and outside the ruling elites, who thought a major war could not happen because it would be against the interests of the rulers. The Russo-Japanese War of 1904–5 led to a revolution which nearly toppled the Czar. Others, particularly on the Left, felt that, on the contrary, war was a welcome way out of the many internal problems facing the rulers. Among academic writers V. R. Berghahn has expressed this view in his *Modern Germany*. The Kaiser and his Conservative supporters feared the growing S P D. Britain's rulers faced civil war conditions in Ireland and industrial unrest in Britain. The Austro-Hungarian and Russian empires faced constant challenges to central authority.

Kaiser Wilhelm II, who had ruled Germany since 1888 when he was

29, was later widely reviled as the man bearing the main responsibility for the war. More recently writers such as Michael Balfour in *The Kaiser and His Times* have described him as a more complex and sophisticated person despite his reactionary political views. A patron of the arts and sciences, he was also reactionary and arrogant. But was his guilt greater than that of the other dynastic heads of Europe? H. W. Koch in *The Origins of The First World War*, has rightly reminded us of the element of Social Darwinism in the 'New Imperialism' of the time. So many members of the elites thought in terms of the survival of the fittest. Koch points out that this attitude was certainly not confined to Germany but was endemic throughout Europe and the U S A.

A. J. P. Taylor believes, rightly in this writer's opinion, that the many who did not favour war have tended to be forgotten. Bits of old newsreel footage and many press photos show cheering crowds and happy soldiers, oblivious to the fate that was awaiting them. It must be remembered, however, that the media were only interested in such demonstrations. They did not cover opposition meetings, nor could they record the private fears of their contemporaries. Taylor points out that the crowds cheered *after* the decision had been taken. Certainly many Socialists and Liberals had no eagerness to go to war. The war was consistently presented as the defence of the homeland or the struggle of David against Goliath. The German Chancellor fed the S P D leaders selective information justifying the war as a defensive measure against Czarist aggression. No doubt out of a mixture of motives they, the biggest parliamentary party, agreed to support the war credits in the Reichstag.

## The Schlieffen Plan in action

At the beginning of the war the Germans attempted to carry out the Schlieffen Plan—a strategy thought out by Alfred von Schlieffen, chief of staff 1892–1906. It was meant to deal with the danger of a war on two fronts by swiftly knocking out Germany's adversary in the west, France, in a lightning move. According to the plan German troops, quickly and effectively mobilised and transported by Germany's efficient rail system, would attack France through neutral Belgium (with its efficient rail system) and Luxemburg. Having knocked out the French, the German armies would then be swiftly transported by rail to attack the Russians. The Plan very nearly succeeded. Unexpectedly strong Belgian resistance proved an important setback for the Germans. The mighty war machine was not on time. But mistakes

13

were made on both sides. The French under General Joseph Joffre had failed to recognise in time that the thrust through Belgium was Germany's main blow. The German advance got to within 15 miles of Paris. Desperate French resistance along the river Marne, and German blunders, dramatically changed the situation. Chief of Staff General Helmuth von Moltke was panicked by confusing reports from the front. Having lost contact with some of his commanders he ordered a general retreat. His forces came to rest about 50 miles from Paris. There they established a fortified line which was to change but little for the rest of the war. Moltke was relieved of his command and replaced by Erich von Falkenhayn.

On the eastern front the Russian invasion was brought to a halt, and heavy casualties were then inflicted on the Russians by Paul von Hindenburg, Erich Ludendorff and Max Hoffmann at Tannenberg and the Masurian Lakes. Even there however the enemy had not been crushed. The much-maligned Czarist armies destroyed or pinned down masses of German and Austro-Hungarian troops until the Russian revolution of 1917. By the autumn of 1914 some German officers were already clear that no easy victory could be expected. Abroad, the German colonies in Asia fell to the Japanese and by 1916 Germany's African possessions had been captured by British and French colonial troops.

## War aims

The military, and many members of the Reichstag and of economic and patriotic organisations, including many university professors, were soon clamouring for an expansion of the German Reich at the expense of its neighbours. Demands included turning Belgium into a vassal state or its full incorporation into Germany, annexing part of northern France and its coastline, taking over Poland and the Baltic states. Later the Ukraine was added to the list. The military were mainly concerned with creating impregnable frontiers, the economic organisations with securing sources of raw materials and the politicians with imposing reparations. It must not be forgotten that many German politicians believed, on limited information, that Germany had been attacked and was fighting a purely defensive war. Nor must it be forgotten that the allies also drew up annexationist plans which were later realised. The Conservatives and National Liberals were strong advocates of such plans, while the left Liberals, Centre and Majority Social Democrats generally took a more conciliatory line. The break-away Independent Social Democrats (see below) openly opposed the war. On 19 July 1917 these three groups, a majority in the Reichstag, passed a resolution calling for a peace based understanding and a lasting reconciliation among the peoples. Chancellor Bethmann Hollweg, who had first believed in a short war and then realised that Germany's situation was deteriorating, had attempted in 1916 to gain U S President Wilson's support for peace negotiations. He failed partly because Hindenburg and Ludendorff were not willing to give up German claims to Belgium. They removed Bethmann Hollweg on 14 July 1917, replaced him with Georg Michaelis, and proceeded to establish a virtual military dictatorship in Germany. Conscription of all civilians between 17 and 60 was introduced, with stricter censorship and more imprisonments of those raising their voices against the war lords.

## New weapons

The German genius for science, technology and organisation, already so apparent in times of peace, revealed itself once again in war. New weapons were brought into play in the hope they would force a decisive conclusion to the war. One of these was poison gas, first used in the spring of 1915 at Ypres. It proved to be of limited effectiveness, especially after gas masks were issued to allied troops. The second new weapon was aerial warfare. In most people's minds aerial bombing in the First World War is associated with the Zeppelin, an airship named after its inventor, Graf Ferdinand Zeppelin. It had been conceived as a civilian passenger carrier, but the military decided it had possibilities as a bomber. Although it was still being sent on bombing missions over England in 1918, it was recognised as ineffective, vulnerable and expensive. In fact, heavier-than-air aircraft were used on a much greater scale, especially in 1917 and 1918 when there were 52 raids by the heavy Gotha bombers. Their offensive against London, which claimed the lives of 857 people and injured over 2000 more, forced the British to deploy many men and machines badly needed in France, to defend the capital.

The German fleet was in a sense a new weapon. At least some of its ships were better constructed and equipped than their British rivals. But only one major naval engagement was fought, the battle of Jutland off the Danish coast on 31 May 1916. The Germans lost six ships, the British fourteen, with correspondingly higher loss of life. Neither side risked another encounter of this kind. In future the Germans attempted to achieve their objectives at sea through the *U-Boot* or submarine. As we shall see, this weapon too had its limitations.

Most of the war, on all fronts, was fought with weapons which had been in use for some time such as heavy artillery, the rifle, the machine gun, forts, blockhouses, barbed wire and, at the beginning, cavalry. Masses of men were flung at each other in desperate attempts to break through the other side's front line. On the Somme, at Verdun and Passchendaele hundreds of thousands of men were sacrificed without tangible result. In the Passchendaele offensive, for instance, the British lost around 265,000 as against German losses of 206,000.

On 1 January 1915 Britain had introduced a total blockade of Germany. This involved stopping and searching neutral ships and confiscating contraband (which included food) as well as intercepting vessels of the Central Powers. Britain ran the risk of antagonising the U S A, which was neutral, by such a policy. The Americans claimed British policy ran counter to the Declaration of London (1909) which dealt with this problem. The Germans made the mistake of starting to sink without warning neutral ships found in the sea lanes approaching Britain. American ships were attacked in 1915, but it was the sinking of the British *Lusitania* (7 May 1915) which brought war closer. This liner went down with the loss of 1153 lives, 114 of them Americans. The Germans claimed it had been carrying munitions. The U S A issued a stern warning after the sinking of the French ship *Sussex* in May 1915 with the loss of more American lives. The Germans then suspended this policy until, in an increasingly desperate situation, Tirpitz re-introduced it on 1 February 1917 against the advice of Bethmann Hollweg.

President Wilson's response to renewed German submarine attacks was to break off diplomatic relations with Germany. A short time later the German leaders committed another blunder which sealed their fate. They attempted to win Mexico for an attack on its northern neighbour promising support for its proposed annexation of Texas, New Mexico and Arizona. Known as the Zimmerman note, this proposal fell into the hands of the British secret service and was released to the press on 1 March. In the same month revolution occurred in Russia, and with the demise of the Czar the Americans had one reason less to be opposed to the allied cause. Finally, in March German submarines torpedoed five U S merchant ships. On 2 April Wilson read his message to Congress asking for a declaration of war against Germany. This duly followed on 6 April 1917.

One aspect of the war which is difficult to understand is the intolerance which was shown to the German communities in the U S A. This had happened in Britain in 1914 with, among other things, anti-German riots. The British royal family had felt obliged to change its name to Windsor on 17 July 1917. In both countries internment of enemy aliens took place. In Texas the governor banned foreign languages, in Wisconsin violence was used against those believed to be pro-German, the teaching of German in schools ceased, German books were removed from public libraries and in one or two cases there were public burnings of German books. The press and cinemas were exploited to promote hatred of 'the Hun'. Under the Espionage Act (1917) and the Sedition Act (1918) the government could suppress any form of dissent. Socialists and pacifists were imprisoned under these acts.

By December 1917 there were 176,000 U S troops in France, by November 1918, when the armistice was signed, the total had reached 1,971,000. In October 1918 a U S force of 1,200,000 broke through the German defences between Metz and Sedan. They were part of a much larger offensive launched by the French supreme commander of the allied forces, Marshal Ferdinand Foch, which finally forced the Germans to sue for peace.

# — 2 —

# From Defeat to Democratic Republic

Disaster threatened the German Empire (founded at Versailles in 1871 after the defeat of France) when in 1917 the mighty weight of the virile United States of America was thrown in behind the Anglo-French alliance. If Britain and France were by that time tired of the war which the European powers had unleashed upon themselves in the summer of 1914, Germany was even more so. By 1918 agricultural production was 40–60 per cent below prewar levels. The official food rations of 1917–18 were well below average prewar levels of consumption. Germans were allowed only about 20 per cent of their prewar consumption of meat, 13 per cent of eggs, 21 per cent of butter, 41 per cent of vegetable fats and about 47 per cent of flour. The official ration could rarely be honoured. Food and other prices had risen dramatically and Germans were working longer hours to meet those higher prices. More than 60 per cent of large and medium-sized factories in the Berlin armaments industry, which worked nine hours a day before the war, worked 10–12 hours a day in 1917. In more than half the factories the workers had to work regularly on Sundays as well. More than a third of those employed in industry were women as compared to about 20 per cent before the war. At the front victory and defeat alike resulted in very heavy casualties. Germany lost nearly two million dead and over double that number wounded in the fighting. In these circumstances it is not surprising that Germans should go on strike, some in anger, others in desperation.

The Russian revolutions of 1917 helped to focus discontent on a level higher than concern for mere material things, important though they were. This revolutionary upsurge in Russia also gave some Germans an example just as it frightened others.

In November 1917 there were demonstrations in Berlin, particularly in the working-class areas, demanding peace. In the same month peace demonstrations took place in certain other German towns as well. Again in November, and at the beginning of December, strikes broke out in a number of important factories. In Berlin, for instance, 2,600 workers at the Daimler Motor Works struck. In January 1918 over 400,000 workers downed tools in Berlin's metal industry. Their demands were political as well as economic. They took up the slogan of Lenin for a peace without annexations or indemnities, and demanded a democratic regime based on universal suffrage. The strike leadership co-opted six leaders, three from the Social Democratic Party, and three from the Independent Social Democratic Party. The Independent Social Democrats were the minority movement of the Social Democratic Party who had been expelled from the party for opposing the world war. Some of them were pacifists, others revolutionaries. They were really only united on the question of the opposition to the war, and then not on the tactics to be pursued, and by their adherance to that ill-defined principle 'Socialism'. Friedrich Ebert, leader of the Majority Social Democrats who supported the war and one of the six coopted leaders, later commented that he joined the strike leadership in order to get the strikers back to work as soon as possible. The strike lasted only a few days but before it ended over a million workers in various parts of Germany had come out and violence erupted, several workers being killed or wounded. Germany was at this time officially under 'state of siege' which meant wide powers for the military and regimentation for the workers; consequently, military courts dealt with thousands jailing them or sending them off to the front. Other strikes followed.

Despite Germany's critical strategic position, due to American intervention, the worsening situation of Germany's Austrian ally and the clamour of many German workers for peace, the Reich's military leaders, Ludendorff and Hindenburg, showed themselves in no mood for negotiations. How they would deal with defeated nations was revealed by the peace of Brest-Litovsk between Germany and Bolshevik Russia agreed in March 1918. This required that large areas of the former Czarist Empire be either incorporated into the Reich or maintained as German puppet states. In the same month a new German offensive was launched on the Western Front which gained some initial success. However, it soon became clear that military victory for Germany was impossible and that with every day complete military collapse drew nearer: Germany lacked the human and material reserves to sustain prolonged military effort and the American troops were pouring into France. In the hope of impressing the Allies and improving the negotiating position, the German military leadership advised the establishment of the broadest possible coalition government in Berlin.

In October Prince Max of Baden took over from Count Georg von Hertling as Chancellor of the German Reich. Prince Max was doubtful about the wisdom of bringing in the Social Democrats for he knew a political price would have to be paid. This price was the introduction of universal adult suffrage and secret ballot in all German Länder or regions (something mighty Prussia did not yet have), the abolition of censorship and acceptance of President Wilson's 14 Points Declaration. The Prince had also rejected the idea of an armistice and only agreed when told by Hindenburg that the armed forces could not hold out even a day longer.

Two Social Democrats entered a new government, Philipp Scheidemann as Minister without Portfolio, and Gustav Bauer as *Straatssekretär* for Labour. These were not very exalted posts for members of a party which in fact had been the largest party in the Reichstag since 1912! The new government included the Centre Party, the second largest in the Reichstag, and the Left Liberals as well as the Social Democrats who entered a German government for the first time. On 5 October the new government approved in principle the change to a parliamentary system in which the Chancellor or Prime Minister would be responsible to the Reichstag rather than to the Monarch, and in which war and peace were the responsibility of the Reichstag as elected parliament of the German people. The Reichstag then went into recess until 22 October while the necessary legislation was being drafted. The Reichstag passed the bills on 26 October but then adjourned until 9 November. Considering the crisis Germany was facing this was remarkable. The slowness of parliamentary developments and the infrequency of that body's deliberations during this period was a sign that Germany's leaders had not yet decided to end the war. On 17 October Ludendorff was still voicing illusions about Germany's military future at a meeting of the Cabinet. Scheidemann sounded a more realistic note by pointing out, 'We have no meat. We cannot provide potatoes ...!' In its telegrams to President Wilson of America negotiating an armistice the German government still prevaricated. As they did so the situation got worse. Wilson hinted strongly that Emperor Wilhelm would have to go and Ludendorff too. The general went on 26 October, the Emperor attempted to hold on. But the developing situation in Germany made it impossible for him to stay.

On Wilson's demand, the Germans had agreed to stop submarine warfare. Now the admirals of the fleet, whose ships had been inactive for some time, decided on their own initiative, without consulting the government, to put to sea and engage the British fleet. In all probability they would have been destroyed and the rank-and-file sailors, who had endured bad conditions for some years, were not prepared to sacrifice themselves in any last-minute, futile, grand gesture. They mutinied and hoisted the red flag. They declared that they would defend Germany against any attack by the British fleet but they would not undertake offensive operations. Had they not taken this action the war might have dragged on with far worse consequences for Germany. They were German patriots who risked being shot as traitorous mutineers. The mutiny started on 30 October. Already, in August of 1917 there had been a mutiny in the fleet. On that occasion two of the leaders, Albin Köbis and Max Reichpietsch, had been court-martialled and shot, many others suffered imprisonment. On this occasion too it looked for a time as though the officers would re-establish their authority for briefly, with the help of marines, they managed to restore 'order'. But as the mutiny was being put down in Wilhemshaven it was breaking out in Kiel (3 November). There it spread to troops stationed in the area and to the citizens of the town. Within days it had spread throughout the coastal towns of North Germany. By the 7–8 November it had spread inland to all major centres of the Reich. In its outward aspects it was similar to what had happened in Russia after February 1917—councils of workers and servicemen were being set up and were either taking over control of the towns or were exercising control jointly with the existing authorities. On 7 November the first royal house fell in Bavaria where a democratic republic was proclaimed. Kurt Eisner became the Prime Minister of a coalition government made up of Independent Social Democrats and Majority Social Democrats.

The leaders of the Majority Social Democrats were under increasing pressure from their rank-and-file to pursue a more militant policy. They feared losing support to the Independent Social Democrats or, worse still, to the Spartacus League, the forerunner of the German Communist Party. They had to demand from Prince Max the abdication of Wilhelm, warning that if this demand were not met they would be forced by their own members to leave the government. Friedrich Ebert further warned the Prince, according to the latter's memoirs, that if the abdication were not announced, there would be a social revolution, 'which I hate like sin'. Both the Majority Social Democratic leaders and the Prince hoped to save the monarchy by securing Wilhelm's departure. This he still refused to do. The Social Democrats therefore left the government and, by the time Wilhelm had agreed to go, on 9 November, the cause of the monarchy was lost in Germany. On that day Karl Liebknecht, one of the Spartacus leaders and Reichstag member, just released from prison where he had been held for opposing the war, led a demonstration to the Berliner Schloss. In the front of the building he proclaimed a German Socialist Republic. Fearing the consequences of opposing such a proclamation, Philipp Scheidemann made his own proclamation of a 'free German Republic' on the same day. For this, for which he had no authority but his own political instinct, Scheidemann was criticised by Ebert. But there was no going back. The next day, as Kaiser Wilhelm II, last of the Hohenzollern monarchs, German Emperor for 30 years, fled to Holland, a mass meeting of the Berlin workers' and soldiers' councils formally elected six People's Commissioners to form a Council to rule Germany. The new Council of People's Commissioners consisted of three Majority Social Democrats, Ebert, Scheidemann and Otto Landsberg, and three Independent Social Democrats, Hugo Haase, Wilhelm Dittmann and Emil Barth. Friedrich Ebert was elected chairman.

Meanwhile, in the forest of Compiègne, Germans and Frenchmen were meeting to arrange an armistice. Marshal Foch of France was the Allies' representative and handed the Allies' conditions to the German commission. The chief German delegate was Matthias Erzberger, a Centre Party member of the Prince Max government, who had been prevailed upon by Hindenburg to go to Compiègne. On 11 November the Germans signed the armistice agreement. Foolishly, the Allies did not require any high-ranking German officer to sign the agreement, though a major-general and a naval captain did sign. Consequently, after the war German militarists were to claim that it was not the work of the German armed forces, who had been 'stabbed in the back' by the politicians.

The coalition government led by Ebert was soon faced with difficult decisions. Its members were men who had suddenly had power thrust upon them. They were used to waging great struggles to get small reforms. Now power was in their hands. What to do with it? Ebert felt that order was to be maintained at all cost. If it were not, and Germany were plunged into anarchy, the people, and particularly the working people (as always), would be the sufferers. He also felt that if the government degenerated into a small, revolutionary junta, it would be forced to take ever more repressive steps to maintain itself (as was happening with the Bolsheviks in Russia). Furthermore, he feared that if a German government appeared incapable of maintaining order the Allies would occupy the whole country. To achieve his primary objective he did two things.

Firstly, as General Wilhelm Groener later testified, Ebert secured the support of the Army High Command for his government. 'We allied ourselves to one another to fight against the revolution, to fight against Bolshevism.... The purpose of this alliance, that we concluded on the night of 10 November was the total putting down of revolution, the re-establishment of ordered government power, the support of such government power by an armed force, and the soonest possible summoning of a national assembly. That was the aim.' They further agreed to the sending of ten divisions of troops to Berlin to carry out the 'disarmament of Berlin, the clearing of Berlin of Spartacists, etc'. Ebert's second aim, as mentioned above by Groener, was the summoning of a National Assembly. On this point there were differences of opinion in the government. The more Left-inclined Independents agreed in principle but thought the Council should get on with the job of transforming the power structure immediately and thus prevent the re-emergence of those capitalist-imperialist forces which were responsible for Germany's present plight. The Spartacists desired immediate action, including the establishment of a dictatorship based on the workers' and soldiers' councils—which they wrongly believed Russia had. They felt betrayed by men like Friedrich Ebert, the professional politicians who, by working-class standards, had long since secured for themselves a good life based on a career in the Socialist movement. Had not such men been the ones who had supported the imperialist war? Was it not a fact that while such men urged caution the reactionary forces were regrouping? Taking up what had been the slogan of Lenin *before* he got power, *Die Rote Fahne*, the organ of the Spartacists, demanded all power to the workers' and soldiers' councils.

On 20 December the first all-German congress of these councils rejected by 344 votes to 98 the demand for a government based on the councils and agreed that on 19 January elections should take place for a national assembly. As these votes suggest, the congress was totally dominated by Ebert's men. The Spartacist leaders Karl Liebknecht and Rosa Luxemburg were unable to secure election to the congress. The congress passed two other significant resolutions which were not to be realised. One of these was a call for the socialisation of all 'ripe' industries, especially coal mining. The other was for the establishment of a People's Militia, a traditional Social Democratic demand, with elected leaders (rather than officers) and responsible to the People's Commissioners. This resolution was an embarrassment to Ebert in view of his alliance with Hindenburg and Groener.

A week before the congress met the promised divisions of loyal troops had arrived in the suburbs of Berlin and General Groener was getting impatient with the slowness of the operations against 'unauthorized military groups' (i.e. Left-wing groups). One of the most important of these was the People's Marine Division which, although now tending to the Left, had been recognised by the People's Commissioners to the extent that they had provided its members with pay. This pay was cut off and in order to 'negotiate' with him the marines seized Otto Wels, Social Democrat Berlin City Commandant.

Under pressure from General Groener, Ebert agreed to troops being used against them. This attack failed and Spartacus demonstrations followed in Berlin, where the offices of the organ of the Ebert party were taken over, and in other German towns. Fighting broke out in various places. On 29 December the Independents decided to leave Ebert's Council of People's Commissioners and their places were taken by Majority Social Democrats.

At the end of December 1918 the Spartacus Leagues decided to break their (by then) very precarious ties with the Independent Social Democrats and set themselves up as the German Communist Party. Against the advice of their two most important leaders, Liebknecht and Luxemburg, they decided not to contest the elections to the national assembly. In this way they showed their disdain for this body and strengthened the suspicions of the Social Democrats and others that their aim was purely armed insurrection. On 6 January the representatives of the new Communist Party, Karl Liebknecht and Wilhelm Pieck, agreed with representatives of the Berlin Independent Social Democrats, the People's Marines and the revolutionary shop stewards, to an armed struggle for the conquest of power. Strikes and the occupation of buildings in Berlin followed. Weapons were distributed but the attempted coup was badly led and ill-coordinated; the result was that the pro-government troops turned the action into a blood bath. The fighting ended on 12 January with the storming by government troops of the Berlin police headquarters. Many of the rebels were shot out of hand. Three days later Liebknecht and Luxemburg, who against their better judgement had supported the rising in print, were hunted down, beaten and shot.

The murder of Luxemburg and Liebknecht (for it was later recognised as murder by the authorities) helped to perpetuate the bitterness which existed between Communist and Social Democrat. This was to be of great importance in the last years of the Weimar Republic. Had Luxemburg and Liebknecht lived they might have led the Communist Party out of the cul-de-sac of mere oppositionism and dependence on Moscow. Rosa Luxemburg had already denounced Leninism long before the Russian Revolution, though she greatly admired the courage and sincerity of Lenin, and by 1918 was disturbed by events in Russia. Had she survived she very probably would have seen through Stalinism.

The armed struggle of the Left in Berlin was not yet at an end. Early in March renewed fighting broke out in the capital during a general strike called by the revolutionary shop stewards to achieve

socialisation of the factories and the dissolution of the Free Corps.*
Gustav Noske, a Social Democrat who had been put in charge of the
Republic's armed forces by Ebert in December, once again acted as the
state's 'bloodhound', as he himself put it. Government troops went
into action killing anyone who was found armed. Roughly 1,200 died
on both sides in the fighting. Skirmishing went on in other parts of the
Reich too but by the end of May the government/Right-wing troops
were in command.

In Bavaria where a Left coalition had been functioning under Kurt
Eisner, an Independent Social Democrat, trouble started when Eisner
was assassinated on 21 February 1919. Eisner was in fact on his way
to the regional parliament to announce his resignation as his party
had been severely defeated in elections held the month before. Eisner
had been killed by a Rightist, but angered by it, one of his supporters
shot the leader of the Majority Social Democrats in the parliament.
Violence now swept through Bavaria. A revolutionary council was set
up and a general strike called. In April the council prevented the
parliament from meeting and then declared a republic based on
workers' councils citing the Russian Soviets as its model. The official
government of Bavaria led by a Majority Social Democrat was not
prepared to capitulate and government troops moved in to settle the
issue. This they did with great brutality, shooting anyone whom they
suspected. A group of 21 members of a Catholic organisation who were
holding a meeting were shot down as suspected revolutionaries. They
were not the only ones. After the carnage the legal government was
allowed to return to Munich.

In January 1919 Ebert had been able to keep his promise to hold
elections throughout the Reich for a national assembly. The Majority
Social Democrats gained 11.5 million votes or 37.9 per cent and 165
seats. To the Left the Independents received 2.3 million votes or 7.6
per cent and 22 seats. The Centre Party's share was 5.9 million votes
or 19.7 per cent and 90 seats. The Democratic Party (left Liberals)
won 5.6 million votes (18.5 per cent) and 75 seats. On the right, the
German Nationalists got just over 3 million votes (10.3 per cent) and
42 seats. Also on the right the German People's Party attracted 1.3
million votes (4.4 per cent) and 22 seats. Minor groups received
another 1.6 per cent of the vote and seven seats. Participation in the
election had been high, 82.7 per cent of the electorate having voted.
Voting was under a new franchise. Women had been granted the vote
which they and male Germans now had the right to exercise from the

* These were armed units of volunteers, including many Right-wing, former officers.
They were officially supposed to protect the frontiers and keep 'order'.

age of 20 (previously it had been from 25 for men). The Social Democrats could claim that in spite of everything their advance was continuing. As a united party they had gained 34.8 per cent of the poll at the last elections of 1912. In 1919 the two Social Democratic Parties had received 45.5 per cent of the vote. It looked as though the parliamentary, gradualist tactic was paying off, for the years before the war had been years of almost uninterrupted advance. That advance appeared to be continuing. Right-wing groups seemed to be on their way out, for their share of the vote had dropped from 36.6 per cent in 1912 to 16.3 per cent in 1919.

From the election results it was obvious that the first elected government of the Weimar Republic would have to be a coalition government. Meeting at Weimar the national assembly elected Ebert President of the Republic by a decisive majority over his Nationalist opponent. Ebert then appointed a government of seven Social Democrats, three Centre Party members, three Democrats and one non-party, Foreign Minister Count von Brockdorff-Rantzau. The Independent Social Democrats had refused to take part in the government.

Apart from the precarious state of law and order the new government faced the problem of negotiations with the Allies and the maintenance of the unity of the Reich.

When Allied peace terms became known in Germany in May 1919 there was great disappointment and equally great anger. The Germans claimed they had expected a peace based on President Wilson's 14 Points and that the terms were not consistent with them. They had neglected to remember that Wilson had no authority to speak for Britain, France or Belgium, and that these states had carried the main effort of the war against Germany. And, of course the terms were, to a considerable extent, based on Wilson's 14 Points. Ebert spoke of the delivering up of the German workers to wage slavery for foreign capitalism. The parliamentary group of the Majority Social Democrats rejected the terms as unacceptable. Scheidemann, as head of the government, and most of his cabinet resigned as a gesture against the terms. He was replaced on 22 June by another Majority Social Democrat, Gustav Bauer, who formed a government of Social Democrats, Centre and Bavarian People's Party. Chancellor Bauer declared that the new government would be prepared to sign if the articles requiring Germany's sole responsibility for the war, and the articles requiring Germany to hand over its citizens wanted by the Allies as war criminals were deleted. The majority of the national assembly voted for this compromise. The Allies refused these concessions; they had earlier granted other concessions, because the Germans, against the terms of the treaty, had just scuttled their fleet at Scapa Flow. Further, captured flags due for handing back to the French had been burned. The Allies warned the Germans of the consequences of any additional delay. In view of this situation the national assembly agreed to give the government a mandate to sign. The Nationalists, German People's Party, part of the Centre and part of the Democratic Party voted against. The Independent Social Democrats had advised voting for the treaty from the start. Their view was that although it was 'a forced peace of the worst kind', they had got to think of the consequences of not signing: continued internment for German prisoners of war, the occupation of Germany's raw materials' areas, the stepping up of the blockade, unemployment, starvation, death and terrible cataclysm—then Germany would still have to sign. This commonsense view of the Independents was in marked contrast to the daydreaming of the Nationalists, and many of the officers. And in view of what later happened in Germany it should be stressed that Ebert and Noske only used their influence in favour of signing when they had heard from General Groener that the military situation was hopeless. In fact he begged them to stay at their posts. Hindenburg, who also clearly understood the situation, sought to evade the responsibility by resigning. The two unfortunate German ministers who signed the Treaty of Versailles were Hermann Müller, a Social Democrat and Foreign Minister, and Dr Johannes Bell.

The main aims of the Treaty of Versailles appear to have been to reduce Germany from the status of a world power to being merely a European power; to rob Germany of its territorial conquests; to destroy Germany as a military power, and to make Germany pay for the devastation Imperial troops had inflicted on other nations. All German colonies were allotted to Allied states as League of Nations' trust territories. The Imperial fleet was also required to be handed over to the Allies but, as we have seen, it was scuttled before this transfer could be effected. The articles of the Treaty dealing with territory stipulated the return of Alsace-Lorraine to France; the creation of an independent Polish state with a 'free and secure access to the sea'; the restoration of Belgium, Romania and Serbia, and the creation of a Czechoslovak state; the carrying through of plebiscites to determine the frontiers with Denmark and Poland; the cession of the Eupen and Malmédy districts to Belgium and the transfer of the Saar to French control under a Leage of Nations' Commission for 15 years; the prohibition of any future union of Germany and Austria. The Treaty reduced the mighty German military machine to an army of 100,000 and a navy of 15,000. It laid down the type and number of ships, forbade submarines, tanks, planes and offensive weapons.

Article 231 stated: 'the Allied Governments affirm and Germany accepts the responsibility of Germany and her allies for causing all the loss and damage', which the Allies and their subjects had suffered 'as a consequence of the war imposed upon them by the aggression of Germany and her allies'. Finally, to enforce the treaty, Allied armies were to occupy bridgeheads along the Rhine for 15 years and the Rhineland was to be permanently demilitarised.

The Constitution of the Weimar Republic, drafted by Hugo Preuss, was accepted on 31 July 1919. It established a federal system with a Reichsrat or house of states and a Reichstag or directly elected house. This was similar to the earlier Imperial Constitution. The President was to be directly elected. There was also provision for a *Reichswirtschaftsrat* or Reich Economic Council, which was no more than lip-service to the idea of economic democracy. The Council played virtually no role in the affairs of the Republic. The Reichsrat was not in the powerful position of the old upper house, but it could delay legislation until overruled by a two-thirds majority of the Reichstag. The latter was the main constitutional organ. Elected for four years it controlled legislation and normally the government. The President did not appear to be in too strong a position on paper, though in practice his position turned out to be very strong. The fact that he was directly elected gave him prestige, and under Article 48 of the Constitution he could employ the armed forces for the restoration of order. In cases of emergency he could suspend most of the constitutional liberties. The same Article empowered the President to rule by emergency decrees. The decrees had to be counter-signed by the Chancellor or responsible Minister, and the Reichstag had to be informed of them and retained the powers of rescinding them. As we shall see, these presidential powers were to be of vital importance later on.

The signing of the Versailles Treaty had incensed many Right-wing officers still more against the Republic. With little else to do with their time, groups of plotters were springing up all over Germany. In March 1920 one such group carried out a coup in Berlin. The originator of this particular plot was not an officer but a civil servant, an agricultural specialist, Wolfgang Kapp. The military figures connected with it were Generals von Lüttwitz and Ludendorff. The coup was actually executed by Ehrhardt's Marine Brigade, a Free Corps organisation. These troops had no difficulty in occupying key buildings in the capital, including the Chancellor's office. Luckily the President and the Government had fled to Dresden from where they successfully called for a general strike. Kapp and his followers were virtually powerless. Most of the army and the police at first remained neutral but slowly turned towards the Ebert regime for fear of worse to come, namely civil war or a more Left-wing regime.

A terrible sequel to the Kapp Putsch was the crushing of the remnants of the so-called 'Red Ruhr Army' which grew out of resistance to the Putsch in the Ruhr.

Thousands of workers had armed themselves and taken over large areas of the Ruhr. In certain instances, they had shown they were more than a match for armed police, Free Corps and even Reichswehr units. After the collapse of the Putsch they were reluctant to surrender their weapons so soon after the loyalty of the official armed forces had proved to be so doubtful. They demanded guarantees against further militarist coups and introduction of the social changes which the Social Democratic leaders had promised endlessly before and after 1918. On 24 March an agreement was reached between representatives of the government and a very wide spectrum of political opinion including the Centre Party, the Democratic Party, the trade unions, Majority and Independent Social Democrats; representatives of local authorities and two Communists though they did not sign for their party. Under the agreement, which became known as the Bielefeld Agreement, the workers agreed to hand over their weapons and return to work. The government side promised to disarm and punish those who had taken part in the Putsch; to disband all anti-republican organisations; to purge the administration of counter-revolutionary elements; to carry through 'as quickly as possible' co-determination in economic organisations and administrative reform on a democratic basis; 'Immediate' socialisation of 'ripe' industries, especially coal and potash; formation of local militias from the loyal republican circles of the population; extension of social welfare legislation; financial help from the state for the dependants of killed or wounded; no discrimination against the workers who had taken part in the struggle or against members of the police or Reichswehr; provided the agreement was loyally kept Reichswehr units would not move into the Ruhr industrial area.

This agreement remained a dead letter in virtually every respect. On 26 March the Weimar coalition was reshuffled with Hermann Müller as Chancellor and the participation his Majority Social Democrats, the Centre Party and the Democrats, but nothing was done to realise the promises given to the Ruhr workers. Most of them handed over their weapons and returned to work, some did not. Reichswehr and Free Corps units were sent into the area and even into towns in the demilitarised zone, thus breaking the Versailles Treaty (quite apart from any consideration of the Bielefeld Agreement). They brutally went about their business, killing both prisoners and wounded, including women. Had Ebert and his colleagues used the opportunity they had immediately after the collapse of the Kapp Putsch they would probably have secured once and for all a democratic, social republic enjoying the support of the majority of the people. As it was, by showing every tolerance to Right-wing plotters but none to workers who had defended the Republic, they alienated countless thousands of politically conscious workers from the Weimar Republic. The Left of the Independent Social Democrats joined the Communist Party and at the elections which followed the defeat of Kapp the Majority of Social Democrats lost to the Left. They did not find much thanks from the right for their actions.

# — 3 —

# Weimar from Crisis to Stability

The elections of 6 June 1920 produced a swing away from the centre parties to the extremes—a result of the heat generated by the Kapp Putsch and discontent with the government. The Social Democrats remained the largest party but lost heavily to the Independent Social Democrats and even to the Communists, the latter being ably represented by two deputies Dr Paul Levi and Clara Zetkin. The Social Democrats felt that continued participation in government with bourgeois parties pursuing measures which were unpopular with many of their supporters would result in further erosion of their base. They therefore left the government and in 1922 were re-united with the Independent Social Democrats. Although they, more than any other party, became associated in the public mind with 'the Weimar System', they did not provide a Chancellor again until Hermann Müller took over for a second time in June 1928 remaining in office till March 1930. After November 1923 the Social Democrats were no longer represented in a Reich government though, as we shall see, they were important in regional government and their man, Friedrich Ebert, was President of the Republic until his death in 1925.

The Centre Party politician Constantin Fehrenbach now took over the government. His party had joined with the Social Democrats in coalition in February 1919 and were participants in all 17 governments to May 1932 (and even after that if one includes expelled Centre Party politicians who remained in office). Thus they, even more than the Social Democrats, could be called the classic party of Weimar.

That during this period they usually had 60-odd seats out of a Reichstag of between 403 (in 1919) and 608 (in July 1932) seats indicates not only their weakness but also the weaknesses of the parliamentary system in Weimar Germany. The partners in the 17 coalition governments were usually united on very little, often carrying on contradictory policies in various ministries, and it is not surprising that by the end of 1932 the governments of the Weimar Republic had existed on average only eight months. In such circumstances interest groups and the permanent 'servants' of the state, the bureaucracy and the military, exercised far more influence than was their due.

## Secret rearmament and the unlikely alliance

The *Wehrgesetz* or Defence Law of 1921 set out the constitutional position of the armed forces in the Weimar Republic. This law paid lip-service to the Versailles Treaty, the democratic traditions of Social Democracy and the developments during the German revolution. The stipulations of the Treaty of Versailles regarding the maximum strength of the forces, their officers and organisation were duly recorded, the President was named as commander-in-chief and even the ghosts of the soldiers' councils crept in. There was an elected *Heerskammer* (Army Chamber) made up of officers, N C Os and other ranks with advisory functions. There were also *Vertrauensträte* in all units mainly concerned with the personal grievances of the ordinary soldiers. The position of the Defence Minister was not very clearly defined. He could issue orders but not commands. Servicemen were not allowed to engage in political activities and even membership of non-political clubs could be banned for reasons of military discipline. Many Social Democrats believed this would prevent soldiers being active in Right-wing parties and organisations. On the whole, however, officers clamped down on Left-wing activity in the barracks and turned a blind eye to or supported, Rightist activities. Although even on paper far from perfect, the *Wehrgesetz* shows the limited value of constitutional devices when democratic consciousness is lacking.

Remarkable in view of the precarious tenure of office enjoyed by his colleagues was the ability of Dr Otto Gessler, a member of the Democratic Party, to retain his position as Minister of Defence which he held from 1920 to 1928. It then passed into the hands of General Wilhelm Groener until June 1932 and from then, until Hitler became Chancellor in January 1933, the post was occupied by General Kurt von Schleicher. Even after that another general, Werner von Blomberg, was Defence Minister until the post was abolished in 1938. This is some indication of the resilience of the old military caste, for Gessler held office with the approval of the Reichswehr even though the generals did not always agree with everything he said or did.

Chief of the army from March 1920 to October 1926 was General Hans von Seeckt, very much an old-fashioned aristocratic officer. He was a monarchist. Of the Weimar Constitution he wrote, 'its basic principles (are) contrary to my political thinking'. Seeckt's military policy, and that of his fellow officers, was secret rearmament while officially keeping to the limitations imposed by the Versailles Treaty. The armed forces were not allowed an air arm, so a shadow air force was built up by expanding, through subsidies, civilian flying clubs where officers trained, training pilots abroad, testing machines abroad and developing a strong civil aviation industry. Likewise the navy tested submarines and other equipment beyond the frontiers of the Reich, notably in Holland and Spain. Further, the Reichswehr maintained a large proportion of N C Os, the backbone of any army, who made rapid expansion after 1933 possible. There were also various military clubs, societies and organisations to foster the military spirit, pass on military knowledge or engage in paramilitary sports activities.

More astonishing than any of these activities was Seeckt's policy of secret military cooperation with Soviet Russia. What could possibly induce military cooperation between old-fashioned German militarists and Russian, in some cases Russian Jewish, Bolsheviks? Firstly, Seeckt was personally pro-Russian, though strongly 'anti-Marxist'. Secondly, both nations were losers of World War I. They felt they had been badly treated by the Anglo-Saxon-French alliance. Thirdly, industrial Germany had much to offer agrarian Russia. Fourthly, some German officers admired the 'strong' government of Bolshevik Russia. Finally, both were hostile to Poland. Poland's existence, so declared Seeckt, 'is intolerable, incompatible with the survival of Germany. It must disappear, and it will disappear through its own internal weakness and through Russia—with our assistance'. As for the Bolsheviks, they regarded one bourgeois capitalist regime much as another and bought where they could.

This cooperation involved the construction of aircraft factories, by Junkers, tanks, artillery, munitions and poison gas factories, the products of which were then used in training by Soviet and German troops. The Germans gave a wide assortment of specialist training to Soviet personnel including staff training to Soviet officers who went to Germany for the purpose. The German Navy too was involved in such cooperation, though much less so due to its suspicion of Soviet Russia and other opportunities.

Russo-German military co-operation continued until Hitler gained power and would not have been possible without the interest of major industrial concerns as well as the military. What about the politicians? What was their attitude to it? Certainly until 1926, when it was attacked by the Social Democrats, most members of the Reichstag were unaware of it. Certainly most of them would have opposed it had they known. The Centre Party Chancellor Wirth

(Chancellor May 1921 to November 1922) knew and approved of it, favouring an Eastern orientation to German policy. He negotiated the Rapallo Treaty which heralded Russo-German *rapprochement* in 1922. His successor Cuno, who lasted until August 1923, opposed such cooperation but was unable to stop it. Stresemann was more sympathetic. The other Chancellors, if they knew about it, were unable to prevent it.

## The Ruhr occupation and Hitler's putsch

Throughout 1921–22 tension continued in Germany. There were rumours of coups and political assassinations (including that of Matthias Erzberger, one of the signatories of the Armistice Agreement, and Walther Rathenau, Jewish Foreign Minister, both were murdered by Rightists). The trials of Germans before German courts for alleged war crimes—mainly the ill-treatment of prisoners of war and the sinking of a hospital ship—further stirred up the nationalists. Worse was to come. The fate of Upper Silesia was still in the balance. By a considerable majority the inhabitants voted in March 1921 to remain in Germany. Polish volunteers, encouraged by the Polish government, anticipated the decision of the Allies to partition Upper Silesia by staging a coup in the area. The French occupying forces did nothing, but the Poles were opposed by German Freikorps who successfully held the Poles. But the Reich government was forced to follow a verbally more conciliatory policy than the Freikorps, which once again increased the wrath of the nationalists. Eventually Upper Silesia was partitioned as a result of a recommendation by a League of Nations' committee drawn from Belgium, Brazil, China and Spain. Their decision was a disappointment to the Germans.

Hatred rather than disappointment was the response of the Germans to the Franco-Belgian occupation of the Ruhr which started in January 1923. Officially it was said that the French sought to ensure punctual delivery of reparations. The move, which was not supported by Britain, was declared an illegal violation of Versailles by the German government under Chancellor Cuno. The Reich government forbade German industry to export coal to France or Belgium, and ordered government officials and other public employees to ignore the instructions of the occupying forces. Many German officials obeyed their government, German workers went on strike. The French military authorities, no doubt remembering bitter situations when the boot was on the other foot, responded with vigour. They jailed hundreds, expelled hundreds more and killed 13 Krupp workers when they fired on strikers.

Faced with so many political difficulties, not to mention economic ones (discussed below), it would not have been surprising if the German governmental system had collapsed. Hitler thought it might – with a gentle push from Bavaria. His amateurish revolt was probably inspired by Mussolini who was busy toppling the Italian parliamentary system after his famous 1922 march on Rome.

Adolf Hitler was born in 1889, the son of a minor Austrian Custom's Official. Like Churchill and some others destined for fame he was not so good at his school subjects, though he made his mark in history classes. He left the *Gymnasium* without graduating with the intention of becoming an artist but he failed to get into the Vienna Academy of Fine Arts and apparently gave up this ambition. For several years he lived on a modest paternal inheritance and from money he earned doing odd jobs. He pursued his interest in architecture at this time.

It was in Vienna, a very politically aware city, that he came to full political consciousness. His views were not unusual for one from his background. As a petty bourgeois he despised the workers. As a German-Austrian he had little time for the lesser breeds of the Empire—Poles, Hungarians, Czechs, and Slovaks. He was conventionally anti-semitic when he arrived in Vienna from the city of Linz. The capital was at that time ruled by a Lord Mayor with strong anti-Jewish tendencies and Hitler was no doubt influenced by this atmosphere. He was probably angered too by finding Jews who were better educated or materially better off than himself. He became a pan-German nationalist in the years before the First World War as he contrasted the dynamism of Germany with the decay of the Hapsburg Empire. At the outbreak of the war he volunteered for service in a Bavarian rather than an Austrian regiment and was twice awarded the Iron Cross. He rose to the rank of corporal.

After Bavaria's brief experiment as a Marxist republic at the end of the war, Munich became a hotbed of Rightist agitation. Hitler attracted the attention of his officers for his Right-wing views and oratorical abilities. They, in fear of Marxism and seeking platforms for their own ideas, assigned him to investigate the activities of a group calling itself the German Workers' Party. He joined this movement, which had been set up by a nationalist locksmith Anton Drexler, and left the army. By the time the party changed its name to the National Socialist German Workers' Party (N S D A P) on 1 April 1920 he was already among its leaders. The N S D A P adopted a programme, taken over from the earlier party, including: the uniting of all Germans in a greater Germany; such a Germany to have a strong central government; abolition of unearned incomes; nationalisation of trusts; abolition of land rents and land speculation; maintenance of a sound middle class; municipalisation of department stores and their lease at cheap rates to small traders; death for traitors and profiteers and, so important after 1933, ban on Jews from holding public office and loss of citizenship, and renunciation of the Versailles Treaty.

In the summer of 1921 Hitler succeeded in fighting Drexler for the party leadership and from then on was the party's Führer, a position which it seems the founders of the movement had not regarded as part and parcel of National Socialism. About this time Hitler got his first financial backers—two wealthy ladies. One of these was Frau Helene Bechstein, wife of the famous piano maker, the other was Frau Gertrud von Seidlitz, who had a considerable holding in some Finnish paper mills. Hermann Göring, famous for his exploits as a fighter pilot, also contributed to Hitler's and the party's upkeep. He had been lucky enough to marry into affluence. Hitler himself did not marry, he was married to the movement and gradually built up an image as an austere, devoted leader. He was a non-drinker, non-smoker and vegetarian. It was in these early years that some of the later internationally-known Nazis joined the movement. Men like Rudolf Hess, son of a German merchant in Egypt and wartime flyer, Max Amann, Hitler's wartime sergeant, and Alfred Rosenberg, the Estonian-German graduate of Moscow University.

Another important, in many respects decisive, figure in the Nazi movement claimed earlier membership than Hitler—a fact probably held against him by his Führer; this was Ernst Röhm. He had served Kaiser and Fatherland as a captain in the army and built up the Nazi movement's military wing, the S A. Early in 1923 Röhm engineered an alliance of a number of militant Right-wing groups including many former officers and N C Os, something Hitler, as a former corporal, could not have succeeded in doing. This brought Hitler on to the same platform as General Ludendorff who was always ready to 'have a go' if he thought he could advance the Right-wing cause.

On 26 September 1923 Gustav Stresemann, who had become Chancellor in August, announced, no doubt to the surprise of those who remembered him as a hardline nationalist during the war, the end of resistance to the French in the Ruhr. He had taken the precaution of getting President Ebert to declare a state of emergency under Article 48 of the Constitution, tantamount to turning the country over to the army under General Seeckt. Seeckt saw his task as maintaining the unity of the Reich and of 'law and order'. However, he had greater ambitions too. He planned to take over as Chancellor and actually drew up a 'government programme' along authoritarian lines. Germany might well have got a military regime at that time had not some Right-wing officers, and later Hitler, jumped the gun. Led by former Major Ernst Buckrucker Right-wing rebels attempted to seize Berlin. Seeckt put down this rebellion. He continued to be pressed by his own officers to take over and in the end it appears to have been a combination of lack of unity on the Right, Hitler's impetuosity and Seeckt's indecisiveness, which saved Germany from military dictatorship in 1923.

Bavaria, which since the fall of the Kaiser had been operating almost as an independent state, was run by an extremely reactionary clique headed by Dr Gustav Ritter von Kahr. After a personal attack on General Seeckt in the *Völkischer Beobachter*, the Nazi newspaper, he ordered its prohibition. The Reichswehr commander General Lossow refused to execute the order and was backed by von Kahr. The situation gradually deteriorated and open secession broke out with officers taking a new oath to Bavaria replacing the one they had taken to the Reich. Hitler hoped to exploit this situation and tried to force the hand of von Kahr, Lossow and police chief Col. Hans von Seisser. He hoped to get them to launch a complete takeover in Munich leading to a march on Berlin. Using the SA he arrested them as they attended a businessmen's meeting in a Munich beer hall. At first reluctant to cooperate with him, they agreed when threatened with a revolver and when they heard that Ludendorff was behind the Nazi leader. Hitler now made a fatal mistake of leaving them in the custody of his subordinates. The three Bavarians slipped away and being enraged by their treatment they ordered troops and police to deal with the Nazis. The putsch of 8–9 November ended in bloodshed with 16 SA and three police killed and many others wounded.

There was bloodshed in other parts of Germany that autumn. In Hamburg the Communists revolted from 23 to 26 October. Ernst Thälmann was in charge and it was hoped that the rising would spread throughout the country. In fact it was put down without too much difficulty. In Saxony and Thuringia Left-Socialist and Communist coalition governments had been established. Seeckt acted with much more decisiveness than he had shown in dealing with Bavaria. These governments were perfectly legal though the Communist partners foolishly called for the setting up of the dictatorship of the proletariat throughout Germany. Workers' militias were formed. Seeckt ordered the Reichswehr in, disbanded the armed workers' organisations and arrested the governments. This action led to the break-up of the coalition government in Berlin due to the withdrawal of the Social Decmocrats. Stresemann fell on 30 November and was replaced by the Centre Party politician Marx who ruled with the help of an enabling act until February of the next year. Stresemann was included in the government as Foreign Minister, a post he occupied until his death in 1929. General Seeckt gradually relinquished control of things after the crushing of the revolts. Why he did so is not clear though he may have felt by so doing he could legally get power by becoming next President. As it turned out his fellow officer Hindenburg was elected to that position after the death of Ebert in 1925. In the autumn of 1926 the politicians felt the position of the Republic had been so stabilised that they could dismiss Seeckt, officially for introducing a member of the old royal family in uniform to a regimental exercise, without any fear of a military coup. They were over-optimistic. The officers had merely changed their loyalty from Seeckt to Hindenburg and he was to lead them and the country into Hitler's lap.

## From inflation to stabilisation

Germany's political troubles of the early 1920s were made much worse by economic problems (in turn to a considerable degree caused by political difficulties). The peace terms, the Kapp putsch, the troubles in Upper Silesia, the coups and rumours of coups, created loss of confidence in the currency and inflation followed. The reparations crisis and the French occupation of the Ruhr led to a catastrophic fall in the value of the mark. Domestic prices became fixed according to the mark's relation to the dollar. In July 1914 this had been 4.2 marks to the dollar; by July 1919 it was 14 marks. In July 1922 493.2 marks were exchanged for one dollar and a year later 353,412.0. Runaway inflation was now fully under way and by December 1923 4,200,000 million marks were needed to purchase one dollar! The situation was so out of hand that shops closed at midday with one set of prices and reopened in the afternoon with another higher set. Those on fixed incomes or with property invested at fixed money values, in government bonds for example, lost everything as did holders of savings bank deposits. This fairly large group of normally conservative people equated their personal misfortune with the Weimar system and were more than ever prepared to listen to the representatives of the old order. But some other people were doing well out of the collapse of the monetary system. Businessmen flourished as their physical assets increased in value daily and even hourly. On the other hand, their debts declined. Obviously, as new loans were advanced those granting them tried to take account of further depreciation of the currency when fixing the rate of interest, but they were never quite successful.

The result was that there was a boom in investment activity as new plant and equipment were being acquired virtually without cost. Great fortunes were made. In this connection the name of Hugo Stinnes is well known. He inherited a coal-mining and shipping firm. After the war the inflation enabled him to expand and diversify his holdings until he became one of the most powerful men in Germany. He used his economic power to gain political influence which he exercised as one of the leaders of Gustav Stresemann's German People's Party, the party which was in government from May 1923 to May 1932, and through his ownership of the newspaper *Deutsche Allgemeine Zeitung*. Stinnes died in April 1924.

Apart from internal measures, such as a radical credit freeze imposed in April 1924, financial stabilisation was brought about by the Dawes Plan, drawn up on American initiative. Named after General Charles C. Dawes, the chairman of the committee which worked it out, the plan was recommended as offering a temporary solution to Germany's reparations difficulties. The Americans hoped, for their part, that the plan would help them to find some outlet for their own excessive gold reserves and markets for their industrial production. Under the plan the Germans were offered an immediate loan of 800 million gold marks, and, though the final reparations total remained unsettled, annual payments of reparations of a size within the Reich's capacity to pay were fixed. In return the Germans had to accept that their railways and the Reichsbank were removed from German control, and the Reparations Commission, under an American financier, Parker Gilbert, exercised a degree of supervision over the Republic's financial arrangements. The Plan, and certain political initiatives abroad by Stresemann, heralded a period of economic recovery and expansion rivalling any other in previous German history. Germany, which for a number of years had been both politically and economically a sleeping giant, now returned to the international scene. One index of this economic return was the expansion of exports. In 1929, despite the loss of Reich territory and of all her colonies, exports were up on the 1913 level by 34 per cent. Germany's share of world production rose from 8 per cent in 1923 to 12 per cent in 1928, and of world trade from 8.1 per cent in 1925 to 9.5 per cent in 1929. Between the years 1923 and 1928 total industrial production was doubled thus overtaking the highest pre-war level. The following figures of production help to illustrate that development:

| Year | hardcoal in mill. tons | brown coal in mill. tons | raw steel in mill. tons | electricity in mill. kWh. |
|------|------|------|------|------|
| 1913 | 190.1 | 87.2 | 20.8 | — |
| 1923 | 62.3 | 118.8 | 6.3 | — |
| 1926 | 145.3 | 139.2 | 12.3 | 21,218 |
| 1929 | 163.4 | 174.5 | 16.1 | 30,660 |

The development of German industry during this period was due to German willingness to learn from American experience of the rationalisation of industry, and to the inflow of foreign investments. Seventy per cent of the latter came from American banks. In 1925 I. G. Farben, the huge firm dominating the chemical and dyestuff industries, was set up. And in 1926 Albert Vögler formed the giant steel trust Vereinigte Stahlwerke A. G. In the electrical industry Siemens had a virtual monopoly.

Naturally, in these conditions of economic expansion the industrial workers were able to improve their position. But not as much as one might have expected. It was only in 1928 that real wages reached the prewar level. And there remained a pool of unemployed though nothing like what was to come.

Unemployment in Germany, 1926–29 (*in millions*)

| Year | | number |
|------|------|------|
| 1926 | January | 2.2 |
| | July | 2.0 |
| 1927 | January | 2.2 |
| | July | 0.9 |
| 1928 | January | 1.7 |
| | July | 1.0 |
| 1929 | January | 2.8 |
| | July | 1.2 |

Many workers improved their housing conditions during these years. This was due to a considerable extent to their own efforts and those of their representatives in, above all, the Länder or regional governments. In the years 1920–30 the workers' building cooperatives alone built some 100,000 homes. Of greater importance was the Prussian housing law of 1918 which empowered local authorities to enact planning measures, provide open spaces, and erect small dwellings and buildings of public utility: it directed further that all districts with more than 10,000 inhabitants must issue police ordinances concerning housing hygiene. The larger towns were required to open offices for the allocation of dwellings and for the control of housing hygiene. The Act of 1918 had been passed because the introduction of universal suffrage had made Prussia a Social Democratic stronghold. Similar measures were introduced in other areas subject to Social Democratic influence. The Reich, again under Social Democratic influence, subsidised house building and controlled rents.

## Stresemann's foreign policy.

As mentioned above, Stresemann's foreign policy helped to produce the international confidence in Germany which produced the conditions for economic recovery. Like the nationalists he wanted to end the encirclement of Germany, German military weakness and foreign occupation. Unlike them he was prepared to seek the friendship of Britain and France to achieve this and prepared for a reasonable compromise settlement in reparations. When that had been brought about, and only then, could the problems of revision of the eastern frontier be approached with any likelihood of success. The Locarno Pacts of October 1925 by which Britain, France, Italy and Germany all guaranteed the Franco-German and Belgian-German frontiers were the first part of his aims and were followed, after some delay, by Germany's entry into the League of Nations with a permanent seat upon the Council. This was in September 1926. Another part of the Locarno agreement was the reduction in the number, and cost to the Germans, of the occupation forces in the Rhineland and the British withdrawal from Cologne on 30 January 1926. Finally, at the beginning of the following year the Inter-Allied Commission of control of German armaments was dissolved. Stresemann's policy of conciliation and gentle revision ran into temporary difficulties later in that year after Poincaré, who had been largely responsible for the Ruhr occupation, replaced the more 'dove'-like Herriot as French Prime Minister. By early 1928 Stresemann was complaining that the Allies were not granting further concessions of the kind his policy of fulfilment deserved. On 30 October he sent an urgent request for a new and final settlement of the reparations question. The Allies agreed and appointed an expert committee to investigate the issue. On 7 June 1929 it produced the Young Plan. Weeks later Stresemann accepted this and got the immediate evacuation of the Rhineland by the British and Belgians, and the promise of French evacuation by the end of June 1930 'if physically possible'. He did not live to see this or the subsequent failure of his policy due to economic and political changes in Germany. Gustav Stresemann died on 2 October 1929.

## The failure of democracy in education

The German education system with its emphasis on obedience and authority had long been the target of Social Democrat and liberal critics of the old order. Once that order collapsed they hoped to be able to do something to alter the education system as well. Apart from any general improvement in standards the reformers sought the breaking-down of the old religious barriers which kept Catholic children separated from Protestant children; the development of a democratic consciousness among teachers which would be passed on to their pupils and, thirdly, the ending of the virtual monopoly by the middle classes of secondary-grammar and higher education. Despite brave efforts the reformers failed to achieve these aims.

As far as standards were concerned, in these areas where the reformers were in charge—Prussia, Hamburg, Saxony, Thuringia— standards did rise. Even in these areas less progress was made in overcoming religious differences though some secular schools were set up in a few areas, notably Hamburg and Berlin. In south-western Germany interdenominational schools were established. The majority of schools, however, remained denominational, so-called *Bekenntnisschulen*. Disagreement over the maintenance of these denominational schools was one of the main differences between the Social Democrats and the Catholic Centre Party which not only prevented the formulation of national educational policy but inter-fered with their cooperation on other issues. Particularly among secondary-school teachers the old monarchical-conservative ideas persisted and they ignored appeals from above for the teaching of loyalty to the Republic's democratic ideals. History textbooks remained nationalist orientated. In the reform-controlled Länder some efforts were made to make secondary education available to children from working class, peasant or poorer homes. In 1925 the *Aufbauschulen* were set up in certain parts of Germany to provide an alternative secondary education for gifted pupils who had completed their elementary school courses, but had, for one reason or another, failed to obtain entrance to a secondary school. Nevertheless, the lack of an adequate scholarship system still prevented most gifted non-middle-class children from getting secondary education. In 1931, the working-class population made up over 50 per cent of the total population, but only about seven per cent of secondary-school pupils were from this social class.

In 1918 Germany was much better endowed than Britain with universities. Greater respect for learning was a possible reason for this. Continuing religious rivalries, the existence of so many independent states in nineteenth-century Germany, and the importance of a legal training in public administration and industry, a training only obtained at a university, were other decisive factors. A number of technical universities were established in the latter part of the nineteenth century, to help Germany develop its technology. Unlike Britain there was a tradition of dependence on the state and senior members of the academic staff had the status of civil servants. Professors were appointed by the state and apart from an attitude of conformity this might have engendered, in Prussia at any rate, Social Democrats were excluded from professorships under a law of 1899. In the few years at their disposal the Weimar reformers could do little to alter this situation. If the great majority of professors were not members of the N S D A P before 1933 they were nationalist inclined.

The situation among the students was not very much different. Again, the great majority were not consciously Nazi-inclined, rather vaguely nationalist though not very political. However, a considerable minority of them were members of the traditionalist fraternities. Most of these had their origins in the struggle against the French, Napoleonic invaders when they had liberal as well as nationalist ideas. But gradually, later on in the nineteenth century, they became reactionary. Membership came to be regarded as a passport to a top job. Moreover membership did not lapse on graduation, former students became much respected *Alte Herren* taking part in ceremonies and get-togethers with each succeeding generation of students. In this way each generation of student members was brought under the influence of the survivors of past generations with all their ideas, prejudices and opportunities for patronage.

Over the Weimar years there were a number of incidents at German universities which seemed to be harbingers of what was to come in 1933. There was the case of E. J. Gumbel, an ex-serviceman turned pacifist who lectured on mathematical statistics at Heidelberg University. He was hounded from 1923 onwards by Right-wing students backed up by teachers. In 1930, by which time he was an 'extraordinary professor', he had his 'licence to teach' cancelled by the Ministry of Education in Baden. This was after protests by Right-wing students over remarks he made about the war while addressing a meeting of socialist students. Prof. Theodor Lessing of Hanover Technical University published an attack on Paul von Hindenburg when the latter was running for President in 1925. He was then hounded for the rest of the years of the Republic. At the start of the campaign his lectures were broken into, mobs stood outside the building and jeered at him, others surrounded him and his family, jostled him and desisted only when he agreed to cease lecturing for a term. In 1930 Günther Dehn was elected by the theological faculty of Heidelberg to a full professorship. A violent campaign was started by nationalist students accusing him of having called the soldiers of the World War 'murderers' and, although an enquiry by the Church authorities proved the falsity of the charge, the appointment was withdrawn under student pressure. There were many examples of Right-wing professors giving encouragement to their cause and denouncing the Republic in their lectures without suffering any inconvenience.

In a few years the two universities of Berlin, the universities of Heidelberg, Halle, Munich, Cologne, Marburg, Greifswald, Kiel, Königsberg, Hamburg, Hanover and Brunswick all suffered from political disturbances. Towards the end of the Republic the universities were radicalised in the way the German people as a whole were being radicalised. The result of the *Astawahlen*, the non-party organisation of the general student body at each university, available for 14 out of 33 universities, or university-level institutions, in 1933, indicated the Nazis commanding majorities in all 14.

## Cultural ferment and political commitment

The Weimar period stands out as an era of intellectual ferment, of rich diversity in motivation and idiom in the arts, of revolutionary content and experimentation in form. The ferment affected all branches of the arts. Here we can only mention some of the significant names, and erect a few sign-posts in literature, the cinema and architecture.

On the Left, the period opened with Heinrich Mann's lampoon of the Germany of the Kaisers, *Der Untertan*, which earned him the hatred of the traditionalists for the rest of his life. Erich Maria Remarque echoed and encouraged the pacifist wave sweeping Europe with *Im Westen Nichts Neues*, a book made famous by Hollywood as *All Quiet On the Western Front*. Arnold Zweig's *Sergeant Grischa* exposed the inhumanity of war on the Eastern Front. In their satirical magazine *Die Weltbühne*, Carl von Ossietzky and Kurt Tucholsky used their considerable talents against militarism, revanchism and authoritarianism. The one later died in a concentration camp, the other despaired and committed suicide in lonely exile. Thomas Mann renounced his earlier nationalism, and recognised the new enemy, laying bare the psychological character of Fascism in his allegorical tale of *Mario und der Zauberer*. In 1931, Erich Kästner, in *Fabian*, narrated the troubles, temptations, and final destruction, of the lower middle class young man in the Berlin of mass unemployment, political gangsterism and avant-garde sex. And Hans Fallada asked, as so many were asking, 'What Now Little Man?', in his novel of the same name. Bertolt Brecht, Ludwig Renn, Anna Seghers, Arnold Zweig, and some other writers, felt the answer was to be found in Communism.

On the right, the poet Stefan George, consciously non-political, published a collection of poems in 1921 entitled *Das neue Reich*. In one of these poems he prophesied that out of the new youth would emerge the new leader. He would set up the new Reich. Deliberately political, Moeller van den Bruck attacked Versailles, the November Revolution, Social Democracy, Liberalism, Democracy and Communism. His *Das Dritte Reich* was at least one of the most influential books of the period. Oswald Spengler fought the same foes, adding a new one, the coloured races. To prevent *The Decline of the West* a strong, new military Reich was necessary. Spengler, together with Ernst Jünger and a host of now forgotten popular writers, stressed the heroics of war, and even went so far as to claim that it was natural, inevitable and invigorating. The book which later became the literary Bible of National Socialism, Hans Grimm's *Volk ohne Raum (A People Without Space)*, whose proletarian hero comes to accept the nationalist credo after learning to hate the British in South Africa, was also written in this period.

Much of German film production between 1918 and 1933 was concerned, like much of production elsewhere, with escapist themes— comedies, adventures in far-off places, detective stories, fantasies and musicals. As the censorship had been abolished in 1918, both the educational and commercial sides of sex could be, and were, fully exploited. But more serious themes were dealt with too, and politics strayed into the cinema.

Serious film directors were preoccupied with the same problems as serious writers. Unlike the writers, they had the problem of financing their projects. The U F A organisation possessed a dominant position both in the production and distribution of films. From 1927 this company was in the hands of Alfred Hugenberg, a reactionary banker, nationalist and later ally of Hitler. Though he did not exploit his position to the full he had no enthusiasm for critical and controversial themes.

One of the directors who did manage to handle controversial themes was G. W. Pabst, an Austrian. His pacifist-inclined *Westfront 1918* gave the public a frank look at the horror of war. In his *Kameradschaft (Comradeship)*, made in 1931, he preached international solidarity with a story about German miners going to the aid of French colleagues, trapped in a mine on the other side of the frontier. Another film made by Pabst in 1931 was his rendering of *Dreigroschenoper* by Bertolt Brecht. All three films still attract film enthusiasts. Two other critical films which have stood the test of time are Leontine Sagan's *Mädchen in Uniform*, exposing the effects of Prussianism in a girls' boarding school, and Richard Oswald's *Captain of Köpenick*, an amusing attack on militarism based on a true story.

*The Blue Angel*, the best-known film of the Weimar era was, unlike the five mentioned above, a U F A production. Directed by another Austrian, Joseph von Sternberg, it tells the story of the decline and fall of a secondary school professor through his infatuation with, and subsequent marriage to, a night-club singer. Emil Jannings, who became infamous for his parts in Nazi films, played the teacher, Marlene Dietrich, who emigrated to America, the singer. This cautionary tale of sex and sadism has been interpreted by students of the German film as symbolic of the destruction of the Weimar system.

More nationalist in tone were the historical and war films directed by Gustav Ucicky and Luis Trenker.

'A hotbed of cultural Bolshevism' was the description given by Hitler to the Weimar Republic's most famous experiment in architecture and design. Founded in 1919 by Walter Gropius, the Bauhaus was conceived as a school which would unite the arts, technology and industry to promote the quality of life. It united the architects Gropius, Ludwig Mies van der Rohe and Marcel Breuer, with painters such as Paul Klee, Wassily Kandinsky and Lyonel Feininger, and others besides. The school greatly influenced the design of furniture, pottery and posters, as well as painting and architecture. Its basic idea was to discard conventional ornamental styles for functional ones of steel, glass and concrete. The new designs were meant to give people a greater insight into reality, and make life easier—especially for women. In Germany their architectural ideas were realised in the complex of Bauhaus buildings at Dessau, the communal theatre at Jena, and the trade union school at Bernau near Berlin.

Politically on the Left, the Bauhaus school had its ideas rejected just as much by Stalin as by Hitler, and by many with money to build in Britain and America. In the postwar era, however, Bauhaus-influenced styles gradually became the accepted convention in the West and, after the death of Stalin, in the East too.

## Hitler in the wilderness

On 1 April 1924 Adolf Hitler faced the judges in a Munich court to hear them pronounce sentence on him for attempting to alter the German constitution by force—the result of his revolutionary escapade of the previous November. He could have got life imprisonment; in fact he was sentenced to five years. Less than nine months later on 20 December he was released from Landsberg fortress. His light sentence was no doubt partly due to the presence of General Erich Ludendorff with him in the dock—the general was acquitted— and to the nationalist sympathies of the judges. Ludendorff, as one of Germany's most famous military men, ensured the presence of journalists from all over Germany and Europe. Hitler used the opportunity presented to get some free publicity. In so many words he told the old ruling classes, 'I want to march with you, not against you'. He actually said: 'I believe that the hour will come when the masses, who today stand in the street with our swastika banner, will unite with those who fired on them'. He was a revolutionary against the revolution (of 1918), a destroyer of Marxism and a friend of the Reichswehr for 'the hour will come when the Reichswehr will stand at our side, officers and men'. Considering he was only a half-educated former corporal, many representatives of the old order must have thought him an arrogant upstart, even a bit mad. But they had to admit he was a courageous fellow, willing to 'have a go' for the old cause, and that his heart was in the right place. And, after all, good old Ludendorff thought him worthy of support. This view of the likely effect of his trial is shown to be plausible when we learn that during his period of internment he received a good many well-to-do visitors at Landsberg. They saw to it that his detention was not uncomfortable.

Hitler did not merely spend his time in Landsberg fortress entertaining wellwishers from high society. He turned his attention to literary activities. He wrote what was to be his autobiography and political testament rolled into one, *Mein Kampf* or *My Struggle*. In its preface he wrote that he realised that men 'are won over less by the written than by the spoken word' but 'Nevertheless, for a doctrine to be disseminated uniformly and coherently, its basic elements must be set down for all time'. We need not say too much about his rambling, two-part, volume written in a style which is a mixture of contemporary popular journalism and south German dialect. The central point of the book is the struggle against the Jews who are at the back of every difficulty Germany had recently experienced. The Jew is 'a parasite on other peoples' who has to lie to convince other people that 'he is not a people but a "religious community", though of a special sort'. In order to infiltrate into a society, he uses a thousand different guises and methods, from debased culture and weakening a nation through intermarriage, to posing as an intellectual benefactor of mankind or a popular political leader. Doctrines such as equality and democracy help the Jew by allowing full freedom to exploit the gullibility of his fellows. Most of all he controls the nation's life through his control of economic affairs especially through the stock exchange. The labour movement becomes 'a pure movement entirely of manual workers under Jewish leadership, apparently aiming to improve the situation of the worker, but in truth planning the enslavement and with it the destruction of all non-Jewish peoples'. Marxism is the doctrine of that movement. Also, 'the Jew by means of the trade union, which could be a blessing for the nation, shatters the foundations of the national economy'.

This then was how the Jews were operating against Germany's interests within the country itself. What about in the international arena? There Germany faced 'chauvinistic France' struggling to turn Germany into a 'hotch-potch of little states'. This is what France fought for in 1914, 'though at the same time in reality it sold its people as mercenaries to the international world Jew'. Britain had fought to annihilate Germany as a colonial and commercial rival but Britain needed Germany as a check to the power of France. As for Russia, it was ruled by 'the scum of humanity' and 'in Russian Bolshevism we must see the attempt undertaken by the Jews in the twentieth century to achieve world domination'. What Germany needed was an alliance with Britain and Italy. With such an alliance Germany could 'break off the soil' the colonial and commercial policy of the prewar period and shift to the soil policy of the future. 'If we speak of soil in Europe today, we can primarily have in mind only Russia and her vassal border states'. In order to justify his aggressive foreign policy Hitler evoked 'Fate' and the 'Court of History'. He was applying the theory of the survival of the fittest to international affairs.

In order for Germany to realise its foreign policy aims it needed a strong internal order, a centralised state, freed from Jews and Marxists and their ideas, practising 'racial hygiene' based on a people trained in will-power and determination.

Hitler was not expecting to win converts with *Mein Kampf* and said this frankly in his preface. This was just as well, for in the years immediately after it was written the Nazi movement did not appear to be getting very far. Membership was rising, but only slowly: 27,000 in 1925; 49,000 in 1926; 72,000 in 1927 and 108,000 in 1928. In these years the Nazi leader had to be largely content with slowly building up his organisation and strengthening his own position within that organisation. He established himself as sole leader to whose decisions all members of the movement were subordinate. He created the S S (*Schutzstaffel* or protective squad) as a special bodyguard bound by an oath of loyalty to his person. That was in April 1925. In 1926 he obtained the support of the crippled, yet intellectually very able, Dr Paul Joseph Goebbels, who had first been attracted to National Socialism by Gregor Strasser's 'Left-wing' version of the Nazi gospel. In that year he deserted the North German Nazi leader Strasser for Hitler who was none too pleased with Strasser's 'socialism'. Despite these successes within the movement Adolf Hitler was not making much impact on the masses outside it.

The elections of 20 May 1928 seemed to augur well for German democracy. Those stalwart supporters of Weimar the Social Democrats increased their vote significantly and their parliamentary strength went up accordingly from 131 to 153. On their left the Communists increased their representation from 45 to 54. The Centre more or less held its position but lost eight seats, being reduced to 61. Stresemann's moderate nationalist German People's Party also lost slightly dropping from 51 to 45 seats. The Bavarian People's Party lost two seats returning 17 members to the Reichstag. The Nationalists, later to be Hitler's allies, faced a slump of support and fell in seats from 111 to 78. As for the Nazis, their strength was reduced from 14 to 12. In May 1924 they had won 32 seats. Their prospects looked bleak yet within two years they were to change dramatically.

# — 4 —

# Weimar Crisis and Capitulation

After the elections of May 1928 President Hindenburg called upon Social Democrat Hermann Müller to form a government. This he only managed to do with great difficulties about a month later. Müller's coalition partners were the Centre Party, the (Conservative Catholic) Bavarian People's Party, the Democratic Party and the German People's Party.

Müller's 'Grand Coalition' was soon faced with a crisis which gave the enemies of democracy in Germany useful ammunition. The outgoing Government and the Reichstag had approved in principle the building of a naval cruiser. This decision had been fought by the parties of the Left at the elections. What now? The Müller cabinet reaffirmed the earlier decision to build the ship. The Social Democratic parliamentary group criticised their ministers for not openly attacking the plan but agreed to continued Social Democratic participation in the government. Agitation, mainly from the Communists, continued over the issue and on 17 November a remarkable scene took place in the Reichstag. The Social Democrats, including the ministers who had agreed it in the Cabinet, voted against the decision to construct the ship. As it turned out, the Social Democrats and the Communists were outvoted on the issue by 202 to 257 in favour. To many in Germany the incident seemed to prove the futility of the parliamentary system. Apart from this it probably led to the weakening of the Social Democratic Party due to internal dissension and loss of grass roots support.

Changes were also taking place in other parties which facilitated the Nazi seizure of power in 1933. After their electoral set-back the Nationalists engaged in post-mortem feuding. The result was that their chairman resigned and was replaced by Alfred Hugenberg on 20 October. As we shall see, this was to be of decisive importance in 1933. The Centre Party changed its leadership about the same time. A party congress elected Professor Monsignor Ludwig Kaas as successor to Wilhelm Marx who had resigned. This represented a shift to the right at a time when Centre-Social democratic cooperation was of the greatest importance for the maintenance of the Republic.

During the summer of 1928 the sixth congress of the Communist International, Comintern, met in Moscow and announced a new line which was of the greatest importance for Germany. It forbade member parties from engaging in collaboration with parties belonging to the Second (Social Democratic and Labour) International. The German Communists from then on treated the Social Democrats as their main enemies, dubbing them 'Social Fascists'. At the 12th party congress of the K P D in June 1929 the Communist leader Ernst Thälmann accused the Social Democrats of trying to establish a fascist dictatorship. The Communists started using up their energies fighting the Social Democrats and in futile attempts to set up their own trade union organisation to rival that under Social Democratic influence. They later recognised, when it was too late, the falseness of these efforts.

The Communists' thesis was wrong and had been thought up in Moscow. It was not the product of a German critique of the Weimar Republic, yet the Social Democrats had a case to answer. They were demanding loyalty to a state which was headed by a militarist Hindenburg. They were in coalition with some profoundly clerical and reactionary politicians in the Bavarian People's Party and the Right of the Centre Party. The state machine was manned by monarchist bureaucrats and 'defended' by monarchist officers who were plotting to destroy its democratic provisions. Further, in the Weimar Republic the industrialists, as in the case of the Rheinish-Westphalian iron industry lock-out of November 1928, could openly defy government decisions on labour disputes. And did not governments in which Social Democrats participate exercise financial stringency when dealing with the unemployed but not when handing out millions upon millions of marks to the enemies of Weimar, the Junkers, to maintain their tottering estates? Finally, the forces of 'law and order', including those controlled by Social Democrats, seemed, in nine cases out of ten, to hit out harder when dealing with Left-wing radicals than when dealing with those on the right. Only a matter of weeks before the 12th Communist congress 31 people had been killed and hundreds more wounded when police, under Berlin's Social Democratic police chief, Karl Zörgiebel, opened fire on a banned Communist May Day demonstration. The Communists had attempted to resist the police and used firearms.

## Opposition to the Young Plan

The 12th Communist Party congress attacked the Young Plan and declared the intention of the party to fight it. More important than Communist opposition to the Plan was that of the Nazis and Nationalists.

As we have seen, the acceptance of the Plan by Germany in 1929 resulted in the withdrawal of Allied occupation forces, and re-established Germany's exclusive responsibility for its own finances and economy. However, it foresaw Germany continuing to make payments to the Allies until 1982! It is only to be expected that very many Germans resented this as, apart from the additional financial burdens it laid upon their shoulders, it was based on the assumption that it was the Germans who were mainly responsible for the horrors of the 1914–18 war. Most ordinary Germans were inclined to think that it was the 'upper ten thousand' in Germany and in the Allied countries who between them shared responsibility for the outbreak of hostilities and that crimes were then committed on both sides. Hugenberg hoped to cash in on the resentment of reparations and of the branding of the Germans as criminals. He launched a referendum campaign demanding that the German people be given the opportunity to vote on the issues related to the Versailles agreement and sub-sequent agreements which followed from it, including the issue of further reparations. His allies in the campaign were Franz Seldte, leader of the paramilitary nationalist Stahlhelm organisation, of which Hindenburg was the most prominent honorary member, and Nazi leader Hitler. In order for a referendum to be held under the Constitution the organisers had to collect the signatures of 10 per cent of the electorate. This they managed to do, most of the signatories residing East of the Elbe. The next step was for the demands of Hugenberg-Hitler to be presented to the Reichstag in the form of a so-called 'freedom law'. This was defeated causing a split in the Nationalist Party. The actual referendum followed and was heavily defeated, only 5.8 million Germans voting in favour as against the 21 million necessary for it to have become law.

Though the referendum vote represented a decisive defeat for the Rightist alliance the campaign leading up to it represented an important step forward for the Nazi movement. Firstly, it helped to establish the Nazis' respectability by associating them in the middle-class mind with respectable Conservative politicians. The alliance with Hugenberg brought Hitler into closer contact with wealthy industrialists. Already since 1923, according to his own testimony, Fritz Thyssen, head of the steel trust, *Vereinigte Stahlwerke*, had been supporting the Nazis. In 1929 Emil Kirdorf, a top man in the Ruhr coal industry, gave assistance to the Nazis. Hitler's destruction of Strasser's Left-wing Nazi organisation about this time and new association with Hugenberg paved the way for others to do the same. The Hugenberg contact further meant that the Nazis had greatly benefited from the Nationalist leader's publicity empire. He owned newspapers, an agency, cinemas and Germany's most important film company, U F A, which produced a weekly newsreel.

When the world economic crisis broke out after the Wall Street crash in autumn 1929 the Nazis were therefore in a position to exploit it. The crisis had severe repercussions in Germany because of the nature of German industry and credit. Roughly one-third of German production was exported by the late twenties. This meant that when other nations started to cut their imports from Germany, German workers lost their jobs. From 1929 to 1933 German exports fell by almost two-thirds. During the years of boom and prosperity German industrial expansion had been financed to a considerable degree by foreign, very often American, loans. About one half of the credits were short term. Obviously, at the first sign of trouble the foreign investors pulled out their funds. These troubles were in the first place economic ones connected with the world economic situation. By September 1930 there were fears about Germany's political future which caused a massive repatriation of short-term credits. This helps to explain why Germany suffered more from the crisis than other highly industrialised nations, except the United States.

### International Industrial Production 1928–31

*1929 output equals 100*

| Year (monthly average) | Germany | USA | UK | France | Sweden |
| --- | --- | --- | --- | --- | --- |
| 1928 | 98.6 | 94.1 | 94.3 | 91.4 | 81.5 |
| 1929 | 100.0 | 100.0 | 100.0 | 100.0 | 100.0 |
| 1930 | 82.4 | 80.7 | 100.7 | 100.7 | 97.1 |
| 1931 | 69.1 | 68.6 | 83.5 | 89.3 | 85.3 |

## Nazism: A mass movement

In March 1930 the Grand Coalition fell apart. Disagreement broke out over the financing of unemployment relief. In December 1929 there were 1.5 million workers on relief and during the next month unemployment grew by nearly another million. The unemployment insurance fund was in deficit and it was considered necessary either to cut down relief payments or increase contributions. The Social Democrats were against the former and the German People's Party, which was closely connected to industry, opposed the latter course. As no compromise was found, Hermann Müller resigned. He died the following year.

Heinrich Brüning of the Centre Party took over from Müller forming a right-of-centre government including many of the old faces from the bourgeois parties of the Grand Coalition. Elections followed in September at which there was what amounted to a landslide to the National Socialists. In 1928 they had only won 810,000 votes and 12 seats. They now received 6.4 million votes and 107 seats becoming second only to the Social Democrats in the Reichstag. The latter won 8.6 million votes and 143 seats, a loss of half a million votes and ten seats. The Communists picked up 4.6 million votes or 1.3 million more than last time. Their strongholds being East Berlin, East Düsseldorf and Merseburg where they emerged as the strongest party. They also did well in Potsdam, Chemnitz, Hamburg, West Düsseldorf and Leipzig. With 77 seats, as against 54 in the outgoing Reichstag, they overtook the Centre Party as third largest parliamentary group. The Centre though increased its representation from 61 to 68 seats, based on an increased vote, together with the other Catholic party the Bavarian People's Party, of half a million giving them nearly 5.2 million votes. The Bavarian People's Party got 19 seats, two more than in 1928. The really big losers of the election were the Nationalists and the German People's Party. The former lost two million votes, leaving them just under 2.5 million, the latter one million, retaining 1.6 million. They were awarded 44 seats (78 in 1928) and 30 seats (45 in 1928) respectively. The small parties attracted over six million votes, some winning, some losing votes. They gained 89 seats.

As the gain in the Communist votes and the loss of votes by the Nationalists and the People's Party indicate, the Nazis did not cash in on the dissatisfaction of the unemployed proletarians. Rather they were able to attract the temporary loyalty of disappointed Right-wing voters. They got their biggest increase in Schleswig-Holstein, East Prussia and Pomerania, in Breslau and Hanover South. In other words, they did well in agricultural districts, especially Protestant ones, rather than industrial areas. They further won over the non-political elements, for another characteristic of this election was the increase in turn out. In 1928 75.6 per cent had voted, in 1930 82 per cent did so. Finally, the Nazis, like the Communists, were attractive to the young, the new voters.

Brüning continued as Chancellor but without a majority in the

Reichstag. He was able to do so only because he was backed by Hindenburg and was able to use emergency decrees under Article 48 of the Constitution, and then inducing enough groups in the Reichstag to vote against their repeal. His answer to this crisis was basically one of deflation. He cut down wages, salaries and prices in an effort to restore confidence in the German financial and industrial system. His efforts met with no significant, immediate success. By the end of 1931 there were some 4.5 million out of work and many others on short-time working.

The Nazis continued their rapid advance. This was made possible by the continuing crisis and by their ever closer ties with the monied circles of the old 'National Camp'. On the 11 and 12 October 1931 they took part in a rally of the Right at Bad Harzburg in Braunschweig. Called on the initiative of Hugenberg, it became known as the Harzburg Front. It consisted of the Nazis, the Nationalists of Hugenberg, the Stahlhelm and other militarist organisations, even the small Economic Party and the German People's Party were represented. Former admirals and generals abounded as did representatives of the old aristocratic families.

Industry was also well represented. Most businessmen were not Nazi supporters, they admired Hitler's anti-Marxism but they worried about his 'socialism'. Some favoured his proposed autarky others feared it could lead to retaliation against German exports. Hitler had meetings on 9 December in Berlin with Fritz Thyssen and Albert Vögler, another leading industrialist, and on 26 January addressed the Düsseldorf Industrial Club. Many attended, few were convinced. As an insurance policy some put money into the N S D A P as well as into the other anti-Marxist parties. Ideally, most of them would have liked an authoritarian regime led by von Papen. Thyssen, however, declared himself for Hitler.

It is remarkable that Hitler's nationalist and business friends did not see through him about this time, did not realise that although they thought they were using him and could tame him, he was determined to use them. They had enough evidence of his arrogant and dangerous ambitions in what he said. They also found him a tough customer in any negotiations for joint action. Once again he exposed himself early in 1932 when he decided to stand against Hindenburg for the Presidency. This was surely a very undiplomatic move? Like the Munich putsch of 1923 it was a move which could have cost Hitler his career. Perhaps more surprisingly, in view of the fact Hindenburg was in the race, Hugenberg's Nationalists also presented a candidate: Theodor Duesterberg, the deputy head of the Stahlhelm. Thälmann, the Communist, was the only other candidate. Hindenburg accepted the nomination of a non-party committee mainly composed of members of the parties he despised, the Social Democrats and the Centre Party and the other moderate groups. Some nationalist groups also supported him. The 84-year-old field marshal needed two attempts to pull off his re-election. On 13 March he won 18.65 million votes to Hitler's 11.4 million. Thälmann attracted 5 million and Duesterberg about half that number. The old man was just 0.4 per cent short of a majority and therefore a second ballot was necessary. Duesterberg decided not to try again and asked his supporters to vote for the field marshal while Hugenberg opted for neutrality between the remaining Right-wing candidates. Hitler found a useful ally in Frederick William, the former Crown Prince. Once again however he lost to Hindenburg by 13.4 million to the field marshal's 19.4 million. Thälmann got just under 4 million. As Goebbels' diary shows, the Nazis were very disappointed with the result even though these two ballots marked a considerable rise in their vote over 1930. One aspect of the ballots worth mentioning is that women, who predominated, voted more heavily for Hindenburg than for any other candidate.

## The Baron's government

Having elected him, the moderates hoped Hindenburg would help them strengthen the Republic. For a brief moment it looked as though their hope would become reality. Just before the regional elections in Prussia, the President issued a decree dissolving the S A and S S. But two days later he was calling for action against Left-wing paramilitary bodies. The President could not get the agreement of the government to ban non-Nazi paramilitary organisations and consequently only the S A and the S S were dissolved. This angered the army leaders who saw the S A as a useful addition to Germany's small Reichswehr. Through General Kurt von Schleicher and the President's son, Oskar, they turned Hindenburg against Brüning. Relations between the two were in any case not good. Brüning had not complied with the President's demand for a cabinet reshuffle to the Right. The breaking point between Chancellor and President came over the government's proposals to cut subsidies to the Junkers' estates and buy up bankrupt ones for smallholders. Hindenburg regarded this as 'agrarian Bolshevism'. Under pressure from President and Reichswehr Brüning resigned.

The appointment of Franz von Papen as Chancellor in May 1932 represented another nail in the coffin of the Weimar Republic. Papen, a wartime cavalry major and a Catholic noble allied to industry by marriage, owed his opportunity largely to Schleicher's influence with the President. Schleicher took over the Defence Ministry in this 'Barons' Cabinet' as it became known, or 'gentlemen's Government' as Papen called it. It would have done justice to the Kaiser for it was made up of aristocratic officers of the reserve with one exception, the exception being the Minister of Economics who was in reality the representative of heavy industry. Most of the ministers had Nationalist connections though formally they were non-party. Papen himself had been nominally a member of the Centre Party but resigned from that party when it criticised his decision to form such a government. Another important fact to note about this government is that five of its eight members went on to serve in Hitler's government of 1933, one remaining a minister until 1945 and some of the others retaining posts in Hitler's Germany.

The government of Franz von Papen was in an even more hopeless position in the Reichstag than that of Brüning had been. Even had they had a firm alliance of Nazis, Nationalists, German People's Party and Economic Party, which they did not, they would not have had a majority. The alternatives were a change of government or fresh elections, the government and the Nazis wanted elections. In order to improve relations with the Nazis further, Papen decided to lift the ban on the SA and SS, an action which could only lead to a new outbreak of disorders throughout the Reich. Another move which made Papen very popular on the Right was the ejection of the Social Democratic-Centre coalition government in Prussia where he made himself Reich Commissar by presidential decree. By this action, he gained control of three-fifths of Germany. Recent elections in Prussia had led to large Social Democratic losses and the coalition was carrying on as a caretaker regime. This furnished Papen and Hindenburg with their excuse.

Three weeks before the election the Papen regime got a boost from the decisions of the Lausanne Conference on reparations. The Young Plan was replaced by a new agreement which scaled down reparations once again and only obliged the Germans to pay when their economic position enabled them to do so. In fact they made no further payments. By 1933 Hitler came to power and he unilaterally abrogated earlier agreements.

As expected, the elections of July 1932 resulted in a great victory for the Nazis. They more than doubled their parliamentary strength returning 230 Reichstag members. This was a greater number of seats than any other party had ever succeeded in winning in the Weimar Republic, or, for that matter, in the Reichstag of the Kaisers. However, as a percentage of the votes the Nazi victory was still behind that of the Social Democrats in 1919 (excluding the Left Socialists) and in actual votes it was behind the number cast for both Social Democratic groups in that year. Moreover the result indicated other, more important, weaknesses of the National Socialists. Compared with the presidential election their advance seemed to be slowing down. And it was being gained very largely, as in 1930, by winning over voters from other Right-wing parties and new voters or those who normally did not bother. Despite their good result the Nazis, even with the other Right-wing groups, were without a majority. Finally, in view of what was to happen later, it should be mentioned that only 37.2 per cent of the votes went to the Nazis, though, admittedly, some of their worst ideas were held by many on the Right.

Of the other big groups in German politics the Social Democrats lost another ten seats, winning 133 seats and 7.9 million votes (against 13.7 million for the Nazis); the two Catholic parties increased their seats to 97, attracting 5.7 million; the Communists also got more seats and votes—89 and 5.2 million; the Nationalists and the German People's Party lost heavily—the former returned 39 members, a loss of 5, the latter only 7, a loss of 23. These parties received roughly 5 million votes.

From the point of view of parliamentary government the elections had made the situation worse than ever. Negotiations followed between Papen, Hitler and Hindenburg. The Centre Party politicians were included as well. These negotiations came to nothing because Hitler was not prepared to be number two to von Papen—who could blame him? What the Reichstag thought of von Papen was shown in September when a Communist censure motion was passed with all groups except the Nationalists voting for it. Seldom had the Reichstag been so unanimous. Papen had attempted to prevent the Reichstag from voting on this and another motion repealing his emergency decree. But Hermann Göring, newly elected as its president, refused to accept Papen's decree, signed by Hindenburg, dissolving the so recently elected parliament. By dissolving the Reichstag again von Papen was gaining months during which he could carry on as Chancellor ruling by emergency decrees signed by the ailing President.

The most important aspect of the elections of 6 November was the loss by the Nazis of over two million votes and 34 seats. The Nationalists improved their position by 15 seats giving them 54. The German People's Party improved its representation too from 7 to 11. These results give us the clue to what had happened: the old Right-wing parties were winning back their middle-class followers. These waverers had been put off the Nazis by Hitler's sectarian ambitions. Göring's treatment of Papen no doubt contributed to this result. Another factor was the sudden lurch to the Left by the Nazis just before the elections. They had supported a Communist-led strike of Berlin transport workers, an unofficial strike at that. The strike continued until after the elections. The anti-working class, bourgeois, supporters of stability and 'law and order' were dismayed at the sight of Reds and Brownshirts picketing together. Nazi losses were also attributable to a decline in turnout from 84 per cent to 80.6 per cent. Further evidence that the high watermark of the Nazi tide had passed was provided in local elections a few days later and even in student union elections. Perhaps this lulled the non-Nazis into complacency.

On the Left the election results seemed to prove that militancy paid off. The Communists again improved their position gaining just under 6 million votes and 100 seats. The Catholics suffered slight losses probably due to the decline in turnout. Social Democratic representation was reduced to 121 for 7.3 million votes. The Communists were no doubt the beneficiaries here.

Once again the elections solved nothing. Once again there was no workable coalition in sight. Hindenburg interviewed the leaders of the Centre and Right-wing groups. Kaas for the Centre Party declared his readiness to take part in a government which included the Nazis. Hitler once again refused to participate in a government which he did not lead. General Kurt von Schleicher, still officially Defence Minister, now attempted to bring together the Left-wing of the Nazi party, the Centre, the trade unions, but not the Social Democratic Party, and the armed forces in a 'strong' government which would introduce a more authoritarian system of government. Schleicher was not very successful in his endeavours, but he persuaded the President to let von Papen go and appoint himself as Chancellor. At the beginning of December the General took over announcing a Cabinet which looked very much like the old one. Military dictatorship appeared imminent. Unlike Papen, however, General Schleicher was realist enough to comprehend that a few officers and aristocrats could not rule a great industrial nation for very long. So he continued in his efforts to win trade-union support as well as attempting to detach the Left of the Nazi party from Hitler. He even tried to bring in the Social Democratic Party. But Otto Wels, who had taken over the leadership after the death of Hermann Müller, was not prepared to form an alliance with Schleicher even when the General offered to ban the Nazi movement. Considering Germany's experience with military men both before and after 1918 this was understandable; knowing what we now know, we can regret it.

Franz von Papen, angry at the way he had been replaced by General von Schleicher, and with plenty of time on his hands, started to intrigue against his erstwhile friend and minister. Although Papen no longer held any official position he still had his powerful friends including the President. The powerful men of industry also wanted a solution and preferably one without the trade unions and the Social Democratic Party. Schleicher's failure to produce a government with any likelihood of success played into Papen's hands. Another factor which helped to break Schleicher was the outcome of the regional election in Lippe, an area with a population of only about 100,000. This was a *Land* in which the socio-economic structure was favourable to the Nazis. They increased their score at the expense of the Nationalists. This helped to convince many influential figures that the Nazis were a necessary part of any government (even though the Social Democrats and the other moderate parties improved their positions in the Lippe election). Papen and Hugenberg reactivated the Harzburg Front. The Cologne banker Kurt von Schröder acted as marriage broker for this alliance. Schleicher also had other enemies in the shape of the East Prussian estate owners who feared his plans for redistributing land to small-holders. They helped to turn the President against him. In the end, however, it seems it was Franz von Papen who persuaded Hindenburg that Hitler was more modest than he seemed and that he and Papen should be given the chance to form a government of 'National Concentration'.

*Johannes Brahms*

*August Bebel, Social Democratic Leader*

*Carl Benz*

*Wilhelm Conrad Röntgen*

*The Kaiser on summer manoeuvres, 1914*

*German troops advancing in Belgium, 1914 (top right)*

*Revolution in Germany, 1918 (right)*

*Albert Einstein*

*Thomas Mann*

*President Friedrich Ebert*

*Richard Strauss*

*Inflation in Germany, 1923*

*The Bauhaus in Dessau, by Walter Gropius*

*Thälmann with uniformed members of the Red Front Fighters*

*Nuremberg: Hitler and Goebbels take the salute*

*Hitler with Hindenburg and Göring, 1933*

*The Reichstag in flames, 1933*

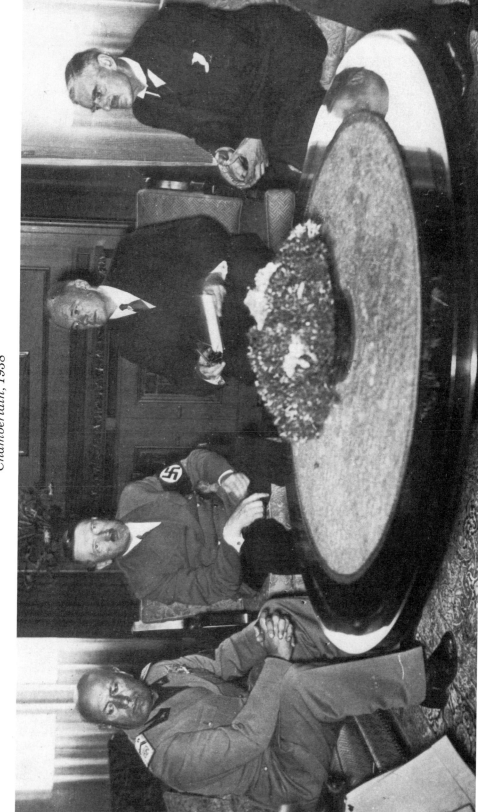

*Hitler meeting with Mussolini and Chamberlain, 1938*

*Russian and American troops in Germany, 1945*

*American troops free inmates of Dachau, 1945*

*The ruins of Berlin, 1945*

*The Nuremberg trials*

(Page 12)

*The Berlin airlift, 1948*

*Chancellor Adenauer with
Churchill in 1951*

*Ludwig Erhard*

*Bertolt Brecht*

*Walter Ulbricht*

*Strengthening the Berlin Wall*

East Germans crowd through the open Berlin Wall, November 1989.

Chancellor Kohl voting in the first all-German elections.

# — 5 —

# Hitler's Germany, 1933–39

It is impossible to pinpoint the moment when Hitler's dictatorship was firmly and irrevocably established. When one considers his position on being appointed Chancellor on 30 January 1933 one can forgive observers at that time for thinking his regime was not likely to last. First of all, his party, the N S D A P, even with its Nationalist allies did not command a majority in the Reichstag. In the Cabinet there were only three Nazis as against nine other members with the apparently key post of Minister of Defence and Vice-Chancellor in non-Nazi hands. The latter post was held by Franz von Papen. Moreover, though Hitler was Chancellor, he was overshadowed in respect and influence by President Hindenburg and Hindenburg was in a position to dismiss him. And the armed forces, which stood on the Right politically, were loyal to Hindenburg, rather than to Hitler. The police forces too were generally not, as they were to shortly become, totally subservient to Nazi wishes. The German press was very largely regional rather than national in circulation and in any case the Nazis ran only 2.5 per cent of all German newspapers. The parties which opposed Nazism also appeared to be in a strong position at the beginning of 1933. They were well organised and, especially the Social Democrats, possessed a large number of loyal, indoctrinated members. The Social Democrats dominated the powerful, though formally independent, trade unions, which had been largely responsible for bringing down one would-be dictator, Kapp, in 1919. Finally, there was the Catholic Church, that authoritarian body which controlled the hearts and minds of about one-third of the population, which was wealthy and had world-wide connections and which had, like the Social Democrats, successfully resisted the attacks of the Kaiser's state in the nineteenth century.

Apart from these factors outside the Nazi party setting limits to its power there were three limiting factors within the movement. The leaders were men with no experience of government and little experience of anything else. The majority of the members were fairly new to the movement which already appeared to be past its zenith.

Nor were the Nazis completely united over their goals. Some stressed their social revolutionary mission while others, including Hitler, proclaimed their nationalist and anti-semitic aims.

Hitler clearly recognised this situation and set about to change it dramatically, both by exploiting available opportunities and by creating opportunities. It is impossible to say whether the Reichstag fire falls into the category of an opportunity exploited or one created. On the night of 27 February 1933 the Debating Chamber of the Reichstag was set on fire with explosive consequences for Germany. Up till 1962 the great majority of historians had assumed that this was the work of the Nazis who wanted a pretext to eliminate their Left-wing opponents and who needed a crisis to panic the electorate into voting for them. Hitler claimed the fire had been started by Communists to signal the outbreak of a Left-wing rising throughout Germany. For months the Nazis tried to pin the crime on a group of Communists including Ernst Torgler, chairman of the Communist parliamentary group and Georgi Dimitroff, a Bulgarian and Communist International official. Also in the dock was Marinus van der Lubbe, a young Dutchman who had been a member of the Dutch Communist Party but was associated in 1933 with a Dutch Left-wing splinter group. Van der Lubbe admitted the crime from the start, steadfastly maintaining that he was the sole culprit. He claimed he had started the fire as a political protest against the Nazis and the capitalist system. The others, despite the torture of five months in chains, denied any responsibility and were eventually acquitted after a well organised international protest action against their trial. Van der Lubbe was convicted and subsequently beheaded on very doubtful legal grounds.

A re-examination of the evidence by Fritz Tobias led him to the conclusion that although the Communists were undoubtedly not involved in the crime neither were the Nazis. The fire was the work of Marinus van der Lubbe alone. However, neither Herr Tobias nor Mr A. J. P. Taylor, who supported this view, were adequately able to explain away some prominent Nazi witnesses, such as Hermann Rauschning and General Halder, who later testified that Hermann Göring, at the time of the fire President of the Reichstag and Prussian Minister of Interior, had boasted he was responsible for the fire.

Whatever the origins of the Reichstag fire it was exploited by Hitler with diabolical brilliance. As the Nazis and their allies did not have a majority in the Reichstag, elections had been set for 5 March. With Göring as head of the Prussian police the Nazi S A could increasingly control the streets in large areas of the country and harass their opponents. On 22 February Göring enrolled large numbers of S A, S S and Stahlhelm members as auxiliary police. The next day the police raided Karl Liebknecht House, headquarters of the Communist Party. Officially they were seeking evidence of a plot. They found no evidence though no doubt the raid yielded material which later helped them to suppress the K P D. As the Reichstag burned four days later Hitler got Hindenburg to issue an emergency decree which he could do under Article 48 of the Constitution. This decree 'for the Protection of People and State' set aside normal civil liberties:

> Restrictions on personal liberty, on the right of free expression of opinion, including freedom of the press; on the rights of assembly and association; and violations of the privacy of postal, telegraphic and telephonic communications; and warrants for house searches, orders for confiscations as well as restrictions on property, are also permissible beyond the legal limits otherwise prescribed.

The same decree gave the central authorities the right to exercise the powers of the organs of regional and local government and introduced the death penalty for a wide range of offences. With one stroke the Weimar Constitution was virtually destroyed. Immediately the arrest was ordered of all Communist members of the Reichstag together with other leading Communists and certain other anti-Nazis. During the night 28 February over 10,000 arrests were made in various parts of Germany. Communist leader Ernst Thälmann was hunted down and taken on 3 March. He later met his death in a concentration camp.

## The Enabling Act and Gleichschaltung

The results of the elections held on 5 March were not as decisive as Hitler had wished. The Nazis got 44 per cent of the seats, their allies 7 per cent. The Social Democratic vote held firm while the Communists did not do at all badly in the situation. The Centre Party actually made slight gains. The main effect of the Nazi propaganda campaign which played on fear of civil war and Red revolution was to drive Conservatives, Nationalists and traditionalists into the Nazi Camp.

When the new Reichstag assembled in the Kroll Opera House on 24 March it was confronted with an Enabling bill giving the government unlimited power for four years. A two-thirds majority was required before this bill could become law. The Social Democrats led by Otto Wels refused to have anything to do with it. Of the 94 Social Democrats who voted against the measure 24 were later murdered. Twenty-six Social Democrats had been prevented from attending as had the 81 Communists who had been elected. They were either under arrest or in hiding. The major responsibility for the passage of the bill with the necessary majority must be held to fall upon the Centre and the Bavarian People's parties, whose combined votes of 92, if cast against the measure, instead of for it as they were, would have increased the minority to 186, or 11 more than was required to prevent a constitutional amendment from becoming law. The Catholic deputies had allowed themselves to be persuaded by Hitler's promises of freedom for the churches. They were influenced too by the pleas of their former party colleague Franz von Papen who was a member of the government asking for supreme power. Finally, apart from Nazi threats, they were influenced by the fact that Hindenburg was still President. They believed he could restrain the government. It is interesting to speculate what might have happened had the Catholic parties not surrendered. Many influential people on the Right, including the President, some in the civil service, some industrialists and officers might have thought again about supporting Hitler. On the Left the Social Democrats and the trade unions, who both later tried to pursue a conciliatory policy towards the Nazis, might have showed more fight.

Having armed themselves with dictatorial powers the Nazis issued further decrees to consolidate their position. On 2 May the trade unions were dissolved; on 18 May the cooperative societies were taken over; on 27 June, the Nationalist leader Hugenberg was removed from his place in the Cabinet; on 7 July, the Social Democrats were deprived of their seats in the Reichstag; and on 14 July, all political parties except the Nazis were outlawed. The democratic institutions of Weimar went the same way as its parties and popular bodies. The Reich Governor Law of 31 March established Reich supervison over the States or Länder. On 30 January 1934 State law was replaced by delegated Reich law. The parliaments of the Länder were dissolved without provision for re-election, and the Länder ministers were henceforth appointed by the appropriate Reich ministers, to whom they were responsible. The Upper House or Reichsrat was dissolved in February 1934. The Reichstag continued to exist as a single-party, rubber-stamping body. It was mockingly described as the most highly paid choral society in Germany: its members received their salaries for singing the first stanzas of the National and Nazi anthems once or twice a year when they were called upon to applaud Hitler's various outpourings and edicts. In November 1933 the non-Nazi members were ousted by a one-party general 'election'. By February 1934 the total *Gleichschaltung* or 'coordination' of all German parliamentary institutions had been achieved.

Dr Goebbels, who on 13 March 1933 had been appointed Minister of Popular Enlightenment and Propaganda, was also very active in the first months after the Nazi take-over. Under a decree issued in June other ministries had to turn over some of their responsibilities to Goebbels' new ministry. The Ministry of Interior gave up the supervision of radio, films, press, theatre; the protection of works of art and memorials, and the regulation of state celebrations and holidays; the Foreign Ministry handed over its propaganda activities abroad. Even material for tourists came under Goebbels' control. As mentioned above, in 1933, the Nazis were not strongly represented in the press. They sought to remedy this situation by banning the 'Marxist' press, by forced sales of newspapers and control of news agencies and personnel. The *Schriftleitergesetz* issued on 4 October laid down that the office of editor was an official position, which could not be held by a person without German citizenship, or who had been deprived of his rights as a citizen, who was a Jew, or who was married to one. In their work editors were placed under various restrictions. The law, especially those parts of it concerned with the functions of the editor, destroyed any possibility of editorial independence. It made it impossible for German journalists to express a personal view of politics. The law gave Dr Goebbels an instrument for the achievement of a complete uniformity of the press: censorship was not necessary because the editor became a *de facto* censor.

The fate of the film industry was the same as that of the press. The film companies were taken over one by one including the largest of them, the U F A, which had belonged to the Nationalist leader Hugenberg. In less than five years the film department of the Goebbels' ministry gained a monopoly position in film production. It goes without saying that the showing of foreign films was strictly controlled. Finally, all journalists, film directors, broadcasters, actors and others at work in the mass media were required to belong to the appropriate Nazi-dominated professional organisation. The results of this on the information and entertainment media we shall examine later.

In Hitler's moves to consolidate his regime the attitude of the armed forces was of the greatest importance. In the person of General von Blomberg, who had been appointed Defence Minister, Hitler found an enthusiastic supporter. Many of the other senior officers were less enthusiastic. Among the junior officers enthusiasm was much more widespread. Hitler lost no time in attempting to win over the senior officers. On 3 February he confided his military and political ideas to the German military leadership. These included the destruction of Marxism and democracy, military equality for Germany, the reintroduction of conscription, and the conquest of living space in the East and its ruthless Germanisation. Of more immediate importance to the officers was the assurance that there would be no moves to bring them under SA or Party control. Hitler was able to give the forces more tangible assurances in June of the following year.

## The 'Night of Long Knives'

Unlike many of his rank-and-file Hitler had never taken the socialist slogans of his movement seriously and had already fallen out with some of his lieutenants, notably the Strasser brothers, because they had. In the summer of 1933 some of his SA men were getting restless and calling for a 'second revolution' to deal with the capitalists, Junkers and reactionaries. At the head of these discontented elements was Ernst Röhm, commander of the SA and Hitler's closest friend in the Nazi movement. In May 1934 Hitler is believed to have negotiated with the military leaders on the cruiser *Deutschland* an agreement which involved their support for him as head of state on the death of Hindenburg in return for the emasculation of the SA. Hitler also intrigued with Göring and Himmler, who saw Röhm as a stumbling block to their own power ambitions, against the SA chief. Meanwhile Papen, angry about the suppression of a speech he had made at Marburg University, inveighed against Hitler to his old friend Hindenburg. When on 21 June Hitler visited the President, he was met by General von Blomberg who warned him that Hindenburg had threatened to declare martial law and turn over power to the armed forces, if Hitler did not reduce tension by dealing with his party radicals. Hitler now acted. He put Göring and Himmler, head of the secret state police or Gestapo, in charge of eliminating 'disloyal' SA leaders in Berlin, while he personally dealt with matters in Bavaria where SA leaders were conferring.

Hitler later admitted that some 77 people had been shot down in that 'night of long knives' on 30 June 1934. After the war the figure of more than 1,000 was given. The victims included not only SA leaders such as Röhm, but also such prominent non-Nazis as General and Frau von Schleicher, General Kurt von Bredow and Erich Klausener, leader of Catholic Action.

Although the 'night of long knives' horrified many people both inside and outside Germany, it misled others into believing that the worst of the Nazi revolution was over, and that Germany would now settle down to a normal existence again. Many of those who harboured such illusions were shocked the following month by the attempt of the

Austrian Nazis, with arms and encouragement from Berlin, to seize power. The coup failed. However, Dr Dollfuss, the Austrian Chancellor, was murdered and the episode created bad feeling between Hitler and Mussolini, who regarded himself as ally and protector of Austria, one of the very few friends Hitler had abroad.

In August 1934 the final consolidation of Hitler's position was achieved. Hindenburg died and Hitler took over the powers of head of state and commander in chief of the armed forces. The title of President was abolished and Hitler styled himself Führer (Leader) and Reich Chancellor. All officers and men of the armed forces were required to swear an oath of allegiance to Hitler personally rather than to the German state or people. This oath was to prove important later on when officers were to claim that they could not support action to remove the Führer because of it.

Hitler's new office was formally ratified by a plebiscite of the German people. One interesting aspect of the 'campaign' – no opposition was permitted—leading up to the vote which is of minor historical importance, was the use of what was claimed to be the political testament of Hindenburg. It praised the Nazis for leading the German nation to 'internal unity'. The testament, which was given the blessing of the President's son, Oskar, is generally believed to have been forged.

## Economic recovery

One of the reasons Hitler had not been prepared to push his Austrian ambitions too far in 1934 was Germany's lack of military preparedness. This was as much a question of economics as of military capabilities. Hitler was also concerned about economic affairs because of the problem of unemployment. Whatever he thought of his promise of 'work and bread' he realised that the continuation of widespread unemployment represented a source of potential instability to the regime. His economic plans therefore aimed at two major objectives—creating jobs and making Germany economically independent as a means of strengthening the Reich's military capacity. Within a few years of taking power the Nazis were able, as the table below shows, to claim success in combating unemployment. Indeed, they were more successful than were the governments of Britain and the U S A and other countries. How were they able to achieve this result?

In the spring of 1933 Hitler issued a proclamation promising a Four-Year Plan 'to rescue the German people, to safeguard German food supplies, and to rescue the German worker through a powerful

Employment and Unemployment in Germany
1932–38 (*in millions*)

| Year | | Employed | Unemployed |
|---|---|---|---|
| January | 1932 | 12.73 | 5.5 |
| January | 1933 | 11.5 | 6.0 |
| September | 1933 | 14.5 | 3.7 |
| September | 1934 | 16.1 | 2.3 |
| September | 1935 | 17.0 | 1.8 |
| September | 1936 | 18.3 | 1.1 |
| September | 1937 | 19.7 | 0.5 |
| September | 1938 | 20.8 | 0.2 |

attack on unemployment'. The measures subsequently introduced were not the product of a specific Nazi ideology of economics. They were rather the type of scheme adopted, though with much less vigour, in many countries in the 1930s nowadays summed up in the term 'Keynsianism'. They were in part based on the 'war socialism' introduced in Germany during the First World War. Further, they were based on measures already undertaken by previous governments.

The Papen government of 1932 had offered tax incentives to businesses to increase the number of their employees. In addition Papen drew up a programme for expenditure on housing, house repairs, land improvement and capital expenditure by the railways and the Post Office. This was followed under the von Schleicher government by the appointment in December 1932 of a Commissioner for the Creation of Employment, who issued, just two days before the Nazis took over, a programme of expenditure on roads, housing, public utilities and inland water transport. Also in existence before 1933 was the voluntary labour service which by the end of the 1932 was 250,000 strong. Its funds were provided partly out of the Reich budget, but primarily from the resources of the Unemployment Insurance Fund. The members of the service were mainly engaged in land improvement schemes. They received food and lodging but no pay. Another scheme worth mentioning was the compulsory reduction of interest on agricultural mortgages. This was introduced in September 1932. Obviously, the effects of these schemes would take time to make themselves felt. When they did so the Nazis were in power and enjoyed the political advantage they conferred. Nevertheless, we should not underestimate the importance of measures initiated by the Nazis, or rather, by Dr Schacht. These were more thorough than those brought in by previous governments, and unorthodox by most people's standards at the time.

Hitler's Four-Year Plan for the abolition of unemployment was given effect by the Law for the Reduction of Unemployment of 2 June 1933. It meant a great extension of public works; tax remissions and subsidies for profits reinvested in industry and agriculture; tax abatements for the employment of female domestic servants (thus reducing the number of women competing with men for industrial or agricultural employment); marriage bonuses for each newly married couple providing the wife did not continue to work outside the home. A separate law, also introduced in June 1933, inaugurated an ambitious scheme for the construction of 7000 km (4,375 miles) of motorways, the famous *Autobahnen*. The general transport tax was raised to help finance this project but taxes on new cars had been abolished in April 1933 to boost the automobile industry. The labour service was greatly expanded and in the early years of Nazi rule was an important factor in reducing the number of unemployed. In January 1933 there were some 180,000 persons engaged in labour service or on some other kind of relief works. By June of the same year the number had risen to over half a million and by June 1934 it was some 800,000. The figure was later reduced as industrial expansion got under way. In March 1935 military conscription was reintroduced, which further helped to mop up the unemployed. It has been estimated that by the time full employment was reached in 1938 about one and a half million men were either doing military service or labour service, and another one to two million were occupied in the service of the Nazi party, the police, and the management of the state-controlled economy.

Another part of the measures introduced in 1933 was designed to foster new industries which would increase the country's defence capacity. Tax exemption was granted for a number of years to enterprises engaged in developing new processes provided these were considered to be of national importance. Under the Second Four-Year Plan announced in September 1936, which was under Hermann Göring's control, much greater emphasis was placed on German economic independence. In order to develop the materials and processes to make this possible the state offered long term contracts with guaranteed profits to firms and went into industry itself. The most important case of the latter was the Hermann Göring Works for the extraction and utilisation of low-grade ore. By controlling imports and subsidies new raw materials such as staple fibre, magnesium and aluminium alloys, plastics, artificial rubber (Buna) and industrial oils from coal were developed. Production of traditional raw materials and agricultural products was given new emphasis. Despite the successes, some of which are benefiting Germany today, the Third Reich was not able to make itself economically independent—as it was to learn to its cost in the war.

All these projects had to be paid for and it was the ordinary people who paid most with lower wages and higher prices. In 1928, a 'normal' year, wage and salary earners received 62 per cent of the national income. Under the Nazis their share fell year by year until in 1938 it was only 57 per cent. It is true that by that time there was work for all and virtual security of employment. In addition, working-class housing projects had continued to expand as under the Weimar regime and the Nazis developed cheap sports facilities and cheap holidays. Six million persons are said to have taken part on such holiday excursions in 1936. But the worker no longer had any freedom to take industrial action, to elect his own representatives or leave his employment without permission.

## Hitler and the Churches

The Nazis were a *Weltanschauungspartei*, a party having a total world outlook which they thought everyone else should accept. They also intended keeping power indefinitely. It was therefore intolerable, from their point of view, that there were any institutions not completely subservient to them and not completely imbued with their outlook. Having achieved the annihilation of organised political opposition and having brought about the control of the organs of government, the armed forces and the information media, they sought to bring those other two alternative sources of ideas and information under their control, the churches and the educational institutions.

In many respects the Catholic Church appeared a greater potential threat to Nazism than the other churches because of its own authoritarian views, the loyalty of many of its followers to Catholicism before all else and its international prestige and ties. The Catholic Church, however, no less than the other organisations which faced the Nazis in 1933, suffered from not knowing its own mind. As we have seen, a considerable number of Catholic clergy had at least some sympathy for Nazism. They were impressed by its old-fashioned moral tone and by its strong line against Communists, Social Democrats, Jews, Masons, Liberals and Anarchists. Its ideas of political and social institutions were similar to the Catholic idea of the corporate state and in Italy, where a party with which the Nazis claimed affinity was in power, relations between Church and State were excellent. And although they had their doubts about the Nazis they feared, particularly after the March elections, that to be too outspoken might lead to a split in the church and tough sanctions against it by the state. At the last contested elections in March 1933 the bishops issued a statement urging the faithful to vote for candidates whose proven character and proven attitudes gave evidence of their concern for the rights of the church. The fact that the bishops had not explicitly mentioned the Catholic parties was exploited by Catholic Nazis. As we have seen, after the elections Hitler promised the Centre and Bavarian People's parties to guarantee the rights of the church in return for their voting for the Enabling Act. The Catholic bishops for their part withdrew their earlier prohibitions concerning Nazism. Catholics were told to be loyal to the state, to carry out their civic duties and to avoid anything subversive. Catholic lay bodies started to declare their loyalty to the new regime. On Hitler's birthday on 20 April 1933 the leader of the Centre Party Monsignor Kaas sent the Nazi leader a telegram of congratulations giving an assurance of 'unflinching cooperation'. This further accelerated the movement of Catholics towards Nazism. The Fulda bishops' conference of 30 May– 1 June issued a pastoral letter which promised loyalty to the new regime though it voiced certain misgivings over the position and treatment of the church. Despite these Catholic moves towards a reconciliation with the Nazis, attacks on Catholic organisations continued. On 28 June a wave of arrests took place in Bavaria. These arrests brought about the dissolution of the Bavarian People's Party on 4 July. The Centre Party was dissolved a day later.

In view of these events it is remarkable how easy the Nazis found negotiations which led to the Concordat signed at the Vatican on 20 July by Papen, for the Reich, and Cardinal Pacelli, later Pope Pius XII, for the Church. Superficially the agreement offered the church much. It accorded it full freedom of profession and public practice of the Catholic religion and the right of the church to manage its own affairs, 'within the limits of laws applicable to all'. It also gave priests certain privileges and continued state subsidies to the church. Most important from the church's viewpoint, Articles 19–25 protected the Catholic educational system. Article 23 even guaranteed the maintenance of existing Catholic schools and the establishment of new ones. The church made concessions on Catholic organisations and on the question of the control of military chaplains. Though the Vatican later commented that the agreement did not imply acceptance of Nazi ideology or methods it undoubtedly gave great international prestige to the Nazi regime at a time when Hitler had few friends outside Germany. It should be remembered that the Vatican and the Weimar Republic had failed to reach agreement on a concordat. Despite the concordat the Catholic Church soon found it had much to complain about in Nazi Germany. Its organisations were harassed, its publications suppressed and thousands of priests were arrested on various pretexts. In 1937 Pope Pius XI decided to protest about the situation in an encyclical, *Mit brennender Sorge*, in which he pointed out that Christianity could not be imprisoned within the frontiers of a single people, within the pedigree of one single race. Nevertheless, most Catholic bishops continued their cooperation with the Nazi authorities and five days after *Mit brennender Sorge* it was balanced by another encyclical which strongly condemned Communism.

The Protestant clergy were probably more enthusiastic about the 'Government of National Concentration' formed by Nazis and Nationalists than were their Catholic colleagues. It had the backing of Hindenburg, a pious Protestant, and the majority of its members were loyal Protestants. But the Protestant clergy were Monarchist, Nationalist and Conservative rather than Nazi and it was now not long before many started to have misgivings about the new regime. Few of them objected to the setting up of a Reich Church which replaced the existing loose association of regional churches, but argument broke out about who was to be its head. Hitler favoured Army Chaplain Ludwig Müller and by propaganda and intimidation succeeded in getting him elected as Reich Bishop. Opposition soon started notably from the 'Confessional Church' led by Pastor Martin Niemöller, a World War I U-Boat officer who had originally backed the 'National Government'. The Confessional Church rejected the authority of the Reich Bishop and the right of the state to interfere in matters of religious faith. Niemöller was later arrested after an outspoken sermon at his church in Dahlem, Berlin. On acquittal, in March 1938, of a charge of an underhand attack against the state, he was immediately taken into 'protective custody' and spent the rest of the Nazi years in concentration camps. In the period 1937–39 hundreds of Confessional pastors were arrested and those who were not lost the state subsidies which formed a large part of their incomes. Most Protestant pastors did not choose Niemöller's road to Calvary, they swore a personal allegiance to the Führer. They were following the traditional policy of their church of acting as a state-supporting organisation. On the other hand, they prevented the Nazis setting up a Nazi-style pagan church.

## Education and culture in the Third Reich

In order to make the educational system subservient to their aims the National Socialists had to centralise it and expel the 'politically unreliable' elements. Full centralisation was achieved in April 1934 when a Reich Ministry of Education was given responsibility for all levels and forms of education from kindergarten to universities though certain Nazi educational establishments remained under NSDAP or SS control. The Nazis kept an eye on teachers through the National Socialist Teachers' League to which 98 per cent of all teachers, including university teachers, in 1942 belonged. All non-Nazi teachers' organisations were dissolved as were all non-Nazi youth and student bodies. Children and young people were under strong pressure to join the *Hitler Jugend* (for boys) or the *Bund Deutscher Mädel* (for girls). By 1938, when Catholic student associations were finally dissolved, the only body open to university students was the Nazi Students' Organisation.

In addition to camping and the usual type of Boy Scouting activities the *Hitler Jugend*, under an Act of December 1936, had the task of educating 'the entire German Youth' in the 'spirit of National Socialism'. Increasingly it put emphasis on the pre-military training of youth. Very many German school teachers were nationalist-inclined before 1933 and welcomed the 'National Revolution'. Probably the majority of their university colleagues shared their views but a higher proportion of them were purged. By May 1939 the Nazis claimed that 45 per cent of university teaching staff had been replaced by good Nazis.

As well as centralising and purging the Nazi revolution affected German education in other ways. Nazi racial doctrines were compulsory subjects at all levels and religious teaching was gradually pushed out. In 1939 prayers were abolished in elementary schools. School discipline became stricter and corporal punishment, abolished under the Weimar Republic, was reintroduced. The whole education system was given a more vocational slant. Courses were also shortened to provide young people with more time for their compulsory military political training. Women's education suffered in the Third Reich due to the official belief that a woman's place was in the home. Consequently there was greater stress on domestic science and nursing for girls to the detriment of their general education. Women found it more difficult to get into the universities and the professions. The impact of war losses forced some modification of this policy.

Despite the positive attitude of many students and university teachers to the Nazi takeover the NSDAP remained suspicious of the universities. It became more difficult than before 1933 to gain admission to higher education. Apart from academic qualifications, only those whose racial descent, physical fitness and record of service to the *Hitler Jugend* were satisfactory found places. These regulations and the greater opportunities available in the armed forces, industry and political organisations, reduced the number of university students by 1939, to less than half that of 1931–2.

In addition to the normal education system the Nazis set up a number of educational organisations of their own. These were supposed to train a specially selected élite for future political and military leadership. The *Napolas* were paramilitary boarding schools of which there were 23 in 1940 with about 5,000 pupils. Even more select were the Adolf Hitler Schools admission to which was open only to those who had, among other things, an unimpeachable family-tree going back to 1800.

What Nazi cultural policy was going to be was shown already on 10 May 1933 when a vast crowd watched the burning of 'decadent' and 'hostile' books in the square in front of Berlin's main University. Condemned were the works of such writers as Heinrich Heine, Thomas Mann, Stefan Zweig and very many others. In literature, painting, architecture, the cinema and the other creative fields artists had either to conform or get out. Jews of course did not have even this choice.

What were these new standards the Nazis sought to impose? If they were not of a directly propagandist nature they had to at least emphasise old Germanic 'folk' traditions or simply suit the personal whims of Hitler. The piece of contemporary literature most favoured by Hitler was Hans Grimm's *Volk ohne Raum* (A People Without Space), the title of which conveys something of the contents. Painting had to be poster-style representational rather than, say, abstract, and was supposed to concern itself with Germanic or Nordic themes. Adolf Ziegler was one of the main protagonists of this kind of painting. In architecture Hitler preferred neo-classical style, a poor imitation of Greece and Rome rather than modern architecture based on contemporary needs and contemporary techniques and materials. Such neo-classical structures were designed by Albert Speer, later Minister of War Production, for the mass meetings and parades held at Nuremberg.

The Nazis realised the importance of the cinema. Dr Goebbels came to realise that people could not be serious all the time; consequently, especially after the outbreak of war, many escapist films were produced. The Nazi film-makers also proved themselves extremely clever in using half-truths for propaganda purposes. An instance of this was the film by Hans Steinhoff called *Ohm Krüger* which was about the Anglo-South African War. The famous actor Emil Jannings played the title role of Krüger, the Boer leader. In the film the Nazis exploited the fact that General Kitchener set up the first concentration camps to intern civilian Dutch South Africans suspected of aiding Boer military formations. Churchill, who was a war correspondent in that war, was shown gloating over the plight of the inmates. As the writer found out when studying in Germany in the 1950s, Britain's 'invention' of the camps was firmly fixed in the minds of even those who were too young to have seen the film and seemed to them to at least greatly reduce German guilt. A film about the Irish struggle for independence, *Der Fuchs von Glenarvon*, the Fox of Glenarvon, and one about the *Titanic* are further examples of skilful exploitation of the half-truth. In addition the Nazis used the documentary technique with amazing results. Two of the best known of this type are Leni Riefenstahl's pictorial epic of the 1934 N S D A P congress and one on the 1936 Olympic Games. Both are still regarded as important by students of the film today. Nazi racial and imperialist policies were allocated their ration of celluloid. In 1940 Viktor Tourjanski produced *Feinde* (Enemies), in order to justify the German invasion of Poland. A little earlier Veit Harlan directed the notorious *Jud Süss* (Jew Süss) to fan the flames of anti-semitic feeling.

Music was more difficult to interpret in a strictly ideological way but the works of Jewish composers were banned.

Quite apart from those of Jewish ancestry, many members of Germany's cultural élite were not prepared to accept Nazi standards and went abroad. There they produced work which has proved more significant than most which appeared in Nazi Germany. There were the writers Thomas and Heinrich Mann, Bertolt Brecht, Anna Seghers, Ludwig Renn and Erich Maria Remarque. Then there were the specifically Jewish writers like Arnold and Stefan Zweig, Lion Feuchtwanger and Friedrich Wolf. These few will stand for the thousands of writers, artists, actors and directors who left Germany. They helped to enrich the countries which took them in. In Britain the high standard of Glyndebourne Opera was a product of the work of refugee musicians. In America Hollywood greatly benefited from refugees. The two giants of modern American architecture Walter Gropius and Lugwig Mies von der Rohe were refugees.

But Nazi Germany became poorer not only in the arts and architecture. Hundreds of university teachers—there were over 300 registered in Britain in 1944—left Germany. About 5,000 medical practitioners entered the U S A from Europe between 1933 and 1940. Many of them were Nazi victims. This number was as many as graduated in one year from all the medical schools in the United States. Worse still, from the point of view of the Nazi war economy, there were the scientists such as Albert Einstein and James Franck, whose theories helped to produce the atom bomb. Hundreds of others worked on various war projects in industry. Finally, many German refugee academics worked for American intelligence agencies as their contribution to the defeat of Nazism. There were the sociologists, Hans Speier, Leo Lowenthal and Max Horkheimer, political scientists such as John Herz and Otto Kirchheimer, philosophers like Herbert

Marcuse, and many others. Among the future Nobel Prize winners who left at this time were: Konrad Bloch (medicine 1964), Ernest Boris Chain (medicine 1945), Max Delbrück (medicine 1969), Bernard Katz (medicine 1970), Fritz Albert Lipmann (medicine 1953), Otto Stern (physics 1943), Eugene Wigner (physics 1963).

## The concentration camp system

Known anti-Nazis who did not manage or desire to go abroad were in danger of finding themselves in prison or, more likely, in a concentration camp for an indefinite period. The first Nazi concentration camp appears to have been set up by Himmler as head of Munich police in March 1933. It was in the grounds and stone huts of a former gunpowder factory near Dachau. It was said to be necessary because the normal prison system could not cope with the sudden influx of prisoners. Other camps were being set up around Berlin, particularly notorious was the one at Columbia-Haus, and in other parts of the country. At the end of July 1933 26,700 persons were in 'protective custody' (*Schutzhaft*). Conditions in the camps were primitive as they were either disused or hastily-constructed premises. Those in charge —S A and S S before June 1934, S S after that date—were virtually free to do as they pleased with prisoners, except that is for a few who the regime wanted to be kept alive for possible future bargains or for propaganda reasons.

The head of the administration of all camps from 1934 to 1939 was Theodor Eicke, a former Imperial Army N C O and later I G-Farben employee in charge of factory security, who at the time of his appointment was undergoing psychiatric treatment. He imposed martial-law conditions as normal treatment for prisoners and not surprisingly many died under torture or from the backbreaking work or were 'shot while trying to escape'. For those who were not so dispatched isolation from the outside world, total insecurity and the thought that they could be detained for life were almost as fearful. By 1937 Eicke had reorganised the camps reducing them to four Dachau, Sachsenhausen, Buchenwald and Lichtenburg. Hardened criminals, vagabonds and homosexuals started to be sent to the camps and were often used as *Kapos* or trusties to oversee and inform on the political prisoners. About this time forced labour was developed in a more systematic form. In the spring of 1938 the S S firm Deutsche Erd-und Steinwerke GmbH (Dest) was founded to exploit quarries and establish brickworks.

It was the job of the secret police to hunt down those destined for 'protective custody'. A law of April 1933 set up the Gestapo (the

German abbreviation for Secret State Police) which however only had jurisdiction in Prussia at that time. Ironically, its headquarters were in Prinz-Albrecht-Strasse in the former H Q of the Communist Party. In Bavaria Himmler was in charge of the political police. He gradually extended his writ until in April 1934 when he became Deputy Chief and Inspector of the Prussian Gestapo, he was *de facto* head of all secret police forces in Germany though in Prussia he was still nominally responsible to Göring. In June 1936 he was appointed Chief of the (now completely centralised) German Police as well as retaining his position as S S Führer. Reinhard Heydrich was his deputy. Heydrich was also head of the *Sicherheitsdienst* (Security Service) or S D. This was set up in 1931 as the intelligence service of the Nazi Party. The Gestapo operated through a network of offices throughout the Reich and a well developed system of informers. In the period October 1935—March 1936 over 1,000 persons per month were arrested by the Gestapo for alleged Left-wing activities alone.

## Persecution of the Jews

Apart from the political opponents of the regime the Jews were the other main category of prisoners in the camps. The first general, organised attack on the Jews was in April 1933 when a boycott of Jewish businesses and professional people was instigated. It was accompanied by much violence. In the same month an Act was promulgated which excluded from the civil service those who had one or more Jewish grandparents. Due to the intervention of Hindenburg specific groups of 'non-Aryans' were excluded from the provisions of the Act. These were those who had held office since 1 August 1914, former front-line soldiers, and those whose sons or fathers had been killed in action. This hit academics too for they were regarded as civil servants in Germany. In the next months various professional organisations—of medical practitioners, dentists and lawyers—expelled their Jewish members or even non-Jews with Jewish spouses. A law of September 1933 prevented Jews from inheriting farms. During the next two years a series of laws and orders were introduced extending the purge of Jews to virtually every profession. When compulsory military service was reintroduced in 1935 Jews were excluded from its provisions. In September 1935 the notorious Nuremberg Laws, so called because they were made known at the Nazi party rally in that city, were announced. They were the Reich Citizenship Act and the Act for the Protection of German Blood and German Honour. The first law deprived Jews of their citizenship and revoked the earlier, more lenient attitude to Jewish ex-servicemen, their dependants and long-serving Jewish civil servants. All were now removed from the public service. The German Blood Act prohibited marriage and extra-marital relations between 'Jews and nationals of German or allied blood' in order to ensure the 'survival of the German race'. It further prohibited a Jew from employing a female national of German or allied blood under 45 years of age in his household. An order dated 17 August 1938 forced male Jews to add the name 'Israel' and female Jews the name 'Sara' to their non-Jewish first names. Jewish passports were marked with the letter 'J' under an order of 5 October of that year.

A number of measures had been introduced during the years 1933–38 to exclude Jews from the economic life of the country. These had not been entirely successful. The Nazis sought a pretext which would give them the opportunity to bring matters to a head. They got this chance when a German diplomat, von Rath, was assassinated by a 17-year-old Jew in Paris on 7 November 1938. The result was a 'spontaneous' outbreak of violence which became known as the *Reichskristallnacht* (Reich Crystal Night). Over 7,000 Jewish shops were destroyed and synagogues burned throughout Germany. Jews were beaten up, about 90 of them killed and some 30,000 herded into concentration camps. Further measures for the 'Aryanisation' of Jewish businesses followed and a large fine was levied on the Jewish community. Jews were also excluded from German schools and universities (this had been already largely achieved in practice), banned from places of public entertainment and cultural institutions and even had their driving licences invalidated. They were ordered to hand over their jewellery and were frequently forced to live together in 'communal Jewish houses'.

During these prewar years Jews were allowed, and sometimes even encouraged, to emigrate. It made it easier for the Nazis to take control of their businesses and clear them from responsible positions without measures which would get them a bad press abroad. However, too many German Jews abroad were witnesses against the Nazi regime. In September 1933 the Haavara Agreement was drawn up between the Zionist organisation and the Reich Ministry of Economics. Would-be emigrants paid in funds to a Trust Company which then used the funds to finance German exports to Palestine. Half of the exports had, however, to be paid for by the Jews in foreign currency. Jews who so contributed were later reimbursed in Palestine by the Company. Some 170,000 Jews had emigrated under this scheme by November 1938. As one might expect, emigration was not very popular among Jews, particularly the older and better-off ones. After all, Palestine was not Europe and emigration, whether to Palestine or elsewhere, invariably meant a considerable financial sacrifice as the true value of properties were never fully realised. There was also the problem of one's profession. Apart from the language difficulty many emigrants found it difficult to start again in their old professions abroad.

Perhaps harder to bear than all the legal actions against the Jews was the cruel social ostracism. Jews found neighbours no longer greeted them on the streets, shops no longer wanted their trade, 'Aryan' friends no longer called. Jewish children no longer had playmates and many Jewish partners in mixed marriages found that husbands or wives sought renewed respectability through divorce. There was the mental anguish and incomprehension of Jews whose families had lived in Germany for centuries, who were Germans to their very roots, who, in some cases, were even old-fashioned German nationalists themselves. Suddenly they were no longer wanted by the community they had admired so much.

## Foreign gambles

Nazi foreign policy in the years before the outbreak of World War II represented a series of bold, even reckless, gambles. Hitler undertook these gambles, often against the advice of the military, because he had a primitive conception of politics and society, especially the politics and society of Britain and France (and of great importance later, of the U S S R and the U S A). It was a case of fools rush in where angels fear to tread. A more sophisticated view would have led to greater caution. His view of Britain was a mixture of admiration and contempt. He admired the British for having built up and maintained the greatest empire the world had ever seen, but he regarded the British ruling élite as effete and decadent, increasingly the pawns of Jewish wire-pullers in the City of London. For him Britain meant the bowler-hatted brigade, armed with umbrellas and elaborate titles and an outmoded view of chivalry. Perhaps Britain was somewhat to blame for Hitler's view for so many of the 'top people' he met were of this variety, members of the Anglo-German Fellowship or The Link, two organisations sympathetic to Germany enjoying considerable support in Britain in the higher echelons. Even among those he met who were not connected with these organisations, many felt he represented a bulwark of 'law and order' at a time when European society was in danger of disintegrating. Many others did not like Hitler but they liked Stalin even less, and they wrongly supposed the alternatives were a strong Germany or Communism in Europe.

It must not be thought though, that the British politicians who had to deal with Hitler were merely ill-advised, gullible fools taken in by anti-Communist patter. Their attitudes of appeasement, like those of their French colleagues, reflected their very real desire to avoid another holocaust. They were impressed by the overwhelming suffering produced by the 1914–18 war. Unfortunately for the world Hitler was not. Unfortunately too for the world very few people could take in the fact that Hitler, the ruler of a great nation, could be totally indifferent to human suffering, his own people's as well as that of other nations. Again, it was difficult to believe that the men around Hitler—the admirals and generals, the industrialists and civil servants, the academics and scientists—would back a megalomaniac and allow themselves to be led to disaster by him. The British and French politicians had two further weaknesses *vis-à-vis* the Nazi leader. They, unlike him, had to seek re-election, and quite understandably the voters were more interested in fighting unemployment than fighting Hitler. Secondly, and this was more true of the British than the French, they felt that perhaps the victors had been hard on Germany in 1919 and that most of Hitler's claims were reasonable even if the man who was voicing them was not.

The claims themselves were never entirely clear. Hitler had always demanded the complete abrogation of the Versailles Treaty which meant restoration of Germany to her 1914 boundaries, the return of Germany's overseas colonies, and military equality for the Reich with the other major European powers. Clearly France would not be ready to surrender Alsace-Lorraine originally taken from her in 1870 after the Franco-Prussian War and regained in 1919. And Poland would not be prepared to relinquish *all* the territory gained at Germany's expense in 1919. But much of what Germany had lost was negotiable and many foreign politicians were sympathetic to the unification of Germany and Austria. An equally resolute, yet more reasonable, more peace-orientated German leader, might have gone a long way to achieving these aims without war.

Hitler's methods in other countries, as much as in his own, caused increasing suspicion. And was the end of Versailles the height of Hitler's ambitions? How important were the statements made in *Mein Kampf*, his book written in 1924, and in the Nazi party programme? These called for German 'living space' at the expense of Russia, and the uniting of all Germans living abroad, which implied a threat to many nations in Eastern Europe. Some Western politicians and experts thought Hitler, like most other politicians, would not be too concerned about not fulfilling pledges made years before he got power. Others took hope from the fact that these aims would lead him into Eastern, and not Western Europe. The latter were impressed by his anti-Communist posturing in the form of the Anti-Comitern Pact of 1936 signed by Germany, Italy and Japan, and the help he gave to General Franco in fighting 'Communism' in Spain. Hitler also misled the anti-Russian, anti-Communist Polish generals by signing a non-aggression pact with them in January 1934. He then moved rapidly in all directions, whether as the result of a carefully conceived plan or in response to the opportunities which presented themselves is in some doubt.

In 1935 he reintroduced conscription in defiance of Germany's obligations. In the same year he negotiated a naval agreement with Britain which greatly improved Germany's naval position. He won back the Saar in 1935 by League of Nations' plebiscite. In the following year his troops reoccupied the Rhineland which had been recognised as part of the Reich but was demilitarised. This made it more difficult for the French and British to help the Czechs and Poles later. Up to this point few politicians in Britain felt very hostile to this apparent assertion of German nation rights. In March 1938 Hitler seized Austria after a campaign of murder and blackmail, though afterwards he held a Nazi-style plebiscite to justify his actions. Once again there were many who were prepared to argue that this was a natural, logical, even historically inevitable development. Austria, without its empire, it was said, was neither economically nor politically viable. Before 1933 many German and Austrian democrats had wanted such a union and, as for the Austrian regime, as it was not very democratic or progressive, its passing would not be mourned.

The next item on the Nazi dictator's agenda was the destruction of Czechoslovakia. This he had talked about, together with the annexation of Austria, at a meeting of his top officers in November 1937. In Czechoslovakia he could use the German-speaking minority as a stick with which to beat the Prague government. Yet again he was able to mislead many reasonable people in Britain and France—as well as some who wanted to be misled—and lead them to believe he was merely interested in the rights of his compatriots outside the Reich. These 'Germans' had never been under German rule. Before 1919 they had been citizens of the Austro-Hungarian Empire. But after 1933 the majority of them increasingly looked to Germany for help and guidance. They supported the Sudeten German Party of Konrad Henlein. Many informed people in the West were coming to have their doubts about the wisdom of setting up Czechoslovakia after the world war. The trouble was the dominant Czechs—about 6.5 million of them—were a minority in their own state. With them were (roughly) 3.25 million Germans, 700,000 Hungarians, 400,000 Ruthenes, 70,000 Poles, and 3 million Slovaks. The latter, like the others, were restless.

They wanted at least autonomy within a Czecho-Slovak state. The Czechoslovak state was more democratic, prosperous and progressive than the other states of central and eastern Europe. Yet the fact that it had not solved the problem of its nationalities made it easy prey for Hitler.

Less than three months after the Austrian Anschluss, Hitler sent a secret directive to the Wehrmacht announcing his 'unalterable' decision to smash Czechoslovakia by military action in the near future. In Czechoslovakia Henlein's supporters stepped up their campaign of demonstrations and terror. In view of the deteriorating situation Britain sent a special envoy, Lord Runciman, to investigate German allegations of oppression in Czechoslovakia. Meanwhile the Führer ordered the German forces to be in a state of combat readiness by 1 October. At the annual Nazi rally in Nuremberg in September Hitler made an angry, threatening speech. There followed a two-day revolt of Henlein's organisation which was put down by the Czechs. War appeared imminent.

Neville Chamberlain, British Prime Minister, had for some time been thinking in terms of a solution based on the Czechs ceding the Sudetenland, the area where most of the German-speaking population lived. Three days after Hitler's Nuremberg speech he flew to Germany, at the time an unusual and indeed courageous step for a 69-year-old who had never flown before, to seek a solution. The crux of his conversation with Hitler was that the Sudeten area would go to Germany and that he would try to persuade British and French colleagues to accept this. The Führer went ahead with his military plans agreeing not to move until he had had a further talk with Chamberlain.

The British Prime Minister had no difficulty in convincing the French, even though they had a mutual assistance treaty with Czechoslovakia, or most of his political friends. Faced with this situation the Czechs were forced to capitulate. They had a treaty with the Russians. But the latter were only required to act if the French did so.

Chamberlain again went to Germany. This time meeting Hitler at Godesberg. The Nazi leader shocked the Prime Minister by raising his demands. In addition to getting the Sudetenland, he wanted the immediate military occupation of the area—to give the impression of a military victory. The whole operation had to be completed by 1 October. It was already 23 September! After much heart-searching the British statesman agreed to put Hitler's terms to his colleagues, the French and the Czechs. The Nazi assured him that he was making his 'last territorial demand' in Europe. The Czechs refused to accept the German demands and mobilised. The French felt obliged to do the same. Britain mobilised the Home Fleet and the auxiliary Air Force. The Nazi dictator appeared to weaken. He sent a letter conciliatory in tone to Chamberlain on 27 September. Chamberlain grasped at this. He warned President Benes of Czechoslovakia that even if Germany lost a world war, Czechoslovakia would still lose the Sudetenland. He proposed the Czechs should accept a limited German military occupa-tion on 1 October of Egerland and Asch—outside the Czech frontier fortifications—and that a commission of Germans, Czechs and British, should quickly decide further areas to be handed over. To Hitler he proposed a conference to work out the details. Apparently it was Mussolini who got Hitler to agree to this. Hitler then issued invita-tions to Chamberlain, Mussolini and the French Prime Minister, Edouard Daladier, to meet him at Munich on the following day. The Czechs were not invited.

The meeting at Munich was not a conference in any real sense, it was a gathering summoned to accept Hitler's demands. The leaders met on the afternoon of the 29 September. By 1 a.m. of the following day they signed the Munich Agreement. It provided for the German Army to begin moving into the Sudetenland on 1 October, and complete the occupation by 10 October. All areas considered to be more than 50 per cent German were to be cleared by the Czechs. They had to leave all installations, including military ones, in good order. They received no compensation.

Chamberlain returned home to a hero's welcome. A man of peace he feared war, especially the bombing of civilians, demonstrated so terribly for the first time in the Spanish Civil War which was then raging. Almost equally he feared the extension of Bolshevik influence in Europe. And, it must be admitted, Stalin's Russia was not a very attractive alternative to Hitler's Germany. He was fully aware of Britain's lack of military preparedness, less aware of Germany's military and economic weakness. Finally, he received little encourage-ment from the U S A whose help had been decisive in the 1914–18 war. He was ill-advised and a poor judge of men—should he not have thought that a man who treated an old man and leader of a great empire in the way Hitler treated him could not be trusted?

In March 1939 Chamberlain was to be completely disillusioned. The remainder of Czechoslovakia was incorporated into the Reich under threat of aerial bombardment. Slovakia masqueraded as an in-dependent state but was *de facto* a German puppet. By May 1939 Hitler was telling his generals, 'Further successes can no longer be attained without the shedding of blood ... Danzig is not the subject of the dispute at all. It is a question of expanding our living space in the East ...' And 'There is no question of sparing Poland ...'

Concerted Anglo-French action in 1933–36 would have resulted in the end of Hitler. His generals feared Anglo-French military moves over the reoccupation of the Rhineland, for instance, and urged Hitler to desist from implementing this policy. Later, an Anglo-French accord with Russia might have achieved the same result. In 1938 General Beck, Chief of the German General Staff of the Army, feared any move against Czechoslovakia would lead to joint British, French, Czech and Soviet action. He was preparing a coup against Hitler to meet such a situation.

Agreement with the U S S R was not to be. Many British, and to a lesser extent French, politicians were suspicious of Stalin. Many of them thought the Soviet armed forces of little military value. Stalin provided them with an additional argument when he purged his top officers as German spies in 1937. Yet in April 1939 there was a tiny glimmer of hope. Chamberlain, largely because of public pressure, agreed to negotiations with Moscow. On the British side these were at best half-hearted. In any case, Poland, Romania and the Baltic states voiced their objections to such an alliance with guarantees covering them. The negotiations dragged on ending in August with the bombshell of a non-aggression pact between Germany and Russia. The Soviets had been greatly disturbed by the Munich Agreement, which opened Hitler's way to the East and indicated Anglo-French preference for dealing with Hitler rather than them. They feared being caught in a war alone, without allies, a war on two fronts. Recently Japan had provoked a series of armed clashes with the U S S R.

The published version of the Hitler-Stalin pact, valid for ten years, declared that neither party would engage in a warlike act against the other or join any third party in any such act. The additional secret protocols placed Finland, the Baltic states and Eastern Poland, 'in the event of a territorial and political transformation' in the Soviet 'sphere of interest'. Bessarabia was also so placed. This gave Hitler the green light for action against Poland. He did not believe that without Russia, Britain and France would act to save Poland. But on 25 August Britain and Poland decided on a treaty of mutual assistance.

On 1 September German forces launched a full-scale attack on Poland the pretext being an attack on the German radio station at Gleiwitz, an 'attack' staged by the Nazis themselves. On the same day Britain and France warned Germany that unless 'all aggressive action against Poland' was suspended and German forces promptly withdrawn they would 'fulfil their obligations to Poland'. On Sunday 3 September with no response from Germany but growing unrest in

Parliament, which had been recalled from holiday, Chamberlain repeated this intention giving the Germans until 11 a.m. to reply. Otherwise, 'a state of war will exist'. The German reply was the sinking of the British liner *Athenia* with the loss of 112 people on the same day.

## USA and Germany

What of America? It is relevant to outline here President Roosevelt's policy towards Nazi Germany in the years before the U S A entered the war. Controversy surrounds the motives and vision of Roosevelt in the 1930s. His actions were certainly isolationist. A pacifist wave had swept across the U S A as it had across France and Britain. Many Americans thought that they had been dragged into the 1914–18 war by the 'merchants of death', the U S arms manufacturers. Europe still seemed a long way away. In addition, many Irish Americans and some German Americans were suspicious of Britain. Hitler's proclaimed anti-Communism and anti-Semitism recommended itself to others, such as Henry Ford. Roosevelt had to consider such sentiments as well as the differing views of his policy advisers.

The three U S neutrality laws passed by Congress in 1935, 1936 and 1937 prevented the legitimate governments of Ethiopia and Spain purchasing American arms thus helping their attackers. The out-break of the Sino-Japanese war in 1937 started a process of change. During the Munich crisis of 1938 Roosevelt called for peace. However, like Chamberlain, he was later forced to see that Hitler could neither be appeased nor relied upon to keep his word. Nevertheless, Roosevelt's immediate response to the outbreak of war in September 1939 was to proclaim U S neutrality and to put the arms embargo and other restrictions into effect. The fall of France in June 1940 (see below) brought about a decisive shift in Roosevelt's stance. In a speech at Charlottesville on 10 June he announced that he would increase U S preparedness and extend to England and France the material resources of America. Rearmament was increased, compulsory military service introduced in September 1940, Greenland and Iceland were occupied, and on 14 June 1941 German and Italian assets in the U S frozen. As in the 1914-18 war there was increasing friction between Germany and the U S over the use of the Atlantic sea lanes for carrying supplies to Britain. When a submarine sank the American destroyer *Reuben James* on 30 October 1941, with the loss of 76 of her crew, Roosevelt ordered the navy to 'shoot at sight' any German or Italian submarines coming into American defence waters.

# — 6 —

# Phoney War, Total War and Total Defeat

Originally equipped by the French, Poland had a large army with a good fighting reputation earned in its war against the Soviets (1920–1). However, when the German forces went into action on 1 September the Poles lacked the necessary modern aircraft, tanks, anti-aircraft and anti-tank defences. Their communications and transport services were weak. German positions in East Prussia and in recently occupied Czechoslovakia gave the Wehrmacht a great strategic advantage. So that, although Poland had relatively large numbers of troops, its outlook was poor right from the start. By 8 September the Wehrmacht reached Warsaw. Any hope the Poles had of continuing open resistance ended on 17 September when Soviet forces crossed the frontier from the East.

In these circumstances it is perhaps surprising that remnants of the Polish forces were still resisting until well into October. Warsaw held out until 28 September when its garrison were forced to capitulate after repeated air attacks which had inflicted heavy civilian casualties and destroyed, among other things, the main waterworks. Poles who escaped created new units in Britain and later in the Soviet Union and fought with distinction on all fronts. Polish agents delivered to the British a German Enigma machine which enabled them to decode secret German radio traffic. Much of this story remains secret but the machine certainly helped the Allies win the war.

Defeated Poland was then divided by Hitler and Stalin. The Soviets advanced to roughly along the Curzon Line (so called because it had been drawn up at the end of the 1914–18 war by the British Foreign Minister Lord Curzon). They could claim that they were only taking back by force what had been taken by force by the Poles in 1920. The area was mainly populated by Ukrainians and White Russians. They further claimed, with some justification, that the Poles had ill-treated these minority peoples. However, neither in 1920 nor in 1939 were the luckless peoples of these areas given any say in what was to happen to them. Germany and the Soviet Union came to a new agreement, officially called the German-Soviet Boundary and Friendship Treaty, concluded on 28 September. The secret part of the Treaty assigned Lithuania to the Soviet sphere of influence and, by way of exchange, gave the Germans the provinces of Lublin and Eastern Warsaw. The partners further agreed not to tolerate 'Polish agitation' in their respective territories. This agreement destroyed any hope that a rump Polish state would be permitted to exist.

In those early weeks of World War II Adolf Hitler was successful in other directions. His navy, which had been considered the weak arm of the German armed forces, scored some striking successes. On 17 September a German submarine sunk the British aircraft carrier *Courageous* off the coast of Ireland and on 14 October the Royal Navy battleship *Royal Oak* went to the bottom while at anchor at Scapa Flow after a daring U-boat attack. Hitler's wildest dreams seemed to be coming true. In the West where Anglo-French forces on one side, and German on the other, watched each other behind well-fortified positions the *Sitzkrieg* (sit-down or immobile war) contrasted greatly with the *Blitzkrieg* (lightning war) in Poland. The British called it the 'phoney war'. In this situation, and with Hitler announcing a 'peace offer' in the Reichstag on 6 October, the German people must have thought that Der Führer was once again delivering the goods and that there would be an early return to peace. In these circumstances, the bomb which exploded in the Munich Beer Cellar on 8 November just a few minutes after Hitler had finished making a speech to the old guard of the Nazi party, was without significance as a manifestation of opposition to the regime.

## Victory in the West

Having knocked out Poland and got some kind of agreement with the U S S R Hitler turned his attention to the West. He rightly concluded that, if left undefeated, Britain and France could only get stronger. He therefore aimed at a quick, yet decisive blow against France which would drive Britain from the mainland of Europe. Britain could then either be starved and bombed into submission or invaded. But before Hitler could turn his thoughts to France his attention was drawn to the situation in Scandinavia.

The Germans were heavily dependent on iron ore from Sweden for their war effort. For seven winter months of each year the ore from near Gellivare had to be hauled by rail to Narvik in Norway. From there it was shipped to Germany. Most of this journey was in Norwegian waters and Norway, like Sweden, was neutral. Winston Churchill, as Britain's First Sea Lord or Navy Minister, asked the

British Cabinet to sanction the mining of Norwegian waters. This was rejected. But in December 1939 Britain saw a chance of intervention in Norway. This was due to the outbreak of hostilities between Finland and the Soviet Union.

The Soviets were concerned with building buffer zones between themselves and the Germans notwithstanding the Hitler-Stalin Pact. They compelled Estonia, Latvia, and Lithuania to sign treaties of 'Mutual Assistance' as a preliminary to taking them over. This gave the Soviet Navy what they considered to be useful bases in the Baltic. Immediately after the signing of the treaties Stalin put pressure on Finland to cede territory which he regarded as vital for Russia's defences. He was particularly concerned about an area where the frontier was only about 20 miles from Leningrad and the island naval base of Kronstadt, and about the lease of the Baltic port of Hangö as a naval base. When agreement was not reached the Russians attacked Finland. Most of the world sympathised with the Finns and were pleased about early Soviet reverses. The British and French intended to send an expeditionary force. This would have had to go through Norway with or without that country's acquiescence. Before such a force could be dispatched the Finns were defeated.

About one month after the Russo-Finnish Peace Treaty was signed, on 9 April German troops started their occupation of Norway and Denmark. This was not the result of Finnish defeat, for already in October 1939 Grand Admiral Raeder had been at work convincing Hitler of the importance of Norwegian ports for the German Navy both to defend German shipping and, offensively, to blockade the United Kingdom. Hitler was convinced that occupation was necessary after an incident in February involving the release of about 300 British seamen who were held aboard the German prison ship *Altmark*. The British destroyer *Cossack* intercepted the *Altmark* in Norwegian waters after it had been given clearance by the Norwegian naval authorities who apparently did not know this ship's mission. In Denmark the Germans found no opposition except for isolated shooting. In Norway things were different. Five German divisions were sent to occupy the main ports and the capital, Oslo. This was a potentially hazardous operation which could have led to disaster for the Germans. Everywhere the Germans met opposition. In the fjord leading to Oslo the guns of the Oskarsborg fortress sank the heavy cruiser *Blücher*, which had several important Nazi officials on board and damaged the pocket battleship *Lützow*. Other German ships had been sunk or damaged when the invasion force had been challenged at the entrance to the fjord. This particular force was compelled to turn back. Nevertheless, the Germans quickly reduced the whole of

Norway. They were able to do this by what became known as the classic Nazi military tactics. These were surprise, command of the air, parachute landings to take important military objectives (in this case Oslo's airport) and the use of internal subversion. In Norway the Germans had the help of Norwegian Nazis led by Vidkun Quisling, a former officer and former Defence Minister. They spread confusion and officers under their influence surrendered their units without a fight. This happened in Narvik. Poor British leadership also saved the day for the Germans.

Two days before the German attack on Norway and Denmark an Allied expeditionary force was due to sail for Norway. This force did not in fact sail as scheduled because of the news that the Germans were heading for Norway. By the time Allied troops were on their way the Germans already controlled much of the country including the vital ports and airfields. Nevertheless the British Navy went into action with some success. During the original German attack British ships and naval aircraft sank two German cruisers as well as smaller vessels. At Narvik, where the British lost two destroyers, they sank, in two engagements, ten better-armed German destroyers and a number of supply ships. In all the Germans lost, apart from these ten destroyers, three cruisers and the use of the badly damaged *Scharnhorst, Gneisenau* (both battle cruisers) and *Lützow* for several months. Allied losses were nine destroyers, one cruiser and one aircraft carrier. The German losses were relatively far heavier than these figures would suggest for their naval forces started off much weaker than those of the Allies. This was to be important when they were contemplating the invasion of Britain.

Three Allied landings took place in Norway. Two near Trondheim, in an attempt to recapture that vital port, failed. The third landing near Narvik succeeded in achieving its objective. On 27–28 May an Allied force of British, French, Poles and Norwegians recaptured Narvik driving the Germans in the direction of Sweden. However, on 10 May the German offensive in western Europe had started and by the end of the month things were going very badly for the Allies. It was decided to withdraw the force in Norway to try to halt the Germans in France. Norwegian resistance then inevitably quickly came to an end. By 10 June 1940 all Norwegian forces had ceased fighting; the government and King Haakon had resolved to continue the fight from London.

One shock for Hitler which partly resulted from the Norwegian campaign was the resignation of the British Prime Minister, Neville Chamberlain, after much criticism of his handling of the situation. Notorious for his appeasement policy before the war, he was replaced by the implacable enemy of Hitler, Winston Churchill. Churchill, who had not done too well as First Sea Lord during the Norwegian campaign, headed a national coalition resolved to prosecute the war to a successful conclusion.

In France and the Low Countries the Allies were defeated by the same factors which defeated them in Norway: surprise, lack of air support, lack of armour, little or no coordination between national forces, apathy and subversion. They were not surprised by the attack on Holland, and even less so by the one on Belgium. They had proposed joint staff talks with Belgium but such talks were rejected.

The Allies did not expect the thrust to come where it did. They were expecting another move similar to the German plan of campaign in 1914, that is, across northern Belgium towards Paris. At Hitler's insistence the thrust was across Luxembourg, southern Belgium and the Somme Valley, with a simultaneous attack on Holland. The aim was to draw the British and some French forces into Belgium and then cut them off from the main French forces. The Germans could then outflank the French fortifications known as the Maginot line. Intensified German security regulations and able use of camouflage concealed the advance of the armoured units, and thus left the Allies in doubt as to which was the main thrust of the offensive. Once again the Germans used parachutists to capture strategic targets. An innovation was the successful use of gliders against strongly fortified positions in Belgium. They also gave the Dutch a taste of the aerial bombardment the Poles had suffered—though German writers today claim the destruction of Rotterdam was due to 'poor communications'. Five days of hard fighting were enough to cause the capitulation of the Dutch forces, though their government and monarch got away to Britain. The Belgians lasted two and a half weeks, capitulating on 28 May with their king at their head. Even with the same forces available, had these countries cooperated with each other and with the Allies before they were attacked the outcome could conceivably have been different.

Abandoned by their friends, the Allies lost no time in getting their troops out of this dangerous situation in which the Anglo-French units, which had gone to the aid of the Belgians, were cut off from the main French forces. On 26 May the order was given to evacuate Allied troops from the perimeter around the port of Dunkirk. An armada of vessels from large naval craft down to small civilian boats manned by volunteers swung into action. Against all expectations, in the nine days which followed, nearly 340,000 British and Allied troops were taken out. Most of their equipment was lost and the diversion of naval vessels from protecting other Allied shipping meant heavier losses in that direction. But the successful evacuation was of the greatest importance to Britain both morally and materially. The lost equipment could be replaced, men could not have been.

One question which baffled the world at the time was how it was that the Germans could not prevent this evacuation. Some Germans argued that Hitler had actually allowed the British withdrawal to give the United Kingdom the chance to save face and then come to terms with Germany. This view rests on the fact that Hitler did halt the advance of German armoured columns for two days between 24 and 26 May. This decision undoubtedly gave the Allies the chance to organise some sort of defence around the evacuation base. Now we know that Hitler's order was in no sense motivated by any desire to placate the British. It was the result of Luftwaffe-Army rivalry, Hitler's own rivalry with his military men and the belief that, as the Allied forces were finished anyway, it was a good idea to regroup the Panzer units before going in for the final kill. Luftwaffe chief Hermann Göring felt the air force, a more National Socialist organisation than the army, should be given a greater share in polishing off the enemy than it had been given so far. Hitler was influenced by this intervention. General Gerd von Rundstedt, one of 12 generals promoted to field marshal in July 1940 for his activities in France, advised Hitler to halt the armoured units to give the infantry time to move up for he feared, if they were too far forward by themselves, they would be in danger of being overrun. Hitler agreed with him in his estimate of the situation. Further, he wanted to show his generals who was boss, for this view was not to the liking of some of them particularly those who hoped to be covered in glory by annihilating the British. The events at Dunkirk showed that the Nazi leadership overestimated (as have many other leaderships since) the role of air power. Their planes were not so very effective against the British Army, though it is true they were hampered some of the time by weather conditions, and they were up against R A F fighters operating from the British side of the Channel. One other factor aiding the British evacuation was that the Germans at first thought Ostend was the most important embarkation port and concentrated their efforts on bombing it.

With the bulk of the British forces out of France along with some of the French, and the rest of the French forces exposed and demoralised, the Germans made rapid advances into the interior of France. By 10 June they were over the Seine. Two days later the French government declared Paris an open city and fled to Tours. On 15 June it was on the move once again. The following day the government resigned and Marshal Pétain, famous soldier of the 1914–18 war, took over the government. He immediately asked the Germans for an armistice. He also had to ask the Italians. On 11 June the Italians had attacked the staggering French in the south, no doubt in the expectation of cheap glory and spoils.

Hitler feared that if he dealt with the French too harshly their government would leave the country and attempt to fight on from one of the French colonies. This would probably have meant that the French fleet would sail for Allied ports and carry on against the relatively weak German Navy. Hitler was no doubt aware of the problems of trying to put the whole of France under German military rule. He therefore agreed to a French government continuing to rule in an unoccupied part of the country. This was roughly the south-east of the Republic, a largely agricultural area. Paris, the northern industrial region and the entire western coast were placed under German rule, though French local administration was to continue in these areas. As one would expect, French forces were to be demobilised and disarmed, their weapons and fortifications handed over in good order and the cost of the occupation was to be paid by France. More questionable was French agreement that their prisoners of war should be held captive in Germany until the end of the war, for was it not already over between the two countries? The French dishonoured their traditions by agreeing to hand over all German citizens wanted by the Gestapo. Worse still, they agreed that all Frenchmen caught resisting the Germans whether in France or anywhere else should be shot. On the vital question of the French fleet, still then in French hands, it was to be disarmed, but left under Vichy control. On 22 June 1940 the French signed the armistice agreement with Germany on the same spot where the Germans had been forced to sign in 1918. This was surely Hitler's greatest moment of triumph!

Some Frenchmen who had escaped from France were determined not to accept the authority of the pro-German 'Vichy French' government under Pétain. One of these was General Charles de Gaulle who had successfully commanded an armoured division. A day after the signing of the armistice he announced that, by agreement with the British, he was setting up a provisional National Committee to work for the recovery of national independence and to honour French alliances. The British government gave French servicemen, who did not wish to join de Gaulle, the chance to return home, but it decided on determined action against French naval vessels whose commanders intended to return them to Vichy France. When the commander of a French naval squadron at Oran, in French north Africa, refused to join the Allies or sail to a French port in the West Indies, the British sank his ships as they lay at anchor.

## Operation Sea Lion—failure over Britain

On 16 July 1940 Hitler issued his Directive No. 16 which began with the words 'As England, in spite of the hopelessness of her military situation, has so far shown herself unwilling to come to any compromise. I have decided to begin to prepare for, and if necessary to carry out, an invasion of England'. However, some months before the German leadership had started to think in terms of such an invasion. He had hoped that Britain would see reason and indeed on 19 July made a speech to that effect in the Reichstag, but at the same time he put in hand plans for an eventual invasion. Two days before his Reichstag speech the Army High Command ordered 13 picked divisions to places on the Channel coast for the first wave of the proposed invasion. And on the same day the Army Command completed its detailed study for landing on the south coast of England. The main thrust was assigned to Field Marshal von Rundstedt. Within a few days the Germans expected to have landed 38 divisions by sea and two by air. The completion of Operation Sea Lion, as the invasion of Britain was code-named, would take about a month so Field Marshal Walther von Brauchitsch told Grand Admiral Raeder, head of the German Navy.

The British government and people took this invasion threat seriously and took what measures they could to prepare for it. Even before the fall of France the government decided to send out of the country all the gold in the banks. Shipments started to Canada on 24 June and by August gold and securities to the value of seven billion dollars had crossed the Atlantic—without apparent loss. Other measures included the setting up of the Local Defence Volunteers, later called the Home Guard, the establishment of a guerrilla-type organisation to operate behind enemy lines in the event of them establishing a bridgehead, and the evacuation of foreigners whose loyalty was questioned to Empire territories. Improvised fortifications were constructed in coastal and strategic areas, road signs removed and pronunciation-tests introduced for persons suspected of being enemy agents! That the situation was grim was admitted by the British Chiefs of Staff who reported at the end of May, 'Should the Germans succeed in establishing a force with its vehicles in this country, our Army forces have not got the offensive power to drive it out'. As well as their commitments at home, it should not be forgotten that the British forces had worldwide commitments.

Hitler knew the British Army must be in bad shape after the evacuation from France but he also realised that to launch a successful invasion the Wehrmacht would have to be in command of the air and the sea. He therefore took steps to bring this about, at the same time hoping that the British would be brought to their knees by bombing, blockade and radio propaganda. On 13 August the Battle of Britain began and on 17 August the Germans established an 'operational area' around Britain, in which all the ships were to be sunk without warning. In February 1940 the Germans commenced broadcasts from the New British Broadcasting Station. Others specifically aimed at Scotland, industrial workers and the 'Christian Peace Movement' were operating from July.

The Battle of Britain began in August and lasted until the end of October 1940. There had, however, been German bombing raids before August and they continued, off and on, for most of the rest of the war. It was on 14 November, for instance, that the notorious attack which destroyed much of the centre of Coventry was launched. The German aim was to gain mastery of the air and to demoralise the population. To this end, they bombed radar stations, airbases, R A F control stations and aircraft factories. Later, in September, they turned their attention to centres of population. From the records available after the war it appears that had they concentrated their attacks entirely on the first set of objectives they might have been successful. Hitler ordered the change because of R A F raids on Berlin which started towards the end of August. These were not very effective but they boosted British morale and caused Hitler and Göring to lose face. The British raids had been ordered by Churchill in response to German bombing of the City of London on 24 August. This bombing was apparently a mistake. However, Hitler had thought before this of terror raids against Britain and from his early days had been a great believer in this kind of attack to demoralise the enemy 'masses'.

The Germans had certain obvious advantages in the Battle of Britain. Their morale was high due to their string of victories over the preceding year. Their bases were fairly close to the targets so that, by the standards of those days, they could send over heavy bomb loads. They greatly outnumbered the British in planes and crews. On the other hand, the British too enjoyed a number of factors in their favour. The British Spitfire was just that much better than the German Messerschmitt 109 fighter. Secondly, it was easier to pick up British pilots who bailed out as they were operating over home territory. Thirdly, the British were very well organised in groups and sectors and, due to the effective use of radar, squadrons could be quickly deployed where they were needed. Some would also claim that the British pilots were just that much better than their German opposite numbers but that claim is difficult to prove. Some Germans believe the opposite to be true because R A F fighter squadrons usually avoided combat with German fighters alone: being numerically weaker they were conserving their energies to deal with German bombers, a more essential task. Another reason for German defeat in the Battle of Britain was undoubtedly lack of determination on the part of Hitler. All the time he harboured the illusion that the British would crack and sue for peace. He overestimated the influence of air power in the same way the Allies were later to do.

The fact that Britain did not crack in the summer and autumn of 1940 greatly strengthened the resolve of all those around the world who opposed Hitler. It influenced the decisions of the neutral states and helped Britain's friends in the United States. Finally, by holding out, Britain provided the base, as well as many of the men and material, for the future liberation of Western Europe.

## An excursion to the Balkans

One reason for Hitler's lack of decisiveness in dealing with Britain was that he had his mind on other things, on a possible attack on the Soviet Union. In July 1940—about the time of the start of the Battle of Britain—he announced to his military leaders his intention to attack Russia. The attack was to start in the following spring. If Germany could smash Russia, so Hitler believed, it could then finish off Britain for the British still counted on the Soviet Union. The invasion would begin in May 1941 and would last five months; then Russia would be smashed!

The Soviet-German agreements of 1939 had not changed much in relations between the two states. True there was increased trade, even trade in military and strategic goods—the Soviets got samples of German planes, tanks, artillery, even the plans of the *Bismarck*—and increased diplomatic activity, but the two dictators remained deeply suspicious of each other. Hitler was busy with his conquests on the field of battle, Stalin was trying to get as much as he could through diplomacy and, as far as small states were concerned, blackmail. Hitler was worried by Soviet advances in the Baltic but he needed Moscow's goodwill and strategic materials at the time and so could not counter such advances. Stalin could not be happy at the easy victories of a regime which had sworn to destroy Bolshevism. In June 1940, when Hitler had his hands full in France, Soviet troops occupied Bessarabia and North Bukovina in Romania. Bessarabia had been seized from Russia at the end of the 1914–18 war, but Bukovina had never formed part of the Russian Empire. It was part of the Hapsburg

Empire before 1919. Hitler feared the Soviets might try to take over the whole of Romania which was the main supplier of oil to Germany. Hitler managed to bring about a change in Romania in September to his own satisfaction, a pro-Nazi government being installed. German 'military advisers' then started to move into Romania. The Russians were naturally uneasy about this and about reports of German troops going to Finland. Officially these troops were on their way to Norway.

In November 1940 Soviet Foreign Minister Vyacheslav Molotov went to Berlin, at Hitler's invitation, to discuss with the Nazi leader future relations between the two countries. Both sides expressed the fears and suspicions outlined above. Molotov wanted clear agreement on specific issues rather than the vague general assurances mouthed by Hitler and his foreign secretary. Speaking to Hitler in a way that few had ever done before, Molotov demanded recognition of Soviet interests in Romania, Bulgaria and Turkey. Hitler urged the Russians to join the pact recently concluded by Germany, Italy and Japan. He claimed that the British were finished and that there would soon be pickings for all in the disintegrating British Empire. Molotov was not impressed, particularly as during his visit the R A F bombed Berlin. Later in the month Stalin made known his conditions for joining the pact with Germany, Italy and Japan. These included clear recognition that Finland, Bulgaria and the Straits, as well as the Persian and Arabian oil fields, were within the Russian sphere of influence.

We shall never know when Hitler decided irrevocably to attack the Soviet Union. We shall never know whether anything Stalin did or said influenced the decision at all. We do know, however, that shortly after Stalin informed him of his terms for joining the pact with the three totalitarian states Hitler issued Directive No. 21. This was on 18 December 1940 and was headed 'Operation Barbarossa'. In it Hitler talked of establishing 'a defence line against Asiatic Russia from a line running from the Volga River to Archangel'. This was to be achieved in a 'quick campaign' of 'daring operations'. It was to commence in mid-May of the following year. The attack would be carried out with the assistance of Finland and Romania, and Sweden would have to be persuaded to permit the transit of German troops from Norway to Finland.

Hitler did not of course unleash his troops on the Soviet Union in May but in June 1941. What caused the delay? It resulted from the need to assist his faltering ally.

In North and East Africa the Italians suffered heavy defeats at the hands of much smaller British and Empire troops in late 1940 and early 1941. By May the British had forced the capitulation of the Italians in Abyssinia. In Greece, which had been invaded in October

1940, things were no better for the Italians. They were driven out by ill-equipped Greek troops to their base in Albania. German troops arrived in North Africa in February and quickly changed the situation. Simultaneously Hitler was preparing intervention in Greece. He had forced Hungary and Romania into the German camp in November. In March Bulgaria and Yugoslavia followed but a military coup in Belgrade reversed the position in Yugoslavia. Instead of dealing with the Greeks by an offensive through Bulgaria, Hitler now decided to finish off both Yugoslavia and Greece at one go. The German attack on Yugoslavia and Greece was launched on 6 April 1941. Yugoslavia was practically surrounded by the forces of the Berlin-Rome Axis and its troops were badly equipped. They were forced to surrender on 17 April. The Greeks, with a little British support, held out on the mainland four days longer. Anglo-Greek forces then tried to hold on to the island of Crete but were overwhelmed by superior forces and, above all, by superior airpower. But the bulk of the British troops managed to get away after inflicting heavy losses on the Germans.

By his onslaught on the Balkans, Hitler had prevented the British from getting a foothold on the European mainland, removed a threat to the, for Germany vital, Romanian oil fields, and eliminated the danger of an immediate second front after the start of the campaign in Russia.

## Barbarossa

Hitler's plan to invade the Soviet Union must have been one of the most widely known secrets in military history. The United States State Department got the news from its legations in Bucharest and Stockholm and passed it on to Molotov. A British agent heard the news and Churchill immediately instructed the British ambassador in Moscow, Sir Stafford Cripps, to inform Stalin. This was in April. Stalin was warned by his own agents, Richard Sorge, who worked in the German Embassy in Tokyo, and the Schulze-Boysen organisation in Germany. Both these sources had reports in by March or even earlier. On 10 June a young German soldier, Communist Rudolf Richter, deserted to the Russians to give them the news. On the evening of 21 June another German soldier, Alfred Liskow of Kolberg, managed to get over to the Russians and warn them. Finally, one hour before the invasion the German N C O Wilhelm Schultz, a Communist mechanic from Eisenach, reached the Soviets severely wounded but managed to get out his warning before he died.

The rumours of the impending attack reached the world press. The official Soviet reaction to these reports was to call them an 'obvious absurdity'. Up to the last minute Stalin tried to placate Hitler by diplomacy and prompt delivery of strategic goods. If Stalin and the Communists had a completely unrealistic picture of the other side, so, as we shall see, had Hitler, most of his generals, and many political and military observers in all countries.

The conflagration which Hitler started in the early hours of 22 June 1941 was the most gigantic military operation in history stretching along a 1,500-mile front. It was also, on Hitler's orders, one of the most deliberately brutal—a result of his ideology and aspirations in the East. Hitler and his colleagues had decided that the Russians and the Ukranians and the other peoples of the Soviet Union were, like the Poles, fit only to be the slaves of the Germans. He therefore sought to wipe out any of them who showed leadership qualities and was totally indifferent to the fate of the rest. As he and most of his generals were completely confident of winning an easy victory, they did not, at first, even try very much to conceal their aims, nor were they concerned to make opportunist promises in order to weaken resistance. Orders were issued not to treat Soviet prisoners of war as other prisoners of war and to shoot certain categories out of hand. The most notorious of these orders was the *Kommissarbefehl* (Commissar Order) issued by the High Command of the Armed Forces on 6 June 1941. This laid down that the political commissars of the Red Army should be 'shot at once' as representatives of Bolshevism. (These commissars were regular uniformed and armed soldiers who could therefore expect to be treated as normal P O Ws.) The German generals tried to justify this and other such orders on the grounds that the Soviet Union had not ratified normal international treaties which protected prisoners. Yet the Soviet Union had requested its protecting power, Sweden, on 17 July 1941, to notify the Germans that the Soviets would adhere to the 4th Hague Convention of 19 October 1907 providing the Germans did so. The Germans chose to ignore this. Finland, Italy, Slovakia and Romania, on the other hand, let it be known that they would respect normal international practice regarding prisoners of war. Of nearly six million Russian troops captured by the Germans only about one million emerged from the camps in 1945; most of the others perished.

During the first few months of Hitler's campaign in Russia all seemed to be going well. Enormous advances were made which compared well with German successes on that front in World War I. In the areas of the U S S R acquired since 1939 many people, who knew Stalinism but not yet Nazism, welcomed the Germans as liberators and this probably speeded their advance. So great were German victories that by the end of September Hitler was instructing the Army to prepare to demobilise some units so that the manpower could be used in industry. The Red Army, he concluded, was finished. Most Allied opinion agreed. In the early stages of the fighting many Soviet troops, when surrounded or out of ammunition or badly led, behaved just like the Poles, French, and even British, had done in similar circumstances: they surrendered in droves. Some, especially the non-Russians, deserted. But many Soviet troops resisted tenaciously even in hopeless situations. And as they recovered from the first shock and the chaos which followed, as they got battle experience and experience with new weapons the resistance grew. Most important of all, morale improved once they started to realise that even Hitler's crack units were not invincible. As early as the beginning of July, along the northern sector of the Finnish front, the SS Kampfgruppe 'Nord', with a Finnish and German Army division, suffered near disaster assaulting the Soviet stronghold at Salla. The five SS battalions employed in the attack were twice thrown back with heavy losses. As they attacked once again, the Soviets launched a counter-stroke which panicked them and sent them reeling back beyond their original lines. On this, and on the more usual occasions, when they pushed their opponents back, the Germans were suffering heavy casualties. General Franz Halder, Chief of the Army General Staff, noted in his diary on 8 October that German Army losses from the beginning of the invasion of Russia were 564,727. This was more than they had sustained on all fronts before 22 June. Generals like Halder had come to recognise, as he wrote on 11 August, 'we underestimated the strength of the Russian colossus'.

If the price was high so was the prize. By the beginning of October the Battle for Moscow had commenced. Moscow was not just the capital of a country, it was the capital of Bolshevism, it was the nerve centre of a highly centralised state, chief rail centre and a most important centre of arms production. In the autumn the German advance started to slow down. Apart from the stiff resistance the highly mechanised German forces suffered in the mud caused by the rain on the poor Russian roads. The mud changed to snow and the Russians could deal with it better than the Germans. On 29 November the Germans of Army Group South were forced to withdraw from Rostov, the gateway to the Caucasus, suffering heavy losses. At the beginning of December Army Group North was held outside Leningrad. Outside Moscow the Germans were also held. Much of their equipment was useless in the severe weather conditions, men and animals became casualties of frostbite, supply trains became an easy target for partisans. In this situation the Soviet leaders brought up reinforcements. Some of these were poorly trained, poorly equipped, but very determined, Moscow factory workers. Many were well-trained and equipped troops brought in from Siberia. Under General Georgi Zhukov and General Ivan Koniev they went over to the offensive. Using ski and sledge troops, cavalry and massive artillery barrages, they forced the Germans back. The Wehrmacht only narrowly avoided a catastrophe similar to that of Napoleon's troops in 1812.

The day after Zhukov launched his 6 December counter-offensive, the Japanese made their surprise attack on the United States Navy at Pearl Harbor. Hitler's response to this new outbreak of hostilities was to declare war on the United States. The United States and the Soviet Union now became allies which meant not only American planes bombing Germany and American troops in action against the Germans in the West, but American supplies for the Red Army through Iran (which had been forcibly brought on to the Allied side by British and Soviet troops in August). The attack on Pearl Harbor also meant that the Japanese were too busy fighting Anglo-American-Chinese forces to attack the Soviet Union. At critical moments, therefore, Soviet troops could be moved from the east to the west.

## Defeat in the desert

The first half of 1942 went well for the Wehrmacht. There were victories in Russia involving gigantic numbers of men and materials, and there were brilliant, but less significant in material terms, actions by General, later Field Marshal, Rommel and his Italian allies in Africa. The African successes came first.

Starting in January Erwin Rommel launched a series of daring thrusts designed to drive the British out of the Middle East, deprive them of the Suez Canal link with their empire, and link up with German forces in the Caucasus. On 20 June the strategic British fortress and port of Tobruk fell to Axis forces. Against the, as it turned out, sensible advice of the Italians, Hitler agreed to Rommel's continued advance into Egypt. At the end of June the German-Italian forces reached El Alamein in Egypt but there they were surprised by the stiff resistance put up by Commonwealth troops equipped with U S supplies and occupying well-prepared positions. The British, from August led by General Montgomery, built up their forces until by mid-October they—150,000 British, Commonwealth, French and Greek forces with 1,114 tanks—were ready to do battle with the Axis.

Rommel had 96,000 men and 500–600 tanks at his disposal. After 11 days of fighting the German commander decided, in defiance of orders, to try to pull back his forces. German military historians attribute Rommel's failure to the break-down of overseas supply lines, the irremediable weakness of Italian armaments, the increasing demands of the Eastern Front for Germany's remaining reserves, and the failure of the Italian fleet (in turn due to lack of fuel and air support). After taking his initial decision to withdraw Rommel hesitated on Hitler's orders. He subsequently lost most of his armour.

November was to be an equally black month for the Axis in Africa. Anglo-American forces under General Dwight Eisenhower went ashore at several points along the coast of (Vichy) French North Africa. There was little opposition, many French officers cooperating with the Allies. Hitler rushed troops to Tunisia to prevent Allied occupation and in the vain hope of expelling Eisenhower's forces. The Germans were however overwhelmed. In May of 1943 the Army Group Tunisia was forced to surrender to the Allies. This surrender marked the end of the fighting in North Africa.

Even worse than the news from Africa in 1942–43 was that from Russia.

## Stalingrad

On 2 February 1943 the last remnants of the once mighty German Sixth Army surrendered to the Russians at Stalingrad. Friedrich Paulus, commander of this army, and his staff, had already been taken into captivity on 22 January. Paulus had consistently refused Soviet demands to capitulate made after the Sixth Army was surrounded on 23 November. He refused because at first he had expected outside help. By Christmas 1942 all hope had disappeared but Paulus held on because of Hitler's order to do so, and because he (rightly) believed that by doing so he was holding down large concentrations of Soviet forces. Perhaps too he hung on because he had not decided his own fate. Hitler promoted him to field marshal on 22 January in the expectation that he would shoot himself. By continuing to resist after November the Field Marshal made inevitable the deaths of thousands of his troops in action, and the deaths of thousands more from hunger, frostbite and disease. In all about 90,000 men, led by Paulus and 24 generals, were taken prisoners. The high-ranking officers were given remarkably good treatment by the Russians, the other ranks, already weakened by their ordeal in sub-zero temperatures, suffered the long march to the camps and years of agony behind the wire. Few of them returned to Germany!

Stalingrad was a great railway centre, a key river port on the Volga and an important producer of tanks and guns. It had acquired some symbolic meaning for the supporters of the Soviet system for it was there that Stalin had defeated White guard attempts to capture it in the Russian Civil War in 1918. Then it was known as Tsaritsyn. Apparently, because of this, Hitler overestimated the psychological and ideological importance of the town for the Soviets.

The basic cause of the German failure at Stalingrad was under-estimation of Soviet military strength and morale. This was not just simply the result of ideologically-based prejudice. It was due to a failure of military intelligence and to the knowledge of the very heavy casualties sustained by the Soviet forces in the first half of 1942. After being pushed back from Moscow the Germans had regained the initiative in the spring of 1942. Hitler sought to capture the Maikop, Grosny and Baku oilfields. Wilhelm Adam, adjutant to the German Sixth Army, quotes Hitler as saying that without these sources of fuel the war was lost. In addition, by taking Sevastopol the Nazi leader intended to gain control of the Black Sea and eventually reach Egypt by the back door. To the north, Stalingrad and Voronezh would be taken seizing industrial areas and making possible an attack on Moscow from the East. Sevastopol was under siege from December 1941. It fell in July 1942. The Germans did not reach Grosny but managed to take the wrecked fields at Maikop. In the north Voronezh was bypassed in July and panzer units pushed on to Stalingrad. Hitler had, by that time, committed the great blunder of aiming at too many objects simultaneously rather than concentrating his forces. At the beginning of the summer offensive in the south they stretched over a 800-km front. The length of this front was later greatly extended. Mounting losses forced the Germans to rely in certain key areas on Hungarian, Italian and Romanian troops, who were poorly equipped and who had little interest in the war.

The factor which turned defeat into disaster was Hitler's order not to retreat, an order which had paid off in the previous winter when the German front was threatened with disintegration outside Moscow.

As we shall see, the battle of Stalingrad was not as decisive as was earlier believed. Still, it was important considering the size of the operation. In psychological terms it seems to have been decisive for both Germans and Russians. This was the first time in World War II that a German army had been destroyed with most of its high-ranking officers preferring life as prisoners of the 'sub-human Bolshevist-Jewish scum' to death. It represented a severe blow to Hitler's prestige for he had claimed Stalingrad had fallen to his army and, worse still, he later promised to save the Sixth Army. Even hardened Nazis felt bitter, disappointed even stunned, by the Führer's failure to fulfil his pledge. What the Sixth Army felt towards the end was revealed years later when the last letters sent by them from Stalingrad were published. These had been confiscated at the time and analysed on the orders of the German High Command. Only 2.1 per cent of the letter-writers were positive in their attitude to the war leadership. Another 4.4 per cent had doubts and 57.1 per cent were regarded by the Wehrmacht experts as rejecting the war leadership.

## Life in occupied Europe

By the end of 1942 National Socialist imperialism had reached the greatest extent of its expansion. Only Sweden, Switzerland, Spain, Portugal and Turkey remained precariously neutral, by making concessions to Germany, the rest of Europe lay at Hitler's feet. How did he see its future? How did he rule it?

Hitler's idea of a German Reich meant at least the Germany of 1914 with Austria and the Sudetenland added to it. This he actually carried through. He further expressed the view that the Baltic states and the Crimea would become part of the Reich. Finland would become a federated state and eventually the German-speaking part of Switzerland and Holland would be incorporated into Germany. The rest of Europe would be under German leadership and the vast areas of Poland, Ukraine and Russia would be colonies whose inhabitants would slave for Germany. Swiftly, on the heels of the Wehrmacht, came the Nazi officials who sought to make this nightmare a reality.

In the occupied East, rivalries developed between the different branches of the Nazi state, party and war machine. This hindered consistency in policy. Broadly speaking, the Nazis were most severe and reckless when they were winning, and a little less so when they were hard pressed or short of labour. Hitler's policy was to exploit these areas to the full for Germany's benefit and everything else was to be subordinated to this end. By various means he sought to destroy the educated classes of the East who were capable of resistance. Education for the subject peoples was to be reduced to the barest minimum, so were public health services. Cheap vodka, tobacco and contraceptives were to be made available to weaken resistance and keep the population down. The traditional imperialist policy of divide and rule was introduced, turning one nationality against another, one religious group against another and all against Jews and Russians.

The policy of exploitation meant colossal exports of raw materials, food and manufacture to Germany at the expense of the indigenous population, reducing them to near starvation. It meant herding millions to work as forced labourers in the Reich. In December 1944 there were over two million of them at work in Germany. For most their status was little better than that of slaves. The third element in this policy was the use of extreme terror against the Eastern peoples. This was partly based on the Nazi view that they were subhuman or *Untermenschen*, partly to smash the growing resistance.

In western Europe the conduct of the Germans was somewhat better. This was particularly so in the early days of the occupation before the resistance movements were organised. Racial affinity and expediency also resulted in better treatment for countries such as Denmark and Holland. These considerations did not save them from immediate exploitation and eventual violence. The Nazis seized the gold and foreign currency holdings of these countries, charged exorbitant occupation costs, confiscated art treasures, paid for Wehrmacht supplies with near-useless paper money, and forced industrial and commerical undertakings into unequal partnerships with German concerns. These countries, like the nations of eastern Europe, were forced to provide millions of workers for the German war economy— over five million of them by the end of 1944. In addition, many of their soldiers, held as prisoners of war, were forced on to war production or farm work. On the whole, they received better treatment than those from the East though they, too, often suffered a great deal.

One of the best-known witnesses of this suffering was Dr Wilhelm Jaeger, a medical practitioner employed by the giant arms concern of Krupps. He recorded how he found French prisoners of war slaving for Krupp, in a camp in Essen, who had been 'kept for nearly half a year in dog kennels, urinals and in old baking houses. The dog kennels were three feet high, nine feet long, and six feet wide. Five men slept in each of them. The prisoners had to crawl into these kennels on all fours ... There was no water in the camp'.

Any opposition to the occupation authorities was crushed as ruthlessly in western Europe as in the east. Potential opponents were rounded up immediately following the invasions. Later a system of concentration camps was established throughout occupied Europe. Thousands were sent to concentration camps in Germany under the *Nacht und Nebel* (Night and Fog) decree. Issued towards the end of 1941, this ordered that suspected resisters should not be tried in military courts in their own countries, which would give publicity to the resistance, but should be sent to Germany in secrecy and there isolated and possibly liquidated.

## *The fate of the Jews*

The worst fate of all in Nazi-occupied Europe was that suffered by the Jews. The Polish Jews were conscripted to do forced labour by a decree of October 1939. About the same time they were required to wear a large yellow star with the word 'Jew' on it. They were increasingly removed to ghettos. The first of these was set up at Lodz in April 1940. Later in the same year another was established in Warsaw; others followed. They were districts surrounded by walls or barbed-wire fences with their own internal administration. Their inhabitants were not allowed out except by special permission of the German authorities. They worked hard for the Germans but, in return, did not even receive subsistence-level rations. The result was death from slow starvation and disease. Into these ghettos were gradually crowded Jews from Germany and the occupied territories, the first Jews from the Reich being deported in autumn 1941. By the end of May 1943 Germany was declared 'free of Jews', although this was not entirely correct.

With the invasion of the Soviet Union in June 1941 the anti-Jewish campaign reached a new intensity. So-called *Einsatzgruppen*, special units of s s and police, were formed to hunt and liquidate Jews, Communists, gypsies and other 'undesirable elements'. These units killed about one million people in mass shootings and by other methods.

The first camp equipped with gassing facilities was Chelmno in Poland which operated from December 1941. However, experiments with gas had been carried out at Auschwitz, set up May 1940, in the autumn of 1941. It was at the notorious Wannsee (West Berlin) conference in January 1942 that Reinhard Heydrich, on the orders of Hermann Göring, discussed with representatives of the various ministries the technical and organisational problems involved in removing the Jews to the East for liquidation. Adolf Eichmann, later executed by the Israelis as a war criminal, was present. It was at this meeting that the term 'final solution' came to be used. In addition to Chelmno and Auschwitz, extermination camps were set up at Belzec, Sobibor, Treblinka and Maidanek. Killings of Jews and others continued in the many other camps, of which in April 1944 there were 20 main camps and 165 subsidiary ones. Heinrich Himmler, as head of the R S H A or Reich Security Main Office, was in charge of the camp system and the liquidations. Heydrich was, until assassinated by Czech patriots in 1942, his deputy. Though the figure of six million Jews exterminated is the one most widely quoted, we do not know exactly how many perished. Rudolf Höss, commandant at

Auschwitz until Decmber 1943, later admitted that, during his service at the camp, 'at least' two and a half million people were executed, and that a further half a million died from hunger and disease. Not all of these were Jews but that was in just one (the largest) camp.

Soon, due to enormous German losses on the Eastern Front, the extermination programme was competing for Jews with the forced labour requirements of the war economy, including the s s enterprises. Auschwitz became, not only the greatest 'factory of death', but also the biggest employer of forced labour. How these 'lucky' Jews were treated was once again recorded by Dr Jaeger. He was talking about a visit to a camp for Jewish women working for Krupps: 'I found these females suffering from open festering wounds and other diseases ... There were no medical supplies ... They had no shoes ... The sole clothing of each consisted of a sack with holes for their arms and head. Their hair was shorn ... The amount of food in the camp was extremely meagre and of very poor quality. One could not enter the barracks without being attacked by fleas ...'

The question is often asked to what extent did the German people know of the bestialities of the Nazi system. Many Germans have denied all knowledge of the atrocities. If one examines the evidence impartially one is forced to conclude that any German had the means to know a good deal about the brutalities of Nazism but that few would have known the full horrors. No secret was made in 1933 of the widespread arrests of Communists and Social Democrats and later of Jews and others. No secret was made of the existence of the concentration camps. The notorious Nuremberg Race Laws were not secret and in many towns the populace saw the ill-treatment of Jews and sometimes the columns of prisoners on their way to the camps. In 1938 all Germany knew about the smashing up of the Jewish businesses, synagogues and homes. True, the Germans were told that the camps were there to re-educate political and other criminals. But did they not ask themselves why workmates, neighbours and friends had disappeared? Why many died in these 're-education camps'? Why the few who were released were afraid of talking about their experiences? During the war millions of Germans served on the Eastern Front: they could not help but see what the 'New Order' meant in the countries concerned. Units of the Wehrmacht took part in the shooting of hostages on all fronts. The Germans who stayed at home saw the millions of slave labourers clearing away rubble or labouring in the factories and on the farms. Did they never ask themselves why these prisoners were in such a pitiful condition? On the other hand, few Germans could have known that their government was systematically exterminating millions of Jews and the Nazi authorities tried to cover up the scale of deaths in the camps. Any German with a minimum of thought and feeling must have been aware that the Nazi system was barbaric. Once they came to this conclusion, could they have done much about it? This is a much more difficult question to answer. Given the nature of the regime, resistance needed the opportunity, which many did not have, and more courage than it is perhaps right to demand of ordinary people. A few found both the opportunity and the courage, though some of these did not realise fully the consequence of getting caught.

## The German resistance

The first Aryan German to be executed for wartime resistance was a communist working in the Junker factory in Dachau. He—his name is unknown—refused to do air-raid protection work, was reported by the works police, arrested and sent to the Gestapo in Berlin. Himmler ordered his immediate execution. This was carried out in Sachsenhausen concentration camp. Although most people have heard of the July 1944 bomb plot against Hitler, the unknown German worker is more typical of the German resistance than are the officers of the July plot. The German workers, Communists and Social Democrats who opposed Hitler, were not attempting any spectacular coup by assassination. They mainly sought to influence their fellow Germans by leaflets, slogans on walls and secret discussions. Sometimes they dared to 'go slow' or even strike. After the war started there were acts of industrial sabotage, help for prisoners of war and slave workers. Among them were Bernhard Bästlein, Franz Jacob and Theodor Neubauer who succeeded in building up a Communist network in about a dozen towns. They all died at the hands of the Gestapo in 1944–45. Some German workers found ways of resisting the Nazis in the armed forces. One of these was Kurt Hälker who, as a member of a three-man group in the H Q of the German Navy in Paris, provided the French resistance with arms and information and later joined them to use their weapons against the Nazis. Hälker survived to be able to tell his story to the author. Less fortunate was a man about whom we know little but who deserves mention. Anton Schmidt's name came up at the Eichmann trial in 1961. He was a Wehrmacht N C O, probably not a member of a group or party, who on the Eastern Front helped Jews to escape. We do not know what happened to him but some of those he helped reached safety and recalled his name for posterity.

In a separate category on the Left were the Communists who were prepared to carry out espionage for the U S S R as a means of defeating Nazi Germany. There was the group known as *Die Rote Kapelle* led by the Luftwaffe lieutenant Harro Schulze-Boysen and there was Dr Richard Sorge's group operating from the German embassy in Tokyo. Most of the members of these groups perished after doing valuable work for the Soviet Union. Finally, working with the Russians, were the officers and men who took part in the anti-Nazi 'Free Germany' Committee. Among these the remnants of the Sixth Army were strongly represented.

Many more Germans than we in the past gave credit for, opposed the Nazis. And, like the Munich lawyer, Edgar J. Jung, and his 'Young Conservatives', and the ill-fated Munich students Sophie and Hans Scholl, they were by no means always on the Left. That their numbers were considerable, we know from the Gestapo files. In August 1942, for instance, 1,761 Germans were arrested for downing tools, 1,583 for illegal contact with foreign workers or prisoners of war. Another 1,210 more detained as 'Marxists', 1,267 as 'reactionaries' and 1,007 as 'resisters'. These were just the main categories of Germans arrested for political matters.

Despite the courage of the many groups and individual resisters the July plotters remain the most significant of the German opponents of Hitler.

The plot of 20 July 1944 was an attempt to kill Hitler and stage a military *coup d'état*. At its centre were military men who were in touch with a number of prominent civilians, the latter were to help form a government after the coup. The civilians included the Social Democrats Dr Julius Leber, who was to be Minister of Interior, Wilhelm Leuschner, Vice-Chancellor, Dr Theo Haubach, Information, and the Christian trade unionists Jakob Kaiser, deputy to Leuschner and Bernhard Letterhaus, Ministry of Reconstruction. The Conservative, former Mayor of Leipzig, Carl Goerdeler, was to be Chancellor and Ulrich von Hassell, former Ambassador to Italy, was to become Foreign Minister. A Catholic lawyer, Dr Josef Wirmer, was to take over Justice, Paul Lejeune-Jung, former Reichstag member, was designated Economics Minister. The provisional Head of State in this shadow regime was General Ludwig Beck. With the exception of Kaiser all the above-listed died in the purge which followed the failure of the plot.

The man who seems to have been the initiator of the July plot was Major-General Henning von Tresckow, Chief of Staff in Central Army Group on the Eastern Front. He was in contact with Goerdeler and other civilian and military opponents of Hitler. Tresckow, descended from a line of Prussian soldiers, had tried for some time to win over fellow officers for a coup. He had not been very successful. Many officers owed their positions to rapid expansion of the forces carried through by Hitler. Their gratitude to him was strengthened by an oath of personal loyalty and by the Führer's brilliant victories up to the end of 1942. The Allied demand for unconditional surrender was a further factor helping to still the consciences of those shocked by the excesses of the Nazi regime. However, had they overthrown Hitler in 1943, by which time it was clear Germany had lost the war, they must have realised they could have got some kind of terms. At the very minimum they would have saved their people from the horrors of continued aerial bombardment, saved them from the horrors of occupation by undisciplined, angry and battle-weary troops, and saved the lives of their soldiers.

After many disappointments, Tresckow gained the active cooperation of a small group of important officers and the passive support of some others. Under the code-name 'Valkyrie' he worked out a plan for the military occupation of Berlin by the rebels. This was completed with the aid of Graf Claus Schenk Stauffenberg, a 37-year-old Wehrmacht colonel, who, after being severely wounded in Africa, became Chief of Staff in the supply section at the HQ of the Reserve Army in Berlin. Stauffenberg was for executing a coup as soon as possible. He realised that delay could only worsen Germany's position. He was aware too that the Gestapo was closing in on the plotters. Because of his position he was able to attend conferences with Hitler. He volunteered to make a bomb attempt on Hitler's life himself. Between 11 July and 20 July Stauffenberg prepared three attempts on Hitler's life. The first two, one of which might have succeeded, he abandoned. Tension mounted as his comrades in Berlin waited for news.

Rumours started circulating in Berlin, the result of vague messages from Hitler's H Q at Rastenburg. General Friedrich Olbricht, Head of Supplies for the Reserve Army, chief military conspirator in Berlin in the absence of Stauffenberg, started the 'Valkyrie' (Walküre) operation by issuing orders in the name of General Fromm. Friedrich Fromm was Commander of the Reserve Army. By the time Stauffenberg and Olbricht arrived at his office Fromm had heard that Hitler was not dead. Stauffenberg's bomb had exploded, killing or wounding several of those present. It might have killed the Nazi leader had not the case, in which it had been placed, been moved when Stauffenberg made his escape. Fromm refused to have anything to do with the attempted coup and was arrested by the conspirators. The rebels, including Beck, now with Stauffenberg, failed to take decisive action to control Berlin.

They did not fortify themselves in their H Q, nor did they seize the radio station, telecommunications centres, Gestapo headquarters or airfields. They did not bring into action one of the few units they were sure of—the paramilitary police under S S General Graf Heinrich Wolf von Helldorf, a fellow conspirator. Their lack of resolve gave the only leading Nazi still in Berlin, Joseph Goebbels, Minister of Propaganda, a chance to act.

Goebbels showed considerable initiative. He knew from Rastenburg that Hitler was alive. He broadcast a message announcing this over the radio. He alerted Hitler's S S bodyguards stationed five miles from the centre of Berlin. He also got the guards' battalion led by National Socialist Major Otto Ernst Remer to move against the plotters in their Bendlerstrasse H Q. This exposed another weakness of Stauffenberg's men: they did not check the reliability of key officers *before* the coup. Remer's men were supposed to be taking over key points in Berlin for the conspirators.

As it became clear that Hitler was not dead and that the rebels did not even control Berlin, doubtful officers, such as Field Marshal Günther von Kluge, Commander-in-Chief West (France), and General Helldorf, dissociated themselves from the coup. This did not save them. Late on the evening of 20 July officers loyal to Hitler on duty at Bendlerstrasse, who had said little during the day but had smuggled in automatic weapons, rounded up Beck, Olbricht, Stauffenberg and others. They released Fromm who allowed Beck to shoot himself and executed the others the same night. He hoped to redeem himself in Hitler's eyes. Fromm was eventually executed by the Nazis.

The plot to save Germany had failed. The courage and patriotism of the rebels did not make up for their lack of competence and ruthlessness. Even so, they might have succeeded had not the great majority of Wehrmacht officers remained loyal to Hitler.

## The break-up of the Rome-Berlin Axis

One of the first jobs Hitler had to do immediately after the bomb explosion at Rastenburg was to receive Benito Mussolini, the Italian dictator. One can imagine both dictators thinking that perhaps, after all, 'Providence' had saved them for a higher purpose. Mussolini had had an escape which was almost as improbable as Hitler's.

Following up their successes in North Africa the Allies had invaded Sicily in June 1943. In the face of mass strikes in the industrial centres and imminent Allied invasion, the King of Italy and a majority of the Grand Council of the Fascist party decided to get rid of Mussolini. They held the former dictator in custody and sought a separate peace with the Allies. An armistice was signed on 3 September and on the same day Allied troops landed in Southern Italy. The German forces in Italy were in a critical position and because of a Soviet offensive on the Eastern Front it was difficult to send many reinforcements. Whatever the reasons, the Allies did not exploit the opportunities open to them. The result was that Field Marshal Albert Kesselring, German Commander-in-Chief in Italy, was able to occupy two-thirds of the country, including the important industrial areas, and to disarm substantial Italian forces.

Not all the Italians were prepared to be disarmed. The Acqui Division stationed on the Greek island of Kefallinia were not. They were attacked and eventually overpowered. Then the 900 Italian prisoners were shot down in cold blood. This, and similar massacres, were carried through by the Wehrmacht, thus exploding the myth that only the SS committed war crimes. Both organisations were later responsible for crimes against Italian civilians. The Italian Navy avoided the fate of the Army and, together with the king and his government, made for Allied-held areas.

Even more dramatic than the occupation of Italy was the remarkable rescue of Mussolini by SS glider troops from a remote mountain-top hotel. The Duce was then set up as a head of the 'Italian Social Republic' in the North. He became a German puppet and was eventually shot by Italian partisans who resisted the Germans and Italian Fascists.

## Operation Overlord

Urged on by Stalin and with growing confidence gained from the landings in North Africa and Italy, the Allies turned their attention to the invasion of north-west Europe. Britain became increasingly a vast arsenal as more and more American men and material evaded the German submarines. In 1942 the Germans had been sinking shipping faster than the Allies could replace it. In 1943 the balance shifted in favour of the Allies, thanks to long-range aircraft, radar-equipped vessels and the mastery of German naval codes using a captured Enigma set from the U 110.

The Western Allies could also be reasonably confident because they knew the Germans could not draw on reserves from elsewhere. Since Stalingrad the Russians had taken an increasingly heavy toll of Germans. In July 1943 Hitler had launched his last great Eastern offensive. Seventeen panzer divisions and half a million men were flung against the Soviets at Kursk. This battle proved to be far more costly and far more decisive than Stalingrad. Now it was the Russians' turn to go over to the offensive, which they kept up to the end of the war. By the end of 1943 they were nearing the Polish and Romanian frontiers.

Despite the apparently good position of the Allies in June 1944 their invasion was faced with dangers which could have proved disastrous. There were the mine-fields to get through. There were the submarines. At key points along the coast there were German heavy naval guns. There was the weather to contend with: bad weather could have made landing men hazardous and landing heavy equipment even more so. The minefields, submarines and guns did not prove to be very dangerous. The weather was a more effective opponent. In the first month after D-day, the Allies lost 261 vessels destroyed or damaged by enemy action, as against 606 by the weather. A sudden gale, contrary to all meteorological experience, blew from 19 to 23 June, destroying landing craft and other vessels. In some respects too, the Allied forces were faced with superior weapons. The British Churchill and the American Sherman tanks were inferior to the German Tigers and Panthers. The quality of the German weapons did not make up for their lack of quantity. Nor did the determination of the s s units make up for their lack of numbers and reserves. From 6 June, the day of the landings, to 23 July, the Germans lost 2,722 officers and 110,357 non-commissioned officers and men, of whom no more than 10,078 had been replaced. Allied losses for the same period were around 117,000. All of them were replaced. Other German disadvantages were lack of air support, which for one thing impeded such reserves as were available due to the destruction of the railways, limited naval power, the growing resistance of the French underground, and lack of a clear plan of defence.

Once Eisenhower and Montgomery had successfully got their troops ashore on the Normandy coast it was only a matter of time before they broke out of the beachhead. By 25 August Paris was taken intact by the Americans and Free French. Some credit for this must go to the German commander General von Choltitz, who refused to obey Hitler's orders to blow up all the bridges and destroy the city. Less than two weeks later Brussels, the Belgian capital, was liberated by British troops and by 11 September the Americans had reached the German frontier. In the same month the Soviets occupied Sofia and reached armistice agreements with Bulgaria, Finland and Romania. The Germans also evacuated Estonia.

In 1944 the Nazis proved that they could be as ruthless as ever and they were not yet beaten. In the East they crushed a rising of the

Warsaw underground with the utmost vigour, after which, on Hitler's orders, the city was razed to the ground. The members of the Polish Home Army met the same fate as the Jewish resisters who, practically unarmed, had gone down fighting a year before rather than be deported like sheep to the slaughter house. The destruction of Warsaw made little difference to the military situation on the Eastern Front.

In the West the Germans virtually annihilated an Allied airborne expedition dropped at Arnhem and Nijmegen in Holland near the German frontier. It was hoped that this force would seize and hold important bridges across the lower Rhine until the main units arrived to outflank the German Siegfried Line. Failure to act on intelligence reports indicating heavy German troop concentrations, including two S S panzer divisions, led to disaster.

It was in the West that Hitler made his last big offensive of the war in the 'Battle of the Bulge'. His aim was, at a minimum, to gain time during which, as he thought, the Western Allies would fall out with the Russians and look for a negotiated settlement with Germany. His maximum aim was to knock the Allies off balance by a sharp, surprise thrust and drive them into the sea, again achieving the same political result. This was not as unrealistic as it sounded. After all, there were differences between the Soviets and the West, and Hitler had succeeded with similar offensives in 1940 and 1941. The Nazi leader greatly overrated his own strength and underestimated that of the Allies. Arnhem had given the Germans some renewed confidence and the Allies appeared to be in difficulties with their supply situation still being largely dependent on the port of Cherbourg. Realising that the enemy had overwhelming air superiority, Hitler planned the blow for December when the weather would interfere with aerial operations. He also sought to create the maximum confusion by using Germans dressed in American uniforms and equipped with American arms. To some extent this tactic succeeded. But many of the luckless Germans who later fell into American hands were shot, as was permitted under International Law.

It was on 15 December that the Germans attacked on a 70 mile front through the Ardennes Forest. The Allies were certainly taken by surprise and initially the Germans had some success. American positions were overrun and the front appeared to be disintegrating. Yet the key communications town of Bastogne held against repeated German attacks and demands for its surrender. This gave the Americans time to regroup their forces. The weather which had been kind to the Germans changed and they soon felt the full force of the mighty Allied air fleets against which they were virtually powerless.

Within a month the Germans had been driven back to their starting point losing some 120,000 men. The offensive had achieved nothing and had robbed Hitler of his last reserves so desperately needed on the Eastern Front. Like the other German offensives this one produced its atrocities. The most widely known of these involved the shooting of at least 71 unarmed American prisoners by the 1st S S Panzer Division near Malmédy.

## 'Terror and wanton destruction'

As mentioned above, Allied air superiority was of great importance in the success of the Normandy landings and in the Battle of the Bulge. But this air superiority over the battle fields was only one aspect of the air war. Another was Allied attacks on targets within the Reich. As early as May 1940 93 R A F aircraft attacked industrial targets in the Ruhr and on 25 August the R A F made its first raid on Berlin. These first raids were more important as morale-boosters to the hard-pressed British than serious military operations. The early raids had been against key targets and had to be abandoned because of German air defences and, in the case of night raids, because of the inaccuracy of night bombing. This led in the course of 1941 to a shift of emphasis to general area bombing of the largest German towns. Though new inventions made precision bombing more feasible and daring precision attacks were mounted, the area of offensive reached devastating proportions after March 1943. One of the outstanding examples of these was the round-the-clock attack on Hamburg by 3,000 bombers between 24 July and 3 August 1943, causing great devastation and loss of life. Such raids were controversial. It was one thing to destroy aircraft and tank factories, blow up synthetic oil plants, blast dams and interrupt communications. It was quite another deliberately to destroy large residential areas, killing thousands of civilians. The idea was to 'bring home to the civilian population of Germany the horrors of war', as one British M P put it to Sir Archibald Sinclair, Secretary of State for Air, who was 'in complete agreement' with this formulation. Such attacks were opposed by an informed minority, men like the Bishop of Chichester, Dr Bell, and the Marquess of Salisbury. The majority of British people no doubt felt that the raids were a legitimate form of warfare against a foe who had introduced it, and who was known to be committing crimes against civilians under German occupation.

The most controversial of these attacks was that on Dresden in February 1945. Sir Arthur Harris, Commander-in-Chief of Bomber

Command, ordered just over 800 aircraft to Dresden on 13 February 1945. In daylight on the next day 400 bombers of the U S Eighth Air Force took up the attack. Third and fourth attacks of 200 and 400 bombers finished off the destruction of this once beautiful town in central Germany. Churchill, putting it mildly, wrote in a memo of 28 March that the attack 'remains a serious query against the conduct of Allied bombing', and implied it was an act of 'terror and wanton destruction'. It has never been established why the attack was made. In general the aim was to support the Russians by hindering the retreat of the Germans, causing chaos and depriving the Nazis of an almost intact city in which to evacuate their administration. The evidence seems to indicate that the Russians did not ask for the raid. In fact they were trying to restrict Allied bombing by establishing a 'bombline' or 'air frontier'. They realised, if the bombing went on, they would inherit a desert. In the above-mentioned memo Churchill made the same point.

The military value of these raids is now in doubt. The German population did not crack, neither did the Wehrmacht. Production of war equipment was actually rising at the height of the bombing. Nevertheless the raids did tie up large numbers of German planes and men who otherwise might have been used against Allied ground forces and especially against the Soviets. The bombing of German fuel supplies was more effective as shortage of fuel did bring panzer units to a halt in the Ardennes offensive and in the battles on the Eastern Front in 1944–45.


## The fall of Berlin

With the failure of the Ardennes offensive by February 1945 the end of the Third Reich came rapidly. Hitler was himself partly to blame for this. He might have withdrawn his still considerable forces from Northern Italy, Denmark, Holland and Norway, and concentrated them in the Reich. He might have attempted to defend the mountainous region of southern Germany and Austria—the so-called National Redoubt—where the Nazis had built some fortifications. Instead he left his forces widely scattered. For the Ardennes offensive he had weakened the Eastern Front. After its failure he transferred units to the East. The armies of the Western Powers swarmed into Germany. Highly mechanised, they advanced at tremendous speed. They were anxious to get to Berlin. But they were not to head in that direction.

General Dwight Eisenhower thought in purely military terms. He felt that Berlin was not an important military objective. More important were the north German ports, and with their capture the isolation of German forces in Norway and Denmark, and the seizure of the 'National Redoubt'. Allied intelligence believed the Nazis would make a last stand in the mountainous area of south Germany and Austria—the so-called 'National Redoubt'. Bernard Montgomery, the British commander, wanted, for personal, patriotic, psychological and political reasons, to give priority to getting to Berlin. He, and Churchill, were convinced that once Berlin, the heart of the Reich, fell, German resistance would crumble. Montgomery further believed that it would make it easier to get on with the Russians if they were deprived of the prestige of capturing Berlin. Eisenhower feared the cost in casualties would be high, too high a price to pay for Berlin especially as it had already been decided that the area around Berlin was to be in the Soviet Zone, and that the city itself would be under joint allied occupation. When Eisenhower made his decision the Soviets were nearer Berlin than Western forces, and appeared poised to take it at any moment. After the war some writers and public figures criticised the Supreme Commander's decision claiming that had the West got to Berlin first, difficulties with the Russians would have been avoided. But at the time the Soviets were still regarded as allies, and as it was believed they would be needed to help finish off the Japanese (no one knew then how effective the A-bomb was to be).

It was left to the Soviets then to take Berlin. They had halted on the Oder, the last main obstacle before the capital, and had been advancing south in Czechoslovakia and Austria. On 16 April 1945 they opened their last great offensive of the war against Hitler's Reich. The Soviet attack was preceded by what was the greatest artillery barrage of World War II. The Soviet force was opposed by Army Group Vistula under the command of General Gotthard Heinrici. Heinrici's men were the odds and ends of the once proud Wehrmacht: Luftwaffe personnel, administrative troops, police turned into infantry, units of the Volkssturm or Home Guard made up of old men and boys. There were soldiers who were on convalescent leave and those previously relieved of military service on health grounds. The whole army was strengthened by the remnants of the S S. It was welded together by fear—fear of what the Russians would do, fear induced by propaganda or knowledge of what the Germans had done in Russia, or what the Russians had done in areas they had already overrun. Those not impressed by such things were usually persuaded to remain by the sight of Wehrmacht officers and men hanging from lamp-posts— executed by the S S for alleged desertion.

The desperate courage of the Germans could not save Berlin from the reckless courage of the Soviets, from the armies of Marshal Georgi Zhukov and Marshal Ivan Koniev. Within days Soviet troops were nearing the centre of the city.

In the Nazi-held prisons S S murder squads were reeking their last vengeance on the prisoners still in their custody. July plotters, Communists, Social Democrats, deserters, those simply caught without papers, those who had uttered 'defeatist' sentiments, and many others besides. Hitler and Goebbels, the Gauleiter of Berlin as well as Propaganda Minister, had refused to evacuate the population, who had to spend days, practically without food or water, in cellars, shelters and the Berlin Underground. For some these havens became their tombs. Whether on Hitler's orders or on their own initiative S S men blew up a tunnel running under an arm of the river Spree and the Landwehr canal. This was a rail link with four hospital trains and many Berliners sheltering in it. Many drowned. Hitler grew indifferent to the fate of his people and ordered a 'scorched earth' policy. He had relied on 'wonder weapons', such as the V 1 and V 2 rockets fired at London, from June 1944 to early 1945. Then he had expected a split in the alliance against him. All hope finally faded once it was clear that the death of President Roosevelt, on 12 April 1945, would not lead to a break-up of the Anglo-American-Soviet alliance. In these circumstances he resolved to kill himself. This he did together with his new wife Eva Braun on 30 April.

Hitler left Admiral Karl Dönitz at Flensburg, as President and Joseph Goebbels, in the Berlin Bunker, as Reich Chancellor. Himmler, who might have been given one of these posts, had deeply wounded Hitler by negotiating with Allied representatives behind the Führer's back. They did not respond. One of the first acts of Goebbels as Chancellor was to attempt the same with the Soviets. They were not interested and Goebbels, together with his wife and children, followed Hitler's example. Himmler killed himself shortly after his capture by the British. Göring was taken by the Americans and poisoned himself after being sentenced to death at the Nuremberg Trials. Not all the Nazis saw the end of the Third Reich as their end. Martin Bormann, Hitler's deputy in the N S D A P, left the Bunker in an attempt to escape, and, though many believe him dead, is still being sought today. General Heinrici lived to tell, in peaceful retirement, of the last days of Berlin. Nor need Goebbels have sacrificed his family. Göring's and Hess' families spent the postwar years in comfortable obscurity in West Germany.

The fate of many ordinary Germans in defeat was a hard one. In the East millions died or were killed either in their homes or attempting to flee to the West. Others were later expelled by the Soviet, Polish or Czech authorities under harsh conditions. Possibly the worst sea disaster in history occurred when the *Goya*, a German freighter, was sunk by a Soviet submarine on 16 April 1945. Out of 6,000–7,000 refugees only 183 survived. It was by no means the only refugee ship to be sunk. Travelling overland thousands of refugees were either shot down or died of exhaustion. Of those who remained in the towns and villages overrun by the Soviets and the Poles many faced looting, rape, forced labour or death. Some died of starvation or disease in internment camps where they had been placed either because of membership of Nazi bodies, or because of some infringement of new regulations or simply by accident.

Historians argue about whether this was deliberate policy or whether it was due to the collapse of discipline. A Soviet propagandist, author Ilya Ehrenburg, incited the Red Army to acts of savage vengeance. On the other hand, it is true the Soviets had suffered bestial treatment at the hands of the German occupiers as part of official Nazi policy. In those circumstances it would have been unreal to expect a totally peaceful 'liberation'. In addition, at the end the Soviet Armies were augmented by surviving POWs and Asiatic troops and, in any case, their high command expected them to live off the land they passed through.

In the West too, the conquerors were not always chivalrous. The Swiss Consul-General in Cologne, Franz Rudolf von Weiss, was dismayed by the conduct of American troops and so was Dr Konrad Adenauer, future Chancellor of West Germany. Some German prisoners, military and civilian, also suffered in the hastily established US camps at the end of the war. Controversy rages as to whether this was deliberate policy or whether it was due to the chaotic conditions that prevailed at that time. On the whole, however, the Germans rightly preferred to see US or British troops arriving than Soviet forces. Fear gave way to feelings of relief when they realised the senseless slaughter, inflicted upon them in the first place by their own leaders, was over.

The last act of the Third Reich was the formal capitulation of its forces to the Western Allies by General Alfred Jodl at Reims on 7 May and by Field Marshal Wilhelm Keitel on the following day to the Soviets in Berlin. Both signatories were later hanged at Nuremberg for their war crimes.

# — 7 —

# Germany Under Occupation

Having defeated and occupied Germany the Allies had to decide what to do with it. At several important wartime meetings the Allied leaders had discussed the matter. Their views changed somewhat according to the military and international situations, the venue and so on. They had to decide on the new Germany's frontiers, on the form the occupation would take, on the compensation Germany should pay, on the political future of Germany, the type of state or states it should construct, and the best means of preventing a recrudescence of Nazism, militarism, or the kind of nationalism which could endanger peace.

Meeting at Yalta, in the Crimea, in February 1945, Stalin, Roosevelt and Churchill agreed that 'the Eastern frontier of Poland should follow the Curzon Line ... They recognise that Poland must receive substantial accessions of territory in the North and West ... the final delineation of the Western frontier of Poland should thereafter await the Peace Conference'. In other words they were recognising the Soviet Union's acquisitions from Poland in 1939, offering Poland German territory in the west and in the north, East Prussia. The Western leaders lost some of their enthusiasm for Polish expansion at Germany's expense as it became clear that postwar Poland would be Soviet-orientated.

At the Potsdam conference in August 1945 the Anglo-Americans found themselves faced with a *fait accompli* by the Russians who had handed over to the Poles all the lands up to the Oder-Neisse Line. The conference decided to place all 'former German territories' east of a line running from 'the Baltic Sea, immediately west of Swinemünde, and thence along the Oder River to the confluence of the western Neisse River and along the western Neisse to the Czechoslovak frontier, including that portion of East Prussia not placed under the administration of' the Soviet Union, 'under the administration of the Polish State'. This was 'pending the final determination of Poland's western frontier'. By this statement the Western Powers were recognising *de facto* Poland's new frontier with Germany even though, in later years, due to the Cold War, they and the West Germans were to emphasise the words, 'pending the final determination'. But by agreeing that 'the transfer to Germany of German populations, or elements thereof, remaining in Poland, Czechoslovakia and Hungary, will have to be undertaken', the Western Powers were making it very difficult to argue in favour of a new revision of Germany's frontiers at Poland's expense. With the loss of the Oder-Neisse territories the Germans forfeited 24 per cent of the entire area of 1937 Germany. The conferences did not deal with Germany's western frontiers. The reestablishment of Austrian independence had been declared an Allied aim by the foreign ministers of the Soviet Union, Britain and the U S A in Moscow on 1 November 1943.

In an agreement of 12 September 1944, signed in London, Britain, U S A and the Soviet Union agreed that the Germany of 31 December 1937 should be divided into three occupation zones, an eastern, a north-western and a south-western. Berlin would be divided in a similar way and would be ruled by an Inter-Allied Commandatura. The Russians would receive the eastern zone but it was not decided, due to Anglo-U S rivalry, which zones the two Western Powers would receive. This matter was cleared up by an agreement of 14 November under which Britain was assigned the north-west and the U S the south-west. On the same day the three powers decided Germany would be ruled by an Allied Central Council. They also made provision for a French zone to be carved from the Anglo-U S zones. It was later agreed, against some opposition from Stalin, to give France a place on the Central Council.

The Yalta communiqué recognised Germany's obligation to pay compensation to the Allied Nations. The nations to receive priority treatment would be those 'which have borne the main burden of the war, have suffered the heaviest losses and have organised victory over the enemy'. Reparations could be exacted from 'the national wealth'—equipment, machine-tools, ships, rolling stock, investments abroad, etc—from 'annual deliveries of goods from current productions' or by 'use of German labour'. Potsdam went into greater detail about reparations. It laid down that the U S S R and Poland were to receive their share from the Soviet Zone and from German foreign investments, and the Anglo-Americans and other nations from the Western Zones and German foreign investments. The conference further granted the Soviet Union the right to substantial reparations, partly in exchange for raw materials and food, from the remaining intact steel, chemical and machine-making plant, in the Western Zones.

What kind of political future could the German people expect? The Potsdam communiqué assured them that 'it is not the intention of the

Allies to destroy or enslave the German people. The Allies want to give the German people the chance to prepare itself to rebuild its life on a democratic and peaceful basis'. Once it had achieved this Germany would once again be able to take its place among the nations. Potsdam implied a united Germany, except for the territories east of the Oder-Neisse Line, in that it spoke of the economic unity of Germany, equal treatment for all Germans, and the setting up of 'a few, important, central German administrative departments'. This was somewhat in contrast to earlier discussions of the 'Big Three'. They had toyed with various schemes for the division of Germany into several states. The most controversial of these was that advocated by U S Secretary of the Treasury, Henry Morgenthau. He wanted boundaries to the east similar, but not as favourable to Poland, as those which came into existence in 1945. Secondly, he wanted the internationalisation of the Ruhr and the Kiel Canal area. Thirdly, France should get the Saar and the adjacent territories bounded by the Rhine and the Moselle Rivers. Finally, he advocated the establishment of a North German state including much of old Prussia, Saxony and Thuringia, and a South German state comprising Bavaria, Wuerttemberg, Baden and some smaller areas. The plan also demanded that the Ruhr 'should not only be stripped of all presently existing industries but so weakened and controlled that it cannot in the foreseeable future become an industrial area'. Morgenthau's proposals never became official policy despite Churchill's and Roosevelt's signatures on the plan at the Quebec Conference in September 1944. The plan did though influence future policy towards Germany.

How did the Allied leaders intend to, in the words of Potsdam, 'assure that Germany never again will threaten her neighbours or the peace of the world'? By complete 'disarmament and demilitarisation of Germany and elimination or control of all German industry that could be used for military production'. To this end all German military, semi-military organisations, even veterans' organisations 'shall be completely and finally abolished'. All Nazi organisations were dissolved, all Nazi or militarist propaganda banned, all Nazi-inspired laws abolished, all war criminals brought to justice. Further, all Nazi members 'who have been more than nominal participants in its activities and all other persons hostile to Allied purposes shall be removed from public and semi-public office and from positions of responsibility in important private undertakings'. On the positive side, German education and the judicial system, administration and local government were to be reconstructed according to democratic principles. Democratic parties were to be encouraged and, 'Subject to the necessity for maintaining military security, freedom of speech, press and religion ... [and] ... the formation of free trade unions shall be permitted'. The Germans were allowed 'average living standards not exceeding the average of the standards of living of European countries' (excluding the U K and the U S S R).

## 'In darkest Germany'

Those Germans who had the time, energy or interest to read the text of the Potsdam agreement might have thought the terms could have been a lot worse, hard though they were in certain respects. Most Germans were concerned with the struggle for personal survival. But most ordinary German manual and office workers, farmers, housewives and pensioners were not afraid of being classed as 'more than nominal participants' in Nazi organisations. Their struggle for survival was concerned with homes, food, jobs and keeping their families together. In the Germany west of the Oder-Neisse Line 20 per cent of all homes had been destroyed. This was made worse by the fact that certain key towns—Berlin, Cologne, Dortmund, Dresden, Düsseldorf, Essen, Hamburg, Magdeburg, Stuttgart, among them—were more than 50 per cent destroyed. In addition, homes had to be found for the millions of Germans pouring in from Eastern Europe. Germany had a housing problem before the war started. In 1939 there was a shortage of about one million homes. In 1948–49 West Germany alone had a shortage of five million homes. The poorer sections of the population were hit harder than the rest. It was the central districts of Berlin, Dresden and Hamburg which had been so heavily bombed rather than the outer, middle-class, suburbs. The problem was increased by the movement of wartime evacuees back to their former places of residence. Some middle-class people lost their homes, in most cases temporarily, to the occupation forces.

The Germans had lived well for most of the war. Food and loot had been available from the occupied territories, and the German economy had not operated as a total war economy for considerable periods between 1939–45. In the last months of the war the situation changed. After the end of hostilities the Germans learned what many Europeans had already learned—what it feels like to be hungry. Production of agricultural products went down. The region which became the Anglo-U S Zone produced, on average, 16.1 million tons of potatoes in the years 1935–38, in 1945 only 12.3 million tons and in 1946 no more than 11.2 million tons. The respective figures for rye, in million tons, were: 2.7; 1.5 and 1.7. The wheat harvest fell in these years from 2.2 million tons to 1.3 millions. Milk production dropped from 12.9

million tons in 1935–38 to 7.4 millions in 1947. Meat and butter supplies were also greatly reduced. Yet in this area there were 4.3 million more people to feed! The situation was worst in the British Zone which was predominantly industrial. Britain was forced to buy wheat in North America and then export it to the British Zone. In his book *In Darkest Germany*, Victor Gollancz, the British Left-wing Jewish publisher, showed great compassion towards the Germans and revealed their plight. He found that in Cologne only 11.7 per cent of children between 6 and 12 years old had completely normal weights, 29.5 per cent were definitely below normal. Gollancz found a similar situation in other towns in the British Zone. Though conditions were bad in Germany it is as well to remember that they were also bad in neighbouring Holland, not very good in the towns of France and Italy, and extremely bad in Poland, the western U S S R, Yugoslavia and other parts of Eastern Europe.

Those German men who had survived the holocaust, and who had either avoided being stuck in P O W camps or who were lucky enough to secure early release, were worried about their jobs. Many factories which had missed being bombed were candidates for demolition or removal as reparations. The reparations hit the Soviet Zone hardest. There, everything from complete factories, sometimes with their key managers, workers and technicians as well, to (some) railway lines were removed to the U S S R. The French Zone was also heavily burdened by reparations. This zone had little industry but its rich forests were exploited in the French interest and its agricultural produce was required to feed the French Army.

More important for France was control over the industries of the Saar, an important centre of the German iron and steel and coal industries. By unilateral actions the French started to reorientate the economy of the Saar towards that of France. Under pressure, the U S A and Britain, but not the Soviet Union, accepted this process. By the end of 1947 a pro-French government was installed in the Saar and the Landtag ratified a constitution proclaiming the Saar's independence of Germany and making it economically part of the French Union. At the time this solution brought the people of the Saar many material advantages. Had the original reparations plans been carried through they would have hit the British Zone very heavily. As it was, as the Cold War got under way, and partly due to it, a more friendly attitude towards the Germans developed, and as a result of the pleas from German businessmen and trade unionists to their renewed contacts in Britain and the U S, these plans were whittled down. American policymakers had also to consider the effect of reparations on demands for U S aid and, in turn, on the American taxpayer. Some firms were put out of business as rivals, others escaped because some Allied firm had an interest in them. The removal of machinery and installations ended completely in April 1951 in the Anglo-American Zones.

The preservation of family units was not easy in the immediate postwar years. First of all there was the obvious difficulty of maintaining contact with one's relatives in the armed forces. As Germany lost the war this became more and more difficult. After the capitulation one could not know what would happen to those taken prisoner. Millions were retained to work in various European countries, some were in the United States and Canada. It took time for contact to be re-established. The large-scale evacuations were another factor causing family members to lose touch with each other. The breakdown of the railway system and the restrictions placed on Germans moving from one zone to another, contributed to the same result.

## The Nuremberg Trials and Denazification

The trials and punishment of war criminals was not a new thing. After the 1914–18 war a few trials were carried through by the victors and there had been demands to 'hang the Kaiser', though these had come to nothing.

This time the Allies were determined to punish the leaders of an evil regime whose innumerable crimes were official policy rather than isolated cases resulting from the over-enthusiasm of a few junior officers. It was hoped the trials of the surviving leaders of the Third Reich would make clear to the Germans, in the words of Potsdam, 'the terrible crimes committed under the leadership of those whom in the hour of their success, they openly approved and blindly obeyed'. Further, they would serve as a warning to future generations. The trials would also demonstrate the determination of the new United Nations' Organisation to act as an effective guardian of international peace and morality, for the Tribunal, which was to conduct the trials, was originated in a U N commission, set up early in 1943. The Tribunal sat at Nuremberg from 20 November 1945 to 1 October of the following year. It dealt with three classes of crimes: crimes against peace, war crimes and crimes against humanity. Accused were the surviving Nazi leaders. Göring, as mentioned above, was sentenced to death but managed to commit suicide. Hanged were: Joachim von Ribbentrop, Hitler's Foreign Minister; Field Marshal Wilhelm Keitel, Chief of High Command; Ernst Kaltenbrunner, Chief of the Gestapo; Alfred Rosenberg, Nazi ideologist and Commissioner for Eastern Europe; Hans Frank, Governor of Poland; Wilhelm Frick, Minister of Interior; Julius Streicher, the most prominent Nazi anti-semite; Fritz Sauckel, head of the slave labour programme; Artur Seyss-Inquart, Governor of Holland; General Alfred Jodl, Chief of Operations of the High Command. Luckier were: Walter Funk, Head of the Reichsbank; Rudolf Hess, Deputy Führer of the N S D A P, who, following his abortive attempt to negotiate with the British in 1941, had spent the rest of the war in British captivity; Admiral Erich Raeder, Commander of the German Navy. They received life imprisonment. Baldur von Schirach, Hitler Youth Leader, and Albert Speer, head of the armaments' programme, only received 20 years each. Baron Konstantin von Neurath, first Nazi Foreign Minister and later Protector of Bohemia and Moravia, was awarded 15 years' imprisonment and Admiral Karl Dönitz, Hitler's successor as Head of State, 10 years. Martin Bormann, Hitler's deputy, was sentenced *in absentia* to death and, as mentioned in the last chapter, is still being sought. Franz von Papen, deputy Chancellor in 1933 and later Ambassador to Turkey, Hjalmar Schacht, one-time President of the Reich Bank, and Hans Fritzsche, an official in the Propaganda Ministry, were found not guilty. These three were later sentenced by German courts but served little time in jail.

Other trials were held at Nuremberg by the Americans alone. The most notable of these were against 'cannon king' Alfred Krupp, prominent lawyers, and the chemical concern of IG Farben. The defendants were found guilty and sentenced to long terms of imprisonment but they were released quite soon in an American attempt to win over West German opinion.

In 1950 General Lucius D. Clay reported, in his capacity of U S High Commissioner for Germany, on the progress made in punishing leading Nazis. Of the 24 most important, he reported, six were executed, six were still serving sentences up to life, and eight had died or committed suicide. The fate of one was obscure and three were still at liberty. Of the 42 persons who held the rank of Gauleiter or regional party and administrative chief, eight were executed, ten had committed suicide or had died; one was shot by the Nazis themselves; 11 were still jailed or interned; while the fate of four was unknown; eight were known to be at liberty, some of these had already served their sentences.

Apart from trials for crimes Germans were liable to denazification procedures. The occupying powers were officially concerned to remove all former Nazis from positions of power or influence. The difficulty was to define the term 'Nazi'. There had been eight million members of the Nazi party and many others who had been members of its affiliates. On the other hand, there were those who had not been members of the Party but who had played a more active role in its crimes than most members. Millions of Germans, particularly in the U S Zone, were required to fill in long questionnaires (*Fragebogen*) about their activities between 1933 and 1945. This could be followed up by a trial before a denazification court. The courts, run by the Germans themselves, placed defendants in one of several categories from 'free of Nazi connections' to 'bearing major responsibility'. They could deprive defendants of their civic rights, fine them or send them to a labour camp.

These courts or tribunals came in for a good deal of criticism. There were great variations in their activities, not only between zones of occupation but even within each zone. Connections helped. Those incriminated Germans who had something to offer the occupying power could often work their passage. Soon all the Allies were prepared to intervene on behalf of experts of various kinds. Little Nazis who had no such expertise to offer often got worse treatment than more prominent Nazis who had. One of the most notorious examples of this is that of Heinz Felfe. He was an officer of the S D, the S S Security Service, as such he was arrested by the Allies. By 1946 he was working for the British intelligence services. They helped to get him denazified and recommended for the German police. To their credit the West Germans, including Dr Gustav Heinemann, later West German President, then Minister of Interior, would have nothing to do with him. The Gehlen organisation, then an intelligence agency run by former Wehrmacht General Reinhard Gehlen for the Americans, recruited him. He became prominent in that organisation and remained so after it became the official West German intelligence agency, B N D. For ten years, however, he was working as a Soviet agent in Gehlen's organisation.

It was not only the occupying powers who intervened on behalf of incriminated persons. The Catholic Church was an influential friend to many of them. In ministries and government agencies they later repaid the Church in kind.

## The return of political life

It is perhaps remarkable that Germans, despite the many mundane yet essential jobs they had to do to ensure their own personal survival, should have any energy left for anything else. Yet thousands of Germans found the energy to take part in political activities once again when the occupation authorities licensed political parties. The

Soviets were the first to allow political activity in their zone. In June and July 1945 they licensed four parties in their zone: C D U, L D P D, S P D and K P D.

On 17 June, 35 persons signed a manifesto of the Christian Democratic Union in Berlin. Among the more significant signatories were: Andreas Hermes, former Centre Party politician and former Reich Finance Minister; Jakob Kaiser, a Christian trade unionist connected with the anti-Nazi opposition; Heinrich Krone, a former Centre Party Reichstag member, and Ernst Lemmer, another Christian trade unionist and former member of the Reichstag. Other important personalities at the meeting were: Dr Hans Lukaschek, former Mayor of Breslau; Otto Nuschke, former Reichstag member; Dr Walther Schreiber, one time Prussian Minister of Trade. Like Lemmer, Nuschke and Schreiber were members of the small, middle-class, middle-of-the-road Democratic Party in the Weimar Republic. Protestant Bishop D. Otto Dibelius also took part in the deliberations. Of the 50 or so leading members, 21 were former Centre Party members, about the same number were former Protestant Conservatives, and 8 or 9 were former members of the Democratic Party. They were united in their view that the old Conservative and old denominational parties should not be re-established. They retained their earlier anti-Marxist and pro-Christian ideas. They wanted to break down denominational barriers and were even prepared to accept members not tied to a particular church provided they recognised 'the Law of natural ethics'. On economic policy they proposed state ownership of mineral wealth and state control of 'monopolistic key undertakings'. Further, they recognised the place, indeed importance, of the worker in the community, and advocated a united trade-union movement.

Partly unknown, because of communications' difficulties, to the Berlin founders of the C D U, other Christian groups were setting up similar groups in other parts of Germany. In Cologne a meeting took place on 17 June attended by 18 former leading officials of the Centre Party. They decided not to reform their old party but to work for unity with local Protestants. Dr Leo Schwering, a librarian and for many years member of the Prussian Landtag, was asked to draft a programme. What emerged was a vaguely Christian Socialist draft. More strongly Christian Socialist were the Hesse C D U based on Frankfurt and greatly influenced in those early days by Dr Walter Dirks. In northern Germany, Schleswig, Hamburg and Bremen the C D U won over a greater number of Protestants and took up a more clearly Conservative position than in the Rhineland, Hesse or Berlin. In Bavaria where they called themselves the Christian Social Union, they were more traditional right-wing clerical in their orientation. There they were also predominantly Catholic.

Who were the mass of members of the new Christian party? In Hamburg, in June 1946, 12 per cent of them were workers, 32 per cent white-collar employees, 10 per cent civil servants, 8 per cent professional people, 14 per cent housewives and 2 per cent unknown. Politically, they were a varied lot. Of the first thousand Hamburg members one was a former Communist, 20 were former Social Democrats, 171 were former Centre Party members and another 5 had belonged to small Christian groups. On the right, 41 had belonged to the moderate Conservative, German People's Party, 36 were from Hugenberg's Nationalists and 254 were former Nazi party members. Of the former Nazis, 36 had held some position in the party. It is difficult to say to what extent the political composition was similar to that of other areas. It is probable that it was similar to other C D U organisations in North Germany, less so to those in other parts. The social composition of the Hamburg party was similar to those of Christian Democratic groups in other urban areas except that, in North Rhine Westphalia, the working class was more strongly in evidence. In South Germany and in Schleswig Holstein the farming community was strongly represented.

Gradually, in the British Zone the local groups of Christian Democrats came together and formed, in February 1946, a party on a zonal basis. Dr Konrad Adenauer, Centre Party politician for many years before 1933 Mayor of Cologne, who had not taken part in the founding of the party, was elected chairman. In the American and French Zones it was not yet possible to set up zonal organisations.

One memorable event in the early history of the C D U was the adoption of the so-called Ahlen Economic Programme by the British Zone Christian Democrats in February 1947. This programme showed the relative strength of the Christian trade unionists in the party at the time. It contained the words, 'The capitalist economic system has not proved suitable to the political and social life interests of the German people ... The content and goal of the social and economic reorganisation can no longer be capitalistic power and profit-seeking, but only the welfare of our people'. The programme was to have little practical significance for the C D U.

Throughout Germany the remnants of the old Liberal parties found the courage to start up their groups again. In Berlin they founded the Liberal Democratic Party of Germany. In Würtemberg they called themselves the Democratic People's Party (D V P). In Hesse they were the Liberal Democrats and in Bavaria the Free Democrats. The term Free Democratic Party was the one which gradually gained complete acceptance in the Western Zones. Led by such former Reichstag members as Theodor Heuss and Reinhold Maier they had more pronounced Liberal, *laissez-faire* views on economic matters than the C D U, and feared the harmful influence of the Church in politics. They were very largely a middle-class party and much more Protestant than Catholic.

The Social Democrats were the oldest German party, a party which had survived persecution before 1900, a party with a large number of trained cadres. The Nazis had done their best to stamp it out and a considerable number of Social Democrats had been murdered, but it was only to be expected that when the Third Reich collapsed the S P D would raise its head again.

In May 1945 Social Democrats in Berlin started to discuss the re-establishment of their party. By 15 June they were ready to issue their programmatic appeal to their countrymen. In their appeal they called for 'Democracy in the state and in the (local) community, Socialism in the economy and in society'. They wanted an 'antifascist, democratic regime and a parliamentary democratic republic'. They advocated the nationalisation of the banks and insurance under-takings, mineral resources and the fuel economy, and the breaking up of the great estates. Significantly, they called for the unity of the working class and warmly welcomed an appeal of the newly refounded Communist Party. Among the Berlin group were the two survivors from a committee of 12, which had been given the task by the last Executive Committee of the old S P D, to carry on the fight in Germany. (The Executive Committee itself had fled abroad.) These survivors were Max Fechner and Richard Weimann. With them were former Reichstag's members Otto Grotewohl and Gustav Dahrendorf, Annedore Leber, wife of July resister Julius Leber, and a number of functionaries of the old S P D. They established a *Zentralausschuss* (Central Committee) with Fechner and Grotewohl as chairmen, and sought contact with their comrades in other zones.

As it turned out, the key figure in the other zones was another former member of the Reichstag, Dr Kurt Schumacher. Schumacher, whom the Nazis had released from concentration camp in 1943 as a very sick man, lived with his sister in Hanover. A man of magnetic personality and great will power, he set about refounding an S P D organisation in Hanover a few days before the American arrival in April 1945. Convinced of his own mission, Schumacher was not prepared to accept the leadership of the Berlin Social Democrats. At the time this was academic, for the occupying powers would not allow organisations embracing all four zones.

A third group of Social Democrats could claim, legally if not morally, that they and they alone, were the true surviving leaders of the Weimar S P D. These were the remnants of the old Executive or Vorstand who had maintained a Social Democratic organisation in London. This group included Hans Vogel, an S P D Chairman, who died in 1945; Executive member Erich Ollenhauer, Fritz Heine and Erwin Schoettle. By the time they were allowed to return to Germany Schumacher had established himself in the Western Zones and the Berlin group were about to unite with the Communists. The Londoners therefore joined Schumacher.

As already mentioned, the Grotewohl-Fechner group had called for working-class unity, this could only mean unity with the Communists. This was bitterly opposed by Schumacher. Why did the Berlin group want unity with the Communists? Firstly, because they believed that the division of the working class in 1933 had assisted the rise of Nazism. Secondly, shared experiences of persecution under Hitler had brought some of them closer together. Thirdly, the Communists seemed to have learned from past mistakes: they no longer called for a Soviet Germany but for a democratic republic; the Communist International had been disbanded during the war which was taken to mean Communist parties would now operate independently of Moscow; the first appeal of the re-established German C P, of 11 June, was politically moderate. Finally, Social Democrats and Communists had common origins as Marxists.

The K P D had been preparing for its re-establishment in Germany longer than any of the three other parties. Of course, officially, it had never ceased to exist. Communist emigrants had carried on its activities from Moscow between 1933 and 1945. Some of these returned on the heels of the Red Army and immediately set about their allotted political tasks. They quickly established their authority over the survivors of those who had remained in the Reich. Ernst Thälmann, party leader until Hitler gained power, had been murdered in a concentration camp. His place was taken by veteran Communist and former Reichstag member, Wilhelm Pieck. Thirteen of 16 signatories of the 11 June appeal had spent the Hitler years in Moscow. They included, apart from Pieck, former Reichstag members Walter Ulbricht, Bernard Koenen and Edwin Hoernle, the writer Johannes R. Becher, Spanish Civil War veteran Anton Ackermann, his wife Elli Schmidt, two Landtag members, Hermann Matern and Gustav Sobottka, and Michael Niederkirchner, Martha Arendsee, Otto Winzer and Hans Mahle. All the other three had been in concentration camps, one, Ottomar Keschke, a former Reichstag member, for 12 years. Franz Dahlem had an impressive record: member of the Reichstag, member of the Central Committee of the K P D, had served in the International Brigade and then in concentration camps. Hans Jendretzky, the third man, had been a member of the Prussian Landtag.

## The *S E D*

The line of the new K P D was to avoid immediate fusion with the Social Democrats. The Communists wanted to build up their own position first and hoped that, even under their own steam, they would be stronger than the socialists. They over-estimated their own strength. The ranks of the Communist cadres had been decimated by Hitler's, and to a lesser extent Stalin's, murder squads. Rank-and-filers, in Germany as elsewhere, had been disillusioned by the sudden switches in Stalin's policies. Many ordinary Germans had been influenced by Goebbel's anti-Soviet hate propaganda and horrified by the behaviour of Soviet troops. And the expulsion of millions of Germans from their homes east of the Oder-Neisse Line did not seem to have anything to do with Socialism or 'Leninist norms'. Still, the Communists had been right when they had warned, 'Hitler means war', and they were obviously the favourite of the Russians. Many of the old supporters re-registered and were joined by some young idealists and, no doubt, by a good many opportunists. But despite help from the Soviets: transport, buildings, printing presses, paper, money, prestige; the K P D found it difficult to match the growth of the Social Democrats. In November 1945 the German Communists received a shock which was to help them to change their minds on the unity issue. The Austrian Communists, who were also being aided by the Soviets in their zone, were severely defeated in the first postwar elections. In addition, they knew that some of the Social Democrats who had originally favoured unity were having second thoughts. So Pieck and Ulbricht decided to act quickly to bring about a Socialist Unity Party which would replace the two existing working-class parties.

In spite of some doubts the leaders of the Berlin-based Social Democrats expressed their approval of such a party and announced their intention to put the matter to a Reich's conference of the party. They were under a good deal of pressure from the Soviet Military Government who made it clear they wanted this party established as quickly as possible. Some of the rank-and-file officials of the S P D, led by Franz Neumann, urged their leaders to put the issue to a vote of the entire party. This Grotewohl and his colleagues refused to do. With the help of the Western Powers, and encouraged by Schumacher,

Neumann succeeded in carrying through the referendum in the Western Sectors of Berlin. There a great majority of members voted, and voted against an immediate fusion of the two parties. They did however vote for fraternal cooperation between the two. Having suffered something of a moral defeat Grotewohl had no difficulty in getting his way at a conference called to decide on unity. The delegates were drawn mainly from the Soviet Zone.

On 21 April 1946 the Socialist Unity Part (S E D) was established. Its joint Chairmen were Pieck and Grotewohl, its joint Secretaries were Ulbricht and Max Fechner. Its writ ran only in the Soviet Zone and East Berlin. In West Germany the S P D and the K P D continued to exist as rivals. In Berlin the S P D was reconstituted and delivered a sharp blow to the S E D in October 1946. In elections for the Berlin city council held in all four sectors the S P D gained 48.7 per cent of the vote as against the S E D's 19.8 per cent. The Christian Democrats won 22.1 per cent and the Liberals 9.4 per cent.

Meanwhile, in the Western Zones of Germany Kurt Schumacher pushed ahead with the building up of a strong S P D. He had come to terms with the Londoners and in May 1946 the first party conference of the West German Social Democrats was held. Schumacher was elected Chairman, Ollenhauer his deputy. The party came out strongly in favour of democracy but also for Marxism and Socialism, including extensive socialisation of industry.

By April 1946 the German working class was once again as bitterly divided as it had been in the Weimar Republic. This time though its division was in no small measure a result of the divisions among the major world powers and their differences were to divide Germany.

## Currency reform and the Berlin blockade

As we have seen, Western policy towards Germany was not entirely consistent. During the war the punitive element had been strong. As the anger of war subsided it started to become more compassionate. There were those who recognised that the Germans could not be won for democracy on empty stomachs. Some Allied statesmen – Churchill was one of them – very soon concluded that a policy of generosity ought to be pursued because the West would need the Germans as allies against the Soviet Union.

No one can say with complete confidence what Stalin's policy was in the war and postwar years. He too had favoured a punitive policy. He too wanted the Germans as allies. Most experts agree he wanted to create a defensive line of Soviet-orientated states in Eastern Europe.

Further, that he wanted to extract from Germany the greatest possible amount of reparations. This was understandable in view of the Soviet Union's enormous losses in men and material, the extent of which the West did not fully appreciate in 1945. If Stalin ever planned a Communist Germany he did not adopt policies designed to bring this about. The annexation of German lands, the reparations, the use of German P O Ws and civilians as forced labourers, the behaviour of Soviet troops, were not calculated to win the hearts of the Germans. Stalin possibly soon came to realise that any attempt to communise Germany by generosity was bound to fail as the Americans did not want a Communist Germany and they could outbid the Russians any time in generosity. Force was another possibility but so long as America remained in Germany this too was out of the question. The early setting up of a non-Communist German government could not be attractive to the Soviets especially if the issues of reparations and Germany's frontiers had not been settled. But the four powers failed to agree on these issues. Perhaps Stalin would have acted differently had be received a large reconstruction loan which he had mentioned to the Americans at the end of the war. The loan was not forthcoming. Russia and the West were separated by 30 years or so of mutual suspicion.

The Western Allies, unable to get agreement with the Soviet Union, initiated measures to rehabilitate their zones economically and unite them politically, thus they set in motion the division of Germany.

The first American move was the offer made in July 1946 by the U S Secretary of State, James F. Byrnes, to merge the United States Zone in economic affairs with that of any other Ally willing to join. The British, desperately short of funds, agreed before the end of the month. By so doing they virtually forfeited their right to pursue their own policy in the British Zone. The Soviets rejected the Byrnes' plan and so, for a time, did the French until the U S and Britain agreed to their Saar plans. In March 1947 the 'Truman Doctrine' was enunciated. President Truman guaranteed the active support of the United States to all peoples resisting internal subversion or external aggression. Initially help was to be given to Greece, Iran and Turkey under pressure from the Soviet Union. The Truman Doctrine was followed in June of the same year by the announcement of Marshall Aid which came after a winter of economic, social and political crisis in Western Europe. General George Marshall in a speech at Harvard University, declared that if the nations of Europe would agree on a combined plan for recovery, the United States would finance it. Although Marshall Aid did not explicitly preclude Soviet participation, the terms were such that it was rightly anticipated that the Russians would not accept them. An intrinsic part of the Aid plan was that the economic recovery of Germany was the key to the recovery of Europe.

It was only to be expected that any policy aimed at the economic rehabilitation of Germany should include a reform of the currency. Once again, as in the 1920s, the German currency was rapidly becoming worthless. Some were saying that Germany was under the dictatorship of the cigarette for it had become a universally accepted unit of value. The practice of barter was widespread. Anything could be obtained on the black market at greatly inflated prices, little was obtainable over the counter in the shops. The Western Allies, therefore, carried through a change of currency in June 1948. Ten old Reichmark had to be handed over for one new Deutsche Mark, though each adult German was given first 40 and then two weeks later, another 20 new Marks. The reform hit small savers the hardest. Owners of land and property got away with little damage. Cash suddenly became short and the shop windows, equally suddenly, became full in order to attract it. For some time the Western Powers expressed the hope that the Soviets would allow a single currency for the whole of Germany, a currency issued on a quadripartite basis. Had the Russians agreed they would have been greatly weakening their power over economic, and political, policy in their Zone. Of course they did not oblige and announced that the new currency would not be permitted to circulate even in the Western Sectors of Berlin. Marshal Vassili Sokolovsky, from 1946 to 1949 Commander-in-Chief of Soviet forces in Germany, in making the announcement, rather enigmatically described the Western Sectors as being part of the Soviet Zone.

There is some doubt about the Western Allies' intentions regarding the introduction of the Deutsche Mark to West Berlin. But they did soon introduce it declaring on 25 June that both the Deutsche Mark and any 'East' Mark would be valid in their part of Berlin.

As part of their reaction to the Marshall Plan and to the six-nation (the Benelux countries and the Western Powers) London conference of March 1948, which allowed the West Germans to draft a constitution, the Russians restricted travel between their Zone and West Germany. This policy was introduced from 1 April. In reaction to the currency reform they extended the restrictions to freight movements between Berlin and the West. The prospects for the West Berliners looked bleak. The Western Sectors were largely dependent on West Germany for their food and fuel, some electricity and gas was supplied from the Soviet Sector.

The right of access to Berlin by the Western Allies had not been laid down in any formal treaty. This is not as surprising as it might seem.

The Soviet Union had recognised the right of its Western partners to sectors in Berlin which would automatically seem to imply the right of access. In any case, the Four Allies had not intended that the four zones should be sealed off from each other. Still, as Russian pressure mounted, the lack of any agreement on access proved embarrassing. Luckily, there was a quadripartite document covering Western use of three air corridors to Berlin from Bückeburg, near Hanover, Frankfurt and Hamburg. From June 1948 to May 1949 these were the only lines of communication between West Berlin and West Germany. If the Russians aimed at driving the Western Powers out of Berlin either to seal off their zone, or give themselves control of the future capital of a united Germany, or merely to demonstrate their capacity to humiliate the West, the blockade of Berlin was a good gamble. Never before had a city been supplied by air, let alone one of 2.4 million people. The Russians had gained experience on the effects of blockades from Leningrad. They had watched the failure of the Luftwaffe to supply the Nazi Sixth Army at Stalingrad, and, in general, Word War II had demonstrated the weaknesses as much as the strengths of air power.

The success of Operation Vittels – as the Americans called the Air Lift – surprised the practitioners as much as it must have surprised Stalin. It was estimated that to keep Berlin alive required a minimum daily transport of 4,000 tons. On the record day, in April 1949, 13,000 tons were lifted into Berlin. The Western Powers had been fortunate when the sectors were originally allocated, in that they got the best airports including Tempelhof. For whatever reasons, the Russians did not withdraw from the Four-Power air control body regulating traffic to and from Berlin. Nor did they interfere with the radio beacon situated in their sector used for guiding Allied aircraft. And, after one of their fighters had caused the crash of a British airliner, they ceased 'buzzing' Allied planes.

The blockade was ended by the Four-Power New York agreement of 4 May 1949 under which the Soviet Union agreed to rescind the restrictions it had imposed, and the Western Powers likewise withdrew restrictions they had placed on communications between their zones and East Germany. This was confirmed at the Four-Power conference in Paris in the following month. The Paris conference achieved little else. Like the earlier Four-Power conferences in 1946 and 1947, it was unable to resolve any of the fundamental differences between the Powers on Germany.

The blockade over, Berlin was to remain divided politically. After being harassed by Communist-organised demonstrators, the non-SED majority of the Berlin city council had decided in September 1948 to transfer their meetings to the West Sectors and to carry through fresh elections in December. They were not permitted to hold the elections in East Berlin where a separate administration was set up. As Berlin's police and university were also Soviet-orientated, a separate police force and the 'Free University' were established in West Berlin in August 1948 and May 1949 respectively. The Western administration was headed by Ernst Reuter, who had been a K P D official briefly in the early 1920s, and then until 1933 and again after 1945 a Social Democratic politician. His opposite number in East Berlin was Friedrich Ebert, son of the first (Social Democratic) President of the Weimar Republic, himself a member of the Reichstag for the S P D. In 1946 Ebert had gone with Grotewohl into the S E D.

## Towards two German Republics

Starting as early as the summer of 1945 the administration of Germany was gradually structured by the Allies into Länder. Some of these, such as Bavaria, Hamburg and Hesse, in the West, and Mecklenburg, Saxony and Thuringia, in the Soviet Zone, were based on traditional German states. Others, such as Bremen, emerged because of Allied needs, in this case the need for a port for the Americans. There was also the need to remove Prussia from the map which was formally done by an Allied decree in February 1947. In all, 11 Länder were established in the West and five in the smaller area of the Soviet Zone. In addition there was Berlin. In the U S Zone a *Länderrat* (Council of States) was established in 1945 to serve the state governments as a coordinating organ for those interstate activities which could not be dealt with properly by individual states. The existence of the Länder later influenced the drafting of the West, and to a lesser extent the East, German constitution. The constitutions of these administrative units tended to reflect the ideas of the occupying power in whose zone they were.

In other respects too the evolution of political and economic structures in the zones resembled the views of the Allies of what was good for the Germans rather than what a majority of Germans would have wanted had they been entirely free to decide for themselves. This was truer of the Soviet Zone than the others, but it happened in the Western Zones to a greater extent than is commonly supposed.

In the Soviet Zone a number of important reforms which probably had the support of the great majority, and the active opposition of very few, were pushed through. On the other hand, Stalinist measures were introduced which made a mockery of the words democracy and

socialism. The first big reform which started in 1945 was the redistri-
bution of the land. The Junkers, the great landowners who had been
such an important pillar of the German Army, and who, although
they were more likely to be Nationalists than Nazis, had played an
important part in undermining the Weimar Republic, had their
estates confiscated. War criminals and Nazi activists suffered the
same fate. Up to 1 January 1949 just over 7,000 properties of over 100
*Hektar* and another 4,200 of less than 100 *Hektar* were taken over.
From these and public land, holdings were found for nearly 120,000
landless peasants and farm workers; nearly 90,000 refugees from the
area east of the Oder-Neisse; 169,000 workers and craftsmen. Additional land was found for 80,000 small farmers, and 45,000 tenant
farmers. Finally, about 40,000 farmers received forest land. This
measure, which amounted to a social revolution in the agricultural
areas, had one serious economic drawback. The smallness of the
holdings, lack of machinery and, in some cases, lack of skill of the new
proprietors, resulted in a fall of productivity on the land. It meant less
food was available for the towns or for export to other parts of
Germany. But in 1945, considering Germany's past, it seemed the
right thing to do. In any case, the Soviets were soon thinking in terms
of collective farms, and Social Democrats, who had long advocated
such a measure, advocated Scandinavian-type cooperatives to counter
the economic drawback. A much less thorough land reform was
carried out in the Western Zones, where the political and social
problems of the large estates were not as great.

Another fundamental reform in the Soviet Zone was the confisca-
tion of all private banks which were then re-organised as Länder and
provincial banks. This measure was introduced in July 1945. More
important still was order No. 124 of the Soviet military authorities
issued on 30 October 1945. It confiscated all German state property;
all property belonging to leading N S D A P officials, leading members
and influential followers; property of the military authorities and
organisations; property of all forbidden societies, clubs and associations; property of other Axis states or their citizens; the property of
individuals on special lists drawn up by the Soviet military authorities. Although some aspects of this reform were later criticised,
especially property on the 'special lists', there is no doubt that the
great majority of Germans in the Soviet Zone agreed with the
measure. Social Democrats, as well as Communists, all over Germany
were calling for similar measures and a great many Christian
Democrats shared their view.

In the Western Zones the Americans saw to it that similar measures
were not implemented there. On 1 December 1946 the people of Hesse

had agreed by 1,081,124 votes to 422,159 to a clause in the Land constitution nationalising the mines, power stations and the iron and steel industry. In August 1948 the parliament of North-Rhine Westphalia nationalised the mines in its Land. In 1947 nationalisation measures had been passed by the parliaments of Bavaria and Schleswig-Holstein. All these measures were set aside by the Anglo-Americans. The U S Military Governor, General Clay, claimed these were matters which could only be dealt with by a German national government but he confided in a colleague: 'If we can thus defer the issue while free enterprise continues to operate and economic improvement results, it may never become an issue before the German people'. The British were pledged to the public ownership of these industries but because of their financial dependence on the U S A deferred to Clay's views. As we shall see in the next chapter, the British did permit the introduction of codetermination which is generally regarded as one of the achievements of West Germany.

In the field of education too reforms were on the agenda. The Russians and their German helpers sacked the great majority of teachers in their zone because of their Nazi pasts. The Russians set up a German Administration for Education in the summer of 1945 to reorganise the education system. All five Länder of the East Zone adopted the Law for the Democratisation of the German School in 1946. It was to rid the schools of the old ideology, break the educational privileges of the old propertied classes, bridge the differences between urban and rural schools, and raise academic standards in the schools. The prewar *Volksschule* was replaced by a *Grundschule*. After eight years in this new basic school pupils went on to a four-year secondary school or received vocational training. Fees for secondary schools were abolished and would-be students from working-class homes were given preference at university. Workers and Peasants' Faculties were also set up to help those who did not have the necessary entry requirements.

In the American Zone the basis for school reforms was the list of recommendations made in September 1946 by a U S Education Mission, headed by George F. Zook, the President of the American Council on Education. The chief proposals were a comprehensive school system, a common six-year elementary school, increased emphasis on social studies and cultural subjects, improved teaching aids and library facilities and educational exchanges. The U S Military Governor followed up Zook's mission, in January 1947, by requiring the Länder in its zone to submit proposals for the reorganisation of education in their areas. Their proposals should be based on 15 principles laid down by the U S Military Governor. These called for equal educational opportunity for all, free tuition, free textbooks and materials, school attendance between 6 and 15 and compulsory part-time education from 15 to 18. As it turned out, most progress towards these goals was made in Bremen, some in Hesse and little in Bavaria. In the British Zone, as in the U S, most progress was made in the Social Democratic-ruled areas, particularly Hamburg. On the whole progress was less dramatic in the West than in the East and many Germans interested in education were depressed by the re-establishment of denominational schools in many areas of West Germany.

In the two halves of Germany organs of two central German governments were gradually evolving. In May 1947 an Economic Council was created for the Anglo-American Zones or Bizonia as they became known. Its job was to formulate and promulgate ordinances on economic matters subject to the approval of an Anglo-American board. Members were to be selected by the regional parliaments or Landtage on the basis of proportional representation. In 1948 a Council of States (*Länderrat*) was added. Its members were mainly the Prime Ministers of the individual Länder together with their chief ministers. The Economic Council became a kind of shadow lower house of parliament with the Council of States becoming a shadow upper house. What about a shadow cabinet? This was known as the Administrative Council and was also created in May 1947. A German High Court was established in February 1948. Although the Western Allies set up these institutions with the help and advice of German politicians and experts, they themselves played an important part in shaping these bodies which, in turn, influenced the form the new West German state was later to take.

In Soviet Germany the occupying power had, by 1946, established 15 central administrative bodies which dealt with matters usually handled by the ministries of a modern state. At first they were merely advisory but by 1947 they had been invested with considerable authority. After the establishment of Bizonia the Russians launched a Permanent Economic Commission in their zone. Two-thirds of its 25 members were appointed by the military administration and the rest by the trade unions and farmers' organisations. The new body took over economic affairs from those of the fifteen central administrative bodies which had been concerned with them. By building up strong administrative organisations packed with reliable people the Soviets were reducing the importance of parliaments and elections in their zone. And, as Austrian experience was to show, even had it come to a non-Communist all-German government, the Russians could have gone on for some time exercising influence in certain spheres, because of the way they had built up the administrative machine in their zone.

It has already been mentioned that the London six-nation conference in February 1948 agreed that the West Germans should start drafting a constitution. At a meeting on 1 July at Frankfurt the Western Military Governors presented the German Minister Presidents (or Prime Ministers) of the Länder with three documents. The first empowered them to convene a constituent assembly by 1 September to draft a democratic, federal constitution. The second document authorised the Germans to investigate the possibility of boundary changes among the Länder. In the third document the Allies set out the powers to be reserved by them in order to further carry out the purposes of the occupation. The Minister-Presidents – five S P D, five C D U, one F D P – not wishing to prejudice the chances of re-establishing German unity, wanted to emphasise the temporary nature of the new part-state. So it was agreed that the constitution-drafting body should be called a Parliamentary Council rather than a Constituent Assembly. It was further agreed that the Council would not draw up a Constitution (*Verfassung*) but a Basic Law (*Grundgesetz*).

The Parliamentary Council met at Bonn on 1 September 1948 and comprised 27 members of the C D U/C S U, an equal number of S P D members, five from the F D P and two each from the Centre Party, the Communists and the German Party. The delegates were elected by the Landtage roughly proportionate to population. As the two major parties were equal, the C D U favouring, the S P D opposing federalism, and the three mini-parties had no united approach, the F D P was able to exercise a disproportionate amount of influence. This party tended towards centralism rather than federalism. But the Americans, and their influence was strong, argued for a decentralised, federal system. General Clay feared the S P D was inclined towards a strong central government because it wanted to be able to raise enough revenue to pay compensation for its nationalisation programme – which he opposed! After a good deal of argument, some of it bitter, the Basic Law was approved by the Council on 8 May 1949 and by the Military Governors four days later. In the same month it was ratified by all the Länder except Bavaria. However, as two-thirds of the Länder had ratified it, Bavaria accepted the verdict of the others and joined the federation. Again after a good deal of argument, the Council decided on Bonn as temporary capital. This did not please the S P D for Bonn was (and is) a stronghold of the C D U and did not have the space or style of a capital. It was, though, convenient for Dr Adenauer who had lived all of his life just outside the sleepy, Beethoven town.

The constitution made provision for a bicameral system with a popularly elected lower house, the Bundestag, and an upper house, Bundesrat, to represent the Länder interests. The upper house is one of the most powerful in the world and is in effect a continuous meeting of Land ministers who vote in accordance with instructions of their governments. The federal government is required to submit all its legislative drafts to the upper house before they go to the lower one, and most bills passed by the latter need the approval of the former. The Chairmanship of the Bundesrat devolves in turn on a representative from each of the Länder. The Länder send delegates roughly in accordance with the size of the population of their Land. Each has a minimum of three, those with populations between two and six millions send four, those with populations of over six millions nominate five delegates. The Federation was given exclusive authority over such things as currency and coinage, weights and measures, posts and telecommunications, and later, after West Germany had regained its sovereignty, foreign affairs and defence, etc. The Länder were granted exclusive legislative authority over a fairly limited range of subjects: education, culture, religious affairs, police, local government, internal administration.

The fathers of the constitution tried to learn from the mistakes of Weimar especially in respect of the Presidency. They got away from the directly-elected, strong President. Under the Basic Law the President is elected for five years by the Federal Meeting (*Bundesversammlung*). This consists of the members of the lower house and an equal number of delegates elected by the state legislatures on the basis of proportional representation. The Bonn President has less power than the Weimar President had. He cannot on his own authority appoint or dismiss a Chancellor, select Cabinet Ministers, dissolve the Bundestag, or declare a state of emergency. The Chancellor, on the other hand, was strengthened as compared with his predecessors under Weimar. According to the Basic Law the Bundestag may express its lack of confidence in the Chancellor only by simultaneously electing a successor and submitting to the President a request for the dismissal of the former Chancellor. After the bad experience of Weimar the framers of the Bonn Constitution decided to throw out the referendum as a legitimate part of democracy. Finally, as a result of the Weimar experience, the Basic Law makes provision for banning parties considered to be operating against the democratic order. Article 21 (paragraph 2) states: 'Parties which, by reason of their aims or the behaviour of their adherents, seek to impair or destroy the free democratic order or to endanger the existence of the Federal Republic of Germany are unconstitutional.' The basic Law did not regulate the details of elections to the Bundestag but, here too, as we shall see, Bonn tried to learn from Weimar. The Basic Law claimed that its framers had acted for all those Germans who were prevented from taking part. According to Article 146 the Basic Law would lose its validity on the day a constitution, freely arrived at by the German people as a whole, came into force.

In the Soviet Zone the military authorities and the German pro-Soviet leaders attempted to match the efforts in the West at constitution-making. There the constitution of 1949 resulted mainly from discussions in three German People's Congresses (*Deutsche Volkskongresse*) between 1947 and 1949. The People's Congress movement had been called into life by the S E D in an attempt to lead the discussions on a future German Constitution. Apart from Communists, and a few pacifists and neutralists, the movement attracted little support in the West. Even in the Soviet Zone the C D U was not at first prepared to cooperate. But its two Chairmen, Ernst Lemmer and Jakob Kaiser were forced to resign, after which the party became more cooperative. The Liberal Democrats sent delegates. In March 1948 the second People's Congress met and elected a People's Council, a kind of shadow parliament. The Communists gradually gained complete control of this body both by purges of the C D U and the L D P D, and by the setting up of two pseudo-bourgeois parties in 1948, the National Democratic Party (N D P D) and the Democratic Farmers' Party (D B D). Both were under the control of Communist cadres from the start. The practice of allowing 'mass organisations' – trade unions, the Free German Youth, Democratic Women's League, League of Culture, Farmers' Mutual Assistance – to send delegates to the People's Congress further increased Communist influence as all these bodies were under Communist control.

In May 1949 the people of East Germany were asked to elect delegates to a third People's Congress. The electorate were presented with a single list of candidates which they could either accept or reject. The S E D had vetted all the candidates through the Anti-Fascist Democratic Bloc to which all parties had to belong. All the mass media campaigned for the official list and no open opposition was possible. It is therefore not surprising that 95.2 per cent of the electorate voted and of these 66 per cent approved the official list. The Congress then approved the Constitution and elected a new People's Council. On 7 October the Council formally constituted itself as the provisional People's Chamber (*Volkskammer*). Meeting as the People's Chamber it unanimously approved a Law on the Constitution of the German Democratic Republic.

The Constitution approved by the People's Chamber need not detain us long for it was not carefully observed in the years which followed. Its preamble asserted that it was 'the German People' who 'have given themselves this constitution'. Article 1 proclaimed:

'Germany is an indivisible democratic Republic; its constituent parts are the German states. The Republic decides on all matters essential for the continued existence and development of the German People as a whole.' The text did not indicate the area in which the constitution was valid. The People's Chamber was the highest organ of the republic, its deputies, subordinated only to their consciences, were elected at universal, equal, and secret elections every four years. Provision was also made for a second chamber to represent the interests of the Länder. This was the *Länderkammer*. The Prime Minister was to be chosen from the largest party represented in the *Volkskammer*. He could not be dismissed until a successor had been found for him. The President's functions were largely ceremonial. He was elected by joint-session of the two parliamentary chambers. Berlin was proclaimed capital of the German Democratic Republic (D D R) but due to the Four-Power status of the city, the Berlin representatives in the People's Chamber had only non-voting status.

Those who had opposed this sham democratic development and those who later actively sought by word or deed to make the German Democratic Republic both German and democratic in reality, were eliminated by Stalinist methods as in the other states under Soviet control. Thousands of Social Democrats, Christian Democrats, Liberals and even some Communists were arrested and interned in former Nazi concentration camps such as Buchenwald and Sachsenhausen. The prison at Bautzen was to become notorious as a place of incarceration for political prisoners. Some died in these prisons or camps, some were sentenced to forced labour in the Soviet Union. Others were later released or were 'bought free' (from 1964 onwards) by West Germany.

# — 8 —

# Adenauer's Germany

## Chancellor by one vote

The election of 14 August 1949 to the first Bundestag did not yield a decisive result. The Christian Democrats pulled slightly ahead with 7.3 million votes (31 per cent). Schumacher's Social Democrats gained 6.9 million votes (29.2 per cent) and the F D P 2.7 millions (11.9). The Communits must have been disappointed with their 1.3 million votes (5.7 per cent) thinking back to their millions in the Weimar Republic. Another 21.1 per cent of the votes were given to seven or so other parties and independents such as the remnants of the old Centre Party, the Bavarian Party, the Right-wing groups like the German Party (D P) and the German Rights Party (D R P).

The result was not too bad for the S P D considering the difficulties it was up against. It was cut off from many traditional centres of Social Democracy—Berlin, Erfurt, Halle, Leipzig, Magdeburg, Dresden—now in the Soviet Zone. The Christian Democrats benefited from the greater proportion of Catholics in the Federal Republic as compared with the Weimar Republic. This ensured them a mass basis for their party. They also got help from the Catholic Church. The American and French military authorities favoured the Christian Democrats and gave them discreet support. Moreover, the Christian Democrats could claim they, together with the F D P and the D P, by holding office, were partly responsible for the Western Zones, improving economic and political situation. Since June 1947 these parties had headed the Economic Council of the Western Zones.

The indecisive result of the election left some room for manoeuvre. But Dr Adenauer was a better negotiator (or intriguer) than Dr Schumacher and had already worked with the F D P and the D P. He managed to prevail over the Left-wing members of his party in this matter. The result was that Adenauer mobilised mass Christian Democratic support for Prof. Theodor Heuss, who was elected Federal President. In return he proposed Adenauer for Chancellor. Remarkably, the proposal was carried by one vote—Adenauer's own! Few would have predicted in 1949 that the 73-year-old Adenauer, presiding over a precarious coalition, would rule for 14 years and become one of the most influential world statesmen. It looked very much as though Bonn would follow Weimar with frequent changes of government.

Dr Adenauer's government faced problems which seemed at least as great, if not greater, than those which faced, and defeated, the governments of the Weimar regime.

There was the problem of unemployment. This was actually getting worse. By the end of 1948 it reached 760,000. During the whole of 1949 it mounted month by month increasing to 1.56 millions by the end of the year.

This problem was complicated by the refugees from the lost territories and from the D D R. In 1950 16.4 per cent of the population of West Germany were from the lost territories, while another 3.3 per cent came from the D D R. On past experience unemployed and refugees added up to political extremism. German industry also faced great problems. It had been disrupted by demolitions, reparations and the division of Germany. Certain branches of industry in which Germany had been leading—aviation for instance—were forbidden. In any case, the interruption of production meant that markets were no longer assured. As well as the unemployed and the refugees, the war victims had to be cared for. In 1952 there were over 1.5 million war disabled in West Germany.

## Economic recovery

Anyone acquainted with the term 'economic miracle' automatically associates it with West Germany, even though, since the Federal Republic's remarkable economic development there have been others—Italy, Japan, Spain and South Korea among them. Certain figures make clear the extent of Federal Germany's 'miracle'. The gross national product of the Republic rose by 61 per cent between 1953 and 1960, compared with 37 per cent on average in the O E E C countries (roughly the Western European states), and 21 per cent in the United Kingdom. In terms of living standards, as measured by the volume of private consumption, West Germany had a 58 per cent rise, in the same period, as against 34 per cent in all O E E C countries and only 25 per cent in the U K. To the extent that non-military government expenditure helped to raise living standards, this aspect of living standards rose more rapidly in West Germany than in Britain. Such expenditure per head increased in the Federal Republic by 71 per cent, but by only 39 per cent in Britain.

How was all this possible? Dr Erhard, Minister of Economic Affairs between 1949 and 1966, and as Director of the Economic Administrative Office of the Anglo-U S zones, the man responsible for carrying through the currency reform, denied there was any miracle. He claims the upsurge was due to the 'honest efforts' of the West German people who had been given, by him, the opportunity of using 'personal initiative and human energy'. Undoubtedly the 'honest efforts' of the West Germans meaning hard work and long hours, was an important factor in getting that part of Germany on its feet again. No doubt too, Dr Erhard's policy of freeing the economy from many inherited controls helped. But there were other, even more decisive factors. Marshall Aid was one of these. West Germany was the fourth largest recipient of such aid which was particularly useful for buying new machinery and raw materials from the U S A. Secondly, Germany had reached a low ebb economically with a great deal of pent-up demand which helped to get the economic resurgence under way. Thirdly, although West Germany had occupation costs to pay, it did not have the heavy burden of armaments in the early years. Later on fairly large sums were put aside for defence but the productive capacity of the nation was not involved and could go on producing goods for export. Because of world-wide rearmament following the outbreak of the Korean war West German goods were in even greater demand. Nor was West Germany burdened with military expenditure abroad, except to a very minor extent, with its devastating effect on the balance of payments. On the contrary, Allied troops in the Federal Republic have helped to swell its 'invisible exports'. West German taxation policies have also been designed to encourage high investment. Taxes on the higher income brackets were relatively unprogressive. There were premiums for savers, subsidies for industry and exemption of overtime from tax which encouraged the practice but aided employers in keeping down the cost. Another very important fact was the situation on the labour market. West Germany had more than one million unemployed until 1955, and more than half a million until 1959. The Republic's rate of unemployment was higher than that of the U K until 1960. This obviously reduced the power of the trade unions to press wage demands. The unions had been hit initially by the currency reform which destroyed their cash reserves needed to finance industrial disputes. In addition, the union leaders were responsible men who were prepared to moderate their policies in the general interest. Codetermination in industry made it easier for them to sell a policy of moderation to their members. Reformed trade union structure made it easier to avoid interunion friction and unofficial strikes. Finally, though the Federal Republic had to contend with a flood of refugees from the East, these refugees represented an educated labour force. Many of them, especially those from the D D R, were highly skilled workers, technicians and managers.

## Codetermination

Demands for some form of codetermination, workers participation in management, as well as public ownership were first heard in Germany in the nineteenth century. With the advent of the Weimar Republic they achieved some, very limited, recognition. These gains were destroyed by the Nazis but stronger demands were made by socialists, Social Democrats, Communists and trade unionists after 1945. As we have seen, these demands were in keeping with the views of the British Labour Government, which was responsible for the main industrial region of West Germany, but it had to defer to American pro-private enterprise policies because of financial dependence on the United States. The British had, however, pushed through certain reforms in 1946 and 1947 which were to be the basis for future German legislation. The Americans were more concerned with decentralisation of German heavy industry and under their influence measures were passed in the Anglo-American zones—Law No 56 in the United States Zone and Decree No 78 in the British—in February 1947, aimed at decartelisation. In the years since West Germany regained its independence this has been largely reversed.

In the early days of the Occupation, German industrialists fell over themselves to get agreement with the trade unions to try and avert complete nationalisation or worse. By the time the Federal Republic had been established the workers in the iron and steel industries had experienced codetermination and were determined to keep the gains they had made and, if possible, extend them. But the employers had regained their confidence and were hoping their friends in parliament would help them to rescind the Allied measures. They were supported by the F D P, and D P and the right wing of the Christian Democrats. In addition, the syndicate of Benelux investors in Germany made representations in Bonn against codetermination together with the American National Association of Manufacturers and the French High Commissioner. The unions prepared strike action to enforce their demands that the arrangements in the iron and steel industry should be recognised and extended to the coal and chemical industries. Only after hard bargaining was a crisis averted.

The Corporation Law of 30 January 1937 recognised three governing bodies of an industrial corporation: the general stockholders' meeting, the supervisory board of directors (*Aufsichtsrat*) and the managing board of directors (*Vorstand*). The *Vorstand* is elected by the *Aufsichtsrat* and carries on the day-to-day business of the enterprise. The Co-Determination (*Mitbestimmung*) Law of 10 April 1951, laid down that the *Aufsichtsrat* of every public company in the iron, steel and coal industries should consist of 11 members, of whom five were to be representative of the shareholders and the other five nominated by the employees. One of the shareholders' nominees must not be a shareholder or official of an employers' association. The five employees' representatives must include one manual and one salaried employee of the enterprise nominated by the Works' Counnil (*Betriebsrat*) after consultation with the trade unions, two nominated by the appropriate trade unions after consultation with the Works' Council, and one other who must not be a trade union official or an employee of the enterprise. The eleventh is elected by the other ten. Under the same law one member of the *Vorstand*, in all there are three members, who is the Personnel Director (*Arbeitsdirektor*), is nominated by the appropriate trade union. His appointment must be confirmed by the Works' Council.

A second law of July 1952 decreed that at least one-third of the members of the *Aufsichtsräte* of all joint stock companies, other than those covered by the earlier law, must be nominees of the employees. Against union wishes the law does not provide for trade-union representation from outside the enterprise on the *Aufsichtsrat*. The same law established works' councils in all enterprises employing at least five people who are 18 or over and having at least three employees over 21. The councils, elected by secret ballot for two years, must be representative of the various trades of wage-earning and salaried staff. The councils discuss everything from complaints from individual employees to holiday arrangements, technical training, proposed mergers and changes in the nature of the enterprise.

There are many problems for the unions connected with codetermination: divided loyalty is just one of them. More important, as new concentration has developed in the economy in the 1950s and 1960s, the unions have found themselves without representation on the new boards running the holding companies.

## Recognition and rearmament

The government which took office in October 1949 was not master in its own house. Some relief was given under the Petersberg Agreement of 22 November 1949 between Dr Adenauer and the Western High

Commissioners (as the former Military Governors were now called). Bonn was permitted to carry on consular relations with foreign countries and participate in international organisations, and was given concessions in the question of demolitions. In return the Chancellor agreed to West Germany joining the Ruhr Authority, set up to control the industries of the Ruhr and dominated by the Western Powers. The New York conference of September 1950 brought new progress for Bonn. West Germany could take up diplomatic relations and its right to speak for the whole of Germany was recognised. West Germany and West Berlin were given a security guarantee by the Western Powers and the Länder were allowed to set up paramilitary security police. The Federal Republic was granted important concessions regarding its industries. Restrictions on shipping and shipbuilding were lifted, it was permitted to produce artificial rubber and synthetic petrol and the situation of the chemical industry was relieved. In 1951 the Republic was recognised as a full member of the Council of Europe and in the same year joined France, Italy, Belgium, Holland and Luxemburg in establishing the European Coal and Steel Community. The Community sought to create a common market for coal and steel by the elimination of restrictions in the trade in these products between the six countries. The treaty setting up the community meant the end of the Ruhr Authority, nullified the main advantages to France of the customs union between France and the Saar, and led to the lifting of the ceiling on German steel production. In July of the same year Britain and the Commonwealth, France and the U S A ended the state of war with West Germany. In September the Foreign Ministers of these three countries declared in favour of the integration of a democratic Germany into a European Community on the basis of equality, the abolition of the Occupation Regime and the cooperation of West Germany in the defence of the West.

These aims were to be realised in May 1952 with the *Deutschlandvertrag*, which ended the Occupation Regime, and the signing of the European Defence Community (E D C) agreement in Paris. At its most basic the E D C was designed to overcome the dangers of a rearmed, nationalist Germany, by creating a European Army, with a West German contingent, attached to the political institutions of a united Europe, with a European Minister of Defence. The E D C never became a reality because the French parliament failed to ratify it. West German rearmament was, however, achieved through the deliberations of conferences in London and Paris in September–October 1954. It was agreed to set up the West European Union which meant extending the Brussels (Defence) Treaty of 1948, signed by Belgium, France, Luxemburg, Holland and Britain and later joined by Italy, to include the Federal Republic. It was recommended that West Germany be admitted to N A T O. There were no hitches with the new plan and the Federal Republic regained its sovereignty in May 1955 and was admitted to the North Atlantic Treaty Organisation in the same month. Under the agreements West Germany renounced the right to manufacture on its territory (though not that to acquire or control) atomic, bacteriological and chemical weapons. It further undertook never to use force to achieve reunification or the modification of its frontiers. There was to be no new German General Staff even though Bonn would raise 500,000 men for N A T O. For their part the Western Powers once again expressed their recognition of the Federal Republic as the only 'freely and legitimately' constituted German regime and therefore the only government entitled to speak for the German people in international affairs. They reaffirmed their view that the question of Germany's frontiers would have to await a peace settlement between a government of a free and united Germany and its former enemies.

Another important agreement of Adenauer's first term was that concluded with Israel and the Conference on Jewish Material Claims Against Germany to pay compensation for the Jewish victims of Nazism. This was in 1952. When it was debated in the Bundestag it met opposition from 238 members, including two Ministers; 402 members, mainly the S P D and part of the C D U, supported it. Indeed, the mere outlining of the development of the Federal Republic's foreign relations in these years wrongly ignores the really bitter debate which took place in the Federal Republic about these issues. We must now look at this debate and see how it affected West Germany's politics from 1949 onwards.

It was widely believed outside Germany that the Social Democratic Party of Kurt Schumacher, and after his death in 1952 of Erich Ollenhauer, was a pacifist party opposed to all rearmament. Although this was the view of many rank-and-filers, it was never the view of the leaders or official party policy. As Schumacher explained in 1950: 'The difference of opinion is not one between those who want to rearm and those who are absolute pacifists ... the big difference is between those who simply want to push through rearmament under the present conditions, and those who reject rearmament unless certain national and international conditions are agreed to.' At the Dortmund Conference of the party in 1952 the Social Democrats set out their conditions for agreeing to rearmament. They were: that an effort be made to establish a European security system within the framework of the United Nations; that the efforts to achieve German reunification be just as strongly continued; that the treaties requiring military obligations of the Federal Republic could be dissolved by the Federal Government if these were found to hinder the reunification of Germany and such treaties should not be binding on a future government of a re-united Germany; that all participants are equal and receive equal treatment so far as defence measures are concerned.

For the Social Democrats then, German reunification remained more important than German rearmament. Schumacher himself was from the area beyond the Oder-Neisse Line, Adenauer was from the Rhineland and was accused of being a separatist in the 1920s. Their backgrounds coloured the views of these two politicians on the reunification issue to some extent. Schumacher also differed from Adenauer in that he saw the danger of Communism in social and economic terms rather than military ones. If the Federal Republic adopted progressive social and economic policies it would not be ripe for Communist infiltration. On the other hand, hurried rearmament brought with it the danger from the militarists who would once again wield tremendous power. Against this Adenauer was a keen protagonist of *die Politik der Stärke*, the policy of strength, meaning military strength. If the West became strong enough it could 'roll back the Iron Curtain'! Once the West became strong enough it could, he said in March 1952, 'conduct reasonable conversations with the Soviet Union'. He did not understand that the Soviet Union was getting stronger too. Once the Soviet Union broke U S monopoly of nuclear weapons in 1949 a decisive weapon was virtually neutralised. Even then the Russians did not relish the thought of a strong, Western-orientated, German military force, backed by enormous economic and scientific power. Just what they were prepared to give up to allay this nightmare we do not know, but in 1952 they made an offer which, though belated, looked attractive and might have been serious.

In its note of 10 March 1952 to the Western Powers the Soviet Government called for a peace conference between the nations whose forces had fought against Germany and 'an all-German Government'. The Soviet Union was willing to offer the Germans complete freedom for German industry to expand and export, German national land, sea and air forces 'which are necessary for the defence of the country', German arms production sufficient to equip such armed forces, German membership of the U N O, full civil rights for all former officers and men of the German armed forces and for all former Nazis, except for those in prison as a result of court action. In return Germany would give up the territories east of the Oder-Neisse Line, it would not join any coalition or military alliance directed against any state which had fought against Germany, and all organisations opposed to peace and democracy would be banned on German territory.

The note also called for the removal of all foreign troops and bases from German territory within one year of the signing of a peace treaty. None of these conditions was really so harsh. Even the one concerning anti-democratic organisations was similar to a clause in the West German Basic Law, though it might have meant, in addition to the banning of outright neo-Nazi parties, the winding up of refugee organisations. This could have represented a political advantage for the C D U and F D P.

One vital point the note did not mention: how the 'all-German Government' was to be formed. Was it to be the result of all-German elections? In a later note of 9 April the Soviet Government agreed to all-German elections being carried through under a commission made up of representatives of the Four Powers. Neither the Western Powers nor the West German Government were prepared to accept the Soviet conditions of German neutrality or recognition of the Oder-Neisse Line. An American note of 25 March demanded that the 'all-German Government ought to be free both before and after the conclusion of a peace treaty to enter alliances which are in line with the principles and aims of the United Nations.' According to the Western view N A T O was such an alliance. Further, the American note stated that the frontiers of Germany must be decided at a peace conference, not before. In a memorandum presented by Dr Adenauer to President Eisenhower of the United States on 29 May 1953 the Chancellor expressed the view that 'no German Government would ever be in a position to recognise the Oder-Neisse Line', though Germany tried to solve the problem of its frontiers in a new spirit of international co-operation.

The majority of people in leading circles in Bonn and other Western capitals regarded the Soviet notes as merely a means to hold up Western defence planning and were therefore not prepared to go beyond repetition of well-known Western views. The Social Democrats, on the other hand, though by no means convinced the Russians were sincere, wanted the West to examine the Soviet proposals carefully. In this they were backed up by small groups of neutralists in the Federal Republic. The most significant of these was one led by Dr Gustav Heinemann, who as a leading Protestant churchman had risen to the post of Minister of Interior in Dr Adenauer's first Cabinet. Heinemann resigned in 1950 in protest against the setting up of paramilitary police formations.

# Adenauer re-elected

The election of September 1953 was fought by the Social Democrats to a great extent on the issues of German reunification and defence. They accused the Federal Government of having failed to make serious attempts to bring about German unity. And they claimed that the policy of Western integration of the Federal Republic reduced it to a position of inferiority and one-sided foreign control. A majority of West Germans did not appear to share this opinion. Many of them had as much fear and hatred of the Russians as the Russians had of them. Though they did not want war, they believed only a show of strength would make the Soviets vacate the D D R and the lost territories. Many of them were impressed by what had already been achieved for West Germany in international affairs. Once again Germany's voice counted and even if foreigners did not love the Germans, they respected them. More Germans still were impressed by the apparent economic miracle at home. True, the prices in the shops were still high, hours of work were long, there was a great housing shortage, and there were about 12 million West Germans living on pensions or welfare payments of one kind or another, quite apart from the unemployed. Yet despite all this there had been a change for the better. The bulging shop windows, the buzzing economic activity throughout the Republic and the export records offered hope.

Of course, it must not be forgotten, that even if the situation had been entirely different the C D U/C S U would have had the mass support ensured by Church backing. The Social Democrats suffered too from the high proportion of women voters—a result of two world wars. In Germany, as elsewhere, women, and especially older women, tend to be more Conservative than men. Many of the younger male working-class, who form a natural reserve of voters for Left-wing parties, had been killed in the war. The Christian Democrats fought a hard campaign, calling the S P D the party of Marxism and claiming 'all Marxism leads to Moscow'. The S P D suffered from two other factors. Firstly, its much-respected leader, Dr Kurt Schumacher, had died in 1952, and there had been little time for the new leader, a sincere but not very charismatic figure, to establish himself. Secondly, in June 1953 strikes and demonstrations had broken out in the D D R and had been put down by Soviet tanks and this tended to convince voters that Adenauer's policy of strength was the only valid one in dealing with the Russians. The turnout of voters rose from 78.5 per cent in 1949 to 85.8 per cent in 1953. Undoubtedly, the higher turnout brought 'unpolitical' voters to the polling stations where they voted C D U/C S U.

The Christian Democrats gained 45.2 per cent of the vote as against

28.8 per cent for the S P D and 9.5 per cent for the F D P. The S P D actually increased its vote in absolute terms and, therefore, the number of its members of the Bundestag. The small parties did not do as well as in 1949. One of the reasons for this was the stiffening of the part of the electoral law designed to eliminate small parties. In 1949, in order to gain representation in the Bundestag parties either had to win a constituency directly, by getting the highest number of votes in that constituency, or had to secure a minimum of five per cent of the votes in any given Land of the Republic. These votes were then distributed according to the principle of proportional representation. Under the new law parties had to gain five per cent of the votes throughout the Federation. This made it more difficult for parties which were confined to particular Länder. The Bavarian Party was the main one of these. It did not secure renewed representation in the Bundestag. The Communists also failed to get back gaining only 2.2 per cent of the vote. The German Party won only 3.2 per cent of the vote but gained a number of constituencies due mainly to electoral alliances with its partners in the government. The Centre Party returned three members in 1953 through an alliance with the C D U. One new party to secure representation was the B H E, the Refugee Party. Founded in 1950 in Schleswig-Holstein it soon became a force throughout the Federal Republic. It was mainly concerned with the problems of the refugees and demands for a return of the Sudetenland and the territories beyond the Oder-Neisse Line. It won 5.9 per cent of the vote and 27 seats.

Excluding the West Berlin members, who were elected by the parliament of West Berlin, the C D U/C S U had won half the seats in the Federal Parliament. This was something new in German politics. Dr Adenauer renewed his coalition with the F D P and the D P and brought the Refugee Party into government as well. The Bonn Cabinet took on a more distinctive Right-wing flavour.

## Restoration

The new Minister who personified this more Right-wing flavour was Dr Theodor Oberländer. A member of the B H E, he became Minister of Refugees. Oberländer was an 'Eastern expert' of the Nazi party and a member of the S S; he was later forced out of office by world public opinion after East German revelations about his past. The Minister of Interior, Gerhard Schröder, was a former Nazi member; Heinrich Lübke, Minister of Agriculture, was later to be in trouble because of his wartime activities; Hans-Christoph Seebohm, Minister of

Transport, became notorious for his utterances on behalf of the Sudeten Germans; Viktor-Emanuel Preusker, Minister of Housing, had been in the S A and S S; Waldemar Kraft, Minister for Special Assignments, was ex-S S. Over a third of the Cabinet, therefore, had doubtful pasts.

People started to talk about a 'restoration' of the Nazis. And indeed the early 1950s saw a massive reinstatement of former officials of the Third Reich and pensions for those who could not be given their old jobs back. In 1952 Dr Adenauer admitted in the Bundestag that two-thirds of the senior officials in the Federal Republic's Foreign Service were former Nazi party members. The same was true of many of the other ministries. Among the more notorious cases were those of Dr Hans Globke, Adenauer's chief personal adviser, who was co-author of the official commentary on the Nazi Nuremberg Race Laws; Friedrich Vialon, a State Secretary whose signature was found on decrees about the disposal of the belongings of Jews earmarked for extermination; and Franz Thedieck, State Secretary, who had the special task in occupied Belgium of 'maintaining close cooperation with the S S', and during whose service 25,000 Belgians were deported to Auschwitz.

Pensions for ex-Nazis, including convicted war criminals (pensions which often compared very well with those of Hitler's victims) were another feature of the restoration. Admiral Erich Raeder was granted a monthly pension of 2,246 D M (about £180 or $550 at that time). The widow of Heydrich, Himmler's deputy responsible for occupied Czechoslovakia, received 1,000 D M per month (about £80 or $200). Anton Kassler, former commandant of Sachsenhausen concentration camp, was paid 6,000 D M (£500 or $1,500) as a kind of resettlement grant. There were very many other similar cases.

Another shocking aspect of the restoration in the early 1950s were the many Nazi doctors who had experimented on patients in concentration camps who found their way back into well-paid official positions. Here one of the worst cases which came to light was that of Dr Hertha Oberheuser. She had been sentenced to 20 years' imprisonment by a U S court for crimes committed in the women's concentration camp at Ravensbrück. She was released in 1952 and was recommended for preferential treatment by the West German Ministry of Labour and found employment in an Evangelical Church hospital. Later she set up a private practice near Kiel. In 1958 the British Medical Association felt obliged to protest against this and similar cases saying, in a resolution, that this was a 'cynical affront to the honour, morals and high ideals of the true practice of medicine throughout the world.'

The problem of what to do with the millions of ex-Nazis was a very difficult one. No democratic society can afford to have for long a large group of its citizens who harbour a deep sense of grievance, reject the system, and feel outside it. They could soon become the basis for a new extremist party. Moreover, many of those who had voted for the Nazis, and many who had joined the party, did so solely because they despaired of Weimar's ability to solve the problem of mass unemployment, defend Germany's frontiers and regain Germany's legitimate place in the world. It is doubtful whether the mass of them were highly conscious anti-semites. Many others joined the Nazi party solely to keep their jobs, or because one stood a better chance of getting a job with a party card in one's pocket. Other Germans, who may or may not have been in the N S D A P, were appalled by revelations about Nazi atrocities, but felt that Germany had paid the price in the mass aerial bombings and the expulsion of millions of Germans from their homes in the East. They therefore felt there should be no more emphasis on Nazi crimes and no more prosecution or purging of, to them, German 'war criminals'. Dr Adenauer was conscious of all these considerations and this prompted him to a generous policy towards former Nazis. No doubt this paid off in votes. As the above cases show, what might have been conceived as a policy based on political realism and Christian charity became a potentially dangerous policy of over-indulgence towards the ex-Nazis.

## Mission to Moscow

No doubt feeling increasingly confident of his own diplomatic skills and under considerable pressure both from the S P D and from his own coalition partners, the F D P, Dr Adenauer decided to negotiate directly with Moscow. He was further encouraged by the more friendly attitude towards the outside world of the Soviet leaders since the death of Stalin in 1953. In May 1955 Austria had regained its independence by a state treaty which led to the withdrawal of the four occupation forces. Austria, however, paid a price Adenauer had not been willing to pay—neutrality. (However, Adenauer's supporters argued that a solution which worked for tiny Austria would never work for mighty Germany.) The Soviet leaders also patched up their quarrel with President Tito of Yugoslavia, a quarrel started by Stalin in 1948. Chancellor Adenauer visited Moscow after these two events in September 1955. He took with him representatives of the opposition led by Prof. Carlo Schmid. He wanted to discuss with the Soviets the question of German reunification and the return of German prisoners-of-war. Little progress was made on the major issue but

Adenauer got a promise on the second and it was not long before thousands of Germans, some of them war criminals, were allowed to return home. Bonn and Moscow decided to establish diplomatic relations which shocked some of Adenauer's political friends. The Chancellor insisted that this did not imply any weakening on Bonn's part and he forced the Russians to accept a note stating that the Federal Republic still did not recognise any of the territorial changes made since 1945. Close on the heels of Adenauer's delegation was one from the D D R. It regained the formal sovereignty for that part of Germany with the right to enter into diplomatic relations with other states. Thus Moscow had diplomatic relations with both German states. If other nations did the same it would make it very difficult for Bonn to claim convincingly that it was the only real German state and the only one entitled to speak on behalf of all Germans. To counter this threat Bonn thought up the Hallstein Doctrine. Though apparently it was formulated by diplomat Wilhelm Grewe, it was associated with the name of Walter Hallstein, State Secretary of the Foreign Office who later became President of the Commission of the European Economic Community. The Doctrine was quite simply that recognition of the D D R by any state would be seen by Bonn as an unfriendly act and Bonn would not have, or would break off, diplomatic relations with such a state. This happened in 1957 with Yugoslavia after she had recognised the D D R. Due to the power of its purse Bonn managed to prevent the nations of the Third World from recognising East Germany. But it could not prevent the East Europeans from recognising Herr Ulbricht's regime and by maintaining the Hallstein Doctrine, West Germany kept itself out of Eastern Europe until late into the 1960s.

Dr Adenauer's failure in the East was overshadowed by new successes in the West. At a conference of the Foreign Ministers of the six countries of the Coal and Steel Community, held at Messina in Sicily in May 1955, proposals were discussed for further advances towards European economic integration. This led in March 1957 to the Rome Treaties signed by the six nations. The first of these set up the Common Market through the progressive reduction and elimination of tariffs and quota restrictions between members, harmonisation of economic policies, and the consolidation of the external tariffs of the six into a single tariff system, applicable to imports from outside the Community. The Treaty seemed to offer the rapidly expanding German industry golden opportunities in a large market. German farmers were later to grumble about the effects of the Treaty on them. The second Treaty provided for the coordination of nuclear research and power projects within the Community.

Another outstanding success for the Federal Republic in this period was the return of the Saar to Germany. This was effective from 1 January 1957 following a referendum in October 1955 in which 67.7 per cent of the Saar people voted for a return to Germany. As the author remembers, German hearts swelled as the barriers between the Federal Republic and the Saar came down.

## Absolute majority

During Dr Adenauer's second term of office from 1953 to 1957 the Federal Republic had regained its sovereignty, become a member of N A T O, joined the Common Market and been reunited with the Saar. It was an impressive record. The Chancellor could also claim he had tried to reach agreement with Moscow, even taking Social Democrats with him to help, and if he had failed there it was not his fault.

In home affairs, although the Federal Republic was a land of sharp social contrasts, unemployment had fallen from 7.5 to 3.4 per cent and some highly desirable social legislation had been passed. The most important measure was the new system of retirement pensions introduced in 1957. Instead of the pensioner receiving a flat-rate payment, which declines as the cost of living rises and which is well below what the wage earner received during his working life, the West German pension is wage- (or salary-) related, and account is taken of the cost of living. This put the Federal Republic ahead of most other countries in this respect. Ironically, West Germany took the idea over from Social Democratic Sweden and the German Social Democrats had done much to make the scheme popular in Germany, but it became law under Dr Adenauer's auspices. The Federal Republic also had a very good house-building record, completing well over half a million houses per annum from 1953 onwards. Once again some of the best results were achieved by Social Democratic-controlled Länder authorities, Bremen, Hamburg, West Berlin, for instance. All this contrasted with the harder life in the 'Socialist' D D R and in the months before the election of September 1957 Adenauer's propagandists tried to link, in the public mind, the 'Socialist' S P D with the 'Socialist' D D R. At one point the Chancellor actually accused some Social Democratic officials of receiving funds from East Germany—a charge he withdrew *after* the election. More legitimately C D U propagandists could claim that in 1949 the S P D had favoured 'planning' rather than a 'free' economy and that they had been proved wrong on this.

Remarkably, despite his apparent successes, Dr Adenauer was not so very popular in 1956. In August of that year public opinion research bodies indicated that within 12 months the proportion of the population favourable to the Chancellor's policies had fallen from 59 to 37 per cent, and according to a poll of July 1956 only 34 per cent of West Germans wanted Adenauer to serve for another four-year term, while 44 per cent believed he should retire. These polls were confirmed by local and Länder elections later in the same year.

One factor in the Chancellor's unpopularity was growing working-class opposition to him. 1956 saw a long and bitter metal-workers' strike which was one of the few really big labour disputes in postwar West Germany. The Bonn coalition was also in disarray. The Free Democrats had not been too happy with the Chancellor's foreign policy. They disagreed when Adenauer had acquiesced in the 'Europeanisation' of the Saar in 1954–55 and again they sympathised with the S P D's view that Adenauer's foreign policy made German reunification more difficult. Early in 1956 some Free Democrats in North-Rhine Westphalia revolted against continued alliance with the C D U. They formed a coalition in West Germany's most important Land with the S P D. This in turn lost the Chancellor his two-thirds majority in the Upper House which could impede constitutional amendments. An angry debate broke out in the F D P which led to all the party's ministers in the Bonn coalition leaving the F D P to form the Free People's Party (F V P). Already in the summer of 1955 a split had developed in the Refugee Party and though its two ministers remained in the government, the party itself went into opposition.

In the autumn of 1956 when the situation seemed far from rosy for Dr Adenauer the Russians once again came to his aid. The Hungarian Revolution of October 1956, smashed by the Soviet armed forces, brought panic-stricken German voters behind the Chancellor. Right up to the election the C D U/C S U exploited this event. In a highly professional publicity campaign, made possible by millions of marks from industrial concerns, the Christian Democratic slogan was 'No Experiments'. Believing, as the Secretary-General of the C D U Dr Bruno Heck put it, that 'The electorate wants a ruler type', the Christian Democrats released a 'Big Brother' poster. This widely distributed poster depicted Adenauer as a serious, sun-bronzed, fair-haired, father figure with penetrating blue eyes which appeared to follow the passer-by. It is believed it helped to convince the women. A majority of valid votes, 54 per cent, were cast by women, and a majority of these went to the Christian Democrats. In other respects too the trends of 1953 continued. The turnout of voters rose from 85.8 per cent to 87.8 per cent. The Christian Democrats were helped by the return of the predominently Catholic Saar a majority of whose population voted C D U. For the first time in German parliamentary history one party, the C D U/C S U, received a majority, 50.2 per cent, of the votes. This gave them 270 seats. The S P D gained 31.8 per cent and 169 seats. Their votes had been swelled to some extent by Dr Heinemann's supporters who had disbanded their own party to join the S P D. The Communist Party had been banned in September 1956 and its voters had undoubtedly turned to the S P D in great numbers. The F D P was reduced to 7.7 per cent and 41 seats. No other parties gained representation in the Bundestag.

## Critical voices

The election results might lead one to believe that critical voices had no place. This was not the case. The cultural scene has not been as exotic as it had been in Weimar but there are those in the theatre, the cinema, among the writers and the journalists who have carried on the critical traditions of the 1920s.

Germany is the classic land of political cabaret and to be sure after 1945 such night clubs were opened in the major cities of West Germany but, the experts say, they have not achieved the standards of the pre-1933 clubs. Wolfgang Neuss of West Berlin was the best-known exponent of this art.

The West German cinema suffered from lack of finance and competition from television and foreign films. Split up into a number of small companies, it had to cater for the less discriminating cinema patron. Most of its production were comedies about rural Bavaria, the so-called *Heimat* (homeland) films, cowboy and detective dramas, and rather superficial war stories. A few directors showed greater courage, among the better known of whom were Wolfgang Staudte and Bernhard Wicki. Wicki, born in Switzerland, made a number of pacifist-inclined films—*The Bridge, Children, Mothers and a General* —and a socially-critical film, *The Miracle of Malachias*, completed in 1961.

Obviously many German writers have been concerned with the events between 1933–45 and there has been a ready market for such literature. Novels about the experiences of ordinary soldiers, which exposed the horror of war, included: Remarque's *A Time To Live And A Time To Die*, Helmut Kirst's *08/15* (and other books), and Heinrich Böll's stories of the Eastern Front. In his *Stalingrad* and *Berlin* Theodor Plievier, an emigrant in Russia who later went West, tried to show life on both sides. Carl Zuckmayer examined the morality of the 'non-political' general in *The Devil's General*.

160

Few writers have dealt successfully with the reality of post-war Germany. The most outstanding of those who have is Heinrich Böll. Born into a Catholic, working class family, in Cologne in 1917, his 'heroes' are those without wordly ambition, the down-at-heel, the war widow, the tenement-dweller. He criticised the priests of his church who were more concerned with saving the young serviceman from the prostitute than from the prostitution of service for Hitler.

Equally original, and equally famous is Günter Grass. In 1959 he published his strange, off-beat, novel, *The Tin Drum*, about a nasty-minded dwarf from Danzig, through whose eyes we see a panorama of the long German nightmare since the 1920s. The book provoked extreme reactions. Grass, only sixteen when the war ended, belongs to the younger generation of more aggressively critical writers. Rolf Hochhuth and Uwe Johnson are among the better-known members of this generation. Hochhuth caused anger and praise for his play *The Representative* in which he bitterly attacked the Catholic Church, and in particular the Vatican, for not condemning Nazism more clearly. Johnson, an emigrant from the D D R, was concerned with the effects of the partition of Germany in his *Two Views* and *Speculations About Jacob*.

Highly critical about the state of West German Society Grass and Hochhuth supported the S P D. Böll, though a Catholic, attacked the S P D for its drift to the Right. He was even more critical of the Christian Democrats.

Given the situation in the West German press it was remarkable that any journalist would chance his arm to strike at authority. The largest newspapers—*Bild Zeitung, BZ, Die Welt*, etc., were the property of one man. The Hamburg 'press lord' Axel Springer was responsible in 1967 for 39 per cent of the circulation of daily papers and over 9 per cent of all periodicals. He was strongly criticised for the pro-cold war, anti-S P D line of his publications. Despite Herr Springer's power, liberal, critical, even some radical, opinions found their way into significant publications in West Germany. Among the 'quality' dailies there are the *Süddeutsche Zeitung* and the *Frankfurter Rundschau* representing the liberal tendency. But up to 1970 both had lower circulations than Springer's *Die Welt* and the more con-servative *Frankfurter Allgemeine Zeitung*. In the popular sector there were no radical papers. Unorthodox views are also found in the highly respected weeklies *Die Zeit* and *Der Spiegel*, and in the illustrated magazines *Stern, Quick* and *Konkret*.

West German television producers and journalists have also been prepared to voice independent and critical opinions over the years—often to their cost! The documentary programme *Panorama* put out by

the North German Broadcasting Corporation (N D R) established itself
in the 1960s as a serious, yet popular, commentary on world events.
But many of its leading staff were removed for offending the Christian
Democrats and other interests.

In East Germany no such critical voices were heard. There, writers,
directors and artists had to fall in line with the S E D's interpretation of
what were suitable themes and how these themes should be handled.
The results were that little new of value was produced. Though such
eminent writers as Anna Seghers, Arnold Zweig, Stefan Heym,
Ludwig Renn, Johannes R. Becher, and, above all, Bertolt Brecht, had
chosen to reside there, their output was small. Many writers preferred
to avoid contemporary problems keeping to the (safer) horrors of the
Third Reich. Some of those who did successfully confront post-war
reality, Wolf Biermann and Christa Wolf, for instance, had their
difficulties. One who did not was Dieter Noll whose *Adventures of
Werner Holt* achieved success in the 1960s, though the most popular
part of this work dealt with the Nazi period. For its cultural image the
D D R had to rely on the high technical achievements of the Berliner
Ensemble, which mainly staged the works of Brecht, its orchestras,
and occasional documentary films such as those by Walter Heynowski
and Gerhard Scheumann.

## The S P D at Bad Godesberg

Naturally the defeat of 1957 was a staggering blow to the S P D and, as
is usual after such defeats, many discussions were held to see how the
party could make itself more attractive to the electorate. Particularly
active were those who claimed the party had lost because it was too
negative, appeared as a narrow, old-fashioned, class-war party, talking in terms of Marxism, and public ownership which confused it in
the public mind with the East German S E D. Further, it was said that
the party was too ambivalent on defence (an important consideration
for many electors) and not friendly enough to the churches in a
country where religion, especially the Catholic religion, was still
important.

The S P D had in fact been slowly changing its views over the years.
Though it called for the common ownership of coal, iron and steel and
energy, the Dortmund Programme of 1952 was neither a thorough-
going Socialist programme nor was it couched in class-war terms. At
one point it called for help for middle-class enterprises. The S P D was
changing because Schumacher had encouraged the recruitment of
middle class members who knew little of Marxist traditions and less

of working class life. These included Prof. Karl Schiller, Prof. Carlo Schmid and Helmut Schmidt, among others. Secondly, some of those who had been emigrants—Willy Brandt, Erich Ollenhauer in the Anglo-Saxon countries or Scandinavia were impressed by the empiricism of their socialists as against the Marxism of continental socialists. On the other hand, they were put off ideology by experience of Nazism and Communism. The latter also reduced their enthusiasm for nationalisation. As far as religion was concerned, as early as 1946 at Hanover, Schumacher had proclaimed that it did not matter how a man came to socialism—through Marx or the Sermon on the Mount. The declaration of the Socialist International at Frankfurt in 1951, signed by the S P D, incorporated this idea. There was no hard evidence that the S P D had lost votes because it had advocated public ownership of the basic industries, or because it was thought to be Marxist and anti-religious. But successive defeats won a majority of the party leaders for a thorough-going attempt to improve the party's image.

One of the most prominent of these was Herbert Wehner who had been a fairly senior Communist in the Weimar Republic. The programme adopted by the Bad Godesberg conference in 1959 by 324 votes to 16 was designed to do just that. The programme called for a 'free partnership' between the S P D and the churches, said that Socialism was rooted in Christianity, advocated protection and encouragement of private ownership of the means of production, and proclaimed the S P D's positive attitude to national defence. Within a matter of months S P D leaders were calling for a united front on national questions.

The S P D was obviously preparing its campaign for the 1961 election. Its Chancellor candidate was Willy Brandt, since 1957 the world-famous Lord Mayor of West Berlin. This time it was going in for a promotion campaign of American style and dimensions. Brandt tried to play the German Kennedy, the latter having become U S President in January 1961, and made a fairly convincing job of it. This time too a crisis was to work in the Social Democrats' favour. This was the renewed crisis over Berlin which started with a Khrushchev speech threatening the Western position in West Berlin in 1958 and ended with the building of the Berlin wall by Walter Ulbricht's regime in August 1961. The building of the wall exposed not only the weakness of the East German regime (it was erected to stop East Germans going West), but showed up Adenauer's claims that the *Politik der Stärke* would lead to German reunification. Another matter which had dented the Chancellor's image was his statement in April 1959 that he would like to stand as Federal President on the retirement of Theodor Heuss in that year. Adenauer was by then 83 years old and said he would give the Presidency the influence it deserved!

When the votes came to be counted in September 1961 they indicated that *Der Alte's* (as Adenauer was nicknamed) popularity was on the wane. The C D U / C S U's share fell to 45.3 per cent and 242 seats. The S P D increased its share to 36.3 per cent and 190 seats, and the Free Democrats jumped to 12.7 per cent and 67 seats. They were the only parties to be returned to parliament. The Free Democrats had gained from the promise made by their leader, Dr Erich Mende, that he would not serve in a Cabinet which Dr Adenauer led. This party also gained for its more positive and flexible stand on German reunification even though it had for years been in government with the Christian Democrats. No doubt too it gained votes from disillusioned middle-class voters who still could not bring themselves to vote for a 'working-class party', the Social Democrats. It is possible that had the S P D given a clearer alternative to the Christian Democrats on national issues it might have gained more ground still.

Dr Mende kept his promise but once again a coalition was formed between the C D U / C S U and the F D P. The Free Democrats, however, got Adenauer to promise that he would retire within two years. Before the Chancellor finally retired he was to face one more great political crisis.

## The Spiegel affair

Adenauer's last crisis concerned action taken against the news magazine *Der Spiegel*, one of the Federal Republic's two leading weeklies. Although not associated with any political party *Der Spiegel* had often criticised various aspects of government policy and had been an outspoken critic of the Bavarian Franz Josef Strauss since he had taken over the Defence Ministry in 1956. The magazine attacked what it considered to be the Minister's personal deficiencies as well as his policies. In its edition of 10 October 1962 *Der Spiegel* published an article attacking the performance of the *Bundeswehr* (armed forces) as revealed in the N A T O exercise 'Fallex'. A police raid, which reminded the public of those of the 1920s and early 1930s, was made on the offices of the magazine in Hamburg. Leading journalists were arrested either in their offices or homes, one, Conrad Ahlers, was arrested by Spanish police while on holiday. The authorities claimed the article was treasonable because it contained military secrets. The proceedings against Ahlers and Rudolf Augstein, the publisher, who was detained in prison for 14 weeks, were given up in 1965 for lack of evidence. The S P D and the F D P alleged that the authorities, in particular Herr Strauss, were guilty of unconstitutional action. Eventually, in 1966 the Constitutional Court divided evenly on that issue. But the resignation of five F D P Ministers in November 1961 caused a political crisis which forced the Defence Minister from office.

Herr Strauss's departure was more agonising because West German Christian Democracy was going through a deep crisis. For years there had been tension between the more socially-orientated, more working-class, 'Left wing' of the C D U typified (until his death in 1958) by Karl Arnold, Prime Minister of North-Rhine Westphalia from 1947 to 1956, and the business wing of the party. The latter group had gained the ascendancy by the early 1950s but the Left remained strong enough to force through certain social legislation. The crisis of the early 1960s was of a different nature. With Dr Adenauer's retirement not far off personal rivalries increased. Dr Erhard, Economics Minister, creator of the 'economic miracle', had surrounded himself with a group of supporters. But they were opposed by the ambitious Herr Strauss who could whip up Bavarian patriotism to support his claims. Strauss also cloaked his ambitions in a vague ideology. He became known as a German 'Gaullist'. His position was supported by Baron von Guttenberg, Wilhelm Grewe, Heinrich von Brentano, who was Foreign Minister from 1955 to 1961, and others. Dr Adenauer also inclined to this view. Very roughly the group stressed Europe's role in economic, political and military terms but, unlike President de Gaulle, they advocated a tough line with the Soviets. Erhard and Dr Gerhard Schröder, Minister of Interior 1953–61, Foreign Minister 1961–1966, looked more to the U S A and the 'Atlantic Community'. As the United States under President (1961–63) John Kennedy, were pursuing a more conciliatory policy towards Moscow, Erhard and Schröder were prepared for small concessions in that direction.

## Franco-German relations

Dr Adenauer's last journey as a statesman was his visit to Paris in January 1963 to conclude a Franco-German Treaty of Friendship. During the visit, the French President questioned Britain's qualifications for entry into the Common Market. As a result when ratifying the Treaty, the Bundestag insisted on inserting a preamble which reaffirmed the West German desire to maintain the Atlantic alliance and admit Britain to the European Community. Because of the differences between France and West Germany over defence and European affairs there was some surprise that the Treaty had been concluded in the first place. In 1966 France was preparing to leave the military side of N A T O and still saw Europe as an association of states; it was not ready for the Common Market to move towards federal structures. West Germany, on the other hand, was strongly pro-N A T O and in favour of European integration. The Treaty had been concluded by two old men who did not get on very well with the young American president John F. Kennedy (1961–3). They felt somewhat left out by the 'special relationship' of the U S A with Britain which had been given new force by Kennedy and British Prime Minister Harold Macmillan. In any case, the Treaty had great emotional appeal for two statesmen who had been brought up hearing about the Franco-Prussian War of 1870–1 and had lived through the two world wars.

The Treaty laid down regular consultations between the French and German leaders and three-monthly consultations of their foreign ministers. It also envisaged security and cultural co-operation. The defence component called for the strengthening of the exchange of personnel between the two armed forces, joint armaments projects and the development of shared concepts of strategy. Among the projects which were developed were the *Roland* air defence missile system and the *Alfa Jet*. On the cultural side a youth exchange programme was set up. In 1964 280,000 young people from the two states had participated in meetings. By 1967 the number had risen to 420,000. This momentum could not be sustained, partly because English was more popular as a foreign language than French or German. In 1987 only 145,525 took part in exchanges.

# — 9 —

# Ulbricht's Leninist State

By the time the German Democratic Republic was set up in October 1949 control by elements subservient to Moscow had been virtually secured. Parliament consisted only of representatives of the five official parties and the 'mass organisations' and was thus a rubber stamp. The parties and the mass organisations had been purged of most leaders who might have displayed any independence, and, in any case, their organisations were held firmly within the corset of the National Front. The radio, cinema and most of the press were under the control of the S E D, as were the police, education and the economy. Apart from the Soviet secret police, an East German security police was being built up. This work was completed with the founding of the Ministry for State Security—*Ministerium für Staatssicherheit*—in February 1950. In all spheres the tendency was towards centralisation. For instance, in July 1952 the Länder were abolished and replaced by 14 weak districts or *Bezirke* subject to central authority.

Despite all these measures unorthodox views were still sometimes heard. Representatives of the churches criticised various aspects of official policy as did members of the C D U and L D P D. C D U Chairman Otto Nuschke spoke out, at his party's congress in November 1949, against single-list elections. Such elections were nevertheless carried through in October of the following year. They followed what was by that time standard practice in Eastern Europe. There was not only a single list with one candidate per seat, but no opposition was permitted. The mass media exhorted the electorate to vote greatly over-simplifying the issues, large numbers of agitators went round urging the reluctant to go to the polling stations, and in some cases they were marched there *en bloc*. On arrival all they had to do was to collect their ballot paper, fold it and put it into the box. Only those wishing to cross out names of the National Front candidates needed to go to the cubicles provided. By so doing they were drawing attention to themselves and it is not surprising, therefore, that few availed themselves of the opportunity. It might be wondered why the regime bothered with such manifestly unfree elections. Yet every regime wishes to appear to be based on the popular will and by showing they can force their citizens to conform, authoritarian systems demoralise their opponents. The Communists also regard their elections as a means of popular education for the 'campaign' lasts for several months, during which the regime's immediate and long term aims are discussed.

Another question which needs clarification is why those in effective control of East Germany maintained five political parties when all had the same aims, methods and policies, and were not allowed even the slightest degree of autonomy. Once again there was the need for window-dressing; five parties look better than one, for there is then the illusion of choice. Secondly, a one-party state might have re-minded the East Germans too much of the Third Reich and led them to conclude the regimes were similar. Thirdly, the four 'allied' parties helped to win for the regime supporters who would not want to join the S E D, officially a Marxist working-class party. As its name proclaims, the Christian Democratic Union sought to win Christians for its objects, which since its sixth party congress in October 1952 had been, 'in the spirit of Christian responsibility, to mobilise all our energies in the struggle for Peace, Unity and Socialism'. Such a party would cater for the tiny handful of genuine Christian socialists or pacifists prepared to cooperate with the Communists, the very much larger group of middle-class business and professional people and some pastors, who tried to save what they could of their old values and way of life, and those who felt they need to indicate some degree of acceptance of the regime but do not want to get too deeply involved. Further, the continued existence of this party meant that many of the original members, who joined before the fate of the C D U became clear, could be 'trapped' in their party and utilised for the regime. Finally, there were those who had been ordered into this party by their S E D superiors.

The membership of the other 'bourgeois' parties is largely made up of the same type of people with the same reasons for joining, except that the N D P D was set up to win over former nominal Nazis and officers for the regime, and the L P D aimed more at the non-church orientated middle class.

The 'bourgeois' parties of East Germany also served as bridges between the D D R and bourgeois groups in West Germany and other countries. The L D P D, for example, had exchanges with the Free Democrats of West Germany and with the British Young Liberals, the C D U with Left-wing Catholic groups, and so on. The S E D found it difficult to make these contacts.

The years 1948–53 were in very many respects grim years in

Eastern Europe. They were the years of Stalin's purges, forced industrialisation and intensified class struggle. East Germany fitted into this general pattern. First there were purges in the Christian Democratic and Liberal Democratic parties designed to remove those who still showed independence. Then came similar moves in the Socialist Unity Party.

In September 1948 the Unity Party's executive committee announced decisions which were to bring East Germany into line with what was happening in the rest of East Europe. In June of that year the Communist Information Bureau or Cominform, made up of the Communist parties of Eastern Europe (excluding the S E D) and those of France and Italy, expelled the Yugoslav party. It was claimed the Yugoslavs had 'pursued an incorrect line on the main questions of home and foreign policy, a line which represents a departure from Marxism-Leninism'. The Yugoslavs were further accused of 'seceding from the united socialist front against imperialism, have taken the path of betraying the cause of international solidarity of the working people, and have taken up a position of nationalism ...' Tito's main 'crime' was his refusal to subordinate the interests of Yugoslavia to those of the Soviet Union, and his refusal to imitate the Russians in every sphere. Stalin feared that Tito would find friends and allies in the other countries of the Soviet bloc. He therefore unleashed a purge which was to lead to the deaths of leading Communists throughout Eastern Europe. The Socialist Unity Party could not for long remain uninfluenced by this development especially as East Germany was under Soviet military rule at the time. The September decisions of the S E D executive represented its recognition of this. The executive called for a 'struggle against nationalism, the slandering of the Soviet Union and Peoples' Democracies, and against the theory of a special "German road to Socialism"'. Another executive decision was the establishment of a party central control commission, similar to that of the Soviet C P, to supervise party members and, if necessary, to discipline or expel them.

The S E D four-day conference of January 1949 was another decisive step along the road to changing the nature of the party. The conference demanded that the S E D must become a 'party of a new type', in other words, a Leninist or Moscow-type organisation. It would accept Leninism including Democratic Centralism, as well as Marxism, and abolition of the parity principle under which former K P D and former S P D members were equally represented at all levels, and become an élite party. In future would-be members had to serve for one or two years, depending on their social background, before they could become full members. The conference decided on the setting up of a Politburo to lead the party, this too was on the Soviet model.

In July 1950 the third congress of the S E D was held. It introduced a Soviet-style constitution for the party including the replacement of the executive committee by a central committee. Walter Ulbricht, widely regarded as Moscow's chief agent in East Germany, was elected secretary general of the party—the key position in any Communist state. Another change in the S E D agreed at this congress was the change in structure. Henceforth, party members would belong where possible to a unit at their place of work rather than where they live, though residential units were not abolished. This again was in line with the K P D and Soviet tradition.

In August 1950 the first major purge in the S E D took place. Stalin had linked 'Titoism' with 'Trotskyism' and both with 'Social Democratism'. In other words, roughly speaking, anyone who voiced doubts about Soviet actions in Germany, or about the wholesale adoption of Soviet methods, norms or terminology, could find himself accused of 'Titoism' or 'nationalism'. Anyone who criticised bureaucracy was in danger of being labelled a 'Trotskyite', or anyone who resisted the destruction of internal party democracy or wanted the trade unions to act as trade unions could be dubbed a 'Social Democrat'. Stalin also regarded the Zionist movement as an international conspiracy working on behalf of United States imperialism, and sent out his emissaries hotfoot to the capitals of Eastern Europe to purge 'Zionists'. Almost anyone of Jewish background was under suspicion.

Those purged in August 1950 fell, it was said, due to revelations at the (notorious) Rajk trial in Hungary. The more important victims included Paul Merker, a senior official in the Ministry of Agriculture, Leo Bauer, editor-in-chief of the East German radio, Lex Ende, editor-in-chief of the S E D newspaper, *Neues Deutschland*, and Willi Kreikemeyer, director general of the D D R railways. In December 1952 Prof. Leo Zuckermann, head of D D R-President Pieck's Chancellory, was accused of Zionism, but he reached West Berlin before he could be arrested. More 'Zionist agents' were 'exposed' in the following month in the V V N, the League of Victims of National Socialism. In May 1953 two members of the Central Committee of the S E D were expelled from the party for allegedly giving away information about illegal party work at the time of Hitler. One man not in the S E D purged at this time was Georg Dertinger, East Germany's Foreign Minister, and deputy Chairman of the C D U. He was accused of enemy activity against the D D R.

Terrible though these purges were, involving the disgrace and harsh imprisonment of many of those 'exposed', the situation in the

D D R did not degenerate in the way it did in the rest of Eastern Europe. There dozens of life-long Communists were brutally treated, humiliated at show trials and executed. In the D D R, on the other hand, virtually all those removed survived to be rehabilitated after the death of Stalin, though by no means all of them got positions equal to those they had lost. It is also only fair to mention that Western intelligence agencies had continually sought to infiltrate East German bodies.

## Socialist construction

Given that Germany was not being treated as an economic whole, the East German leaders were in a difficult position. Their part of Germany was not, as often commonly supposed, without industry. But its industries were mainly light industries—textiles, consumer goods, automobiles, office machinery and light engineering products of all kinds, optical equipment, electrical goods and chemicals. Most of these were dependent on raw materials or parts from other areas of Germany. Attempts to replace these from within the D D R meant heavy, in some cases, uneconomical, investments. Another disadvantage suffered by the Soviet Zone/D D R was the heavy dismantling by the Russians. Their zone suffered about twice as much as the Western zones. In addition, the Russians demanded goods from current production which were, in many instances, not traditional manufactures of this area; fulfilment of these demands required heavy investments which held down living standards. The East German economy suffered further from loss of key workers, technicians and managers to the West. Some did not want to work for a 'socialist' regime, some, in the early years, feared being forced to work in the Soviet Union, many did not appreciate being forced into political activities after working hours, even more sought better living standards and a more relaxed atmosphere in the West. Between 1945 and 1961 just over 3 million Germans whose homes were in the Soviet Zone/D D R migrated to West Germany. During the same period some 2.7 million Germans from the lost territories, who had been quartered in the Soviet Zone/D D R, moved West. Of course, many of these were not employed in industry.

In order to try to make their state independent of West Germany the D D R leaders, starting with the first five-year plan of 1951–55, invested large sums in the energy and iron and steel industries. Dismantling cost the Soviet Zone 85 per cent of its very limited steel rolling capacity. The area is poorly endowed with hard coal and its brown coal capacity was reduced by about 40 per cent by dismantling. The extraction of the relatively plentiful brown coal was given priority and a great many technical problems were solved in order to enable it to be used in the metallurgical industry. But production costs remained high in that industry and heavy dependence on brown coal was a factor in the relatively high costs of East German industry as a whole. The most publicised project in the brown coal industry was the 'Schwarze Pumpe' complex near Hoyerswerda started in 1955. In the iron and steel industry the most important project was that at Eisenhüttenstadt on the East German-Polish frontier. Supplied with coke from Poland this was an entirely new development with a new town, known as Stalinstadt from 1953 to after the 20th congress of the C P S U in 1956. The D D R's efforts to build up its steel industry are indicated by the following figures:

Per capita Production of Rolled Steel (*in kilograms*)

|  | D D R | Federal Republic |
| --- | --- | --- |
| 1946 | 5 | 50 |
| 1958 | 70 | 300 |
| 1964 | 170 | 430 |

Despite East Germany's progress in this field it remained a very large importer of steel. Another industry which commanded large investments was shipbuilding. This hardly existed before the war in what had become the D D R. It too had suffered from dismantling. It was built up to provide reparations for the Soviet Union and after they formally ended remained dependent on orders from the U S S R.

All these reparations and investments in slow-maturing projects required sacrifices, great sacrifices of the East German people. Living standards did not rise in the way they were doing in the Federal Republic in the early fifties. This became widely known in East Germany through the West German radio, letters from friends and relatives in the West, and Western visitors. Naturally dissatisfaction spread. Often between 1952 and 1989, the author heard ordinary East Germans comment: 'We work as hard as they do. We are no less skilled. Why should we be worse off than they are? Are we alone responsible for the war?' In 1952 new sacrifices were imposed. It was announced that the D D R would build up its own 'national armed forces' as well as the basis of Socialism. This was proclaimed as the East German response to the Federal Republic's signing the European Defence Community Treaty a few weeks before. The D D R already possessed certain paramilitary forces which were officially part of the police. These were re-organised and expanded. An intensive recruitment campaign was launched. Officially this was voluntary but a good deal of pressure was used to persuade the reluctant. As a result of the war and migration to the West the D D R was short of labour and the expansion of the 'People's Police in Barracks' caused further strain on the nation's resources. The new forces had to be housed, fed and equipped. Only by new burdens could the necessary means be found.

The Economic Plan for 1953 sought to find the means by a great increase in the productivity of the labour force and by a new wage structure based, to a much larger extent than before, on piece work. In April 1953 food prices were increased and in May it was announced that the work 'norms' for industrial workers would be raised, which meant more work for the same money.

One would have thought such measures alone would have given the state and party officials enough to do as they involved reorganisation, paper work and much propaganda activity. But at the same time due to the decision to commence socialist construction the class struggle was being intensified. More nationalisation measures were being put into effect, a collectivisation drive in agriculture got under way, there was more discrimination against students from non-working-class homes, the intelligentsia lost some of their privileges, and the churches came under increasing pressure. These measures were largely self-defeating because they led to more East Germans going West which in turn caused greater difficulties in every sphere of society.

## Revolt in June and the 'New Course'

Since the death of Stalin in March 1953 the Soviet leaders had been taking stock of their inheritance and had reversed some of his policies. Early in June they advised the Politburo of the S E D to do the same in the D D R. Most of the discriminatory measures were then rescinded but confusion remained about the work norms of the industrial workers. Did the 'New Course' cover them?

On 16 June about 80 building workers on the main 'Stalinallee' site in East Berlin went on strike against the higher norms. The next day strikes and demonstrations took place in many parts of East Germany. In some places they were orderly and peaceful, in others not so peaceful. Some were concerned solely with economic grievances, others demanded the resignation of the government and free elections. In East Berlin, where violence did take place, demonstrators were joined by West Berliners, some of whom were undoubtedly agents for Western organisations. R I A S the Radio in the American

Sector (of Berlin) was of key importance in spreading news of the strikes and so encouraging further strikes and demonstrations. The 'revolt' soon ended when Soviet troops took up key positions in the towns throughout the D D R and martial law was proclaimed. Although they admitted that their 'mistakes' were an important cause of the strikes, the S E D leaders sought to show that the events of 16–17 June were part of a plan for their overthrow worked out by Western intelligence agencies. They have failed to offer much hard evidence of this. In West Germany the events of those days became known as the People's Revolt, which in fact they were not. Most of those involved were workers, few members of other social classes took part. Secondly, the extent of the strikes is generally widely exaggerated. Research carried out for the West German Ministry for All-German Affairs indicates that 372,000 workers downed tools. The same source estimates that there were some 8 million workers in the D D R at that time which, if correct, means that about 4.5 per cent of the D D R's industrial workers stopped work. East German estimates worked out higher! From their accounts the percentage would be 5.5. Nor did the rising end in a blood bath. Western estimates put the number of those killed at 21. The number of wounded was higher.

The June revolt shook the East German leaders and their supporters. They resolved to continue the New Course appeasement policy. They also looked for scapegoats. One of these was Max Fechner, Minister of Justice, who was condemned for 'hostile activities'—he had upheld the right to strike—and imprisoned. Rudolf Herrnstadt, editor-in-chief of *Neues Deutschland*, was removed together with Security Minister Wilhelm Zaisser, and the Secretary of the S E D Berlin organisation, Hans Jendretzky. Herrnstadt was given a post in the state archives, Fechner and Jendretzky were later rehabilitated.

## The 20th Congress and Wolfgang Harich

In the years after 1953 the D D R's policies and priorities were influenced to a great extent by the more conciliatory attitude of the Soviet leaders to the West, an attitude summed up in the term 'peaceful coexistence'. On their own account though they attempted to 'build socialism' at home and gain recognition abroad. They remained somewhat uneasy about their position fearing a Soviet sell-out. This was particularly so in 1955 when the Soviet Government joined the Western Powers in signing an Austrian Peace Treaty and withdrawing from that country. In that same year West Germany established diplomatic relations with Moscow without making any concessions on the question of the recognition of the D D R or Germany's post-war frontiers.

For Herr Ulbricht in particular the second half of the fifties was worrying. 1956 brought the 20th Congress of the Soviet Communist Party with Khrushchev's dramatic anti-Stalin speech. Ulbricht, as a man who had served Stalin faithfully, could not be sure he would not be sacrificed on the altar of 'de-Stalinisation' and coexistence. Perhaps luckily for him, the Hungarian revolution came in October 1956 and there were troubles in Poland. Both were partly the result of 'de-Stalinisation', both frightened the Soviet leaders. Ulbricht appeared to have things under control in East Germany, so why not leave well alone? The D D R did not entirely escape the consequences of the 20th Congress. The East German leaders made statements in line with Moscow's reappraisal of Stalin. Streets, institutions and Stalinstadt, named after him, were renamed. His books and photographs of him were removed. Those purged by Stalin's edict were rehabilitated.

The official de-Stalinisation measures were not regarded as adequate by some party intellectuals. Dr Wolfgang Harich, lecturer at the S E D's own school and editor of the official journal of philosophy, became spokesman for such individuals. Harich was in touch with circles in Poland, Hungary and Yugoslavia as well as the West German Social Democrats. He wanted intellectual freedom, more say for the workers, a more positive role for the East German parliament, more emphasis on raising living standards and the revitalisation of the S E D together with a refurbishing of its ideology. The East German leaders obviously feared his influence for he was arrested, brought to trial in March 1957 and sentenced to ten years' imprisonment. He was, however, released in autumn 1964.

## 'Overtake the West'

By the time of the 5th Congress of the S E D in 1958 Walter Ulbricht could feel more confident than before. He had got those who might have opposed him, the most senior of whom was Politburo member Karl Schirdewan, removed from the party leadership. In the Politburo he was surrounded by colleagues who, apart from Otto Grotewohl who died in 1964, remained with him throughout the sixties. East German living standards remained lower than those prevailing in West Germany, but they were tolerable and improving. His government seemed to be winning the confidence of the D D R people. The numbers going West was declining. In 1959 'only' 143,917 left, the lowest figure since 1949. Internationally Ulbricht had the backing of the Soviet leader, N. S. Krushchev, who attended the congress. The colossi of the world communist movement, the U S S R and China, were at one, and Soviet space achievements helped to convince comrades they were on the winning side. The optimism of the congress was indicated by Ulbricht's promise that by the early 1960s the D D R's per capita levels of consumer consumption would outpace those of West Germany. This promise was to prove totally unrealistic. The congress endorsed the introduction of polytechnical instruction in schools which aimed at giving school children some knowledge of elementary technology and the factory or agricultural system at an early age. And, for those who wished to go on to higher education, the new edict laid down a year's compulsory practical work in the economy. This was in line with Soviet education. Like earlier S E D congresses, the fifth made a number of proposals on the German issue. These included a defensively rearmed, neutral, united Germany, based on the frontiers of 1945, which had emerged from a confederation of the two German states.

## The Berlin Wall

The optimism of 1958–59 did not last. Measures aimed at 'the comprehensive construction of Socialism', including virtually total collectivisation of the land and more nationalisation, led to economic difficulties and both to an increase in the number of refugees going West. This in turn increased the strains and stresses of East German life and produced yet more refugees. Mr Khrushchev's ultimatum, which amounted to a demand that the Western powers recognise the D D R or suffer interference with their position in West Berlin, created uncertainty and further contributed to the outflow of people from the D D R. In some cases too West German firms, short of labour with a booming economy, recruited East German workers with promises of higher wages. With just over 199,000 of his citizens lost in 1960 and a further 155,000 in the first eight months of 1961, Herr Ulbricht was forced to take drastic action. On 13 August 1961 the Eastern part of Berlin was sealed off from the Western part and the construction of the Berlin Wall begun. In addition, the frontier with West Germany was strengthened. Even so, another 50,000 or so East Germans managed to cross to the West by the end of the year. The Wall was a scar bisecting a great city. It was physically ugly, morally uglier still. Up to the end of 1968 over 60 people died while attempting to cross it. Altogether, at least 137 people were killed trying to reach West Germany from the D D R during this period.

# — 10 —

# East Germany in the Sixties

Many East Germans feared that the closing of the Republic's Berlin frontier in August 1961 would lead to repression and renewed austerity. Their worst fears were not realised. Those caught trying to get to West Germany were jailed, and there was some toughening of the official attitude to certain 'pampered' groups, such as building workers, who had earned very high wages by East German standards before the Wall. But, on the whole the regime was a little less hard than before. East Germany was on the verge of a mild 'thaw' which was to last until the end of 1966.

The main features of East German life in the 1960s were the spreading of prosperity, more genuine discussions between the rulers and the ruled on important, though mainly non-political matters, coupled with continued rigidity in political and intellectual affairs. The prosperity and a greater measure of international acceptance helped in the consolidation of the regime.

## The New Economic System

Under Mr Khrushchev cautious reforms of the Soviet economic system associated with the name of Professor Yevsei Liberman were introduced in 1962. In 1963 the Sixth Congress of the Socialist Unity Party announced similar reforms for the D D R. Among the principal authors of the East German reforms were Erich Apel, who had studied and worked in the Soviet Union, and Günter Mittag.

The reforms were given the rather ponderous title of the New Economic System of Planning and Managing the Economy. The main ingredients of the new system were: the restoration of profit as a measure of economic utility and stimulus to growth; less rigid planning and more power for the directors of the 80 'socialist trusts' (V V B's) into which the major part of industry was divided; a more creative role for the banks with a discriminatory credit policy designed to reward or penalise the 'socialist trusts' according to their varying performances; more emphasis on quality as against mere quantity of production, and concentration on the products best suited to East German skills, capacities and raw materials. The congress decisions meant greater concentration on the traditional patterns of industry in this part of Germany.

When they heard the news the East German people were no doubt somewhat sceptical. This was by no means the first shake up of the D D R's economic system. Each new change had been heralded as progress, and each time they had been bombarded for months by the mass media with the details of the new changes, exhortations to study them and promises of better times. The promises and forecasts made at the last congress in 1958 regarding living standards had proved hollow. This time there were fewer specific promises and the results were more convincing.

Of every 100 households in East Germany in 1958 only 5.1 had television sets, whereas in 1965 the number was 48. In 1958 only 2.1 per cent had refrigerators, but in 1965 the figure was 26. Washing machines were found in 1.6 per cent of households in 1958. By 1965 the figure had risen to 28 per cent. By this time more East German homes possessed television sets than did the homes of Austria, France, Italy and Switzerland. The progress they still had to make is indicated by a comparison with the situation in Britain in 1965. In that year 39 per cent of British homes were equipped with refrigerators, 56 per cent with washing machines and 88 per cent with T V. In the second half of the sixties further progress was made in the D D R. By 1969 48 per cent of East German households had fridges, the same number washing machines and 66 per cent television receivers. But despite this progress the party leaders had still not redeemed their 1958 pledge to provide their people with more consumer goods than the West Germans. And although East German architecture had recovered from the stultifying effects of Stalinism by the time of the Sixth Congress, and many respectable, even pleasing buildings of contemporary design were erected in the following years, the housing situation remained critical by the end of the sixties. The modest housing targets were still not being fulfilled.

In other respects too East German living standards lagged behind those of the advanced nations of Western Europe. Private motoring started in earnest in the 1960s but by 1970 the D D R remained one of the most undermotorised industrial countries in the world. The standard and variety of clothing available in the shops left much to be desired compared with that found in neighbouring Western countries. This situation resulted to a considerable extent, from very large exports of textiles and clothing. And despite the growth of foreign travel in the 1960s, many East Germans felt bitter about the fact that they were unable to holiday in Western countries or even in Yugoslavia. The only people who really felt deprived, however, were the old age pensioners and they were allowed to journey to the West or emigrate if they so desired.

On the positive side, partly due to emigration, there was no unemployment and most East Germans, including all industrial workers, got a statutory five-day week in September 1967. Not all West Germans had this. The health service, which had suffered from migration of personnel, improved (though it could not provide the increasingly complex medical technology and drugs available in the West). Basic education opportunities followed by apprenticeships were good (though many school buildings were old and neglected and schooling was regimented).

## Havemann, the Intellectuals and the changing Élite

The new interest in economic reform from 1963 resulted in a modicum of academic freedom in East German universities. This was especially true for those engaged in teaching or researching in subjects essential for the New Economic System—economics, mathematics, statistics, and the newly discovered cybernetics and sociology. Just how limited this freedom remained, however, was indicated by the case of Professor Robert Havemann.

Havemann joined the Communist Party in 1932 and was later sentenced to death by the Nazis for his anti-regime activities. His researches were regarded as so important—he is a physical-chemist— that the sentence was not executed. After the war he was in trouble with the Americans in West Berlin for his opposition to U S nuclear arms. He was appointed to a chair at the Humboldt University of East Berlin and eventually became a member of the East German Academy of Sciences. Apparently it was a series of lectures given by Havemann in the autumn and winter of 1963–64 which got the professor into trouble again. These lectures, later published in West Germany under the title *Dialektik ohne Dogma?* by the Rowohlt Publishing Co., amounted to a call for democracy in the D D R. 'What is necessary, what is a condition of life for Socialism, and what was lost during the period of Stalinism, is Democracy. Socialism cannot be achieved without Democracy'. Havemann claimed he was speaking as a good Leninist. The professor also attacked capital punishment, still a penalty in the D D R in 1970 though rarely used, arguing, 'In the last resort the death penalty is only demanded in order to be able to kill political opponents'. He showed even greater courage by attacking academic colleagues who, without any knowledge of the natural sciences, rejected 'Western' scientific theories because they did not fit in with their own dogmatic view of Dialectical Materialism. Such people had discredited Dialectical Materialism and the D D R. They were still at work. Their theories were still being widely publicised in the D D R even though the Soviet Union had discarded them.

Havemann's courage was rewarded by his removal from the university and his expulsion from the Academy of Sciences. He was given research work. His plight brought support from the American Nobel Prize Winner, Linus Pauling, who urged the East German Academy President, Prof. Werner Hartke, a former Nazi party member, to 'take immediate action to revoke the unjust and improper dismissal of Professor Havemann'. Pauling himself had been awarded an honorary doctorate of the Humboldt University.

Professor Havemann was a popular lecturer at the Humboldt University. Yet neither his removal nor other events of the 1960s caused much opposition among East German students. Can we conclude then that they, unlike their West German colleagues, were supremely content? This was not the case. True, in certain respects, East German students were in a better, or rather a different position from students in the Federal Republic. The great majority of them, unlike those in West Germany, received monetary grants and they were likely to have been more carefully selected. As a higher proportion of East Germans were studying science and technology they were less involved in controversial issues than their colleagues in the arts and social sciences. East German courses were more vocation-orientated and the D D R's students were more likely than West German students to know that they had secure jobs to go to. Moreover, Ulbricht's students could feel that their state, as the friend of those idols of student rebels the world over, North Vietnam, the Arabs and Castro's Cuba, was more worthy of support than the Federal Republic.

Yet East German students had their grievances. At least some of them were known to feel overburdened by compulsory subjects— Marxism, maths, Russian and a second foreign language, and sport— which all students were required to do. Some ached from the strain of too much extra-curricular activity for the S E D or from what were, officially, voluntary vacation shifts on farm or building site or in the Republic's factories. It would have been surprising too if all were satisfied with their material conditions. Most East German students, if they could have experienced them, would certainly have regarded the living and working conditions of British counterparts as luxurious. Most East German students regretted the lack of opportunity to travel to western countries. Some of the idealistic and more sensitive minority no doubt shared some of Robert Havemann's preoccupations. This was shown during the Warsaw Pact countries' invasion of Czechoslovakia in 1968 when a few young people, including the sons and daughters of prominent S E D members, issued leaflets and daubed slogans denouncing the action. But the majority of East German students were probably no different from the majority elsewhere. Concerned with successfully completing their studies, and embarking on their careers, they had little taste for politics. The Berlin Wall and the fate of earlier opposition to the regimes of Eastern Europe had helped to convince them that making the best of what they had was preferable to fighting a hopeless cause.

Between 1952–70 over half a million students had graduated from East Germany's universities and technical institutions. They were to a great extent responsible for the D D R's recent achievements and of these they were proud. Their collective and individual successes gave them a common consciousness. Many of them occupied positions of responsibility which they might not have gained had they lived in the Federal Republic. Such positions became available after early postwar purges, and the flight of senior colleagues to the West, or were created by expansion. In some cases, those holding such positions knew they had been favoured as students because of their working-class background. These factors, as well as fear of the secret police and growing alienation from the West welded the D D R's élite to the system. This should not be taken to imply that the members of this new mass élite were uncritically behind the regime—far from it— but they were unlikely to want to put their hard won gains in jeopardy by attempts to bring about sharp and sudden changes in the D D R. Their attitude depended on a number of factors including the satisfaction of their material expectations and their degree of participation in decision making.

This postwar generation of technicians, managers and members of the professions was gradually taking over the top positions from the older generation. The latter were, except for the salvaged remnants of the prewar bourgeois intelligentsia, often old Communist all-round functionaries rather than the academically trained specialists.

We can see the advance of this new generation in the Central Committee of the Socialist Unity Party. By 1964 well over 90 of the Committee's 181 full and candidate members could be placed in the category of the specialists. At the very top of the Party, in the Politburo, which was formally elected by the Central Committee, the old generation still dominated in 1970. Remarkably, this had changed but little by the mid-1970s, Walter Ulbricht apart. Who were the members of the Politburo, the rulers of the German Democratic Republic in 1970?

Walter Ulbricht, aged 77, had held the key position of first secretary of the S E D since 1950. He thus had more experience of power than any other Communist leader except for China's Mao Tse Tung and Enver Hoxha of Albania. As Chairman of the Council of State since the death of President Pieck in 1960, Ulbricht was head of state. He started life in a working-class home in Leipzig and, on leaving school, became an apprentice cabinet-maker. Conscripted into the army he opposed the 1914–18 war and became a founder member of the German Communist Party. By the early 1920s he was a full-time Communist official and by 1923 a member of the Central Committee. In the years which followed he served the Soviet Union, as the 'first Socialist State', faithfully, living in the U S S R from 1933 to 1945. The Soviets rewarded him with their support. This was the basis of his success. It was nonetheless remarkable that he should have survived so many major upheavals, so many twists and turns of Soviet policy.

Apart from Walter Ulbricht, the most experienced East German politician was Willi Stoph. Born in 1914, he joined the K P D in 1931. He was a truck driver in the German Army during the war, but his official biography credits him with 'illegal anti-fascist activity' between 1933–45. A former Defence Minister, he had been Prime Minister since the death of Herr Grotewohl in 1964, as well as member of the Politburo and of the Council of State. Erich Honecker was widely expected eventually to replace Ulbricht as S E D secretary, as he was Ulbricht's deputy. Born in 1912, the son of a miner, he became a K P D member in 1929, and spent ten years in prison under the Nazis. Hermann Matern, a veteran Communist, and Friedrich Ebert, former Social Democrat and son of the President of the Weimar Republic, were long-standing members of the Politburo. Both were well into their seventies and becoming less active in politics. Herbert Warnke (68), head of the trade unions, and Prof. Albert Norden (66), in charge of propaganda, could also be considered nearing the end of their careers. Of the younger members, Dr Günter Mittag (born 1926), a member of the Council of State, and one of the authors of the New Economic System, was the most prominent.

The members of the Politburo were a fairly homogeneous group. All, except Albert Norden, the son of a Rabbi, were from working-class backgrounds, and most were in the pre-1933 working-class movement. Contrary to common belief, few spent the war years in Moscow; most were either emigrants or in jail.

## *A new deal for women*

As mentioned above, to some limited extent, the rulers of the D D R had attempted to start a dialogue with their people. There was something like a genuine discussion on educational reform in the 1960s and on the Family Law of April 1966. Many feminists in West Germany and other countries regarded the new law as a great step forward in the fight to achieve full equality for women. The Family Law obliged both partners in marriage to do their share in educating any children they had, and in doing the housework. Both had the duty to contribute towards the maintenance of the family, though 'a spouse who has no income or means contributes through housework towards the upbringing of the children'. The Law broke new ground in respect of property. The property that each partner had on marriage remained their own, as did any gift acquired during the marriage. Property of any kind obtained during the marriage by work became the joint property of both. This implicitly rewarded women who spent their time as housewives and mothers. Another 'advanced' feature of the Family Law was that it did not grant the wife automatic right to be kept by the husband. In most situations she would have that right—as a fulltime mother, in sickness or old age, or during periods of study. In the latter case the husband had the duty to give her all the assistance he could, and could not force his wife to take up unskilled work if she preferred to undergo professional training. On the other hand, the Law made it more difficult to be a 'mere housewife' without family responsibilities.

East German women, as a group, had to face greater difficulties than their sisters in the Federal Republic. A far higher proportion of them were engaged in the economy and yet they had endured greater difficulties shopping, greater difficulties in finding dry-cleaners, hair-dressers and launderettes, and greater difficulties in getting repairs done. This situation had been changing for the better. And it must not be forgotten that East German mothers did at least find it much easier to get their children into nurseries than did mothers in Western countries.

It was impossible to say just how East German women viewed their government, how they reacted to the advantages and disadvantages of living in the D D R. As in other countries few women took part in politics. Only about 26 per cent of the S E D members were women, and in 1970 only one woman, Margarete Müller, had reached candidate membership of the Politburo. Another woman, Dr Grete Wittkowski, was President of the State Bank, and there were women members of the Council of State and Council of Ministers. With official encouragement women had been gradually taking on jobs and entering professions formerly monopolised by men.

## The Socialist Constitution of 1968

At the seventh congress of the S E D in 1967 Walter Ulbricht called for a new constitution for the D D R. Within a year a new constitution had replaced that of 1949. Why this change? The official explanation was that the D D R had become a socialist state and needed a socialist constitution. This might have been part of the truth. But more important was the leaders' determination to emphasise the sovereignty of the D D R, its difference from West Germany, and to underline to the world, and the people of East Germany, that there was no going back on their version of socialism. The new constitution was also in line with changes in some of the other East European states. Perhaps too, it was designed to offer hope to the East German people, that the dictatorial methods which had made the old constitution a dead letter would soon be a thing of the past.

Article 1 of the new constitution made clear the intended change. The D D R was described as 'a socialist state of the German nation', instead of merely a 'democratic Republic'. Unlike the old constitution, the new one recognised the leading role of the 'Marxist-Leninist party' and the 'socialist ownership of the means of production'. A number of rights of the individual were deleted—the right to strike and the right to emigrate, for instance. As for the formal institutions of the state, the Volkskammer lost some of its power to the Staatsrat (Council of State), which was set up after the death of President Pieck in 1960. In the Staatsrat its Chairman directed its work. Thus Herr Ulbricht's *de facto* power in this body was formally recognised. The government or Council of Ministers (Ministerrat) lost some of its power to the Council of State and was entrusted mainly with economic affairs. In turn the Council of Ministers was given more independence vis-à-vis the Volkskammer.

All in all, the constitution of 1968 was a little more realistic than that of 1949, and somewhat more authoritarian. Whether the provisions of the constitution would be observed was widely doubted.

## Into Czechoslovakia

Apart from giving unswerving support to the Soviet Union and the Warsaw Pact, the D D R's main preoccupation in foreign affairs was the battle for recognition. It found no difficulty in gaining recognition from the other Communist states including China. And after the rapprochement between Moscow and Belgrade, Tito and Ulbricht exchanged ambassadors in 1957. After Fidel Castro won power in Cuba that state forfeited its relations with Bonn by recognising the D D R. But until 1969 the D D R failed to win recognition from either the Western states or from any of the countries of the Third World. Only in 1969 was the D D R able to improve its official representation abroad. More will be said about this in the next chapter.

With its Warsaw Pact allies the D D R enjoyed, at the official level at any rate, good relations in the 1950s. They were united by ideology (except for Poland and Hungary in 1956), had common economic interests—and common fears about their own survival. In the case of the U S S R, Poland and Czechoslovakia, there was the additional fear of West German 'revanchism'. The greater flexibility shown by Bonn in the 1960s and its trade offensive in Eastern Europe caused Ulbricht some worries. He feared his allies would be prepared to exchange ambassadors with Bonn without getting assurances on frontiers and recognition of the D D R. Only in the case of Romania were these fears realised. The same might have happened in the case of Czechoslovakia but for the intervention of the Warsaw Pact forces in August 1968. Whether or not Herr Ulbricht played any significant role in persuading the Russians that something had to be done about the situation in Czechoslovakia, it is safe to assume he was worried about it. The liberals associated with the name of Alexander Dubcek, who took over the Czechoslovak C P in January 1968, were engaged in experiments which Ulbricht must have feared would catch on in the D D R. The East German frontier with Czechoslovakia was open, and thousands of East German tourists visited the country in 1968. An S E D Politburo resolution of 25 July 1968 regretted that the Czechs underestimated 'the anti-socialist forces at work in their country and the dangers of interference from Bonn'. Subsequent meetings between delegations of the other Warsaw Pact parties with the Czechs, including an encounter by Ulbricht and Dubcek at Karlovy Vary on 12 August, apparently did nothing to still the fears of the Soviet, D D R, and other East European leaderships. The result was that their tanks and troops poured into Czechoslovakia on 21 August.

The D D R officially regained its sovereignty in 1955 but in its relations with the U S S R it remained less than equal. The relations were governed by the massive Soviet military and security presence in East Germany and by the fact that roughly three-quarters of the D D R's trade was done with the Soviet Union. Nevertheless Western observers noticed a somewhat more independent attitude on the part of East German leaders during the 1960s. This was believed to be due to the D D R's growing economic strength, its apparent stability, the great need for the Soviet Union to find allies in the Communist camp against China, and, perhaps Herr Ulbricht's personal conviction that he was far more experienced at the top than any of the Soviet leaders. The relations between the two states were formally governed by treaties signed in 1955 and 1964.

# — 11 —

# West Germany in the Sixties

The time between Dr Erhard assuming office in 1963 and his next appointment with the electorate, in September 1965, was not an easy period for him. It would have been difficult for any man to fill Adenauer's shoes, and the ex-Chancellor, despite his advanced age, still wanted to play a role in German politics. He remained a member of the Bundestag and as Chairman of the C D U criticised his successor. In effect he claimed Erhard was becoming soft on the 'Reds' and was endangering West Germany's good relations with France. This naturally encouraged his rivals to remain active. But he had troubles in other directions. There was a growing crisis in the Ruhr, a continuing crisis in agriculture and a new crop of scandals connected with Germany's dark past.

The crisis in the Ruhr mining industry did not suddenly arise in 1963. It had been going on since about 1958 and was similar to that facing the coalmining industries in other countries: oil was replacing coal as a means of cheap, economical fuel and therefore only the most efficient mines would survive in the shrinking market. In 1958 West Germany used 125.2 million tons of hard coal. The amount in 1963 actually rose to 127 million tons, but fell in 1965 to 114.4. In 1967 it was down to 97.1 million tons. The amount of mineral oil rose year by year over this period from 27.3 million tons in 1958 to 124.8 million tons in 1967. The amount of natural gas, though still small, rose greatly over the same period. In about the same years some 250,000 miners lost their jobs. Subsidies, tax on oil and protection against foreign coal were the main weapons used to fight the crisis. Nevertheless, in the sixties it appeared to be a losing battle. Critics have claimed more could have been done to attract outside industry to the area.

The crisis of West German agriculture is illustrated by two figures. Firstly, between 1949 and 1965 the number of farms declined by 488,000. Secondly, between 1950 and 1965 the number of those working in agriculture fell from over five million to just under three million. As was only to be expected the farmers were increasingly angry and demanded a ban on imports.

## Trouble in the Bundeswehr

Another headache for Dr Erhard was the controversy which sur-rounded the retirement, in 1964, of Vice-Admiral Hellmuth Heye, the Parliamentary Commissioner for the Armed Forces. Due in large measure to the efforts of the Social Democrats, the West German soldier has far more rights than either earlier German soldiers or the soldiers of most other countries. He is supposed to be a 'citizen in uniform': as such he can take part in political activities, join a trade union, though not strike. If he commits a serious offence, he will be tried by a civilian court for there are no military courts in the Federal Republic. On the Swedish pattern a Parliamentary Commissioner (*Wehrbeauftragter*) will work to protect the rights of individual soldiers and take up their grievances. Because of opposition from the right it took over a year and a half's discussion before the first Commissioner was appointed. He was an ex-general and was sub-sequently dismissed for alleged homosexual offences. His successor was ex-Admiral Heye who came from an old military family and had been a C D U member of the Bundestag. In three articles published in 1964 in the weekly magazine *Quick*, and in an interview in *Der Spiegel*, the Admiral claimed that there was a danger that the Bundeswehr was developing into a 'state within a state'. When told by his critics that such allegations belonged in his annual report to parliament rather than in a popular magazine, Heye retorted that after two and a half years in the post he felt more drastic action was required to make parliament and public take note. The Admiral was subsequently forced out of office. Heye's view that all was not well in the Bundeswehr seemed to be vindicated by a number of cases of brutality, involving deaths of servicemen, which came to light in 1963–64.

Differences over the running of the armed forces, the rights of servicemen and so on led, during the Chancellorship of Dr Erhard, to the resignations or dismissals of three top officers including General Trettner, Inspector General of the Bundeswehr.

That the struggle between the traditionalists and the democrats in the Bundeswehr still was not solved as West Germany entered the seventies was indicated during the 'Grashey Affair' at the time of the Grand Coalition. General-major Helmut Grashey, deputy commander of the West German Army, delivered a lecture, early in 1969, at the staff academy of the Bundeswehr in Hamburg. In his lecture he said it was time to throw out the ideas of the 'citizen-in-uniform' which, he claimed, had been merely a concession to the S P D. He attacked the Commissioner and the civil administrators of the armed forces.

Grashey's superior, General Albert Schnez, commander of the Federal Republic's land forces, shielded Grashey from attack. He himself had failed to get a top N A T O post because of Dutch objections based on his wartime record. After the setting up of the S P D-F D P coalition in 1969, Helmut Schmidt, Social Democratic Minister of Defence, ordered the removal of Grashey, from the Defence Ministry to another command. Grashey, however, decided to retire. In a semi-secret report to his staff officers, which became public in January 1970, Schnez fully endorsed the views of his subordinate.

Over the years the Bundeswehr was plagued by rumours of corruption, allegations of military inefficiency, and accidents often caused by faulty equipment. Just one example, up to May 1970, 120 Starfighters had crashed with the loss of 56 pilots.

## Election 1965

The differences in the Christian Democratic camp remained bitter and deep before, during and after the election of 1965. Remarkably perhaps in these circumstances, the C D U/C S U emerged once again as the strongest party with 47.6 per cent of the vote and 245 seats. But the Social Democrats also improved their position winning 39.3 per cent and 202 seats. The Free Democratic vote slumped to 9.5 per cent and this gave them 49 seats. The F D P was less credible than it had been in 1961 as a party of new initiatives in both foreign and internal policy, for of course it had once again been enjoying office with the Christian Democrats. The S P D, which in 1961 had campaigned for television sets for old-age pensioners, clean air and 'modern weapons' for the Bundeswehr, became even vaguer in 1965. This might have cost it votes. Most of its hard policy campaigning was done for it by its intellectual fringe headed by the famous author Günter Grass. He saw his task as winning over floating middle-class voters who might otherwise vote F D P or for the neutralist splinter group the German Peace Union (D F U). He spotlighted the 'forgotten' issues such as the recognition of the Oder-Neisse Line and legalised abortion because '10,000 women die every year in West Germany from the consequences of illegal ones'. Another famous and controversial intellectual, Rolf Hochhuth, author of *The Representative*, wrote a pro- S P D paperback. It is doubtful whether the intellectuals made much impact. And they were in serious danger of being disowned by the party leaders who were playing it safe. One serious election analyst, Prof. Erwin K. Scheuch of Cologne, wrote after the election that the S P D had undoubtedly gained from its attempt to woo the Catholics but, he continued, 'it was badly advised when it believed it had to do away with policy'. It had underestimated the electors. Willy Brandt was later to admit that he too thought the party had concentrated too much on its 'image' and not enough on policy. One ugly aspect of the campaign, and it was not the first time it had happened, were the continuous attacks on Herr Brandt because he was born illegitimate and because he had been an emigrant. What should have been a mark in his favour, his wartime journalistic activities in Sweden against Nazism, was used to discredit him. So dispirited was Herr Brandt after the election that he announced his intention of retiring as Chancellor Candidate of the S P D.

It took Prof. Erhard a good deal of hard bargaining to resurrect his coalition with the Free Democrats. And as the leading Hamburg weekly *Die Zeit* commented, 'Erhard is building a coalition in which all the participants are dissatisfied'. Another leading paper, *Die Frankfurter Allgemeine Zeitung*, thought the coalition was in danger of developing the 'neurotic turbulence of a Strindberg marriage'.

Apart from the growing crisis in the Ruhr coal-field and arguments about Länder finance, two of the major problems which faced the Erhard government were what to do about the new nationalists and the student revolt.

## The New Nationalists

Numerous attempts had been made in West Germany over the postwar period to found a successful far-Right party. Up to the 1960s the most successful had been the Socialist Reich Party led by Col. Otto Ernst Remer and Fritz Dorls (among others). Set up in October 1949 and openly Nazi, the party achieved notable successes in the Land elections in 1951 in Lower Saxony (11 per cent of the vote) and Bremen (7.7 per cent). It elected 16 members in Lower Saxony and 8 in Bremen. In October 1952 the party was banned as unconstitutional. This ban did not stop the setting up of new Right-wing parties every year since 1952. These were all without success. One party did manage to stand out among the many Right-wing groups. This was the German Reichs Party (D R P) established in 1950. Two of the more significant leaders were Adolf von Thadden and Wilhelm Meinberg, holder of the Nazi party's gold medal, former S S officer and Nazi member of the Reichstag. Perhaps more important than the D R P in these years as a means of carrying out Nazi ideas were the products of many far-Right publishing houses. The most important of these was that belonging to Dr Gerhard Frey publisher of *Die Deutsche National-*

*Zeitung und Soldaten-Zeitung* and other journals. Dr Frey boosted circulation by attacks on S P D politicians as traitors, attacks on Israel and with articles designed to show stories about Nazi crimes were myths and that in reality the Allies were the war criminals.

After the setting up of the National Democratic Party (N P D) in November 1964 the fortunes of the far Right appeared to be improving. The hard core of the new party were former members of the D R P. They joined together with remnants of the Refugee Party, and other Right-wing groups. Fritz Thielen of the D P was elected Chairman. His Vice-Chairmen were Wilhelm Gutmann (Refugee Party), Adolf von Thadden and Heinrich Fassbender (a veteran of several far-Right failures).

Despite the limited time available to it, the new party gained about 600,000 votes or 2 per cent of the valid votes in the Federal election of 1965. It was in 1966 that the world started to take notice of the N P D. At the Land election in Hamburg held in March of that year it managed 3.9 per cent of the poll. This rose to 7.4 per cent in Bavaria and 7.9 per cent in Hesse in November. The party gained representation in both regional parliaments. Its success was a factor in the fall of Dr Erhard. The F D P, on the other hand, failed to return any of its members to the Bavarian parliament. The formation of the Grand Coalition of the Christian Democrats and the S P D at the end of the year helped the N P D to further successes. Between April 1967 and April 1968 it gained seats in Schleswig-Holstein, Rhineland-Pfalz, Lower Saxony, Bremen and Baden-Wüttemberg. The 'rise' of the National Democrats caused a healthy reaction among German trade unionists, students and many other West Germans. However, it should be pointed out that the party had gained 'only' 60 seats out of a total 849 in these Länder parliaments.

Who were the nearly two million West Germans who had given their votes to this party of revenge and resentment? They were more likely to be Protestant than Catholic, especially Protestants in Catholic areas. They were more likely to be inhabitants of villages, small and middle-sized towns than large towns. Those in small businesses, officials and the middle classes were over-represented among N P D voters but N P D supporters came from every occupation and social group. Trade unionists were under-represented among N P D supporters; refugees over-represented, though not remarkably so. Men tended to vote N P D more frequently than women. The party attracted all age groups but the Nazi generation (30 to 59) was strongly represented and it did best in what were the hard-core Nazi areas in the 1920s and early 1930s. It also did well in areas where there had been a relatively high proportion of non-voters. It made gains from the F D P, to a lesser extent from the S P D, and from the C D U/C S U.

The members of the N P D were similar to its voters. Their political backgrounds were, as one would expect, more markedly far right. In 1966 twenty per cent of the members were former Nazi party members. As the party expanded its membership this sank to 9 per cent by the end of 1967. Of 18 members of the party's first Federal Executive Committee 12 were former active Nazis. At the Land level, 300 of the party's 446 officials in 1968 had earlier far Right connections. But only 14 of its 60 members of Länder parliaments were former Nazi party members.

In their programme and political utterances, although they stressed that they stood by the constitution of the Federal Republic, the N P D leaders advocated measures which bore a striking resemblance to those advocated by Nazi and nationalists before and after 1933. Xenophobia is one of the key elements of the N P D programme as published in 1967. The very first words are 'foreign power', which 'oppresses divided Germany in a divided Europe ... The Germans still bend to the will of the victors who have divided Germany and Europe among themselves'. The N P D is presented as an organised protest against materialism which can only be overcome by recognising past ideals that are now despised. The older generation wrongly sits in the dock while the young are seduced to turn away from German history. In this way Germany is capitulating spiritually as well as it did militarily, with the result that foreign rule will become permanent. As far as the state is concerned, the N P D wants strong government, with a strong President directly elected by the people. All laws introduced under the influence of the victors are to be removed from the statute book. In education the N P D calls for a national, centralised educational system, based on proven German methods. Experimentation is to end. Education must be based on the natural connection between People and Fatherland, Family and Homeland (*Heimat*). The economy is to be based on entrepreneurial initiative and state planning. Government expenditure must be curbed. But German agriculture must be protected and encouraged, the workers must be guaranteed their jobs against foreigners. Codetermination should not mean outside trade union officials in the factories. In its defence policy the N P D demands a policy aimed at European defence: 'We need a military force strong enough to deter every possible enemy'. Foreign troops should be withdrawn from Germany. The Bundeswehr needs a soldierly spirit, must be free of trade-union or any other political influence, and must be free of civilian administrators. Former Waffen-S S men should be given the same treatment as other former members of the German armed forces, and former P O Ws must receive compensation which is at least equal to that of former political prisoners. The N P D rejects the view that Germany alone was guilty for the last war and demands the return of 'East Germany', meaning the territories beyond the Oder-Neisse, and the Sudetenland. The Federal Republic has the responsibility for 'Middle Germany' (D D R).

What were the causes of the National Democratic Party's relative success in the second half of the 1960s? With the magnetic and authoritarian personality of Dr Adenauer out of the way Right-wing voters, not very committed to Christian Democracy as such, possibly felt the new C D U/C S U leadership no longer represented their aspirations. Secondly, the Free Democratic Party's Left-wing was becoming more vocal and was attracting to the party other Left liberals. Prof. Ralf Dahrendorf, the noted liberal sociologist, son of a S P D politician and critic of German traditionalism, joined the F D P in this period. Thirdly, the spread of 'Gaullist' ideas and the failure of the Western Allies to achieve German reunification helped to create the new nationalism. In 1965, according to a poll carried out by the Emnid Institute, 69 per cent of West Germans put the reunification of Germany before European unity. In 1951 only 55 per cent had done so. (In the period 1955–56 over 75 per cent had done so.) Perhaps too, the fact that the N P D leaders tried hard to appear, by far-right standards, sensible, respectable, middle-class spokesmen, operating within the constitution, helped it to gain old-fashioned nationalists and former Nazis grown 'soft' in the affluent society. The economic recession of 1966–67 certainly provided the party with coal-miners and farmers who felt they had been forgotten by the orthodox politicians. The setting up of the grand coalition of Christian and Social Democrats in December 1966 strengthened this feeling. The machine politicians, *die Bonzen*, appeared to be ganging up against *der kleine Mann*, the 'little man' or the man in the street. Resentment against foreign workers was also a likely cause. According to figures published by the Ministry for Economic Affairs in Bonn, there were 329,000 foreign workers in West Germany in 1960 (1.5 per cent of the labour force). The number rose year by year until it reached 1,313,000 or 6.1 per cent of the labour force, in September 1966. It then started to fall. Finally, the N P D appealed to Refugee party and D P members who had not managed to find a home in one of the other three parties.

With growing concern abroad and demonstrations, sometimes, ending in violence, every time the N P D held a major meeting, the Federal Republic's major politicians were under increasing pressure to find a solution to the N P D. There were those who argued that the mere existence of such a party was an insult to Hitler's victims and that therefore the party should be banned. Others believed that any attempt to drive the N P D underground would make matters worse, especially as it appeared to be keeping within the letter of the law. Some worried about the Republic's image abroad, others about the bait it offered to Left-wing student militants. Some of the more Right-wing Christian Democratic and Free Democratic politicians feared that any action to ban the National Democrats would cost them the support of their own more extreme followers, who sympathised with many of the things said by N P D politicians. The most embarrassing aspect of the N P D's success was that it would qualify for public funds. Under the Party Law (*Parteiengesetz*) of July 1967 West German political parties have the right to financial assistance from public revenue. It was later laid down that parties gaining 0.5 per cent of the vote would qualify. By the start of the 1970s the Federal Republic had not decided what to do about the N P D.

## The Grand Coalition

As mentioned above, Prof. Erhard was under fire from his own colleagues, as well as the opposition, and was faced with the rise of the N P D, with the student revolt and with an economic recession. The number of unemployed, though small, started to rise. Another blow fell in July 1966. At elections in North Rhine-Westphalia the Social Democrats made considerable gains coming within two seats of winning an absolute majority. Erhard's critics in his own party were emboldened by this result. In August Herr Eugen Gerstenmaier, C D U President of the Bundestag, told the world that it was time Erhard went and that he himself was prepared to take his place. The Chancellor's fate was virtually sealed on 27 October when the F D P announced its intention to withdraw from the government. Erhard countered by reallocating F D P posts to his Christian Democratic Ministers. But the following day he had yet another problem. The Bundesrat decided to reject the budget proposals. The Land elections in Hesse a matter of days later finished off 'rubber lion' Erhard. Though the S P D only achieved a slight increase in its already absolute majority, the 2.4 per cent decline in the C D U vote was seen as a defeat for Erhard. The following day the Social Democrats, with F D P assistance, got a motion through the Bundestag asking Erhard to give parliament a chance to vote on a motion of confidence. By 10 November the Christian Democrats had agreed on a new Chancellor candidate, Dr Kurt Georg Kiesinger, Prime Minister of

Baden-Württemberg, and nominee of Franz Josef Strauss. Who would the Doctor seek as his coalition partners?

The Free Democrats were not enthusiastic about renewing their partnership with the C D U/C S U. The Christians were not very attracted to them. There was bad feeling because of the break-up of the government, and they still opposed Strauss, and, in any case, were not strong in numbers. The Social Democrats had the numbers, and in recent years had come to favour a 'Grand Coalition' with the Christian Democrats. They had the backing of (C D U) Federal President, Heinrich Lübke. Would the Social Democrats accept Franz Josef Strauss? They had strongly attacked him in the past but the chance of office helped them to modify their opposition to him. For them it was a very difficult position. Herr Erich Mende, F D P leader, could not guarantee that all his group would support a mini coalition of S P D and F D P. Even had such a government been formed with the full backing of all the F D P group it would have rested on a small majority. It would have inherited an economic crisis which, had it got worse, could have seriously dented the image of the S P D. Such a government would have favoured a more flexible Eastern policy, but, it was argued, it would be under sharp attack from the Christian Democrats for being soft on the Reds, or as a government of 'renunciation politicians', that is, those prepared to renounce Germany's interests. Further S P D leaders, notably Herbert Wehner, argued that if they could enter a strong government, they could prove to the electorate that they were competent ministers and this would improve their chances at the next election.

Dr Kiesinger's government included the following prominent politicians: Herr Brandt, as Vice-Chancellor and Foreign Minister, Prof. Karl Schiller (S P D), Minister of Economics, Herr Strauss, Finance Minister, Dr Gerhard Schröder (C D U), Defence Minister, Herbert Wehner (S P D), Minister for All-German Affairs, Dr Gustav Heinemann (S P D), Minister of Justice, and Paul Lücke (Interior), Kai-Uwe von Hassel (Refugees) and Hermann Höcherl (Agriculture) of the C D U/C S U, and Georg Leber (Transport) and Carlo Schmid (Bundesrat affairs) of the S P D. In all there were eleven, including the Chancellor, C D U/C S U Ministers, and nine Social Democrats.

The new government gave the S P D their first taste of office since before 1933 but rank-and-file members, including parliamentarians, were far from happy about it. They found a spokesman in Günter Grass. In open letters to both Kiesinger and Brandt he attacked the Chancellor. 'Is there not in the S P D/C S U/C D U a man with a clean enough record to take over the office of Chancellor?', he asked. He was of course referring to the fact that Dr Kiesinger had been a member of the Nazi party and had held a highly responsible post in the Foreign Office under the Nazis. Grass argued that Kiesinger's appointment helped to make the N P D's ex-Nazis respectable, an argument the National Democrats were later to use themselves. They also pointed out that Prof. Schiller had been a Nazi party member. To make matters worse, in the first year of the Grand Coalition the recession deepened and the S P D's electoral stock fell. In three regional elections in that year it lost ground.

When Herr Brandt took over as Foreign Minister it was expected that Bonn would make at least a partial reappraisal of its policy towards the D D R and East Europe. Brandt's policy was that of 'small steps' towards minor improvements in relations between East and West. The Foreign Minister also felt that the Hallstein Doctrine had outlived its usefulness. During Dr Erhard's term of office Bonn's relations with the Third World had worsened. Its close relations with Israel had led to a deterioration of its relations with the Arab states. In October 1964 Herr Ulbricht had paid a state visit to Cairo and Bonn had sought revenge against President Nasser by recognising Israel. Ten Arab states then broke off diplomatic relations with the Federal Republic. Under Adenauer, Bonn had broken off relations with Yugoslavia and Cuba when they recognised East Germany. The Arab states did not give full and formal recognition to the D D R but the danger was that they would do so making it so much more difficult to resume relations with Bonn in the future. The Social Democrats could not persuade their colleagues to abandon the Doctrine mainly because of the attitude of the C S U. In 1969 Egypt, Iraq, Sudan, Syria, South Yemen and Cambodia recognised the D D R. Bonn no longer had relations with the five Arab states but complications arose with Cambodia. Bonn did not break off relations as such but recalled its Ambassador declaring he 'is and will remain recalled'. This provoked Cambodia to break off relations. In Eastern Europe the Federal Republic had achieved success by establishing diplomatic relations with Romania in January 1967. This had represented a dent in the Hallstein Doctrine for Romania retained its ties with East Berlin. Bonn claimed that it was prepared to make exceptions in the case of the Soviet Bloc states because they were not free to decide between the two Germanies. Because it would not recognise the Oder-Neisse frontier or the D D R, or sign the Non-Proliferation Treaty, or clearly renounce a nuclear role, the Federal Republic was unable to establish formal relations with any of the other Warsaw Pact countries though in 1968 it once again exchanged ambassadors with Belgrade. Yugoslavia retained its relations with the D D R.

## The S D S and the student revolt

Certainly up to the mid-1950s German students tended to be conformist in their political views. Towards the end of the 1950s some change was noticeable. This was provoked by rearmament including the reintroduction of conscription which directly affected students, the campaign against nuclear arms, the changes for the better in Eastern Europe, the failure of Adenauer's policy to achieve reunification, the struggles of countries like Algeria for independence, the emergence of new social models in China and Cuba, the 'Leftward' trend in the Vatican and the other churches, and the poor conditions which the students had to put up with. The scandals concerning ex-Nazis and the *Spiegel* Affair (see p. 164) in the early 1960s further contributed to make students more critical of their society.

The changing pattern was seen in the development of the S D S, *Der Sozialistische Deutsche Studentenbund*, the Socialist German Students' League. This body had been set up after 1945 as the official Social Democratic student body and for years had been regarded as one of the most moderate of the European socialist student organisations. However, at a congress held at Frankfurt in the summer of 1959, the S D S turned sharply Left just at a time when the parent body was turning Right. In the following year the S P D dissociated itself from the S D S. Deprived of the main sources of its funds, the S D S might have failed but for the assistance it received from certain Left-wing academics—Professors Wolfgang Abendroth of Marburg and Ossip K. Flechtheim of the Free University of West Berlin were the most prominent—who formed a sponsoring society, *Der Sozialistische Bund*. The S D S was able to hold its own against the new Social Democratic University League (S H B).

The Free University of West Berlin had by this time gained a special position in higher education in West Germany. Modelled on American lines, its structure had encouraged its students to take a greater part in running things than was traditionally the case at German universities. In this way its students gained in self confidence. It had built up a high reputation for its political science teaching, thus attracting to it some of the more critical students attracted to that discipline. Both parts of Berlin became competing markets of world culture and ideas which the students savoured drawing from both. The Free University admitted a fair number of refugee students from the D D R some of whom claimed to be Marxist and socialist, but against the S E D. Large numbers of students came from West Germany proper, some of whom sought to avoid military service by studying in West Berlin (where the conscription law was not in force). Given this special position of the Free University it is not surprising that the increasing critical awareness of West German students should manifest itself there.

In the 1960s the S D S was able to organise a number of headline-making demonstrations in West Berlin. The first of these was in December 1964, when several hundred students demonstrated against the then Congolese Premier, Moise Tshombe. In February 1966, 1,500 students took to the streets against American policy in Vietnam in a march authorised by the authorities. In December of the same year 1,000 students defied the police to make a similar protest. In April 1967 2,000 turned out against American Vice-President Hubert Humphrey. In between there were several demos, including a sit-in involving 3,000 against the university authorities for preventing the use of official buildings for political meetings. More dramatic was the reception given the Shah of Iran who had abuse and tomatoes hurled at him. On that occasion, 2 June 1967, a 26-year-old student Benno Ohnesorg was shot in the back by a plain-clothes policeman. A demonstration of 4,000 followed to protest against the shooting, and silent marches were held throughout West Germany on the day of his funeral, involving 100,000 students.

1968 and 1969 saw more student demonstrations and more violence in many parts of West Germany. The approaching federal elections raised the temperature and made students more political. So did the student revolt in Paris in May 1968, the N P D, the assassination attempt against S D S leader Rudi Dutschke in April, the continuing Vietnam War and the passage of the emergency powers' laws (*Notstandsgesetze*) by the Federal Parliament. The fact that the bulk of the members of the Bundestag belonged to the government parties seemed additional proof that West German democracy was a sham. During this period the S D S moved further and further away from the traditional Marxist, state-socialist ideology, in favour of a mixture of the teachings of the Russian anarchist Bakunin, the American 'New Leftist' Herbert Marcuse, Mao Tse-tung, and the South American revolutionist Che Guevara. Trotsky and Lenin also gained, or retained, a few admirers.

Despite the successes of the S D S it remained a small body amongst the total student population. In the autumn term of 1966 the Christian Democratic student organisation (R C D S) with 2,200 members was the largest student political society. It was followed by the S H B with 1,500 members. The S D S came third with 1,200 and the League of Liberal Students (L S D) fourth with 900. A year later the S D S had 2,500 members, the S H B, which was moving in the direction of the S D S, 2,000, and the L S D 1,100. The R C D S was in a state of complete stagnation. Nevertheless, all these student bodies put together represented only a small proportion of the student body of nearly 300,000 students in the mid-1960s. The traditionalist fencing fraternities (*Verbindungen*) had more members. And a survey published in *Der Spiegel* (19 June 1967) showed that the great majority of students had no clear, and certainly no Leftist, political orientation. However, many students could be won for occasional S D S activities because of a vague concern for some of the issues mentioned above, and a feeling of dissatisfaction about conditions at the universities and in the schools.

German schools were overcrowded and especially in the agricultural areas conditions were bad. In the 1950s the number of single-class schools with one teacher for all grades was actually increasing. The war had caused great destruction of school buildings. Even so, in 1961, 50 per cent of them dated from before 1905. Traditional regional differences had been accentuated by the federal system. In Hesse, with a population of about five million in 1965, 11.6 per cent of the appropriate age group were able to pass the *Abitur*, the university matriculation exam, in 1964. In the Rhineland, with a population of about three and a half million, only 5.1 per cent got their *Abitur* in 1964. As Prof. Dahrendorf, for one, has often pointed out, it was still very difficult for working-class children to get an education commensurate with their abilities. Children from agricultural areas, Catholics and girls were others who could be described as the educationally underprivileged. This lack of opportunity was indicated by the fact that only about four or five per cent of university students in West Germany were from working-class homes, although the majority of people were working class. In Britain and the D D R a higher proportion of students were from the blue collar class. In the early 1960s about one third of the West German population lived in towns of over 100,000. At the same time 53 per cent of students at West German universities came from these towns. Unlike those of Britain or East Germany most students in the Federal Republic in the 1960s had to finance their studies themselves. This obviously made it more difficult for the less well off. It meant too that the majority of better-off students were dependent on their parents. In 1965 Prof. Dahrendorf, in *Die Zeit* (23 April), summed up the situation of the German universities as follows: the German university admits too few students; of those who are admitted too many leave without qualifying; those who do complete their studies study too long; what they learn is too little in terms of quality and quantity.

## Brandt becomes Chancellor

As we have seen, after the S P D joined the Grand Coalition it suffered a number of electoral reverses. In 1969 the climate of opinion started to move more in its favour. The economy took a turn for the better and this became associated in the public mind with Prof. Karl Schiller, the Social Democratic Minister of Economics. Only Chancellor Kiesinger was regarded as more popular among the government politicians. In March the S P D got another boost by the election of Dr Gustav Heinemann to the Federal Presidency. The election took place earlier than expected because of the unscheduled retirement of Heinrich Lübke. For some years the East Germans had attacked Herr Lübke claiming that he had designed and built concentration camps during the war. This he had always denied. In January 1968 the weekly *Der Stern* broke the news that J. Howard Haring, an American hand-writing expert who had worked for General Motors, I B M and Shell, as well as for the District Attorney of New York, had stated his view that signatures on wartime blueprints of concentration camps were undoubtedly Lübke's. Pressure on Herr Lübke grew until he was finally forced to go.

Dr Heinemann was opposed by Dr Schöder in the Federal Meeting. About 90 per cent of the Free Democratic delegates voted for the Social Democrat indicating to the S P D as *Die Frankfurter Allegmeine Zeitung* saw it, that they could be reliable coalition partners. Dr Heinemann was the first Social Democrat to be President in Germany since the death of Friedrich Ebert in 1925.

The federal elections of 1969 were hard fought considering the two main contenders had been, and were still during the election, in a coalition government together. The changes were not dramatic. With 15.2 million votes (46.1 per cent) the Christian Democrats received only 300,000 fewer than in 1965. The S P D gained over 14 million votes, an increase of roughly 1.2 million, which represented 42.7 per cent of the poll. The Social Democrats increased their parliamentary strength by 22 giving them 224 seats as against 242 for the Christians. The F D P slumped from over 3 million votes to 1.9 million (5.8 per cent) emerging with 30 seats, a loss of 19. The dreaded N P D attracted 1.4 million votes (4.3 per cent) which did not qualify them for representation in the Bundestag. The Left-wing A D F gained only 197,570 (0.6 per cent).

The Social Democratic gains were made predominently in white-collar, dormitory areas, for instance, around Cologne and Bonn, in Hamburg and the nearby districts in Schleswig-Holstein. The S P D failed to attract more working-class support but it got itself across to the younger white-collar and professional people. This could be a long-term danger to the Christian Democrats for as the economy changes there are more of these voters. They tend to be either indifferent to or, at least, less bound to the churches, a fact which has led a minority in the C D U/C S U to ask whether they ought not to drop the 'C' from the title of their party. West Germany is becoming more urbanised and since 1961 it has gained less support than the S P D in these areas. In the towns of over 100,000 inhabitants it gained 62 seats in 1957 as against 27 for the S P D. In 1961 the figures were 41 and 49, in 1965 30 and 60, and in 1969 14 and 76 respectively. In 1965 33.2 per cent lived in such towns. These people were more convinced by the S P D's 'We'll create the modern Germany' than the C D U/C S U's 'It depends on the Chancellor'. The Christian Democrats argued: We built the affluent society without the S P D; look at the state of 'Socialist Britain'; the S P D's 'soft' line on Eastern policy had been exploded by the Soviet invasion of Czechoslovakia; and the student agitators were close intellectually and even personally to the S P D. These arguments did not have the desired impact.

The Free Democrats of Walter Scheel lost ground as a result of their recent swing to the Left. The results indicated that the C D U and the N P D had gained from F D P losses. That a great many of those who gave their second vote to the F D P wanted a coalition with the S P D was indicated by the fact that they gave their first votes to the candidates of Brandt.

The Left-wing A D F or Action for Democratic Progress undoubtedly suffered from its association with Soviet Communism. It was an alliance of the neutralist D F U, the recently formed German Communist Party (D K P, not to be confused with the K P D which still claimed to exist underground) and other tiny groups. The D K P failed to condemn the Soviet action in Czechoslovakia. Most S D S students and supporters would not consider voting for these orthodox Communists and those associated with them. The A D F was hit as well by the argument that a vote for it was a wasted vote.

Herr von Thadden's candidates lost some of their protest support when the economic situation improved. There is no doubt that the long-sustained campaign against the N P D frightened off some people who thought it was not respectable.

The Christian Democrats fumed against the possibility of the S P D/F D P coalition and offered talks to the leaders of both parties. After the success of the coalition negotiations between the Social and Free Democrats, Herr Brandt was elected Chancellor on 21 October by 251 votes to 235 with 5 abstentions and 4 invalid. As a successful candidate for Chancellor must receive more than half the votes of the

Bundestag's total membership he needed 249 votes. Thus he was elected by a margin of only two votes. All S P D and F D P members were present and it can therefore be assumed that three of the F D P had either abstained or spoilt their papers.

The main appointments in the new coalition were: Willy Brandt, Chancellor; Walter Scheel, F D P Leader and former Minister for Economic Aid, Foreign Minister; Prof. Karl Schiller, former Rector of Hamburg University, Minister of Economics; Helmut Schmidt, former wartime Lieutenant and veteran S P D defence spokesman, Minister of Defence; Hans-Dietrich Genscher (F D P), Minister of Interior; Georg Leber (S P D), the leader of the Building Trade Union, Minister of Traffic, Posts and Telecommunications; Josef Ertl, the right-wing Bavarian Free Democrat, Minister of Agriculture. A non-party appointment, that of Prof. Hans Leussink as Minister of Education and Science, caused some surprise. Herr Leussink is a professional engineer and former Rector of the Karlsruhe Technical University. In all the Cabinet comprised 12 S P D members, 3 F D P and Herr Leussink. One important S P D member not in the government was Herr Herbert Wehner, Minister for All-German Affairs in the Grand Coalition. Herr Wehner took on the important job of leading his party's group in the Bundestag.

The most pressing problem calling for immediate action was a revaluation of the currency. From 1952 onwards West Germany had a surplus on its foreign trade and many economists believed the Mark was undervalued. A huge surplus in 1967, partly the result of a drop in imports brought on by the recession, and the international monetary crisis of November 1968 brought renewed demands from West Germany's allies to revalue the mark. As the Christian Democrats opposed this nothing was done. The controversy became dramatic during the election with Kiesinger and Strauss opposing, and Schiller favouring, revaluation. In two days the equivalent of $540 m. flowed in. The foreign exchange markets were closed temporarily. The old government allowed the mark to 'float'. The new Cabinet at its first meeting revalued the currency by 9.28 per cent which made West German exports dearer abroad and foreign imports cheaper. This decision, like that to float the mark, hit Federal Germany's agriculture. Measures to protect it brought the old government into conflict with the other members of the Six. After hard bargaining the new mini-coalition was permitted by the other Common Market states to grant subsidies of various kinds to West German agriculture.

The new coalition faced some tough problems, the principal one of which was how to stay in existence, and attacks on government policy by former F D P leader Erich Mende did not augur well for its future.

# — 12 —

# The Social-Liberal Coalition

## Brandt and Ostpolitik

The 13 years 1969–82 were a period in which West Germany seemed to gain a greater importance, a new stature, in the international community. This was made possible by the Federal Republic's continued economic expansion, and by its active diplomacy. The *Ostpolitik* of the early years of the S P D-F D P coalition laid the foundations of this new influence.

Willy Brandt outlined his policy towards Poland in a press conference after his election as Chancellor on 21 October 1969. He welcomed the idea of opening diplomatic relations in the near future. A week later he indicated his view of relations with the German Democratic Republic. He reiterated the traditional West German position on the unity of the German people, commenting, 'Even if there exist two states in Germany, they are not foreign countries to each other; their relations with each other can only be of a special nature'. He then went on to offer the East Germans negotiations at government level without discrimination on either side, which should lead to contractually agreed co-operation. For the first time a West German Chancellor had recognised the existence of the German Democratic Republic. Willi Stoph, Chairman of the Council of Ministers of the D D R, found Brandt's statement full of contradictions but 'there was a hint in it of a more realistic assessment of the situation created in Europe as a result of the Second World War'. On this basis, Walter Ulbricht presented a draft treaty on relations between the two German states to President Heinemann. After more statements, some delays, correspondence and backstairs diplomacy, Brandt and Stoph met at Erfurt (D D R) on 19 March 1970. The people of that ancient town gave Brandt an enthusiastic welcome which seems to have taken the politicians of both states somewhat by surprise. The two heads of government conferred again in the West German town of Kassel on 21 May. In the meantime the two states had signed a postal agreement and Bonn announced measures aimed at helping the other Germany to export more to the Federal Republic and thus reduce its trade deficit. As a further gesture to the S E D, the Bundestag repealed the so-called 'safe conduct' law. Highly offensive to the East German leadership, this had granted certain S E D politicians immunity from prosecution on visits to West Germany. It had been originally introduced at the time of the abortive S P D-S E D talks of 1966. Negotiations also followed with the U S S R, Brandt fully understanding that on their success depended the future of relations with East Germany. A treaty on the renunciation of force was signed in Moscow on 12 August 1970 by the two states. Thus 31 years after the signing of the notorious Hitler-Stalin Non-Aggression Pact the Federal Republic and the Soviet Union had agreed on a treaty which made a genuine contribution to peace and understanding. Article 3 bound the two nations to respect the territorial integrity of all states in Europe within their existing frontiers, including the Oder-Neisse line and the frontiers between the D D R and the Federal Republic. The treaty opened the way for the other agreements which followed. In December the Federal Republic and Poland signed a treaty Article 1 of which stated that the signatories agreed that the Oder-Neisse line 'shall constitute the Western state frontier of the People's Republic of Poland'. With the initialling of the treaty the Polish government announced its intention to allow those ethnic Germans who wished to leave for the Federal Republic to go. The position of West Berlin was regulated by the Four Power agreement of 3 September 1971. The west gained Soviet recognition of the close ties between West Berlin and the Federal Republic and its guarantee of the unimpeded movement of people and goods between the Western Sectors and West Germany. West Berliners were, in future, to have normal opportunities to visit East Berlin and the D D R for tourist, cultural and business reasons. In return the Western Powers recognised, once again, that the Western sectors are not part of the Federal Republic or governed by it. The treaty put paid to the West German practice of holding important state occasions in West Berlin, such as the election of the Federal President or plenary sessions of the Bundestag. The West Germans were, however, authorised to maintain a permanent liaison agency in West Berlin. In return the Soviet Union gained the right to install a consulate-general there. The three Western Powers, by signing the treaty, did not give up their view that the whole of Berlin remained under Four Power control. Even after they later recognised the D D R they still continued to exercise their right to send patrols, unhindered by the East Germans, through East Berlin. As for the West Germans, the three Western Powers had pointed out in 1949, 1954 and 1967 that West Berlin was not a *Land* of the Federal

Republic. For them West German laws had not applied in West Berlin, only identical laws agreed by the parliament of West Berlin. The military service laws and the emergency powers laws of the Federal Republic, for instance, did not apply in West Berlin. From the standpoint of the Four Powers, therefore, West Germany was losing nothing by the 1971 treaty.

The most fundamental of the treaties which arose from the *Ostpolitik* was the so-called Basic Treaty (*Grundvertrag*) between the Federal Republic and the Democratic Republic. Signed on 21 December 1972, it obligated both states to develop good neighbourly relations on the basis of the aims and principles of the United Nations' Charter. The two states further agreed to respect the sovereignty of each other, to renounce force, to work for disarmament and to solve the practical and humanitarian problems which stood between them. In 1974 the Federal Republic and the D D R agreed to exchange special representatives, not ambassadors, having diplomatic status. In a letter to the East German government Herr Brandt reaffirmed that the Basic Treaty did not contradict West Germany's aim to work for the right of self-determination of the German people and for German reunification. In 1973 there were other great strides forward in *Ostpolitik* with the establishment of full diplomatic relations between West Germany and Finland, Czechoslovakia, Hungary and Bulgaria, the admission of the two German states into the United Nations and the opening of the Helsinki Conference by 32 states of Eastern and Western Europe, Canada and the United States.

Herr Brandt had no easy time in trying to get the *Ostpolitik* accepted in Bonn. Many Christian Democrats claimed that he was giving much away and getting very little in return. With his slender majority he was abandoning some of the most cherished principles of all previous administrations—the position of West Berlin as a *Land* of the Republic according to Article 23 of the Basic Law, the right of the Federal Republic to speak for all Germans, the non-recognition of the D D R, the rejection of the Oder-Neisse frontier and the right to their *Heimat* of those expelled from beyond it, and the Hallstein doctrine. The reality of the situation was, however, that West Germany's ability to enforce its claims weakened with every year which passed. The world felt West Germany had re-emerged in a way which no one had dreamt of in 1945 or even 1949, and should be content to acquiesce in these losses. By clinging to its old claims West Germany was inviting suspicion and hostility in Eastern Europe, and growing impatience in the West. Though there were critics of Brandt's *Ostpolitik* in the United States, Bonn's most powerful ally was seeking détente with the Soviet Union and therefore welcomed

Brandt's basic approach. As for the Soviet Union, this period was a good time to negotiate with the Kremlin leadership. They feared that the growing Sino-American friendship could be at their expense. By landing a man successfully on the moon in 1969 the Americans had shown that the Russians had no advantage over them in this area. For these, and other, reasons the Soviets were prepared to come to the conference table. The initiatives of the S P D-F D P government greatly increased the prestige and moral stature of the Federal Republic in all those states which had been belligerents in the Second World War. Nor did the Basic Treaty do anything to lessen the feeling of kinship between the citizens of the two Germanies. As former Governing Mayor of West Berlin Brandt knew better than most Bonn politicians the realities, in human terms, of the division of Germany. This was also true of some of his colleagues. Herr Genscher, F D P Minister of Interior, was born and brought up in Halle (D D R) and still had relations there. Professor Schiller was born in Breslau, now in Poland, and Annemarie Renger, S P D Bundestag President was born in Leipzig. Egon Bahr, who did so much of the negotiating with the East Germans on Brandt's behalf was born in Treffurt (D D R). His aim, like Brandt's was, in no small degree, to improve the situation for those millions of Germans suffering through the partition. This they certainly did. The two million West Berliners could now visit the D D R without much difficulty. Once again they could phone their relations in the other half of the city. Between June 1972 and May 1978 19.58 million visits by West Berliners were recorded in East Berlin or East Germany proper. In 1977 alone there were 3.4 million visits by West Berliners in the D D R including East Berlin. The three million or so Germans who had left the D D R between 1949–1971 could once again visit their relatives without the danger of being arrested as deserters. In 1976 3.1 million West Germans visited the D D R, in 1977 2.9 million did so. Because of the Basic Treaty roughly 6.5 million West Germans living in the frontier areas became eligible to visit the frontier region of the D D R. In 1977 around 443,000 such daily visits were made. In the other direction it proved easier for old age pensioners from the D D R to visit West Germany. In addition, up to the end of 1977 an estimated 215,000 East Germans under retirement age had been able to visit the Federal Republic on 'compelling family business'. This included attending weddings, funerals, etc. The *Ostpolitik* also resulted in many thousands of ethnic Germans from Eastern Europe being permitted to emigrate to West Germany. In both political and human terms Brandt's policy was a success. His personal achievement was recognised in 1971 when he was awarded the Nobel Prize for peace, the first German to be so honoured since Carl von Ossietzky, the pacifist, in 1935.

## Domestic reforms

Brandt was anxious that his government should be a reforming administration and a number of reforms were embarked upon. More money was spent on education at all levels and the school leaving age was raised to 16. Retirement pensioners got more as did other welfare claimants. Tenants were given more rights. A law was passed to encourage wider share ownership by workers and other rank-and-file employees. Efforts were made to improve the motorways and railways. The Brandt government was also far sighted enough to decide to establish an oil reserve *before* the oil crisis of 1973. It came too late, however, to make any difference when the oil embargo was imposed. The age of majority was reduced to 18 giving the vote to an additional 2.5 million young people. Believing the Federal Republic should be able to compete more effectively with the D D R in sport, the government gave more federal aid to sports' organisations. This did not halt the tide of D D R successes. At the Mexico Olympics (1968) West Germany had gained only five gold medals against the D D R's nine. Subsequently, at Munich (1972) and Montreal (1976) the D D R increased its lead. At Montreal it was second with 40 gold compared with the U S S R (47), U S A (34) and West Germany (10). Nevertheless, West Germany's olympic achievements compared well with those of Britain, France and Italy. All these improvements were fairly non-controversial, all were well within the Federal Republic's financial means.

Much more controversial was legislation connected with codetermination. This met with opposition from the Right-wing of the F D P and the majority of the Christian Democrats. One argument used was that such legislation would frighten off foreign investors, especially American investors. In November 1971 the *Betriebsver fassungsgesetz* (Factory Constitution Law) was passed with the votes of the S P D, F D P and 21 Christian Democrats. This strengthened the right of individual employees to be informed and to be heard on matters concerning their place of work. The Works' Council (*Betriebsrat*) was given more authority and trade unions were given the right of entry into the factory provided they informed the employer of their intention to do so. It is convenient to mention here that after years of argument a new Codetermination Law came into effect on 1 July 1976. This improved employee representation on the supervisory boards of companies outside the coal and steel industries. The main provision was that in the 650 major companies accounting for 70 per cent of West German output, the employee representatives on the boards were increased from one third to one half. Though this represented a big improvement from the employees' point of view, it did not give them the kind of parity representation enjoyed by their colleagues in coal and steel. First of all, the chairman is agreed by both sides. But if share-holders and employees cannot agree on a chairman the shareholders' nominee becomes chairman. Secondly, out of the ten employee representatives, one must be a senior executive. Of the rest, three are trade union nominees, usually leading trade union officials from outside the firm, and the other six are various categories of employees from within the firm.

## Youth and terrorism

The Bundeswehr continued to grow under the Social Democrats as under the Christian Democrats, so did the number of conscientious objectors to military service. In 1968 11,952 had applied to be recognised (5,588 were so recognised). In 1970 19,363 applied for recognition (9,351). By 1977 the number of applicants had risen to over 70,000. With over 495,000 men under arms in 1979, the West German armed forces were second only to the French in numbers in Western Europe. The West Germans spent more per capita on arms than Britain or France, but less per capita as a percentage of gross national product. The S P D-F D P regime continued to expand provision for alternative service for objectors, usually in hospitals or agriculture, and cut conscription from 18 to 15 months in June 1972. Brandt's Chancellorship seemed to augur well for the reintegration of the minority of potentially Left-wing students into more conventional political movements. Despite the increasing numbers of conscientious objectors, to a considerable extent this did in fact happen. But a small minority of the minority remained so alienated from society that they were prepared to use violence to change it. Led by Andreas Baader, a drifter and adventurer, Ulrike Meinhof, journalist and daughter of a curator, and Gudrun Ensslin, a philosophy student and pastor's daughter, the so-called Baader-Meinhof gang pulled off a jail break, held up banks, bombed police stations, and attacked American Army camps and the Right-wing Axel Springer press building in Hamburg. The violence was frightening, especially for the great majority of West Germans for whom the greatest political catch-phrase was *Sicherheit* —security. The reaction of the S P D-F D P government was to rush through a whole series of measures, in June 1972, tightening up the firearms regulations, extending the power of judges to hold suspects in custody, extending the range of activities of the para-military *Bundesgrenzschutz* (Federal Frontier Defence Force) and of the *Verfassungsschutz* (the West German equivalent of the American FBI). Baader, Meinhof and some others were arrested in June 1972. Some of their confederates continued with their acts of violence. In February 1975 the chairman of the West Berlin C D U, Peter Lorenz, was kidnapped and ransomed. In April the West German Embassy in Stockholm was seized and blown up. The terrorists concerned were apprehended but not before two diplomats had been killed. The wave of violence reached its climax in 1977. In April of that year Baader, Ensslin and Jan-Carl Raspe were sentenced to life imprisonment, Meinhof had committed suicide in prison. In revenge Baader's comrades murdered Siegfried Buback, Chief Federal Prosecutor, and his driver. On 30 July Jürgen Ponto, Dresdner Bank chairman, was killed resisting a kidnap attempt. Hans-Martin Schleyer, President of the Federation of German Industry, a leading employers' organisation, was kidnapped after a battle in which his driver and three bodyguards were killed. Among the demands of the kidnappers was the release of 11 convicted terrorists including Baader, Ensslin and Raspe. To reinforce their demands the urban guerrillas joined forces with the Palestinian Liberation Organisation (P L O) to hijack a Lufthansa airliner with 86 passengers and crew on board. Eventually the plane was allowed to land at Mogadishu in Somalia. A brilliant rescue operation by the *Bundesgrenzschutz* was mounted. The three leaders, held in Stammheim prison near Stuttgart then killed themselves in a last act of defiance. Herr Schleyer was murdered. Terrorism had been defeated—at a price. More legislation, giving the police wider powers of search and arrest, and making it possible to bar defence lawyers from trials of suspected terrorists, was introduced. All that the Baader-Meinhof group had achieved was a slightly more authoritarian Federal Republic with Bonn's government quarter looking like an armed camp. Not too much significance should be attached to the terrorists, they had less of a cause than almost any other group operating in Europe, the Middle East or South America.

If the West German reaction to terrorism was understandable, it was more difficult to understand the so-called *Berufsverbot*. On 28 January 1972 the heads of the governments of the *Länder* chaired by Willy Brandt, had agreed principles for dealing with public employees (*Beamte*) who were members of political extremist organisations. Basically, they decided, public employees would have to undertake to uphold the Basic Law. Membership of organisations which fought against the constitutional order would usually result in a conflict of loyalties, in these cases the employer would have to decide what to do. This agreement of principles led to a good deal of controversy. The practice of vetting public officials was not new, nor was the restatement of the principles and the publicity given to a number of individual cases. Usually, the teachers, postmen, engine drivers and minor officials excluded from the public service were leftists and many were members of the German Communist Party (D K P). The problem was that the D K P, since 1968, was a legal organisation. Totally committed to Moscow it remained among the least attractive of Western Europe's Communist parties. However, was there any danger in allowing its members, and there were very few of them, going about their lowly tasks in the public service? Was not their exclusion from the public service another step along the road to fear, suspicion and conformity? Such actions provided no protection against the thousands of Soviet bloc spies in the Federal Republic. That there was a danger of undue conformity was revealed by the *Wehrbeauftragter*. The first S P D member to hold this position, Karl Wilhelm Berkhan, found that conscripts were reluctant to stand up for their rights. He believed this was in part the result of increased unemployment which made young men fear taking risks.

## Election 1972

Willy Brandt as Chancellor lived, in political terms, if not recklessly, then at least dangerously. He had a small majority and a coalition partner with a record of previous splits and defections. At a stroke his majority was halved when three F D P Bundestag deputies, including former leader Erich Mende, joined the C D U in October 1970. Worse was to come. In October 1971 came the first anti-*Ostpolitik* defection from the S P D, followed by two others in February 1972. When the Budget was rejected on 28 April 1972 by 247 votes to 247 with one abstention, it was clear an election could not be far away. On 16 May Dr Günther Müller, former Chairman of the Young Socialists, was expelled from the S P D for (right-wing) anti-party activities. This reduced the coalition deputies to just half (248) of the Bundestag deputies with full voting rights (that is, all the deputies except those from West Berlin). The treaties with the Soviet Union and Poland were ratified because most of the Christian Democrats simply abstained (after American representations) rather than voting against them. Another blow was struck against the Brandt administration when Karl Schiller resigned on 7 July over differences on economic policy. In this situation of Parliamentary stalemate Brandt deliberately got himself defeated on a confidence motion by getting his cabinet to abstain. On 22 September President Heinemann could announce fresh elections.

Brandt's victory was by no means certain. His government came under attack from right-wing defectors, including Schiller, who left the S P D altogether before the elections, and the left-wing Young Socialists. The Christian Democrats, led by the moderate Rainer Barzel, attacked the government for selling out the national interests and for damaging the market economy. There were also doubts about the administration's ability to deal with the terrorists. During the Olympic Games held in Munich in September, Palestinian terrorists killed 11 Israelis and one police officer during a police battle to free Israelis held hostage. The results of the elections held on 19 November came as a shock to the C D U/C S U. Only once before in its history had the S P D done better. In terms of seats the S P D won 230 (224 in 1969), the C D U 176 (193), C S U 48 (49) and F D P 42 (30). With 45.9 per cent of the popular vote the S P D had, for the first time, outdistanced the C D U/C S U (44.8). The Free Democrats had improved their position from 5.8 per cent to 8.4 per cent. The N P D vote had slumped to a mere 0.6 per cent and the D K P got only 0.3 per cent. The S P D owed their success to the increased support they had received from youth, women and the working class. There can be no doubt that Brandt's personal popularity had been a crucial factor in the victory.

Willy Brandt's personal triumph was short-lived. In April 1974 Günter Guillaume, a personal assistant to the Chancellor, was arrested as an East German spy. Brandt resigned on 6 May taking upon himself the political responsibility for what he called his carelessness in the affair. It was widely believed he could have continued and resigned for personal reasons. He had been Chancellor for nearly five years, which was longer than Kiesinger or Erhard, and was in the Adenauer class in terms of his significance. Aged 60, he remained in the Bundestag and was active as S P D chairman.

The Bundestag elected Helmut Schmidt Chancellor by 267 votes to 225, including three coalition deputies, on 16 May. Schmidt (born 1918), the son of Hamburg school teachers, had studied economics at Hamburg University before taking up politics. He had been the Interior Minister in the Hamburg *Land* administration (1961–5), chaired the S P D Bundestag caucus (1967–9), served as Defence Minister (1969–72), Minister of Economics and Finance (July–December '72) and Finance until May 1974. The new Foreign Minister was Hans-Dietrich Genscher (F D P). Other important appointments included: George Leber (S P D) Defence, Egon Franke (S P D) Inter-German Relations, Hans Apel (S P D) Finance, Professor Werner Maihofer (F D P) Interior. The only woman member of the government was Dr Katharina Focke (S P D) Minister for Youth, Family and Health. This ministry was, up to 1980, almost the only one held by women.* In 1961 Elizabeth Schwartzhaupt (C D U), the first woman minister in the history of the Federal Republic, was appointed to it by Dr Adenauer. Schmidt's administration comprised 11 S P D members and four F D P.

## Honecker takes over the D D R

Brandt's *Ostpolitik* represented both an opportunity and a challenge to the S E D. On the one hand, the East German leaders welcomed relations with Bonn and the non-Communist world with all the advantages international recognition would bring. On the other they feared their fragile stability could be shattered by Bonn's embrace. As we saw above (p 196) several Arab states and Cambodia started off a wave of recognitions of the D D R in 1969. By the end of the year 11 states of the Third World had recognised East Berlin. The break-through with the Western industrial states came after the signing of the Basic Treaty with the Federal Republic. Switzerland was the first such state to recognise the D D R in December 1972. Belgium was the first N A T O state to accord recognition to East Germany (27 December). Britain and France waited until 9 February 1973. The United States and Canada were among the last states to agree recognition in September 1974 and August 1975 respectively. That the D D R was not going to let past political quarrels and propaganda stand in the way of diplomatic relations was shown when it took up full relations with Iran in December 1972 and Franco Spain in January 1973. Both regimes had provided the East German media with many anger-filled hours in the past. In the case of Iran, oil was a consideration. It is not clear what the D D R was to get out of rushing into relations with Spain. When Erich Honecker was photographed with President Ford of the United States, and then Chancellor Schmidt at the Helsinki Conference on Security and Cooperation it was for the S E D a dream come true. The party felt it had stormed the final summit, taken the last stronghold, in the long war for recogni-tion. The East German leaders believed such symbolic pictures must surely give them the seal of approval in the eyes of their own people. The photographs emphasised, they believed, the point once again that even the West had recognised that there was no alternative to the S E D in the D D R.

The man who had fought so hard for this dream to come true, Walter Ulbricht, died on 1 August 1973. Ulbricht had been deprived

* Marie Schlei was Minister for Economic co-operation, 1976–78

of much of the glory and credit for what was happening by being forced to resign as First Secretary of the SED in May 1971 just before the VIII Congress of the party. As expected, Honecker took his place. Ulbricht was given the purely honorary title of 'Chairman of the SED' and was allowed to remain head of state. But his true position was indicated by the speed with which speech writers forgot he had ever had anything to say, his portraits disappeared, institutions named after him were renamed, and he was downgraded in the history books. In October 1972 the Council of State was deprived of most of its power. By the time Ulbricht died physically, he had long been dead politically. His modest funeral was the outward recognition of this. He had to pay the price for being, in his final years as SED boss, just a little independent of Moscow, for wanting to drive a harder bargain with West Germany than the Soviet leaders needed, and perhaps not least, for keeping Erich Honecker waiting too long.

## New Constitution

Herr Honecker immediately re-emphasised the Soviet connection. This was given formal expression in the new constitution of October 1974. Article 6 declared that the DDR 'is for ever and irrevocably allied' with the USSR. Gone was Article 8, paragraph 2 of the 1968 constitution which pledged the DDR to work to overcome the division of Germany. (In most other respects the basic elements of the 1968 constitution remained.) The Friendship Treaty between the DDR and the USSR of 7 October 1975 bound East Germany even more closely to the Soviet Union. Eternal friendship between the two was the promise contained in Article 1. Economic co-operation and integration became obligatory under Article 2, and Articles 4 and 8 bound the two states to give military assistance to each other in case of attack. Article 9 seemed to deny the possibility of any separate East German foreign policy, for it stated that both would consult each other, in the interests of both states, on all international qustions and would act from a common position. The East Germans proved to be good allies for the Soviet Union, backing its line in the international Communist movement, at the UN, and giving economic and military aid to the Soviet Union's clients in the Third World especially Vietnam, South Yemen, Ethiopia, Mozambique, Angola and the African National Congress guerrillas in Rhodesia.

In his domestic policies Erich Honecker attempted to secure his own position by getting his own men promoted, swung for a time to the 'left' in his economic ideological policies, tried to placate his people with the limited means available, and confronted the domestic challenge caused by better relations with West Germany.

In his personnel policy Honecker pushed those who had been associated with him in his long years as head of the Free German Youth (F D J). One of his associates, Horst Sindermann, became Chairman of the Council of Ministers (Prime Minister) in October 1973. Honecker's rival, Stoph, was kicked upstairs to the powerless Council of State. Though the old men of the Politburo seemed to take a long time to fade away, Honecker contented himself with having others promoted. Following the pattern of the Soviet Politburo, the Minister of Defence (1973) and the Minister for State Security (1976) became full members of the Politburo. Honecker revealed his own appetite for power by taking over as Chairman of the National Defence Council in 1971. This body would run the D D R in time of war. He also was formally elected Chairman of the Council of State in October 1976. In this he could claim he was only following the good example of the Soviet leader Leonid Brezhnev. In general Honecker tended to down grade economic experts in the first years of his stewardship, preferring instead political/ideological specialists like himself. Later he was forced to some extent to reverse this because of the D D R's economic difficulties. Thus Willi Stoph was reinstated as Chairman of the Council of Ministers in 1976, and the economic expert Günter Mittag reverted to his previous role as Central Committee secretary for the economy. He had lost this in 1973.

In economic/ideological questions Honecker swung 'left' in his first years as S E D Secretary. This could have been merely part of a campaign to show his allies that the D D R was a truly orthodox Soviet bloc state and to let his own people know that better relations with the Federal Republic did not mean there would be any convergence of the two German systems. One such measure was the nationalisation of the remaining mixed and private firms, in order, as the S E D put it, to further the development of Socialist production relations, and remove 'certain symptoms of recapitalisation in the D D R'. This happened in April 1972. At that time these enterprises were responsible for over 14 per cent of national income. They employed nearly two million adults as against nearly 6.7 million employed by the socialist sector. They were mainly in food and textiles. This measure was possibly a sop to still the anger of some because of the relatively high standard of living of those in the semi-private and private sectors. Later this policy was partially reversed. Starting in July 1974 Honecker used the term 'Communist' in reference to the members of the S E D. In contrast to previous policy he put much more emphasis on the K P D of Thälmann at the expense of the old S P D. Again, this could have been part of the policy of *Abgrenzung* (delimitation) between the ideology of the West German S P D and the S E D. Later on this emphasis was toned down, probably because of the negative reception it got from the D D R population and even the ordinary members of the S E D. At the IX Congress of the S E D in May 1976 there were 1,914,382 members and 129,315 candidate members of the S E D out of a total population of only 16.89 millions. In the writer's experience many of them were merely fellow travellers. In such a situation and with an acute shortage of labour the S E D leaders remained limited in what they could do both politically and economically. It is significant that between the VIII and IX congresses the proportion of party members from the intelligentsia had risen while the proportion from the manual working-class had fallen. There is a clue here to the failure of the 'left' line. The S E D programme adopted in 1976 in the end represented a compromise between the old 'independent' Ulbricht emphasis on the uniqueness of the D D R's Socialism and Honecker's emphasis on the Soviet orthodoxy of the D D R. The new S E D statute agreed at the IX Congress in May 1976 also represented a compromise. However, Herr Honecker followed the Soviet example of changing his title from First Secretary to General-Secretary—a title last used at the height of Stalinism, 1950–53. Finally, the new *History of the SED* published in 1978 marked some retreat from the 'left' line of the early Honecker period with Ulbricht reappearing, but some rewriting of history to give Honecker a more prominent role!

## Raising living standards

The S E D leaders continued to attempt to raise the standard of living in the 1970s. No doubt there was a sincere desire to see their people enjoying a better life, but, in addition, they realised that improved contacts with West Germany made this of paramount political importance. In 1980 the citizens of the D D R still measured their own success by comparing their life to that of their relatives in the West. The possession of consumer durables continued to rise in the D D R. In December 1973 a new currency law permitted D D R citizens to accept foreign currency gifts of up to 500 Marks (then £125). They could continue to receive gifts in kind as well. This law was designed to encourage West Germans to give their relatives West marks (badly needed by the D D R), encourage East Germans hoarding them to spend them, raise living standards of significant numbers of East Germans and end a potentially dangerous situation which put many East Germans outside the Law (by illegally holding foreign currency). The new ruling did all of these things. It led to a boom in the Intershops which sold Western goods against Western currency only. It also created antagonisms between those who possessed Western currency and those who did not. It exposed once again the weakness of the D D R Mark. It led to those with badly needed skills—plumbers, painters, carpenters, bricklayers—who were self-employed or who did private work in their own time, to demand payment in West Marks. In 1979 a weak attempt was made to rectify this situation.

In 1971, 1972 and again in 1976 old age pensions were increased by higher percentages than ever before. The lowest paid workers were also given some improvement in their pay. To halt the decline in the birth rate generous allowances were granted to mothers with longer paid leave as well. Interest free loans were available to young couples to buy furniture and other fittings. If they got on with having a family they could, depending on how many children they had, avoid repaying the loan altogether. There was indeed some improvement in the birth rate but experts did not think this would be a long term trend. The high divorce rate, the large number of women employed and the changing attitudes of women would seem to confirm this view.

At the end of the 1970s the economic situation of the D D R appeared gloomy. The Republic had been hit by the world energy crisis with the Soviet Union, the main oil supplier, increasing its prices in accordance with world trends. The D D R increased its indebtedness to the U S S R and Western states to maintain living standards. The world slump and the D D R's shortage of labour restricted its economic activities further.

## Abgrenzung

As we have seen, in the Constitution of 1974, and in many other ways, the S E D attempted to deny that Germany existed. It is interesting that the 1974 Constitution was not, unlike that of 1968, put to a referendum. There was fear it would provoke too much discussion. The introduction of compulsory military training in schools in 1978 was more political than military in its intention acting as a kind of ideological rearmament. There was much discussion too about 'real existing Socialism' meaning the D D R's version not that of the S P D, Eurocommunists—like the Spanish and Italian Communists—or Czech reform Communists. That the S E D leaders did not welcome any reform ideas imported from the West was made clear to its intellectuals. Those who did not understand the message were fined (author Stefan Heym), put under house arrest (Robert Havemann), jailed (S E D author Rudolf Bahro), forcibly ejected from the D D R (folk singer Wolf Biermann and author Reiner Kunze) or allowed to leave (jazz singer Christiane Wunder and others).

By 1980 the S E D had largely failed in its *Abgrenzung* policy. Although the majority of the D D R's citizens had not experienced any other political system, they still seemed to regard West Germany as their closest neighbour. They continued to watch West German television and found it difficult to accept the official view that the Federal Republic headed by the S P D and the F D P represented a threat to anyone.

## Election 1976

When Helmut Schmidt took over as Chancellor in 1974 he faced the problems associated with the world energy crisis. The Federal Republic too, like other industrial states was facing inflation and unemployment. In the regional elections the S P D lost ground. By the time the Federal elections came round in 1976, politically, the situation did not look all that rosy for the coalition. Yet the Federal Republic had weathered the international economic crisis better than almost any other industrial state. Indeed, the independent Hamburg weekly, *Die Zeit* (11 June 1976) showed that between February 1973 (Schmidt had been Chancellor since May 1974) and March 1976 West German prices increased by 20.5 per cent. This compared with an increase in Switzerland of 22.6 per cent, U S A 30.2, Holland 32.5 and much higher increases in Britain, France, Italy and Japan. In the election campaign it was easy for the S P D-F D P to win the battle of statistics whether the figures related to employees' incomes, public sector debts, strikes, growth or unemployment. No wonder the S P D quoted the London *Financial Times* and the American *Newsweek* referring to the Federal Republic as a model. If unemployment, low compared to many other industrial states, was up, so was unemployment pay at 68 per cent of the previous wage. Retirement pensions had been doubled since 1969 and there were many other social improvements. The Christian Democrats claimed they wanted freedom instead of socialism, less bureaucracy, and a tougher line with the East. This time the Christian Democrats presented Dr Helmut Kohl as their Chancellor candidate. Herr Kohl, a tall, friendly, 46-year-old Catholic, who had been the Prime Minister of the Rhineland-Palatinate from 1969, lacked the Bonn and international experience of Chancellor Schmidt. In his own party Kohl was a moderate. Once again the S P D faced the anger of Franz Josef Strauss, the fury of the Axel Springer press, the money of big business and the restrained but clear opposition from the Catholic Church. Despite all this, the Social Democrats must have been disappointed with the results.

The S P D vote fell to 42.6 per cent, roughly their 1969 position. The F D P proportion went down to 7.9 per cent, only twice had they been lower—1957 and 1969. The Christian Democrats could be well pleased with their 48.6 per cent share. Only in 1957 had they gained a higher proportion of the vote. The losses of the S P D were right across the country and were not confined to any one group, though they lost in middle class Catholic areas more than in any others. They had lost the advantage among the first-time voters. As usual the Christian Democrats had done well among the old. The real winner of the election was Herr Strauss whose C S U had done better than ever in Bavaria. In near civil war conditions in the Christian Democratic camp Herr Strauss was chosen to lead the C D U/C S U in the 1980 election. Worries about the economy and about easier divorce and abortion (in Catholic areas) probably go a long way to explaining the S P D's difficulties. Many S P D members felt the party should have offered the voters, especially the young, a little bit of idealism, even utopianism.

With a majority of ten the S P D-F D P coalition managed to retain office up to 1980. It pursued a policy of cautious reform at home and cautiously flexed its muscles abroad. Save only perhaps in its industrial democracy and certain aspects of its welfare system, it would be going too far to describe West Germany as a model. It still had the problems which faced the other industrial states—inflation, unemployment, the dangers as well as the opportunities produced by the micro-chip, pollution, the maldistribution of wealth, the integration of a considerable alien workforce, the dangers inherent in the growth of police power to deal with modern crime, the risks involved in maintaining a large military establishment. Yet the Federal Republic seemed to be able to cope better than most of its friends, neighbours and rivals.

## The Greens

Schmidt's managerial pragmatist style did not commend itself to many young West Germans who were searching for both idealism and new thinking. They found a new party to vote for, the Greens.

The Greens developed out of earlier protest movements especially the student protest movement of the 1960s (see chapter 11). Some of the earlier protesters were integrated into the new S P D/F D P establishment after 1969, a tiny handful became urban terrorists. Others remained outside the mainstream of politics, unconvinced by Brandt's social-liberal coalition. That coalition, as led by Schmidt from 1974, disappointed many young idealists by its reliance on the nuclear deterrent and nuclear power, and its attempts to maximise growth. Inevitably, a section of the rising generation sees any existing government as too orthodox for its taste and responsible for all the unsolved problems of society. Some of those in West Germany were influenced by new thinking on ecological issues, women's rights, gay rights, minorities and educational reform, both German and American as well as Mao's 'cultural revolution'. The intellectual collapse of orthodox, Soviet, Communism made it easier for other 'outsider' movements to attract adherents. At first about 1973, citizens' initiatives were formed at local level on specific issues such as opposition to a nuclear power station or a new road or a runway extension. In 1972 the Federal League of Citizens' Initiatives for Environmental Protection (B B U) was established by groups mainly from Baden-Württemberg, which opposed the setting up of a nuclear power station at Wyhl. By 1977 the B B U had over 300,000 affiliated members in 1,000 groups. In December of the same year a green party was founded in Lower Saxony and in the regional election in the following June it secured a vote of 3.9 per cent. In the same month a 'rainbow list' put up candidates in Hamburg, gaining 3.5 per cent. In October 1978 green lists in Bavaria and Hesse gained only 1.8 and 1.1 per cent respectively. The first success at the regional *Land* level came in Bremen in October 1979 when the green list gained 5.1 per cent and 4 seats in this traditionally left-wing city state. Success followed in Baden-Württemberg in March 1980 where the Greens won 5.3 per cent and 6 seats. By the federal election of 1983 the Greens had also gained seats in West Berlin, Hamburg, Hesse and Lower Saxony, a total of six of the eleven regions of West Germany.

For the election to the European parliament in 1979 the Greens had been forced to establish a national political party. This was achieved at Frankfurt am Main on 17–18 March 1979 by 500 delegates of widely differing views and interests, from moderate ecologists to extreme Marxists. Its top candidates in the European election were: Petra Kelly, an administrative counsellor with the Economic and Social Committee of the European Community; author Carl Amery; artist Joseph Beuys; and Herbert Gruhl, author of the influential *Ein Planet wird geplündert* (1975, *The Plundering of a Planet*). The new party gained 3.2 per cent, not enough to win seats but a respectable vote for a new party. It fell back to only 1.5 per cent in the federal election of 1980 but this was probably due to fear of splitting the anti-Strauss S P D vote. In most cases a vote for the Greens was a vote lost to the S P D.

Who were the Green voters? Research revealed that they were more likely to be men than women, single than married, Protestant than Catholic, at home in large towns than in small towns or villages, middle or upper class than blue collar. They were over represented among the 18–24 age group and among those with the *Abitur*, the university entrance certificate. In fact, Green supporters were the best educated of the electorate. The Greens had found supporters among the greatly expanded student population.

## Election 1980

The main issue at the election of 1980 was whether Bavarian C S U leader Franz Josef Strauss was fit to be Chancellor of the Federal Republic. His utterances during the election were not designed to placate worried voters. Moderate right-of-centre voters gave increased support to the F D P, which gained 10.6 per cent, its best vote since 1961. The S P D gained slightly as well (42.9 per cent) with the combined C D U/C S U falling to 44.5 per cent, their worst vote since 1949. As Vice-Chancellor and Foreign Minister Hans-Dietrich Genscher (F D P) had committed his party to remain in coalition with the S P D. The F D P ministers, Genscher and Gerhart Baum (Interior), Otto Graf von Lambsdorff (Economics) and Josef Ertl (Food, Agriculture and Forestry), remained at their posts in a government of 17 ministers. There were virtually no changes in the S P D team, the key members of which were Hans-Jochen Vogel (Justice), Hans Matthöfer (Finance), Hans Apel (Defence), Egon Franke (Inter-German Relations) and Herbert Ehrenberg (Labour and Social Policy). The only woman minister was Anje Huber (Youth, Families and Health).

Soon after the election it became clear that there were mounting tensions between the F D P and the S P D on economic issues, and between Schmidt and his party over defence and security policy. Like the rest of the world the Federal Republic had been hit by the second oil crisis of 1979 and the recession that caused rising costs and rising unemployment. Unemployment at 1.8 million in 1982 was higher than at any time since the 1950s although this compared well with other European states. The majority of the S P D wanted to maintain high levels of spending on welfare and industrial assistance, the F D P sought spending cuts and balanced budgets. Schmidt was under pressure from his own parliamentary group a sizeable number of whom represented the left of the party. There were also those on the trade union wing who wanted high public spending. Security issues caused even greater tensions within the S P D.

## Progress in Europe

An excellent English-speaker, Helmut Schmidt felt a good deal of sympathy for Britain and the U S, but the circumstances of the 1970s caused him and Hans-Dietrich Genscher to re-examine West Germany's position. The U S appeared weakened and unsure of itself. In 1971 an attempt was made to get the Senate to vote to withdraw U S troops from Europe. Although it was defeated, it indicated American doubts. The U S revealed itself to be highly vulnerable to world oil price rises in 1973, following the Fourth Arab-Israeli War. Europeans looked on in fascinated horror when President Nixon (1968–74) was forced to resign over the Watergate affair. The U S withdrawal from Vietnam in 1973, although welcome, showed the limits of American power. In Europe, too, things were changing. There was the fall of the Greek military regime and the Portuguese dictatorship in 1974, the death of Franco in 1975 followed by the end of dictatorship in Spain. The E E C was being expanded, with Britain, Denmark and the Irish Republic joining in 1973, followed by Greece (1981) Spain and Portugal (in 1986). The S P D used its financial resources with positive results to help democratic socialists in Greece, Portugal and Spain. Schmidt decided also to upgrade Franco-German relations. One sign of this were his 22 official visits to France, over 8 years, compared with 14 to the U S, 13 to Britain and 9 to Italy. In his 14 years in office Adenauer visited France 22 times, the U S 9, Britain and Italy 6 times each. Chancellor Kohl sustained this level of visits after taking over in 1982. Up to 1989 all German Chancellors since 1949 had visited France more than Britain. Schmidt (and Genscher) were concerned about developing the European Economic Community into the European Community (E C), a move which involved its members more and more in their own defence, thus creating at least a 'European pillar' of N A T O. Schmidt found much common ground with President Giscard d'Estaing (1974–81), with whom he developed a good personal relationship.

Franco-German initiatives were important in cementing and developing the E C. Finally in 1979 the European Parliament was directly elected for the first time, though this was in line with the original treaties which had provided for this at an early stage. In 1981 Genscher and Italian Foreign Minister Emilio Colombo presented a proposal for a European Union. The proposal came at a time when the world economy was in recession, suffering from the second oil shock which followed the Iranian revolution and the start of the Iran-Iraq war. It called for more power for the European Parliament; majority decisions in the Council of Ministers (instead of one state being able to veto decisions agreed on by the others); the E C developing its own common policy on foreign and security issues; a common cultural policy aimed at creating a European identity; harmonisation of laws; co-operation in the fight against crime and terrorism; and, above all, greater economic integration. Over the decade which followed, the E C went in this direction and the Single European Act, passed in 1986, was a practical expression of this.

## Controversy over new missiles

Following the period of East-West détente in the 1970s, after the end of the Vietnam war in 1975 and the signing of the Helsinki agreements (C S C E) in the same year, tensions started rising again by the end of the decade. In 1975 Soviet-backed Cuban troops were brought into Angola. In 1979 a Soviet-backed regime won the civil war in Nicaragua. There was the Soviet invasion of Afghanistan in December 1979 and in 1981 a military regime took over in Poland and the free trade union movement, Solidarity, was brutally crushed. Although it had nothing to do with the Soviets, the fall of the Shah of Iran in 1979 was also a worry for the West because of the Islamic fundamentalist nature of the regime which replaced him. Under its ailing leader, Leonid Brezhnev, the Soviet Union appeared to be drifting into the hands of its military. Already by the mid-1970s the Soviet Union had started deploying S S-20 missiles in Europe. This was a weapon not of deterrence but of pressure on West Europe, especially on the Federal Republic, and was intended to strengthen both a feeling towards neutralism and the political uncoupling of West Europe from the U S A. Those who were forced to this conclusion and thus advocate a suitable N A T O defence posture ran the risk of being called cold war warriors, the fermenters of increased alienation and a new arms race. So much progress had been made in the 1970s and towards détente with the Soviets, by the president of the U S, Richard Nixon, that it was difficult for many to grasp that the West could be facing a renewed threat.

In Germany Helmut Schmidt had been a strong advocate of defence throughout his political career. Now he had to face this new situation. Many in the S P D were not ready for it. He attempted to square the circle by putting forward the so-called 'double-track' option. This involved détente and deterrence, the offer to the Soviets that if they dismantled their own theatre nuclear weapons (mainly the S S-20s) the West would desist from deployment of its new intermediate-range nuclear missiles (I N F), Pershing-2s and Cruise. This approach was adopted in December 1979 by N A T O.

Chancellor Schmidt continued to pursue the *Ostpolitik* his predecessor, Willy Brandt, had inaugurated. Here he had strong support from all sections of the S P D as well as his Vice-Chancellor, Hans-Dietrich Genscher. He visited Moscow in 1974 and 1980, and Brezhnev visited Bonn in 1978 and 1981. Schmidt met East German leader Erich Honecker at Werbellinsee (D D R) between 11 and 13 December 1981. The final day of the visit coincided with the announcement of martial law in Poland. Schmidt had sought better relations with that Communist regime also, giving credits and economic aid. Right-wing critics felt, whatever the earlier achievements of *Ostpolitik*, the current Schmidt-Genscher phase was based too much on appeasement and one-sided concessions. By the beginning of the 1980s the West had new leaders—Ronald Reagan, Margaret Thatcher and Francois Mitterrand—who favoured a firmer approach to the Soviets. Schmidt began to look isolated.

## *The fall of Schmidt*

It was no surprise when Chancellor Helmut Schmidt was ousted from office on 1 October 1982 by a constructive vote of no-confidence. In his place Helmut Kohl, Chairman of the C D U since 1973 and C D U Bundestag group leader since 1976, was elected with the votes of most of the F D P who had broken their coalition with the S P D. As mentioned above, the F D P had come increasingly into conflict with Schmidt and the S P D over economic policy, and Schmidt had fallen progressively out of favour with his own party over a wide range of issues. In April 1982 the S P D congress had swung left, demanding much more comprehensive co-determination in industry and new taxes to finance job-creation schemes. The congress also moved left on defence, attacking the U S A for allegedly promoting a new arms race.

Helmut Schmidt did not share the views of the S P D congress in these vital policy areas. He knew that they would be opposed within his cabinet and would not win a majority in the Bundestag. His S P D Finance Minister, Hans Matthöfer (to April 1982), felt there was an urgent need to reduce the growing official debts of the Federal Republic. This was the view of the four F D P ministers especially Minister of Economics, Otto Graf Lambsdorff. This alone could have caused the breach between the S P D and the F D P. In August 1982

223

Lambsdorff set out in a memorandum an alternative economic strategy which involved drastic spending cuts but which he thought would lead to economic growth. This was rejected by the S P D and on 17 September the F D P ministers resigned. It must be pointed out that Schmidt threatened them with dismissal if they did not.

Schmidt hoped he could get the President of the Federal Republic to agree to dissolve parliament and call new elections leaving him in office during the transitionary period. This would have helped the S P D slightly. It was an unrealistic proposal as the F D P had agreed to join a coalition with the C D U/C S U and in theory they commanded a larger majority than the previous S P D-F D P coalition (279 as against 271). On 1 October they elected Helmut Kohl as the new Chancellor.

# — 13 —

# Kohl's First Term

When he took office as Chancellor on 1 October 1982 Helmut Kohl did not appear very secure. He had failed in the 1976 election against Helmut Schmidt and many thought he had not sparkled in either public or parliamentary debates since then. Moreover, his coalition partner, the F D P, looked in bad shape. It had suffered defections to the S P D, including the F D P's general secretary, Günter Verheugen and the prominent women members Ingrid Matthäus-Maier and Helga Schuchardt. The first two returned to the Bundestag on the S P D list in 1983. Others, like Dr Hildegard Hamm-Brücher, remained in the F D P but were unhappy with the change. An attempt was made at Bochum on 28 November 1982 to establish a Liberal Democratic party independent of both the existing F D P and the S P D, but this party subsequently failed. Kohl had his old troubles with the Bavarian C S U and he inherited economic problems.

## Election 1983

The S P D and its sympathisers strongly attacked Kohl for his method of achieving office, forgetting that the S P D had itself come to office in 1966 by such means and remained there for three years without facing the electorate. Kohl, however, was prepared to go to the country and ask for a mandate, which he got on 6 March 1983. The C D U/C S U got its highest percentage poll since 1957 (48.8), the S P D went down from 42.9 to 38.2, while the F D P looked precarious with only 6.9 per cent (down from 10.6). The Social Democrats had suffered losses to the Greens who entered parliament with 5.6 per cent and the F D P had lost votes to the S P D. Helmut Schmidt did not stand as his party's Chancellor candidate and it was difficult for the S P D to find a replacement for this highly popular politician. Hans-Jochim Vogel (born 1926), the S P D candidate for Chancellor, was a moderate and a man of great experience. A Catholic lawyer, he had served as S P D mayor of Munich, Minister of Town Planning and then of Justice; yet he lacked the charisma of Schmidt and presided over a divided party. Kohl, on the other hand, had a towering physical presence and spoke with conviction. The main issues of the election were defence and the economy. Kohl came out strongly for N A T O, the double track decision and the Federal Republic's close relationship with the U S A. He reminded audiences that they had U S troops in West Germany and free trade unions. In Poland they had Soviet troops and no free unions. It was simple but effective. Most voters believed that Kohl's government, backed by business, was more likely than the S P D to solve the problem of unemployment, which had reached the highest level since the early 1950s. Kohl probably benefited slightly from the swing to the right in the U S A and Britain headed by the powerful figures of Ronald Reagan (1981–89) and Margaret Thatcher (1979–90). The French socialist President, François Mitterrand, seemed to come to his aid as well. He visited Bonn on the twentieth anniversary of the Franco-German Friendship Treaty in January 1983 making a strong speech closely supporting Kohl's stand on defence, commenting 'the missiles are in the East, and the pacifists are in the West'.

The composition of Helmut Kohl's government remained virtually the same after the election as before. The F D P lost agriculture, being reduced from four ministers to three. The main government members after Kohl were: Hans-Dietrich Genscher (F D P), deputy Chancellor and Foreign Minister; Friedrich Zimmerman (C S U), Interior; Gerhard Stoltenberg (C D U), Finance; Otto Graf Lambsdorff (F D P), Economics; Manfred Wörner (C D U), Defence; Norbert Blüm, from the blue collar wing of the C D U, Labour and Social Policy. The other F D P minister was Hans Engelhard at Justice. In the 17-member government the only woman was Dorothee Wilms (C D U), Minister of Education and Science. Later the government was increased by three, with Professor Rita Süssmuth (C D U) becoming Minister for Youth, the Family, Women and Health in September 1985; Walter Wallmann (C D U), Minister for Environment, Protection of Nature and Nuclear Safety from June 1986; and Wolfgang Schäuble (C D U), Minister for Special Tasks from November 1984.

## The economy in the 1980s

In the 1980s economic liberalism became fashionable world-wide to a greater or lesser degree. The main protagonists of this cause were Ronald Reagan in the U S A and Margaret Thatcher in Britain. Both these countries already had, in any case, stronger traditions in this direction than most others. The European Community (E C) with its determination to create a single internal market by 1992 placed great emphasis on the free market. The new economic liberalism meant the reduction of the role of the state as far as possible, with deregulation, the scaling down of publicly funded welfare programmes and the abandonment of subsidies. This ran counter to the traditions of most of Europe (excluding Britain) and Japan which were corporatist. Here, the state played a major regulatory role, engaged directly or indirectly in economic activity, business and labour, and sought to avoid conflict through negotiations. Most professions were highly respected but also highly regulated. Subsidies were regarded as a normal part of economic life and the welfare state prevailed.

The C D U/C S U had fought its campaigns in 1976, 1980 and 1983 on the slogan 'Freiheit statt Sozialismus' (Freedom instead of Socialism) yet in office it revealed a reluctance to abandon the 'socialism' of its predecessor. It remained more 'socialist' than Labour governments in Australia and New Zealand, or the Spanish Socialists. After a false start the French Socialist government also genuflected to the new ideology of economic liberalism. By comparison, Kohl's government was very mild. It did go in for a degree of cuts in public expenditure and privatisation but its measures were in no way comparable to Thatcher's programme. Some public shareholdings—such as the Federation's shareholdings in Volkswagen, Veba and the Salzgitter AG—were sold but other sell-offs were prevented from within the coalition (the Bavarian C S U stopped the sale of Lufthansa). In 1990 Finance Minister Theo Waigel announced that in 1983 the Federation had been financially involved in 808 firms and by 1990 this had been reduced to 132. The state had received D M 7.4 billion from the sales.

The forces opposing any dramatic change in public policy remained well-entrenched in central and regional government, the parties and other organisations. The vast subsidies to West Berlin and the border areas could not be cut, nor the monies for the cultural programmes abroad (so vital to promoting West Germany's image). The publishing and printing trade was heavily dependent on public bodies. Many branches of industry remained locked into the Federal Republic's defence effort. Although there were cuts in student funding, spending on research and development and adult education remained high (by international standards). Subsidies to the German Democratic Republic went up. The vast welfare programme was only slightly dented and help for, among other things, housing, agriculture, ship-building, the political parties continued.

The critics of this corporatism abroad and within the Federal Republic pointed to falling growth. Growth in the 1950s had been around 8 per cent, 4.5 per cent in the 1960s, 2.7 per cent in the 1970s, but only 1.7 per cent between 1980 and 1988. By comparison, Japan's growth rate in the 1980s was 4.1, in the USA it was 2.6, Britain managed 2.1 and France 1.9. This was, however, only one indicator. Of these and many other states, only Japan had a better record on inflation than Germany in the 1980s. Federal Germany also had record trade surpluses. In part this was because of the falling price of oil and raw materials but all the industrial states benefited from this too. Britain enjoyed the North Sea oil bonus which West Germany did not. The Federal Republic also had to cope with increasing numbers of refugees which Britain did not (see below). West Germany had a higher Gross Domestic Product per capita than Britain, France or Italy, though it had fallen slightly behind Japan and remained well behind Canada and the USA.

By the end of the 1980s the West German economy was booming, even before German unity got under way. By contrast, Britain's economy was faltering as was that of America. German success was, to a considerable extent, due to the widespread view that the stamp 'Made in Germany' was the guarantee of quality and good design. It was also the result of West Germany's ability to deliver on time. All of this was the result of Germany's industrial culture including its industrial and professional training and its so-called corporatism. This is not to say that Germany had no need of change to meet the challenge of 1992 and the single market within the European Community.

## The East German economy

Like the West German economy, that of East Germany was affected by the general recession of the early 1980s. It found it increasingly difficult to export its industrial goods to the West and when trade did improve it was hit increasingly by cheap competitors. When the price of oil declined so did its revenue from exports of oil products, which were the biggest single source of hard currency and the biggest item of trade with West Germany (its main trading partner after the Soviet Union). Textiles and clothing, chemical products and services brought in roughly equal amounts of revenue from West Germany, followed by agricultural products. Dependence on oil meant dependence on a highly fluctuating market. The textiles and clothing market relied on cheapness and style, neither of which East Germany was strong on. Chemicals brought heavy pollution and agriculture had to be greatly subsidised. The 'services' included use of transit routes between West

Germany and West Berlin and forced minimum exchanges of D-mark by West German tourists. It did not add up to a solid and dynamic export trade.

The East German economy had at least 14 difficulties which got worse as time went on. Its products required too many raw materials and too much energy to manufacture, relative to the products of Western industrial nations. It attempted, for political reasons, to produce too many different goods. It took too long to get new ideas and new products onto the market. Due to the cumbersome planning system bottlenecks occurred leading to breakdowns in production. There was too much red tape, too much paper work and too much supervision of the wrong kind. The poor transport system and poor water system reduced the efficiency of the economy. The population suffered from the lack of everything, from sink plugs and toilet paper to spare parts for domestic appliances and vegetables; this led to endless queueing. The appalling state of housing reduced morale and hindered labour mobility. Labour remained scarce due partly to both poor organisation and low productivity. Excessive reliance on female labour led to increased absenteeism. Lack of internal competition reduced the need to innovate. The absence of a proper pricing system led to an unrealistic evaluation of goods and services. The heavy burden of defence and security drained men and materials both badly needed elsewhere. The East German economy did most of its trade with its partners in Comecon, the members of the Council for Mutual Economic Aid, dominated by the Soviet Union. These were backward economies with little ability to help each other to modernise. Finally, political desires, even fantasies, took precedence over economic common sense. As the economy plunged deeper into difficulties in the 1980s the S E D leaders decided on what was to prove their last gamble.

At the XI congress of the S E D in 1986 Honecker announced a new, revolutionary five-year plan which was supposed to transform the East German economy into one of the most modern in the world. The idea was to concentrate on the new 'key technologies'—microelectronics, C A D/C A M, automation, robotics, nuclear energy, laser technology and biotechnology. Older delegates must have remembered the similar ambitious plans of Ulbricht which came to nothing. Once again everything was to be sacrificed for a few top priority projects. Vast investments, including hard currency, were poured into them, while other parts of the economy were starved of resources. In May 1990 Wolfgang Biermann, for many years head of Zeiss Jena, one of the D D R's most prestigious enterprises, admitted to *Neues Deutschland* that only by clandestine purchases of equipment for making silicon chips from the West was his firm able to progress to produce its own 1 megabit chips in the late 1980s. Politburo member Günter Schabowski was later to say it was like attempting to invent the bicycle for the second or third time. At a time when microchips were being sold 'by the sack' abroad, the D D R was producing them at an astronomical cost.

## Inter-German relations

Despite the deterioration in relations between the U S A and the Soviet Union between 1979 and 1986, to the surprise of some the change of government in Bonn brought no change in the relations between the two German states. Elements within the Christian Democratic camp had criticised the S P D/F D P coalition for being too soft on the S E D regime. In government they pursued the same policy. This was partly because Genscher remained Foreign Minister and he helped to ensure continuity. Having been born and brought up in Halle, he had a personal interest in the D D R. But many in the C D U/C S U felt the same. Frau Kohl, for instance, had grown up there too. But the truth is, few in the coalition believed there was really a chance to re-unite Germany in the near or even medium term. Like the previous government, what they sought was an improvement in relations, a lowering of tension, higher living standards for the East German people and a little more freedom: a more tolerable life in general. The Kohl government sought to wring concessions out of Honecker's regime using its economic muscle for this purpose. In 1983 and 1984 Honecker was compelled to seek credits in Bonn. The D D R was granted a D M 1 billion credit in 1983 and D M 950 million in July 1984. In exchange the D D R dropped the minimum exchange requirement demanded from children and later that required of pensioners visiting the D D R. There was also a modest increase in the number of East Germans under pensionable age allowed to visit the West on 'urgent family business'. The D D R however, was not a free agent. It knew it could only go as far as Moscow allowed it. On 2 August 1984 the Soviet paper *Pravda* expressed doubts about the credits, claiming Bonn was using them to gain more influence in the D D R with the ultimate aim of re-unification. This was the era of Yuri Andropov (1982–4) and Konstantin Chernenko (1984–5) in the Soviet Union. The wartime generation of leaders were breathing their last breath. The D D R was forced to sacrifice its participation in the 1984 Olympic Games in Los Angeles where it expected to do very well. By so doing the S E D leaders were reducing their credibility in the eyes of their people. Honecker also had to postpone (until 1987) a projected visit to

Bonn, agreed when he met Chancellor Schmidt in 1981. Honecker believed he badly needed this trip to convince his own people that he wanted better relations with West Germany and that he was totally accepted by the Bonn political establishment. Moscow, for its part, wanted to set the pace in the relations between the two German states.

Inter-German relations continued to improve throughout the Kohl era with ever increasing contacts. Ambitious West German politicians felt obliged to visit Honecker to demonstrate that they were doing all they could to improve relations. The trip of Franz Josef Strauss to East Germany in July 1983 caused something of a sensation. Undoubtedly one reason for his journey was to assert his independence vis-à-vis his colleagues in Bonn. Whatever his reasons, he was a welcome guest as far as the S E D was concerned. Honecker convinced himself that such important guests must help prove to the East German people that he was their legitimate, independent leader and that there was no going back to a united Germany, the D D R was a permanent part of the European landscape.

## The churches and dissidence in the D D R

In both halves of Germany, politicians felt under pressure to improve inter-German relations. The relative success of the Greens in the West encouraged young people in the East to think dangerous thoughts.

In the D D R compulsory military training in secondary schools was introduced for 15- and 16-year-olds from September 1978. Undoubtedly, the S E D saw this as a means of indoctrinating young people to counter the growing indiscipline and disaffection that it could sense. Many young people found life in the D D R grim and restrictive. Most lived in poor housing, under constant attempts to regiment them, limited entertainment possibilities and virtually no foreign travel. The numbers having to cope with growing up in broken homes were high relative to most other modern states. As elsewhere, there was growing juvenile delinquency, though this was given very limited acknowledgement. More and more people, including many young ones, applied to leave the D D R for West Germany.

Increasingly, thinking young people turned to the churches for intellectual stimulation and practical help. These were a minority but a growing one. The churches had been given a limited amount of freedom in the hope they would co-operate with the S E D's 'peace' campaigns and help give the D D R respectability. A meeting between

Honecker and the executive committee of the League of Evangelical Churches in the D D R, the main Christian body in East Germany, on 6 March 1978 had emphasised the S E D's recognition of the churches' role in a socialist society. The church side was led by Bishop Albrecht Schönherr, who some felt was a little too conciliatory towards the S E D. However, the churches were being drawn more and more into a stance of opposition. They voiced their objection to military training in schools and called for an alternative to military service, similar to that available in West Germany.

In 1984 there was a wave of embassy occupations by East Germans seeking to emigrate to the West. Eventually, they were allowed to leave after secret negotiations. In March of that year the evangelical church synod at Görlitz urged the S E D to create the conditions which would persuade people to stay. This call was repeated by the same body in the same town in 1987 when the value of the nuclear deterrent and military service were also questioned. In July 1987 in Dresden, at the first organised meeting of the D D R's Catholics, 80,000 Catholics heard Cardinal Joachim Meisner call for more career opportunities for Christians who were still being discriminated against. By that time events in other Warsaw Pact states, including the Soviet Union, were influencing the mood in the D D R.

## Election 1987

The elevation of Mikhail Gorbachev to the leadership of the Soviet Union in 1985 was to have a decisive impact on Germany. 'Conservatives' in both parts of Germany were confused by the new Soviet leader. His style, rhetoric and, not least, actions, soon made him the most popular foreign statesman among Germans. In the Bonn coalition, F D P Foreign Minister Genscher worried some of his Christian Democratic colleagues who were concerned that he was being taken in by Gorbachev's smile. More than anyone in the government, Genscher was pushing for detente and was thus in touch with the popular mood. Of German politicians, Genscher was revealed in surveys to be the most popular. He then retained this position right up to the subsequent elections of 1990.

By contrast, Helmut Kohl and the new Social Democratic contender for the Chancellorship, Johannes Rau, Prime Minister of Northrhine-Westphalia, failed to capture the public's enthusiasm. Kohl appeared to many as either inept or pandering to hardliners in his own camp. In 1986 he caused ructions by comparing, in a *Newsweek* interview, the public relations skills of Gorbachev with those of Goebbels. Kohl and his party colleagues reasserted the view that the 'German Question' was still open. Kohl restored the concept of the 'German Fatherland' and was the first Chancellor in two decades to address large rallies of bodies representing the refugees from the lost territories.

Compared with the S P D, Kohl and the C D U/C S U were not under quite the same pressure from the Greens. However, the nuclear disaster at Chernobyl in the Soviet Union in May 1986 caused world-wide concern. Kohl's response was not to abandon nuclear power but to set up a Ministry for Environmental Protection and Reactor Safety headed by Walter Wallmann, Mayor of Frankfurt am Main. Worse was to come, with large-scale spillages by chemical companies into the Rhine in the winter of 1986. In view of all this Kohl was heartened by the regional election result in Lower Saxony where the C D U/F D P coalition was returned with a one seat majority in 1987. The C D U vote fell, the S P D vote remained static, the F D P and the Greens improved their positions. It could have been much worse for Kohl.

Johannes Rau was the successful leader of West Germany's biggest *Land*. In 1985 he led his party to an absolute majority (52.1 per cent) in the regional election. He beat off the Green challenge, who failed to break into parliament by achieving only 4.6 per cent. This success helped him win the nomination to lead the S P D's challenge to Kohl. His main problems, however, were that he was too moderate, not decisive enough and his party spoke with several voices. Its main theme was neither anti-nuclear, anti-growth nor anti-N A T O, but it used greenish rhetoric against the coalition. It was also far more 'realistic' on the German issue, a majority of leading S P D members believing it to be closed. None of this was enough to appease the Green corner in the political arena.

There was internal strife in all the West German parties in the 1980s, but it is no exaggeration to say that the Greens really did succeed in spite of their infighting. The public financing of political parties and the television coverage of environmental issues were decisive factors which helped them throughout the period. The Greens were split into so-called *Fundis* and *Realos* (fundamentalists and realists). The first-named rejected compromise, including coalitions, and were sceptical about parliamentary institutions compared with the value of mass, direct action. The realists were prepared to join in coalitions with the S P D and play a constructive role in parliaments rather than just using them for propaganda or obstruction. The bulk of Green voters favoured the realist position as did the majority of the parliamentary group in the Bundestag, with the executive committee inclining to the 'fundi' position. Because they opposed 'personality cults' and strongly favoured basis democracy (leaving the local party branches to decide major policy issues), the Greens had difficulties with their leading personalities and public image. Their representatives in the Bundestag were supposed to surrender their mandates after only two years. This made it more difficult for them to build up an effective parliamentary cadre. This policy was opposed by both Petra Kelly and General Gert Bastian, formerly commander of the Bundeswehr's 12th armoured division, two of the Greens, most effective parliamentarians. Despite their divisions, in the period 1983–7, the Greens had made advances at regional elections in all but one *Land* (Saar), and were represented in 7 out of 11 parliaments. In Hesse they had forced the S P D into an agreement with them in June 1984, converting this into a full coalition in October 1985. Josef 'Joschka' Fischer as first Green minister was put in charge of environment and energy. The Greens had also gained 8.2 per cent in the European Parliament election of 1984 thus achieving representation for the first time.

In the election of 25 January 1987 'only' 84.3 per cent of the electorate voted. This compared with 89.1 in 1983, 88.6 in 1980, 90.7 in1976 and 91.1 (the highest ever turnout) in 1972. The decline could be attributable in part at least to the weather. It remained higher than recorded in any post-war elections in the U S A, Britain or France. The C D U/C S U vote slumped from 48.4 per cent to 44.3. The S P D vote moved from 38.2 per cent to 37. The winners were the F D P up from 7 to 9.1 and the Greens, up from 5.6 to 8.3. For the C D U/C S U it represented the worst result since 1949. Genscher's more softly-softly approach to the Soviet Union had won over some moderate conservatives. In Bavaria the more strident critics of 'Genscherism', the C S U, saw their vote fall from 59.5 per cent in 1983 to 55.1 in 1987 on a lower turnout. Strauss' claim that a tougher line would win more votes did not appear to be true.

## Women and politics

The advance of the Greens had highlighted the fact that West Germany had not made much progress towards better representation of the sexes. In the 1980–3 Bundestag only 8.5 per cent of members were women. This increased to 9.8 per cent in the 1983–7 parliament and 15.4 per cent in the 1987–90 parliament. This great increase was due largely to the Greens. In the late 1980s the Greens had the biggest number of women enrolled as party members (33 per cent), next came the S P D (25), F D P (24), C D U (22) and C S U (14). By the 1980s the earlier differences between the sexes in voting habits had been largely eroded.

The following table shows voting behaviour by sex for the different parties in the federal elections of 1980, 1983 and 1987. The figures are expressed as a total percentage of the vote:

|         |       | men and women | men | women |
|---------|-------|---------------|-----|-------|
| CDU/CSU | 1980: | 44            | 44.2 | 43.7 |
|         | 1983: | 48.5          | 47.7 | 49.2 |
|         | 1987: | 43.8          | 42.5 | 45.1 |
| SPD     | 1980: | 43.5          | 43.1 | 43.9 |
|         | 1983: | 38.9          | 38.4 | 39.4 |
|         | 1987: | 38.1          | 38.5 | 37.8 |
| FDP     | 1980: | 10.6          | 10.5 | 10.8 |
|         | 1983: | 6.7           | 7.2  | 6.3  |
|         | 1987: | 8.7           | 9.2  | 8.3  |
| Greens  | 1980: | 1.4           | 1.6  | 1.2  |
|         | 1983: | 5.3           | 5.9  | 4.8  |
|         | 1987: | 8.0           | 8.3  | 7.7  |

The percentages reflect the slightly greater appeal in 1980 of Chancellor Schmidt over Strauss among women voters, with the lingering advantage enjoyed by the C D U/C S U among older women voters reasserting itself in 1983 and 1987. Despite their large number of women candidates, the Greens clearly attracted a higher percentage of voters among men as compared with women. This was 'normal' for a new and 'revolutionary' party.

## Honecker in Bonn

Kohl retained his cabinet mostly as it was in the period between 1983 and 1987, although Graf Lambsdorff had been forced to resign in June 1984 after being charged in the Flick affair. Lambsdorff's replacement as Minister of Economics, Martin Bangemann (F D P) kept his post until he went to the European Commission. Manfred Wörner stayed on at the Ministry of Defence until he was elected Secretary General of N A T O, the first German to hold this post, in 1988. Dr Dorothee Wilms (C D U) was moved from Education and Science to the key post of Inter-German Affairs; one of her first tasks was to help prepare for the much-delayed visit of Honecker to Bonn.

Honecker finally arrived in Bonn on 7 September 1987. It was the first visit by an East German head of party and state. He was received with all official pomp on his five-day trip. Although the D D R's Foreign Minister Oskar Fischer was greeted by Frau Wilms not by Genscher, one could have been forgiven for thinking that at last the two German states were permanent and had recognised the division of Germany as permanent. This was what Honecker and the S E D wanted. Kohl criticised the Wall and President von Weizsäcker alluded to German unity by remarking that the citizens of the two German states were part of the same nation, a nation which had not started with Bismarck nor ended with Hitler.

The visit was successful as an event which further eased tension. Nothing spectacular happened or was achieved apart from the signing of three agreements on science, technology and the environment. Kohl accepted an invitation to visit the D D R. Honecker went on from Bonn to visit his old home in the Saar and then his new friend Franz Josef Strauss in Munich.

## Scandals galore

In the 1980s the Federal Republic was hit by a series of scandals which shocked the public and the political establishment alike. In December 1983 General Günter Kiessling, Deputy Supreme Commander of Allied Forces in Europe, was dismissed by Defence Minister Wörner, accused of homosexual activities likely to compromise his position. The General was later reinstated after the Minister admitted the charges were false. Shortly afterwards Kiessling was pensioned off with great military pomp at a ceremony attended by Wörner and General Bernard Rogers, N A T O Supreme Commander in Europe. Surprisingly, the Minister held on to his post despite widespread criticism. There was also strong criticism of the Bundeswehr's security service (M A D) the body which had alerted Wörner to the alleged activities of Kiessling. A shake-up of M A D was announced.

A real security scandal was the defection of Hans Joachim Tiedge, a senior official of the internal security service (B f V) of West Germany, to the D D R in 1986. Tiedge had been living a dissipated life for some time but no action had been taken. The case was just one of many in the 1980s involving defections to the East or conviction in the West on spy charges. Many involved single, middle-aged women, like Margaret Höke, a senior secretary in the President's office for 21 years, who was arrested in 1986 on spy charges.

Perhaps the affair of the so-called 'Hitler diaries' was as much farce as fraud. The weekly *Stern* paid out D M 9,340,000 for these diaries between 1981 and 1983, when they were revealed to be forgeries. Two men, including a *Stern* reporter were jailed in 1984 for the fraud. A considerable amount of the money was not recovered. The affair revealed the continuing interest in Hitler as well as the gullibility of the so-called quality press and the fallibility of experts.

The resignation in April 1986 of three senators (ministers) of Eberhard Diepgen's C D U/F D P West Berlin government on bribery and corruption charges rather tarnished the good name of local government. The most senior of them was Diepgen's deputy and as Senator for Internal Affairs was in charge of the police. The charges concerned payments from a Berlin developer and helped to give the Greens in the city a new impetus.

The Flick affair threatened to bring discredit on the whole political establishment. This involved allegations that Graf Lambsdorff, as Minister of Economics; Rainer Barzel, President of the Bundestag; and some others had assisted the Flick group of companies in tax evasion on party contributions. In 1987 Lambsdorff was convicted of these charges but acquitted on corruption charges. Lambsdorff was fined; a Flick official was also fined and given a suspended prison sentence. It was not claimed that the Graf or Barzel had sought to enrich themselves.

Worse still was the scandal which engulfed the German Trade Union Confederation (D G B). This involved the union-owned *Neue Heimat* group, Europe's largest construction concern. *Der Spiegel* was responsible for exposing malpractice and corruption which brought *Neue Heimat* to the verge of bankruptcy. It had to be liquidated with all its affiliates, including the jewel in the crown of the D G B's commercial empire, *Die Bank für Gemeinwirtschaft*. To some degree this sorry story must have damaged the idea of trade union alternatives to capitalism.

In 1987 a scandal, also brought to light by *Der Spiegel*, hit the Schleswig-Holstein government in a *Land* ruled by the C D U since the 1950s. Reiner Pfeiffer, a close adviser to the Prime Minister of Schleswig-Holstein, Uwe Barschel, alleged in a signed document that his boss had instigated a campaign of dirty tricks against his S P D rival, Björn Engholm. This included false rumours about Engholm's sex life, tax situation and views. Barschel repeatedly denied the charges. Subsequently, on 11 October 1987, his fully-clothed body was found in the bath in his room in a fashionable hotel in Geneva, Switzerland. He had died from an overdose of medication. Gerhard Stoltenberg, Federal Finance Minister and Chairman of the Schleswig-Holstein C D U, later apologised to Engholm and the S P D, admitting that Barschel had not told the truth and had seriously damaged

237

respect for state politics and for the C D U. In the regional election in September 1987 the C D U gained 42.6 per cent of the votes (1983: 49 per cent), the S P D 45.2 (43.7) and the F D P 5.2 (2.2). Fresh elections were held in May 1988 with the C D U falling to 33.3 per cent, its lowest vote since 1958, with the S P D share rising to 54.8, its best result ever, and the F D P falling back to 4.4. Engholm was elected Prime Minister.

A more painful and embarrassing scandal than the others was the discovery that the former Chairman of the Central Council of Jews in Germany, Werner Nachmann, had been embezzling the funds. This came to light after his death and was revealed in 1988 by Nachmann's successor, Heinz Galinski. Apparently, between 1980 and 1988 Nachmann had misappropriated D M 33 million of funds given by the West German state as compensation to the Jews for Nazi crimes.

One should make neither too much nor too little of these incidents. Many other democracies (not to mention the non-democratic states) suffered from such scandals in the 1980s. The Socialist governments of Austria and Greece, big business in Britain and the U S A, the Reagan administration and the governments of Italy and Japan all had their problems of this type.

## More opposition in the D D R

In preparation for Honecker's Bonn visit the D D R Council of State issued decrees on 17 July 1987 abolishing the death penalty (which had rarely been used for many years) and introducing an amnesty, which it was claimed would lead to 24,621 convicted prisoners and another 1753 in pre-trial detention being released. Within weeks of Honecker's Bonn sojourn his security police were cracking down on dissidents. They raided an ecological library in the Church of Zion in East Berlin making several arrests, confiscating documents and equipment. Those arrested had been involved in publishing two magazines *Grenzfall* and *Umweltblätter*. On 10 December 1987 a number of people were taken into custody because they wanted to present a declaration to the D D R's United Nations' Association, demanding an open and truthful democratic society. In both cases the prisoners were released after a short time but some were advised to go to West Germany or face possible legal action against them. According to Günter Schabowski, the S E D leaders felt a sense of outrage when an unofficial group attempted to join the annual demonstration (17 January 1988) commemorating the murder in 1919 of Rosa Luxemburg and Karl Liebknecht (see chapter 2). The unofficial group aptly quoted the words of Luxemburg, criticising Lenin and advocating free discussion. There were over 100 arrests including the former S E D members Vera Wollenberger and Stephan Krawczyk, a banned song-writer and singer, his wife Freya Klier, and Bärbel Bohley, a painter who had clashed with the regime before. Widespread protests followed in both German states and all the parties in the Bundestag condemned the arrests. By 24 January, 54 of the arrested were already in Giessen, West Germany. The three named and some others were forced to leave the D D R, others who left were glad to get out. There were more arrests at various times in 1988, in many cases of those who like Wollenberger, Krawczyk and Bohley wanted to see the S E D moving in the direction of Gorbachev's reforms in the Soviet Union. Increasingly East German church leaders were voicing criticisms of the situation.

Despite the arrests in the D D R and the S E D's attitude to Gorbachev's style of leadership, relations between the two German states continued to improve in 1988. One new feature was the many towns in the West which were finding twinning partners in the East. This development started in 1986 with Saarlouis in the West and Eisenhüttenstadt in the D D R. In that year three twinning agreements were signed. In 1987 there were 16 such agreements and in 1988, 23. Another remarkable development was that the President of the Bundestag was commissioned to investigate the possibilities of official contacts with the D D R parliament, the Volkskammer. In the past such contacts had been frowned upon on the grounds that the Volkskammer was not a real parliament. The other sign of improvement, a result of popular pressure in this case, was the great increase in East Germans below retirement age being allowed to visit relatives in West Germany 'on urgent family business'. In 1980 only 40,422 were allowed out; in 1985 the figure had crept up to 66,074. In the following year it was between 244,000 and 300,000 according to West German estimates and, according to the D D R reached 1,290,000 in 1988. Both the S E D and the Bonn government were repeating some of their long-held tenets, yet in practice the frontier between their two states seemed to be melting.

## S E D and Gorbachev

Officially all was well between the S E D and its brother party the C P S U in the 1980s. The last years of Brezhnev followed by Andropov and Chernenko were years when the C P S U seemed paralysed at the top. This gave the S E D leaders more leeway. They were themselves remarkably active in the international arena despite their age and state of health. When Gorbachev took over in Moscow in 1985 the ruling Politburo of the S E D consisted of 26 full or candidate members. Among the top leaders Honecker was 73; head of government Willi Stoph 71; Minister for State Security Erich Mielke 78; Defence Minister Heinz Hoffman 75; Volkskammer President Horst Sindermann 70; economic supremo Günter Mittag 59; ideology expert Kurt Hager 73; International Secretary Hermann Axen 69; Harry Tisch trade union boss 58 and crown prince Egon Krenz 48. Many of them were ailing. Honecker, with the help of Mittag and Mielke, appears to have decided most issues with general policy discussions rarely taking place. They were totally isolated from both the people and even the lower levels of the S E D, due partly to the impossibility of open discussion on any issue and also to their privileged life-style. Western visitors usually courted them rather than criticised them. They could however avail themselves of West German media reports and easily verify that they were, when critical, usually accurate.

Open criticism of the Soviet leader was difficult and they therefore claimed that whereas the Soviet Union needed glasnost (openness) and perestroika (restructuring), the D D R did not because the situation there was quite different. Firstly, since it was on the frontier of the ideological and military divide between the Warsaw Pact and N A T O the S E D therefore had to be more disciplined and vigilant than its comrades elsewhere. Secondly, the D D R was far more advanced than the Soviet Union and had long ago solved some of the fundamental problems facing the C P S U. Its economy was well-organised and modern, unlike that of the Soviet Union. It had kept a degree of private enterprise, which Gorbachev had started to legalise, and was now extending this. It also had better functioning parties and mass organisations than existed in the Soviet Union. There was an element of truth in all of this but not enough to make any fundamental difference. Since the mid-1970s the S E D had been a little more tolerant of private business at the very low level of corner shops, small snack-bars, services and the like. The four satellite parties: Liberal Democrats (L D P D); Christian Democrats (C D U); Democratic Farmers (D B D); and National Democrats (N D P D), were given a higher profile in the 1980s. But these were not changes of any fundamental importance.

The S E D's attitude to the Gorbachev line was put by veteran ideologue Kurt Hager who, in an interview in the West German *Stern* (10 April 1987), asked rhetorically, 'If a neighbour changed his wallpaper in his apartment, would you feel you had to do the same?' More directly Margot Honecker, Minister of Education, speaking at the ninth East German Pedagogic Congress (13 June 1989) condemned those who talked about the free market economy and pluralism. She had no doubt they sought 'not the strengthening of socialism, but the return to capitalism'. The S E D also identified itself as a friend of the hard-line leadership in China which had crushed the student demonstrations for democracy in Beijing with tanks. In a report to the S E D Central Committee (22 June 1989) Joachim Hermann, the S E D Secretary responsible for the media, reported how the D D R media had refuted 'Western horror stories' about the Beijing massacre. With these sort of statements from their leaders the East German people could have little hope that reform was on the way. One other cause of dismay was the falsification of the results of the local 'elections' in May 1989. For once far more people had been prepared to take a risk and vote against the official list. The S E D decided that direct falsification was the only answer. It was only prepared to admit a slight increase in the 'no' vote, 141,845 or 1.15 per cent. In this situation more people decided to attempt to vote with their feet.

## Historians in conflict

Kohl was the first German leader in East or West to have been born too late to have served in the war or to have been involved with the Nazis. This was true of 14 other members of the 19-member government of 1987. Only four, including Genscher, Zimmermann, Stoltenberg and Oscar Schneider (C S U) Minister for Planning and Building, had seen wartime service. Most of the others, however, still remembered the war as children, several had been refugees. Despite the passage of time, the Nazi years remained ever present not only in childhood memories, school books, museums, visits to concentration camp sites and anniversaries, but also in the media, feature films and even the hunt for Nazi criminals.

Like previous Chancellors since 1949, Kohl fully acknowledged Germany's responsibility for Nazi crimes. Speaking on 9 November 1988, on the 50th anniversary of anti-Jewish *Reichskristallnacht*, at the rebuilt West End synagogue in Frankfurt, he said that event, 'remains with us. In pain and in shame it is part of our present'. He called the Nazi attempt to exterminate the Jews, 'unique genocide'. Kohl's words were well-chosen, coming as they did at a time when the German academic community was locked in the so-called *Historikerstreit*. This consumed the energies of a small number of German historians in determining their views on Germany's past, above all recent past, and was played out in the mass media. The principal

241

contestants were Ernst Nolte, Andreas Hillgruber and Michael Stürmer (an adviser to Kohl), on the one hand, and Jürgen Habermas, on the other. In the respected *Die Zeit* in July 1986 Habermas accused the three of 'apologetic tendencies' in relation to recent Geman history. What was at stake was whether there was anything to salvage from Germany's past which could form part of a patriotic attachment, and whether the attempt to wipe out the Jews, the Holocaust, would be 'relativised', and German guilt lessened, by comparing it to other crimes. Habermas believed what the Germans needed was a *Verfassungspatriotismus*, in other words, patriotism based on the Federal Republic's Basic Law. For him German history was too flawed to offer a democratic identity for Germans in the 1980s. Stürmer rejected this view arguing the need to identify with the positive aspects of Germany's past. Hillgruber and Nolte were more concerned with putting the Nazi experience into the context of twentieth century European and world history. Nolte did not, in fact, deny that the Holocaust was unique, but that did not in itself preclude comparison with other crimes. Nor could any of the three be accused of flirting with the idea of West Germany loosening its ties with the E C, N A T O and its other Western commitments. Habermas seemed to think the 'revisionism' he rejected was the ideological counterpart to the political change of 1982.

Perhaps the argument was more intense because it was played out at a time of increased, right-wing activity in West Germany (see chapter 14). It was also a time when the Soviet authorities and Soviet historians were saying more about Stalin's crimes which made it easier still for some to excuse Hitler by reference to Stalin.

Over forty years after the end of the 1939–45 war, with new generations, more facts available, more time to digest those facts and the experience of other tragedies, it was only natural that the perspectives would begin to change, even more so among younger historians like Stürmer. The truth was that by the end of the 1980s mass education had failed to eliminate cultural illiteracy in Europe, North America and elsewhere, including knowledge of the crimes casting shadows over the pasts of many states. Also, the determination against placing Nazi crimes in a comparative historical and international perspective could be interpreted as a form of racism practised against the Germans. Remarkably few people accused the Russian or other Soviet peoples over the crimes of the Soviet state, which had already existed over seventy years compared with the twelve years of the Third Reich. Was it not possible for Russians to deny the 'achievements' of the Soviet state yet feel a sense of patriotism engendered by an identification with such twentieth century Russians as, for instance, Gagarin, Pasternak, Plekhanov, Sakharov, Shostakovich, Solzhenitsyn, Stravinsky and Zhukov. Could such great twentieth-century German and European figures as Konrad Adenauer, Heinrich Böll, Thomas Dehler, Thomas Mann, Martin Niemöller, Klaus von Stauffenberg, Kurt Schumacher and Richard Strauss not form the basis of a German, democratic, patriotism? Such patriotism is normal and in no way contradicts the aim of building a united Europe.

# — 14 —

# German Unity Restored

The annual convention of the C D U in June 1988 was not a happy one for Helmut Kohl. Since the election of 1987 the party's fortunes had sagged. Membership, which had risen from 287,000 in 1968 to a high of 735,000 in 1983, had fallen steadily to 693,000 in 1988. Membership of the rival, but allied C S U, had also peaked in 1983 at 185,000 (74,000 in 1968), falling slightly to 184,000 in 1988. The membership of the coalition partner, F D P, had risen to 87,000 in 1981 (57,000 in 1968) but had fallen to 64,000 in 1986 and then had risen to 65,000 in 1988. By contrast, the opposition S P D had peaked with 1,022,000 in 1976 (732,000 in 1968) falling year by year to 910,000 in 1987 and remaining at that figure in 1988. Green membership was estimated at 44,000 having risen from 18,000 in 1980. In five out of six regional contests between 1987 and 1988 the C D U vote had fallen. In Hamburg, for the first time since the fall of Schmidt in 1982, an S P D/F D P coalition had been formed at *Land* level in August 1987. The economy was not performing well by post-war German standards. Kohl's prestige in the opinion polls was low. There was talk in the C D U of finding a successor.

One year later there was still no joy for Kohl. In the *Land* elections in Schleswig-Holstein and West Berlin the C D U had failed and it had lost support in the election to the European Parliament:

Election to European Parliament in percent

|  | 1984 | 1989 |
|---|---|---|
| SPD | 37.5 | 37.3 |
| CDU | 37.4 | 29.6 |
| CSU | 8.5 | 8.2 |
| FDP | 4.8 | 5.6 |
| Greens | 8.2 | 8.4 |
| Republicans | — | 7.1 |

The C D U had to fear a new challenge on the right which could put them out of office at the elections in 1990 as the N P D had in 1969 (see chapter 11). The new challenge was from the so-called *Republikaner* (R E P) or Republicans.

## *Schönhuber's Republikaner*

The R E P caused a minor sensation when they broke into the West Berlin parliament gaining 7.5 per cent in the *Land* election in January 1989. The defeat of the F D P there, combined with the R E P success, led to the removal of the C D U from office and the formation of S P D/Green coalition. A few weeks later the right-wing N P D gained 6.6 per cent of the vote and six seats in the Frankfurt local elections. The R E P also did well in the two districts where they put up candidates. In June the R E P gained 7.1 per cent of the vote in the election to the European Parliament. If the votes of other candidates are taken into account the far-right gained nearly 9 per cent. The R E P gained 6 of West Germany's 81 seats. The success of the R E P hit the prestige of the Federal Republic abroad and worried the politically responsible at home.

The R E P had been formed in 1983 by disaffected members of the C S U and Franz Schönhuber, the former presenter of a popular chat show on Bavarian T V. The former C S U members thought that Franz Josef Strauss was going soft on Communism by his visits to the D D R and the help he gave to Honecker to secure a credit deal. Schönhuber had lost his job after he had published a book recounting his experiences in the wartime Waffen-S S. In the book Schönhuber did not identify with the Nazi regime and subsequently he dissociated himself from it in several interviews, such as the one in *Der Spiegel* (6 February 1989). The main planks of his party's programme were law and order, restrictions on foreign immigration, German neutrality between the Soviet Union and the U S A, and pan-European integration on Gaullist lines. At the 1989 European election the R E P strongly opposed further moves to integrate the Federal Republic into the European Community. They also wanted a 'decriminalisation of German history' which, they believed, had been dominated by the views of the Second World War victors.

Surveys conducted by the Konrad Adenauer-Stiftung in 1989 revealed that R E P supporters tended to be in the 18–29 age group, men rather than women, blue-collar or self-employed rather than white collar employees, lived in small rather than large towns and had weak or no church affiliation. R E P supporters also tended to be over represented among those who had only completed basic education. In some respects, therefore, they were different from earlier far-right supporters. Some observers have pointed out that the R E P was successful among young people at a time of high youth unemployment. In 1987, for instance, 16.5 per cent of those aged 20–24 were unemployed compared to 8.9 per cent for the population as a whole. There has also been speculation that the R E P appealed more to those in the insecure sectors of the economy who feared job competition from newcomers. The death of Franz Josef Strauss in October 1988 had left a gap on the right in German politics, especially but not only, in Bavaria. Schönhuber hoped to exploit the opportunity presented by the empty stage.

The N P D had been in existence since the 1960s. It had been a complete failure though it is true that it more than doubled its percentage of the vote in 1987 compared with 1983, 0.6 as against 0.2 per cent. In 1989 it had about 7,000 members. Unlike the R E P its activities were monitored by the Federal Office for the Protection of the Constitution (B f V). On the extreme right there were also a number of tiny, openly Nazi organisations, in some cases engaged in political violence. In its 1989 annual report the B f V recorded 103 acts of violence by right-wing extremists, 12 of these involved arson, 52 bodily harm and one death. According to the B f V far-right bodies, including the N P D but not the R E P, had about 35,000 members in 1989. They had increased each year since 1986 when the total was 22,100.

Worrying though the R E P were, they were simply part of a wider European phenomenon of parties hostile to the existing political establishment and to foreign immigrants. These included the French National Front; the Italian M S I; the Swiss Vigilants, Action National and the Autopartei; the Vlaams Blok in Belgium; to a degree the Freedom Party in Austria; and the various anti-tax and 'progressive' parties in Scandinavia.

## Political violence

One shock which the political establishment had to face was the apparent widespread support for the R E P among the police. Police pay and conditions had fallen behind those in other occupations over the years and the police were, in some areas like Berlin and Frankfurt, under severe strain during demonstrations. At one particularly bad incident on 2 November 1987, two policemen were shot dead by masked participants at a demonstration at Frankfurt airport commemorating the clearing of a 'peace village' six years previously. The village had been part of the campaign against the extension of the runway. The police faced violence when sent to clear the increasing numbers of squatters in West Berlin and they were also still facing urban terrorism in the shape of the so-called Red Army Faction (R A F). This terrorism, which had been contained in the late 1970s, erupted again in the 1980s. In the 1970s the main targets had been individuals like Hans Martin Schleyer, President of the Federation of German Industry, who was kidnapped and then murdered in 1977. In the 1980s the main targets were U S military installations or places frequented by allied servicemen. On 30 November 1989 the R A F blew up and killed Alfred Herrhausen, chief executive of Deutsche Bank, West Germany's largest. Their previous successful assassination was in 1986. The police also had to deal with I R A attacks against the British forces in Germany, Arab attacks on American property and factional fighting between foreign groups.

In 1990 assassination attempts on Oskar Lafontaine, S P D candidate for the Chancellorship, and Wolfgang Schäuble, Federal Minister of Interior were both disturbing and perplexing. Lafontaine was stabbed in the neck by a mentally disturbed woman but he made a good recovery. Schäuble, who was shot in October by a mentally unstable drug addict, returned to work in December though confined to a wheelchair. The attacks made it more difficult for politicians to meet the public.

## Changes in the C D U

In the summer of 1989 Kohl got rid of the C D U Secretary General Heiner Geissler who was regarded as being on the social welfare orientated left-wing of the C D U. He was made a scapegoat for the party's lack of success and was replaced by Volker Rühe a handsome younger man. Geissler instantly became popular with the public, more popular than Kohl: in Emnid opinion poll published in *Der Spiegel* 25 September 1989, Geissler came fifth in popularity, Kohl fourteenth. Professor Rita Süssmuth, no longer a minister but President of the Bundestag since November 1988, got the highest rating, followed by Genscher; Lothar Späth, C D U Prime Minister of Baden-Württemberg; Björn Engholm, S P D Prime Minister of Schleswig-Holstien; and Heiner Geissler. There then followed four S P D leaders, two C D U leaders, one F D P member and Theo Waigel of the C S U all ahead of Kohl. The party preferences expressed were C D U/C S U 40 per cent, S P D 39, Greens 9, F D P 8 and R E P 4. The same survey revealed that of those polled, 66 per cent felt the government was doing too much for civil servants, 54 too much for big business and 47 per cent too much for ethnic German immigrants. On the other hand, 61 per cent believed the government was not doing enough for pensioners, 55 for the unemployed, 51 for those on social security and 44 for farmers. The only comfort for the C D U/C S U was that it was increasing its support again (as was the S P D) and that support for the R E P was already falling.

## The D D R's hot summer

The leaders of the D D R, it used to be said, feared a good summer. Bright sunny weather, like that of 1961, only served to make young people think of holidays in far away places, which for them included Stuttgart, Munich and Cologne. The summer of 1989 was a good one and it was the summer of a year which had seen much political drama in East Europe. In June the first multi-party elections in Soviet Europe since 1946 had taken place in Poland. Open competition was allowed for the 100 seats of the Polish Senate and 35 per cent of the seats in the lower house. The free trade union movement, Solidarity, won 99 of the Senate seats as well as many of the others it was permitted to stand for. A Solidarity-led government was formed. Hungary too was heading for democracy with the Communists having already resigned themselves to a life in opposition. On 2 May Hungary, one of the few places abroad East Germans could go to, opened its frontier to Austria, pulling down its frontier fortifications. This event reached the East German population via West German T V. Soon hundreds, and then thousands, of East Germans were making the trip. Many crossed into Austria illegally. More dramatic still was the announcement by Hungary on 10 September that it would not prevent East Germans leaving for Austria or attempt to send them back to the D D R. By this time thousands were already in West Germany. Thousands of others had sought refuge in the West German embassies in Warsaw, Prague and Budapest.

These events revealed the lack of support for the East German régime. The obscurantism of the S E D leaders, a worsening supply situation, events in neighbouring states had all played their parts in deciding people to leave. Negotiations produced freedom for the D D R citizens in the embassies. On 5 October eight special sealed trains left Prague carrying 10,000 East Germans. Foolishly the East German leaders had insisted that they go via the D D R so that the regime would save face by officially expelling them. As the trains moved slowly through Dresden, police fought off other East Germans attempting to board them. The first large scale disorder since 1953 occurred.

On 7 September a demonstration of around 200 people, peacefully protesting against the local election fraud of 7 May, was broken up with force, many arrests followed.

The Politburo of the S E D appeared paralysed. Honecker was reported to be seriously ill, even dying. Some members were on holiday. The leader of the L D P D, Manfred Gerlach, whose party had long been a satellite of the S E D, decided to open his mouth and make a sober, modest, yet clear, call for change. His call went unheeded. On 19 September Bärbel Bohley, back in the D D R, wrote to the Minister of Interior announcing the setting up of New Forum on 10 September according to article 79 of the D D R constitution. Shortly afterwards a group calling itself Democracy Now was formed. On 25 September 6,000–8,000 people took part in what the S E D *Leipziger Volkszeitung* (26 September) called an 'anti-socialist mob' in Leipzig. The next day brought the announcement of the Social Democratic Party (S D P) of the D D R. The staff of the prestigious Berliner Ensemble, Brecht's theatre, issued a call for reform on 29 September. On the same day activists of the official S E D-controlled union at the Bergmann-Borsig engineering plant in East Berlin wrote to F D G B Chairman Harry Tisch calling for change. All these 'manifestos' were moderate, all assumed that both the D D R and 'Socialism' would continue.

## Revolution in Autumn

A visitor to East Berlin on 7 October could have been forgiven for thinking the regime was in full control. There was the usual military parade to celebrate the setting up of the D D R in 1949, with mass bands, goose-stepping elite troops, heavy tanks and other hardware. Taking the salute were the members of the Politburo, headed by Honecker, and with them, Mikhail Gorbachev. Not far away another demonstration of a different kind was beginning. It walked to the Palace of the Republic, where the official party had gone to feast, shouting, 'Gorby', 'We are staying here', 'Stasi out', 'Gorby help us' and 'New Forum'. The presence of Western camera crews made it difficult for the police to intervene. Soon they did however and with considerable brutality. The Berliners were not alone, mass demonstrations were taking place in Leipzig, Dresden, Jena, Plauen and Potsdam.

On 18 October it was announced that Honecker had resigned 'for health reasons' and had been replaced by Krenz. In reality Krenz and Schabowski with the agreement of most of their colleagues had plotted to have Honecker, together with Mittag and Hermann, removed. Krenz, as a former S E D Central Committee Secretary for Security, a protégé of Honecker and someone who appeared to have endorsed the Chinese Communists bloody repression earlier in the year, lacked credibility. He did his own cause no good by seeking election as head of state. Although he achieved this aim it was virtually the first time some members of the D D R parliament had voted against an S E D proposal. The demonstrations intensified and so did the flow of refugees. On 30 October according to the East German news agency A D N, around 200,000 people demonstrated in Leipzig demanding the legalisation of New Forum and 'all power to the reformers'. Other demonstrations took place in Halle, Schwerin, Karl-Marx-Stadt (Chemnitz), Poessneck, Cottbus and Magdeburg. The same source reported demonstrations on the following day in Weimar, Meissen and Meinungen. More demonstrations took place at these and other towns in the days and weeks following. In the face of this massive opposition there were further resignations from the Politburo on 2 and 3 November: Axen, Hager, Mielke, Tisch, Alfred Neumann and Erich Mückenberger. The heads of the satellite parties and mass organisations fell thick and fast. Discipline in the armed forces was breaking down. To make matters worse the Czechs had opened their frontiers on 3 November making it easier still for East Germans to get to West Germany. The whole of the Politburo resigned and was replaced by a new, smaller one of 11, made up of 9 survivors from the Honecker era and 2 new faces. On that day, 8 November, New Forum was legalised.

## Berlin Wall opened

The unbelievable happened on 9 November. That night Schabowski announced to astonished world media representatives that the D D R was opening its frontiers, including the Berlin Wall, immediately. It is still not clear exactly how the decision was taken. That same night there were scenes of rejoicing on both sides of the Wall as tens of thousands crossed from East to West. They did so in an orderly manner and most of them went back. This resulted in some S E D leaders drawing the wrong conclusions. As Schabowski wrote later in his book *Das Politbüro*, he and some of his colleagues thought this measure would stabilise the D D R, in fact it marked the beginning of the end.

The government was reorganised with Hans Modrow (aged 61) at its head. Until then he was S E D Secretary for Dresden and a new member of the Politburo; he was considered to be sympathetic to

Gorbachev. The four satellite parties were given more weight than previously, 11 out of 28 portfolios. Parliament then voted on 1 December to delete from the constitution reference to the leading role of the S E D in the D D R. On that same day a committee investigating abuse of office and corruption under Honecker presented an interim report. It angered ordinary East Germans and dismayed the S E D faithful with details of the luxurious life-style of the D D R's top politicians. They were angered too by glimpses television gave them into the special hospitals for the elite which were a world apart from the inadequate health facilities for the majority of East Germans. Two days later the entire Politburo and Central Committee of the S E D resigned. A 25 member committee was given the task of preparing a special congress. Morale in the S E D fell fast. Between October and early December membership dropped from 2.4 million to 1.2 million. Krenz resigned as head of state on 6 December, Gerlach being elected in his place. On the same day an amnesty was announced for mainly political prisoners. The factory fighting-groups were being disbanded and the Ministry of State Security abolished. Democratic elections were promised. By that time the demonstrators in Leipzig were calling for German re-unification. Each day brought the Communist dictatorship closer to extinction.

## Western reactions

In October 1989 polls showed that two out of three West Germans did not expect to see German reunification by 2000. Yet in September, 88 per cent had said they favoured it. Many in the West German political elite thought like Minister Wolfgang Schäuble, who in January 1988 told David Marsh of the *Financial Times* that reunification was not on the agenda at the moment, 'it would lead to instability and the danger of a neutralised Germany'. But he found the division unnatural. In the S P D camp there were many who wanted to drop the idea of reunification altogether. Egon Bahr, who had played a key role in the formation of the Brandt approach to the D D R in the 1960s (see chapter 12), was, by 1988, calling talk of reunification 'hypocritical'. He believed relations between the two German states would be further improved by West Germany abandoning the aim of reunification. The S P D as a party had not gone this far, but it had set up a joint commission in 1982 with the S E D on fundamental values. Given the history of Stalinist Communism's attempts to undermine Social Democracy, it was a dangerous gamble. However, in the documents it produced, both sides made concessions. The S E D, in a joint 1987 statement went a little way in the Gorbachev direction. It implicitly led the S P D nearer to giving up on German unity.

Reaction to events in the D D R in the West was a mixture of joy, fear and caution. Everyone applauded the peaceful demonstrations urging reform. There was some fear that the situation could get out of hand and provoke Soviet intervention. There was caution in word and deed, no one wished to be seen as interfering. Genscher remarked (*Der Spiegel*, 25 September 1989), that Bonn would continue as before with the D D R. 'We do not want to destabilise the D D R in the future. But we cannot remain indifferent, if we learn that the D D R is destabilising and isolating itself by refusing to reform.' At that point in time Western governments did not expect German unity to be re-established. The S P D showed its support for the reform forces by recognising the S D P as a sister party.

## Kohl's 10-point plan

The first dramatic statement from the West German side was Kohl's ten-point programme of 28 November. His most controversial proposal was point 5, 'We are prepared to take a further decisive step, namely, to develop confederative structures between the two states in Germany. A legitimate democratic government in the D D R is an unrelinquishable prerequisite.' All his other points were really built around this. He had taken excellent advice from those who really seemed to understand what was going on in the D D R. His Western allies were not too pleased. At that time, however, he did not realise with what speed the issue would be settled.

By December top politicians were giving credibility to the Modrow regime. James Baker, U S Secretary of State, British Foreign Minister Douglas Hurd, President Mitterrand of France, the new Czech democratic president, Vaclav Havel, as well as a host of West German politicians, made the journey to East Berlin. On a visit to Minsk (6 December) Mitterrand and Gorbachev were cool on German unity. By 22 December the French president was becoming more enthusiastic. He said in Leipzig that France would not stand in the way of German unity. Gorbachev had warned Honecker about the need for reform but it is not clear at what point he became reconciled to German re-unification. He needed West German economic aid and had become convinced that the D D R was bankrupt and that there was no N A T O threat. Margaret Thatcher, Britain's Prime Minister, was worried about the political and economic dominance of a united Germany in Europe. Increasingly, however, it mattered little what any of them thought, the East German people were going to achieve unity either by constitutional means or simply by moving west en masse.

## Relations with Warsaw and Moscow

Genscher, even more than Kohl, had a breath-taking schedule of international meetings, in a situation which changed from day to day. In many respects, Poland was his biggest potential headache. The older generations of Poles still remembered the horrors of Nazi occupation in a country which had suffered more than most, first from Nazism and then from Communism. As a means of staying in power the Communist regime had played on fears of German 'revanchism' since 1945. As millions of Poles had been settled on German territory from Danzig and Stettin to Breslau and Gleiwitz, and a German minority still lived in Poland, such fears could be exploited. After years of improvement, Polish–German relations came to a standstill in 1980–1 as a result of the suppression of Solidarity. Genscher's visit to Warsaw in January 1988, and the Polish Prime Minister's visit to Bonn in January 1989, marked a positive turning point. Kohl's visit to Warsaw in November 1989 saw the conclusion of 11 agreements and a joint communique on the 'firm foundation' of the 1970 Warsaw Treaty. These were based on the underlying policy of continuing German economic help, civilised treatment for the German minority in Poland (which had been deprived of its cultural freedom) and recognition of the Polish–German frontier. Interestingly it was reported in *Die Welt* (2 June 1990) that 75 per cent of the 500 German minority candidates allowed to stand for the first time in Upper Silesia in local elections had been successful. They had stood in 38 of the 63 local councils in Oppeln. Kohl appeared to stumble over the frontier issue in February–March 1990 when he seemed to be placing conditions on the final recognition of Poland's western frontier. Perhaps he had been surprised, even shocked, when Germans living in Poland had greeted him on a visit as 'our Chancellor'. Perhaps he felt the need to give a signal to former refugees living in West Germany that he understood their case. The matter caused Genscher embarrassment and annoyance but was soon cleared up when Kohl admitted he too had made mistakes.

For Kohl and Genscher the breakthrough on German unity came on their visit to Moscow on the weekend of 10–11 February 1990. By then they had good relations with the Soviet leader and he in turn seemed to trust the West Germans. On a previous visit to Moscow in October 1988 the Germans had been told by Gorbachev that attempts to reverse the 'historically-produced' division of Germany would be 'incalculable, even dangerous'. On that occasion Kohl admitted he would probably not live to see reunification. Between then and February 1990 the Soviet leader's visit to the Federal Republic had taken place in June 1989; this could hardly have failed to make a great impression on him. *Der Spiegel* (5 June 1989) reported poll findings which revealed that 73 per cent of Germans had a positive attitude to the Soviet Union. This compared with only 13 per cent in 1983. It also published a poll showing that Gorbachev was much more popular in West Germany than Bush, Mitterrand or Thatcher. He had been confronted by scenes of almost hysterical enthusiasm for 'Gorby', the kind of enthusiasm he did not experience in the Soviet Union. He needed West German help and they were ready to oblige. In any case, he had seen the rapid demise of the S E D regime. In February 1990, Gorbachev agreed to the principle of German unity, leaving it to the Germans themselves to decide the timing and the method. They reassured the Russians on the question of frontiers, economic aid and other matters but insisted on Germany remaining in N A T O. Later that month (24–25 February) Kohl and U S President George Bush agreed on German unity; Germany remaining in N A T O; and the U S A continuing to act as guarantor of stability in Europe. They also accepted the special status of what was still the D D R. After reunification Soviet troops would remain there for a transitional period and N A T O troops would not be introduced. A number of other consultations were held on the basis of 'two plus four' meaning the foreign ministers of the four victor powers of 1945 and the foreign ministers of the two German states. These were not however decisive. Once Kohl had the agreement of the superpowers he was virtually home and dry.

## *Free elections in the* D D R

Due to the deteriorating situation in the D D R, elections scheduled for May had to be brought forward to 18 March. One problem was that West Germany, which had given humanitarian aid to the D D R, was not prepared to help with fundamental restructuring until a democratic government was in place. The Modrow government had been expanded on 2 February by opposition members joining it as members without portfolios. They were supposed to monitor the work of particular ministers and help decide overall policy.

With the elections on the horizon the different groups attempted to become more and more like West German parties. The old Communist S E D sought to give itself a face lift by changing its name first to the

S E D–P D S, then to simply the P D S, short for Party of Democratic Socialism. Under the leadership of Gregor Gysi (42), a lawyer who had not held office under the old regime but was the son of a Communist official, it claimed to be a broad left party clear of Stalinism but holding to what had been positive in the D D R's 40 years. It was not expressly against German unity. It had the advantage of a D D R-wide organisation, large funds, many thousands of full-time functionaries and others fighting for their jobs. It also gained advantage from its man Hans Modrow leading the government.

Other groups, which had hesitations about German unity, were grouped in *Bündnis 90* (Alliance 90) made up of New Forum, Democracy Now and the Initiative for Peace and Human Rights, the Greens and several other groups like the United Left (V L). They all agreed that the D D R had useful experiences to offer West Germany, wanted some kind of democratic, ecological socialism to be retained, and were neutralist and pacifist. The V L was Marxist.

As it turned out the three most significant groups were the Alliance for Germany, the League of Free Democrats (B F D) and the S P D. The Alliance comprised the C D U which had been a satellite party but had transformed itself as early as its special December 1989 congress, the new German Social Union (D S U) and the new Democratic Awakening (D A). The C D U had the clear advantage over its partners with its D D R-wide organisation and its very name. The B F D was made up rather late from the old Liberal Democrats with the new F D P and the new German Forum Party (D F P). The S P D had been the S D P (see above) but had sensibly changed its name and lined up with the West German sister party. All the new parties suffered from lack of funds, organisation, offices and equipment, media and experience. Had it not been for the help they got from West German parties and widespread television coverage in both parts of Germany the election would have been a farce.

By the time the elections approached it became clear that the key issue was how fast and by which route German unity would be restored. The Alliance and the B F D favoured the D D R simply applying to join the Federal Republic under article 23 of the Basic Law. This was the simplest way and the fastest route. The S P D wanted a slower process involving the two parliaments setting up a commission to draft a new constitution which would have to be ratified. The S D P/S P D had been very popular initially as the party of Willy Brandt, who had done so much to improve inter-German relations. He was warmly welcomed when he spoke for his colleagues in the D D R. The S P D lost ground once the C D U had been recognised as a party by the West German C D U and once German unity became the central issue. Polls in March revealed that 91 per cent of East Germans favoured unity and only 5 per cent were against. But whereas only 35.3 per cent of those polled wanted it very quickly, support was higher amongst Alliance supporters with 57.5 per cent wanting this. Neither the statements of the then leader of the East German S P D, Ibrahim Böhme, (41) nor those of Oskar Lafontaine, the West German S P D's Chancellor candidate designate, helped matters. Lafontaine was for ever stressing the difficulties on the road to unity. Kohl attracted over 1 million people at six meetings he addressed in the D D R.

## Alliance for Germany wins

On a pleasant sunny day 93.4 per cent of the East German electors voted on 18 March in the first free elections in that part of Germany since 1932. The turnout was higher than at any West German election since 1945. It is more remarkable when one considers that some of those on the register had left for West Germany and were not, therefore, able to vote. The result was an unexpectedly resounding victory for the Alliance:

|  | votes | percent | seats |
|---|---|---|---|
| CDU* | 4,711,000 | 40.6 | 163 |
| SPD | 2,526,000 | 21.8 | 88 |
| PDS | 1,892,000 | 16.3 | 66 |
| DSU* | 728,000 | 6.3 | 25 |
| BFD | 609,000 | 5.3 | 21 |
| Alliance 90 | 336,074 | 2.9 | 12 |
| DBD (Democratic farmers) | 251,000 | 2.1 | 9 |
| Greens/UFV | 271,000 | 2.0 | 8 |
| (including Women's League) |  |  |  |
| DA* | 106,000 | 1.0 | 4 |
| NDPD (National Democrats) | 44,000 | 0.4 | 2 |
| DFD (Democratic Women's |  |  |  |
| League) | 38,000 | 0.3 | 1 |
| VL | 20,000 | 0.2 | 1 |
| others | 53,000 | 0.5 | – |

* Member of Alliance for Germany. The D B D, N D P D and D F D were formerly Communist satellites which had transformed themselves in varying degrees.

The victory of the Alliance was rightly seen as a victory for Kohl and for the fast route to German unity. Lothar de Maizière, leader of the C D U, had campaigned very much in Kohl's shadow. The West German Friedrich-Ebert-Stiftung reported that its research indicated that the Alliance gained the votes of 58 per cent of the blue collar workers, 47 per cent of the white collar employees, 43 per cent of the pensioners but only 32 per cent of graduates. The Alliance got its biggest success in Karl-Marx-Stadt (60.7 per cent). Thus the workers had clearly shunned the so-called 'workers' state' and its party. The S P D gained its highest vote in East Berlin (34.8 per cent). The P D S also scored its highest vote (30.2 per cent) there. As Berlin was the home of many of the Communist elite, functionaries of state, party and mass organisations, journalists and institute intelligentsia, this was only to be expected. Alliance 90 likewise got its best result (6.3 per cent) in Berlin. It had remained a party of the unorthodox intellectuals, who had received considerable media attention but lacked organisation and had been unpopular due to their attitude on German reunification. The B F D got its best vote (10 per cent) in Halle, the home of West German Foreign Minister Genscher. There were few differences between men and women voters but it was noticeable that the S P D scored best among the 59–69 and 70 and over age groups. These were the people most likely to remember the old S P D traditions of many areas of the D D R. The C D U did equally well across the age groups. The P D S got its best vote among the 29–39 age group.

On 6 May 75 per cent of the D D R's voters turned out again to vote in local government elections. Once again the C D U emerged as the biggest single party with 34.4 per cent. Its closest rivals the S P D and the P D S gained 21.3 per cent and 14.6 respectively. The Free Democrats attracted 6.7 per cent.

## D D R: *A grand coalition government*

One of the first things the new Volkskammer did was to agree unanimously a statement on 12 April recognising the D D R's joint responsibility for the wrongs done to the Jews, Poles, Soviet peoples and Romanies and Sintis. It reaffirmed the Oder-Neisse frontier with Poland and confessed shared guilt for the crushing of the 'Prague Spring' in 1968.

After the March election a grand coalition government of the Alliance, S P D and B F D was formed in the D D R under Prime Minister Lothar de Maizière. Markus Meckel (S P D) was appointed Foreign Minister and Peter-Michael Diestel (D S U) was deputy Prime Minister and Minister of Interior. Pastor Rainer Eppelmann (D A) who had been in trouble under Honecker as a conscientious objector to military service became Minister of Disarmament and Defence.

## Monetary, economic and social union

On 1 July 1990 the two German states were formally joined in a monetary, economic and social union. This was the result of a treaty signed in Bonn on 18 May. It committed the two states 'to achieve in freedom as soon as possible the unity of Germany within a Europe peace order'. The D D R was committed to introducing the social market economy and the federal system. West German law and practice were to be introduced as soon as possible. The (West German) Deutsche Mark was introduced into the D D R as sole legal tender. Wages, salaries, grants, pensions, rents and leases as well as other recurring payments were converted at a rate of one to one. All other claims and liabilities in D D R Mark were to be converted to the Deutsche Mark at the rate of two to one. On the day of the introduction of the Deutsche Mark there were long queues of excited East Germans outside the banks all over the D D R.

The industries of the D D R now faced full competition from West German products as well as goods imported into West Germany. Most East Germans preferred West German products even, in some cases, when there was little difference and despite the higher cost. They were losing orders in the East too. As East European states freed their trade they switched from D D R products to West European ones. Soon unemployment in the D D R was rising rapidly.

## Privatisation in D D R

One of the biggest concerns of both German governments was to privatise the East German economy. To this end the Volkskammer voted on 17 June to establish a *Treuhandanstalt* (trustee corporation) to run state property until it could be sold off. The new body was headed by Detlev Rohwedder, Chairman of the West German industrial giant Hoesch, and Reiner Maria Gohlke, Chairman of the West German railways. There were many difficulties. One was the question of ownership. A joint declaration of the two German governments (15 June 1990) agreed in principle to ensure that property, except for that taken over between 1945–49, be returned to the original owners. This made it more difficult to sell until the old owners had had the opportunity to make their claims. Another problem was that western investors would be reluctant to go to areas lacking infrastructure and services such as good roads, rail connections, accommodation, information technology, telecommunications, health and recreation facilities, banking and insurance services, component suppliers and sympathetic and well-organised local and regional administrations. What the D D R did have was a relatively well-educated work force.

The easiest properties to deal with were those nationalised by Honecker in 1972. They were small enterprises and many of their former owners were interested in getting them back. Much more painful was the problem of houses and other dwellings. In many cases the homes of those who had fled the D D R had been sold or let, with priority given to those loyal to the S E D. Former refugees went back demanding the return of the family home. Most would not be rich individuals, just middle class people for whom the dwelling represented the bulk of their property. The two governments resolved that no one would be made homeless because of claims of this sort, and the former owners would have the right to compensation.

Close on the euphoria of monetary union came another cause for celebration when West Germany won the World Cup in July. This was the third time it had won this prestigious football prize, the previous two being in 1954 and 1974. According to the *Financial Times* (10 July) national team manager, Franz Beckenbauer, commented after unity 'the choice (of players) will become even bigger, and nobody will be able to beat us for years. I'm sorry for the rest of the world, but that's the truth.' Hundreds of thousands of young Germans, from East and West, were on the streets in all the big towns, draped in the German flag. There were pockets of violence, particularly in Hamburg and Berlin. Germany, like several other European countries, including Britain, was no stranger to football hooliganism.

## Unity Treaty agreed

One sad if, as it turned out, minor development on the road to unity was the break up of the D D R grand coalition on 20 August. The S P D decided to withdraw over policy and personal differences, which at that late stage were of little consequence. It was a shame that a party that had done so much for East German freedom was not represented in the government at the moment of re-unification.

On 23 August the Volkskammer voted, with nearly three-quarters of the members voting in favour, for 'the entry of the D D R to the area of jurisdiction of the Basic Law' according to article 23. The next step was for Wolfgang Schäuble, Federal Minister of Interior, and Günter

Krause, D D R State Secretary in the Prime Minister's office, to sign the *Einigungsvertrag* (Unity Treaty) on 31 August. This treaty was then ratified by the two parliaments on 20 September. On the following day the Bundesrat formally accepted it by a unanimous vote. In Bonn, 440 members voted in the Bundestag for the treaty with only 47 Greens voting against and 3 abstentions. In the Volkskammer the vote was 299 in favour, 80 against and 1 abstention. Volkskammer opposition to the treaty came from the Communist P D S, Alliance 90 and the Greens. The Federal President, Richard von Weizsäcker, signed the treaty on 24 September. Unity congresses were held by the various parties in the same month.

## Two plus four Moscow Treaty

The last major formal act covering the external aspects of German unity was signed in Moscow on 12 September by the foreign ministers of the four victor powers—France, the Soviet Union, the United Kingdom and U S A—and the foreign ministers of the two German states. Lothar de Maizière represented the D D R because of the earlier withdrawal of the S P D from the coalition. Article 1 states that the united Germany 'has no territorial claims whatsoever against other states and shall not assert any in the future'. Article 3 committed Germany to 'renunciation of the manufacture and possession and control over nuclear, biological and chemical weapons.' Germany agreed to cut its conventional forces. Under article 4 the Soviet Union agreed to withdraw its forces from Germany by the end of 1994. Until the completion of this withdrawal (article 5) no foreign or German troops integrated into N A T O would be allowed on the territory of the former D D R. However, with German agreement, the troops of the three Western powers would remain in Berlin until the Soviet withdrawal. Following the Soviet withdrawal, German N A T O forces could be stationed in the former D D R, but not foreign troops or nuclear weapons. Under article 6 Germany had the right to belong to alliances (in effect N A T O). The four victor powers agreed to 'terminate their rights and responsibilities relating to Berlin and to Germany as a whole.' Germany and Poland signed a treaty confirming the Oder-Neisse frontier on 14 November in Warsaw.

## Political and military unity

A remarkable yet hardly noticed ceremony took place on 24 September when the D D R, represented by Epplemann, was officially released from its obligations under the Warsaw pact. It had been agreed that members of the lower ranks of the D D R armed forces could apply to become part of the Bundeswehr after unity had been realised. Military unity was achieved on 3 October when Gerhard Stoltenberg, Federal Minister of Defence, took over what was left of the East German armed forces at Straussberg, near Berlin, their former headquarters.

German unity was finally restored on 3 October in Berlin. The mass official celebrations then took place before the Reichstag and (only yards away) the Brandenburg Gate on the night of 2–3 October with Brahms, Beethoven and Mendelssohn on the musical programme, an impressive firework display, searchlights and the singing of the national anthem. It was a highly emotional but dignified occasion with hundreds of thousands of participants watched by millions on television around the world. Messages flowed in from the world's leaders with the President of Czechoslovakia, Havel, commenting, 'The war is over!' Only the Israeli leader, Itzhak Shamir, expressed 'mixed feelings'. To represent the former D D R in the Bundestag there were 144 former members of the Volkskammer: 63 C D U, 33 S P D, 24 P D S, 9 F D P, 8 D S U and 7 Alliance 90. Five former D D R ministers, including Lothar de Maizière, became federal ministers without portfolios.

## Regional elections 1990

1990 had not started off badly for the S P D, with a win in the regional (Land) election in the Saar. Opinion surveys also put the S P D ahead of the C D U/C S U nationally. The mood went against the S P D by the time of the East German elections in March but in May the Social Democrats were out in front again with success in the regional elections in Northrhine–Westphalia and Lower Saxony. From May until October it was downhill all the way with slight gains from then until the December election. As for the Greens, although they failed again in the Saar (2.6 per cent) they held on in Lower Saxony (5.5) and got into the parliament of Northrhine–Westphalia winning 5 per cent, a gain of 0.5 per cent.

In the elections for the re-established East German Lander—New Brandenburg, Mecklenburg–West Pomerania, Saxony, Saxony–

Anhalt and Thuringia—on 14 October, the C D U lost ground in all but Saxony. The S P D improved its position in all five, but only in Brandenburg was it enough to enable the S P D to form a government. The P D S took losses in all five but the Alliance 90/the Greens made gains in all. Finally, the F D P improved its position everywhere except Saxony. In West Germany, Kohl remained unpopular until May, rapidly improving his position after that time. His S P D rival, Oskar Lafontaine, fell back in public esteem. By November Kohl was the preferred candidate for the Chancellorship of 57.7 per cent of the electorate, compared with only 35.8 who wanted Lafontaine. What seems to have happened is that questions such as immigration, unemployment and the environment were replaced by German unity as the key issue. Inevitably Kohl, and Genscher, scored heavily, with constant media attention. In addition, Lafontaine stressed the difficulties ahead, including the soaring costs of German unity. Most experts disagreed with him.

## Booming economy

In April the five leading independent economic forecasting institutes gave a very optimistic picture of the impact of monetary union on the West German economy. Subsequently the West German economy did boom, partly because of the extra demand generated by East German consumer spending. By the end of the year the German economy compared well with the other major industrial economies:

Economic indicators in percentages at December 1990

| | Inflation | Interest rates | GNP | Industrial growth production | Unemployment | Balance of payments $ billion |
|---|---|---|---|---|---|---|
| Canada | 5.0 | 11.38 | 0.5 | −2.8 | 9.1 | −14.7 |
| France | 3.6 | 10.31 | 2.2 | 1.1 | 8.9 | 5.8 |
| Germany | 3.0 | 9.35 | 5.5 | 5.2 | 6.7 | 50.2 |
| Italy | 6.5 | 12.50 | 3.0 | −0.6 | 9.9 | −28.0 |
| Japan | 3.6 | 8.25 | 5.4 | 6.5 | 2.1 | 39.3 |
| UK | 9.7 | 14.00 | 0.6 | −1.5 | 6.2 | −27.2 |
| USA | 6.3 | 8.25 | 1.0 | −0.6 | 5.9 | −96.4 |

## Kohl's victory

The only question still open on 2 December 1990 at the first election for a united German parliament since 1933 was the size of the Bonn coalition's victory. As it turned out it was larger than expected. Turnout was down, only 78.6 per cent in the West and 74.7 per cent in the former D D R. This could have been due to a certain apathy in the face of what seemed to be the coalition's inevitable victory. Overall the C D U gained 36.7 per cent, the C S U 7.1 and the F D P 11. On the opposition side, the S P D won 33.5 per cent, West German Greens 3.9, P D S 2.4 and Alliance 90/the Greens 1.2. The West German Greens were eliminated from parliament because they failed to attract 5 per cent of the vote. The election law allowed parties to stand in just one part of Germany 'election region West' or 'election region East'. This was designed to give the significant but smaller East German parties a chance of representation. As Alliance 90/the Greens and the P D S both got more than 5 per cent in the 'electoral region East' (6. and 11.1 respectively) they both were awarded seats. The far right was soundly beaten. The R E P gained 2.3 per cent in the West and 1.3 in the East (overall 2.1).

Even in the West the S P D vote was down compared with both 1987 and 1983, 35.7 as against 37 and 38.2. In the West the C D U vote was up slightly from 34.5 in 1987 to 35.7. In the East, however, it gained 41.8 which compared with 40.8 at the March elections. The F D P was up in both West and East, in the West from 9.1 in 1987 to 10.6 in 1990. In the East it gained 12.9 compared with 5.3 for the B F D in March. Alliance 90/the Greens with its 6 did better than it and the Greens had done fighting separately in March (4.9).

The only consolation for the S P D was that it had increased its vote compared with March in all five *Länder* of the old D D R. There was the slight consolation for Lafontaine that at least in the Saar his party's vote rose from 43.5 (in 1987) to 51.2. In the other West German regions the S P D took losses. The situation for the Greens was not hopeless as they would be represented in the Bundestag by Alliance 90 and they remained in most regional parliaments.

There were more women elected to parliament than ever before.

Women in the Bundestag in percent

| 1949 | 1953 | 1957 | 1961 | 1965 | 1969 | 1972 | 1976 | 1980 | 1983 | 1987 | 1990 |
|------|------|------|------|------|------|------|------|------|------|------|------|
| 6.8 | 8.8 | 9.2 | 8.3 | 6.9 | 6.6 | 5.8 | 7.3 | 8.5 | 9.8 | 15.4 | 20.4 |

With 64 the S P D had the largest number of women members elected in 1990. The C D U/C S U came second with 44 and were followed by the F D P with 16. The P D S had 8 and Alliance 90/the Greens 3.

## Problems facing the new Germany

German unity had been restored with remarkable smoothness. As some had long believed, it had only needed the green light from Moscow to make it happen. No wonder Chancellor Kohl praised Soviet leader Mikhail Gorbachev for his part. There had been no deaths along the road and virtually no violence. It was what Engels must have imagined a working class revolution would be like in an advanced nation where the 'immense majority' wanted it, the few holders of power could not stop it.

The new Germany does, however, face considerable problems. The economic problems of the former D D R are immense; but there are other ones too. Probably over 1 million citizens of the former D D R reject the Federal Republic and its values. Many of these will be strengthened in their convictions by their difficulties in finding new employment. Most of the 80,000 former full-time officials of the State Security Service (S S D or Stasi) are among these, so are thousands of former officers of the armed forces and some former police officials. They include many full-time functionaries of parties and mass organisations, a significant number of professors and other academics, school heads, higher officials in the state apparatus, journalists, state pensioners in the art world, many higher level managers in industry and collective farm chairmen and other officials.

Another problem is what to do about those who committed crimes for and on behalf of the S E D regime, or simply abused their power on their own behalf. Most of the former members of the Politburo were arrested. Many were later released on health grounds. Some remain in prison awaiting trial. What is to be done about those who were pressed into service by Mielke's Stasi? At the end of 1990 the archives of the State Security Service were in a chaotic state. It will take years to sort them out. Revelations about both East and West Germans who worked for the Stasi will undoubtedly continue to haunt the public life of the new Germany for many years to come. In its report to the Volkskammer at the end of September, the parliamentary committee investigating members of parliament stated that 12 ordinary members and 3 ministers were so badly incriminated they should resign immediately. All the main parties were affected. Dr Axel Viehweger (B F D), Minister for Building resigned immediately. Before that Professor Dr Kurt Wünsche (B F D) had given up his post as Minister of Justice because of his earlier career in the S E D government. Ibrahim Böhme, former Chairman of the S P D in the D D R had been forced to resign even though he denied Stasi activity. It was very sad that Lothar de Maizière felt he had to resign in December 1990 as the accusations against him continued to gain strength. In the united C D U he had been elected as Kohl's deputy Chairman. No doubt there would be other casualties.

Bonn will have to come to terms with the fact that a not insignificant number of its own officials high and low worked for the Stasi. Colonel Joachim Krase, who died in 1988, was second in command of M A D. He is said to have worked for the Stasi and helped to bring down General Günter Kiesling, in an effort to topple Defence Minister Wörner (see chapter 13). Three days after German unity Klaus Kuron of the B f V admitted having worked for the Stasi since 1982 for financial gain. At the same time Gabriele Gast of the B N D was arrested. She had been delivering information to the D D R for 17 years. As former East German intelligence officers are 'coming in from the cold' Bonn is getting a clearer picture of espionage in its own corridors of power.

A problem of quite a different order is what to do about the mass influx of foreigners and ethnic Germans into Germany. At the end of 1988 there were 4,489,100 foreigners living in West Germany, 43 per cent of whom had lived there for 15 years or longer, only 29.1 per cent or 1,307,900 had acquired the right to stay in the Federal Republic indefinitely. In the last year for which figures are available, 1987, there was a net inflow of 117,741 foreigners, that is excluding ethnic Germans or refugees from the D D R. The biggest groups were from Poland (47,703), Turkey (20,521) and Yugoslavia (9,734). Then followed Iranians (6,566), Romanians (6,456) and Italians (5,823). A significant number of these were asylum seekers. The problem is not simply one of resources, the factional fighting of various rival groups also presents difficulties. The B f V estimated that in 1989 there were 97,250 members of foreign extremist groups active in the Federal Republic. Turks, Iranians, Yugoslavs and Sikhs fought their fellow countrymen on German streets.

As the economic situation in East Europe has worsened and the freedom to migrate has improved the numbers of ethnic Germans arriving in West Germany has increased:

Ethnic German migrants to West Germany, 1985–9

| 1985 | 1986 | 1987 | 1988 | 1989 | 1990 |
|------|------|------|------|------|------|
| 38,968 | 42,788 | 78,523 | 202,673 | 377.055 | 397,000 |

The Germans are coming to realise that their country is a multicultural society. But they will be pressing for a European solution to the refugee problem.

## Relations with Moscow and Washington

A delicate problem for the Germans would remain their relations with the Soviet Union. In November 1990 Gorbachev was again in Bonn. This time he was in a more embattled state than in 1989; he was far from popular at home. He returned to the USSR with a package containing a non-aggression pact; a trade, science and technology cooperation agreement and a labour and welfare accord. A month later he and Kohl were appealing to the German public to send aid to the Soviet Union where conditions of near starvation had engulfed many urban areas. The Germans had to be careful about their relations with the Soviet army still on their soil until 1994. They were paying to maintain the Soviet troops in Germany and to build homes for them in the Soviet Union. They were appalled to find out just how badly these soldiers lived. They were embarrassed by Soviet deserters and crimes committed by Soviet troops. It needed tact, compassion and diplomacy to deal with a situation of this kind.

Some tact was also needed in relations with the United States. In the postwar decades the Americans had been the rich, glamorous, liberators whose attractiveness and positive qualities had been personified by President John F. Kennedy. As the authoritative veteran journalist, Marion Gräfin Dönhoff, writing in *Die Zeit* (30 November 1990), commented, the Vietnam war cast a shadow on the previously unmarred image of the Americans, particularly in the eyes of the young. No one had believed, she wrote, the Americans capable of the My Lai massacre. After that US—German relations were less starry-eyed and instead were based more on common interests. According to Dönhoff, Germans had become sceptical about the USA's world role, 'The Europeans do not wish to be forced to collaborate in such activities as the bombing of Libya or Panama. They regard with a certain scepticism Washington's tendency to act as world policeman ...' The 1990–1 Gulf crisis brought out the differences once again. Neither the USA nor Germany wanted war in the Middle East, both agreed that Iraq should withdraw from Kuwait. But the Germans placed more weight behind exploring all peaceful channels to achieve this than the Americans. When Americans expressed dismay that the Germans were not being more active in the war effort, the Germans reminded their friends of the enormous burdens they faced over German unity, including the billions to help the Soviet Union—an aim both countries regarded as desirable. The Germans also pointed out that the Basic Law prevented them from deploying military forces outside the NATO area. By the end of 1990 they did nevertheless send some warplanes to Turkey, a NATO state, to help in its defence against an (unlikely) Iraqi attack. In addition, it had 19 ships on patrol. By February 1990 Germany had spent the equivalent of £5,651 million in the allied cause.

The relations between the Americans and the West Germans had changed in other ways too. The Federal Republic had become extremely affluent despite a high level of defence expenditure, aid and welfare programmes. By contrast, the U S A had become less affluent. By the 1980s American servicemen were glad to get part-time jobs in any capacity in the towns where they were stationed. The U S were heavily in debt to their European ally as revealed by figures in the *Statistical Abstract of the United States 1990:*

Current account balance with main US trade partners million $

|  | 1986 | 1987 | 1988 |
|---|---|---|---|
| France | −577 | +173 | −1,419 |
| Japan | −53,792 | −55,368 | −49,975 |
| W. Germany | −17,773 | −18,263 | −20,841 |
| UK | −12,122 | −11,326 | −12,658 |

Even before the coming of German unity the Americans were looking for big savings from their garrison in Germany. The end of the cold war will mean that most of the 250,000 U S troops will leave. An estimated D M 12 billion flowed annually into the West German economy from spending by the U S military in the 1980s. There would be gains and losses on both sides. In defence terms N A T O was becoming more Europeanised and, due to the N A T O-Warsaw Pact agreements of 1990, much smaller. One other source of friction between the U S A and the European Community, rather than between the U S and Germany, was the question of agriculture. The U S argues that the same rules of free trade should apply to agriculture as apply to trade and industry. The E C believes this is an impossible request as it would mean the decline of most of West European agriculture. The Gatt negotiations in Brussels in December 1990 broke down over this issue. Despite the differences which have emerged over the years Frau Dönhoff was right when she concluded in her article, reassuring her American friends, 'Our system of values is so closely linked to yours and our way of life so similar to yours that I cannot conceive of anything that could separate us.'

## Germany and the E C

The European Community did not hesitate to welcome the prospect of the re-establishment of German unity. It merely saw Germany being enlarged rather than a new state joining. Germany did not expect, and was not offered, any increase in its seats and votes in the Commission or in the Council of Ministers. It was not clear whether the Federal Republic would increase its representation in the European parliament even though it now had nearly 17 million more inhabitants. Moreover, with the likelihood of the expansion of the E C with Austria, Norway and other states joining, Germany's formal significance would decline somewhat. Germany was in tune with France, Italy and the other E C members, except Britain, who wanted the Community to move rapidly towards monetary, social and political union with a foreign affairs and defence dimension.

Relations with Britain were dented somewhat as Margaret Thatcher revealed coolness towards German unity, and when her friend and senior member of her government, Nicholas Ridley, made some damaging remarks about the Germans and the E C. He apologised and resigned. His chief lost popularity both among the public and among her parliamentary colleagues. Certainly one of the important factors in this decline was the Prime Minister's negative attitude to the further development of the E C. Most British people it seemed, did not like their country to be isolated from its neighbours. After Margaret Thatcher was ousted in a party revolt in November 1990 and replaced by John Major, the Germans became cautiously optimistic about an improvement in Anglo-German relations. Germany and Britain were joined by indissoluable ties in the E C. For Britain, Germany was as important as the U S in terms of trade. As an export market it was, in 1990, more important than Australia, Canada, Hong Kong, India, Israel, Japan, Malaysia, South Africa, the Soviet Union and Singapore put together. The Gulf War brought fresh attacks on Germany from sections of the press. The *Daily Mail*, a paper which had supported Hitler and the British Fascists in the 1930s, wrote (6 February) of 'The Shame of Germany' because some Germans did not wish to serve in the Gulf.

## German aspirations in the 1990s

Hitler would have thought the Germans of the 1990s were not fit to survive, and Bismarck would not have been too impressed. Most other people would be relieved to read the results of a survey for the

*Süddeutsche Zeitung* (4 January 1991). It revealed that 40 per cent of Germans saw Switzerland as a future model for Germany. Sweden was the second most popular model attracting 29 per cent of Germans. Japan and Italy came next with 10 per cent each. The Western liberators—France, U S A and Britain—were scarcely regarded as models. They attracted 8, 6 and 2 per cent respectively. When asked with which country Germany should have good and close relations in the next ten years the Soviet Union was well ahead with 59 per cent, next came the U S A with 44 followed by France with 36. On being asked which states Germany should have less intensive relations with, 32 per cent mentioned Israel, followed by China with 26. East Germans were more likely to name Israel than West Germans. The survey was conducted at a time when Israel was in the news because of the deaths of Palestinians. An amazing 71 per cent wanted to see a European federal state created in the 1990s. The nationality of the head of that federal state was a matter of indifference to 40 per cent. When asked in which directions Germany should strive to be an example to the world 85 per cent said in environmental protection and 77 mentioned social security.

Another question asked for a list of areas where the state should spend more money, again the environment led with 86 per cent, followed by health care, social welfare and housing, all with 56 per cent. Next came help for the old (51), public transport (40), nurseries and kindergarten (37), all ahead of economic development (23), science (23), schools (21), internal security (21) and road building (20). At the bottom of the list were development aid (16), art and culture (8), integration of foreigners (7) and sport (5). There were no votes for defence. Asked about their fears for the year 2000, damage to the environment again topped the list.

Despite the low priority given to integration of foreigners, 48 per cent thought there should be more tolerance of foreigners, and only 17 per cent said less. This was one of a list of values at the top of which came readiness to help others (78) and respect for the old (67), courage to stand up for one's beliefs (64) and tolerance of people whose views differ from one's own (63).

Differences on the role of women could be seen between the old D D R and West Germany. When asked in which area women should have more influence, eastern respondents were more conservative than those in West Germany. Easterners named, in order, family, education and training, social life, then came science, law and politics. In the West politics came first followed by law, education and training, science, family, social life and art. To the question whether more women should go out to work in the next ten years 48 per cent were in favour, 51 against; in the old D D R only 30 per cent were in favour but 69 per cent against. In both parts of Germany 58 per cent were for abortion on demand. A hint of East German authoritarian indoctrination was revealed when 69 per cent of old D D R respondents revealed they would like to see more discipline in the schools (in the West 44), more police on the streets (65 East, 25 West) and more respect for state authority (40 East, 20 West).

Germany started its new life with the good will of its neighbours and partners in the European Community. According to the magazine *European Affairs* (April 1990), the three opinion polls conducted in all the member states between November 1989 and October 1990 revealed in each country a majority in favour of German unity. In the last poll the majorities in favour were: Spain 85, Ireland 85, Germany 84, Italy 83, Portugal 83, France 77, Belgium 73, Greece 73, U K 72, Netherlands 70, Denmark 69 and Luxembourg 60. It was a good result by any standards. The same source quoted President Mitterrand as saying,

Should we have clung to our memories of the world wars, to a sort of exclusion imposed on the Germans as an 'intrinsically dangerous' people, an intolerable people which must be safely enclosed behind (theoretical) barbed wire? This would have been unthinkable. The Germans—through their history, their culture, their thinking, their character and their works—have not merited such a judgement.

David Marsh, Bonn correspondent of the *Financial Times* (29 December 1990), described Helmut Kohl as a 'modest statesman' who had not let his massive successes of 1990 go to his head. These qualities were desperately needed in the Chancellor whose country was being thrust into greater leadership in the new Europe, unable to remain just an economic giant at the same time as being a political dwarf.

# — Appendix 1: —

# Biographies of 152 Germans, 1871–1991

**Adam-Schwaetzer, Irmgard** (1942–   ), born in Münster she gained her doctorate in pharmacy in Bonn in 1971 and worked for industry in Germany and Brussels for several years. She joined the F D P in 1975 entering the Bundestag in 1980. She was a strong supporter of the F D P's coalition shift from S P D to C D U/C S U in 1982. From 1982 she was the Secretary General of the F D P until her appointment as party Treasurer in 1984. She served as State Secretary in the Foreign Ministry 1987–91 and then as Minister of Housing.

**Adenauer, Konrad** (1876–1967), a Catholic, he studied law and economics at Freiburg, Munich and Bonn. Mayor of Cologne, 1917–33, member of Centre Party, 1906–33. He was sacked by the Nazis for alleged embezzlement but on appeal got a pension. Arrested by Nazis in 1934 and 1944. In 1945 the Americans appointed him Mayor again, shortly afterwards the British fired him. He was C D U Chairman to 1966, Chancellor of Federal Republic of Germany (F R G), 1949–63, Foreign Secretary as well 1951–55. He was one of the architects of what became the European Community, of Franco–German reconciliation and German–Jewish reconciliation. His first wife, Emma, died in 1916. They had three children. In 1919 he married Gussi they had seven children.

**Augspurg, Anita** (1857–1943). Studied law at Munich she founded, with Lida Gustava Heymann, the German Association for Women's Rights in 1902. With Heymann she set up in 1915 the International Executive for Lasting Peace (later renamed as International Women's League for Peace and Freedom). She and Heymann opposed the Nazis and were forced into exile in Switzerland where they died in 1943.

**Augstein, Rudolf** (1923–   ), born in Hanover he served as a lieutenant during the war. From 1946 he published the weekly *Der Spiegel* achieving outstanding success and widespread recognition. He was very briefly an F D P member of the Bundestag, 1972–3.

**Baader, Andreas** (1944–1977), a member of the so-called Red Army Faction, a terrorist group, he was convicted in 1968 of setting fire to a department store. He committed suicide in prison.

**Baden, Prince Max von** (1867–1929), heir to the throne of Baden, as Chancellor of Germany in 1918 he tried for a peace agreement on lines of Wilson's 14 points, he proclaimed abdication of Wilhelm II and thus end of monarchy in Germany.

**Barzel, Rainer** (1924–    ), C D U/C S U Chancellor candidate in 1972, he served as President of the Bundestag, 1983–4. A Catholic born in East Prussia he was Minister of All-German Affairs, 1962–3.

**Baudissin, Graf Wolf** (1897–    ). Although he studied law (Berlin) and agriculture (Munich) he was a professional soldier from 1930 serving under Rommel. He took part in the rebuilding of the Bundeswehr in the 1940s and 1950s and was one of the authors of the concept of the 'citizen in uniform' which brought him into conflict with traditionalists. He retired from the forces with the rank of Lieutenant-General, serving as Director (1971–84) of Hamburg University's Institute for Peace Research and Security Policy.

**Bebel, August** (1840–1913), master turner, co-founder S A P D/S P D, leader to 1913, member Reichstag, 1867–81, 1881–1913. He was the leading architect of Europe's first mass democratic reform party and an early champion of women's rights.

**Beckenbauer, Franz** (1945–    ), was an apprentice with an insurance company before taking up football with F C Bayern. As manager of the German Nation Football Team (1984–90) he led his team to victory in the World Cup in Italy in 1990.

**Beckmann, Max** (1884–1950), born in Leipzig he attended the Weimar School of Art then went to Paris where he was impressed by Cezanne's painting. After a period in Florence he returned to Berlin where he soon became a prominent painter. Service as a medical orderly in the 1914 war greatly influenced his work which had elements of both Expressionism and New Objectivity. The Nazis regarded his work as decadent and he settled in Amsterdam, later going to New York where he died in 1950.

**Becher, Johannes Robert** (1891–1958), son of a Bavarian judge, he was a foundation member of the K P D. He spent the Nazi years in Moscow and became the D D R Minister of Culture. A poet, he became an exponent of Socialist Realism.

**Becker, Boris** (1967–    ), youngest winner of the men's tennis singles at Wimbledon, the first German to win and winner on three occasions: 1985, 1986 and 1989.

**Benz, Carl Friedrich** (1844–1929). Having founded his company in Mannheim in 1883 he built the first successful automobile in 1885–6.

**Bergmann-Pohl, Sabine** (1946–    ), born in Eisenach. A medical practitioner and specialist in respiratory complaints, she joined the East German C D U in 1981. After the free elections of March 1990 she was elected President of the *Volkskammer*, head of state. After German reunification on 3 October she was appointed Minister for Special Tasks in Chancellor Kohl's unity government.

**Bernstein, Eduard** (1850–1932), son of a Berlin Jewish engine driver he started work in a bank. Because of Bismarck's anti-socialist laws he went to live in Switzerland and then London. His experiences led him to 'revise' Marxism. He served as an S P D member of the Reichstag where he became one of the opponents of the 1914 war.

**Bethmann, Hollweg Theobald von** (1856–1921), Minister of Interior of Prussia and then Reich, Chancellor and Prime Minister of Prussia, 1909–1917.

**Beuys, Joseph** (1921–1988), born into a strict Catholic family in Krefeld, he served as a pilot in World War II. In 1947 he began studying art in Düsseldorf. In 1961 he was appointed professor of monumental sculpture at the Düsseldorf Academy of Arts but was dismissed in 1972 for admitting all the students who had failed the admissions procedure. By this time he was well-known as a left-wing political activist; he stood as a Green candidate on several occasions. He was perhaps the most influential post-war German sculptor.

**Biedenkopf, Kurt** (1930–    ), a Catholic and a lawyer by training he was the youngest rector of a German university (Bochum) at 37. He served as Secretary General of the C D U, 1973–77 modernising the party structure. In 1990 he was elected Prime Minister of Saxony in the first democratic regional election there.

**Bismarck, Otto Fürst von** (1815–1898), Prussian diplomat in St Petersburg and Paris, 1862 Prime Minister and Foreign Minister of Prussia, Chancellor of Germany, 1871–90. Known as the 'Iron Chancellor' is regarded as the father of German unity and of the German colonial empire which he founded in 1884.

**Blüm, Norbert** (1935–    ), a Catholic toolmaker born in Rüsselsheim he gained his university matriculation certificate at evening classes. He studied philosophy, theology, history and German gaining his doctorate (Bonn) in 1967. He represents the blue collar wing of the C D U and has served as Federal Minister of Labour since 1982.

**Böckler, Hans** (1875–1951). He was an influence in the rebuilding of the trade unions in West Germany after 1945, becoming the Chairman of the D G B in 1949.

**Böll, Heinrich** (1917–1985), born in Cologne the son of a Catholic joiner, he worked in a bookshop before military service. His first novel *Der Zug war pünktlich* (*The Train Was On Time*), set in the war, appeared in 1949. He then wrote a series of highly successful novels and short stories, becoming an important, if unofficial, cultural ambassador for West Germany. In 1972 he was awarded the Nobel Prize for Literature. He became increasingly critical of West German situation, fearful of nuclear disaster and the restrictions on personal freedoms. His short *Die verlorene Ehre der Katharina Blum* (*The Lost Honour of Katharina Blum*, 1974) is typical of this period.

**Bohley, Bärbel** (1945–   ), an East Berlin painter by profession, she campaigned against the militarisation of life in the D D R. She was briefly imprisoned in 1983 and later (1988) expelled from the D D R, she returned in 1989 and helped found New Forum. She was elected to the Volkskammer in 1990.

**Bormann, Martin** (1900–1945), he was effectively head of the Nazi party organisation, 1941–45, after Rudolf Hess flew to England. He was a ruthless ideologue who sought to implement extreme Nazi race measures. He is believed to have been killed trying to leave Berlin in 1945.

**Brahms, Johannes** (1833–1897), born in Hamburg he lived in Vienna from 1862. The son of a double bass player he played in taverns as a child to supplement the family income. He did not write his first symphony (of 4) until 1875 when he was 42. His music was described as 'a romantic spirit controlled by a classical intellect.' Although widely recognised abroad since, in his own lifetime he remained very much in the German cultural area.

**Brandt, Willy** (1913–   ), born Herbert Frahm, joined splinter group S A P in 1931, emigrated 1933 living in Norway, and from 1940, Sweden. Active in socialist emigre politics. He returned to Germany in 1945 as a Norwegian journalist. Schumacher and Reuter were his political mentors, persuading him to work for the Berlin S P D. He was member of Bundestag 1949–57, 1957–66; Mayor of (West) Berlin; S P D Chancellor candidate, 1961, 65; Foreign Minister and Vice-Chancellor, 1966–69; Chancellor, 1969–74; Chairman S P D 1964–   ; Chairman

Socialist International, 1977–80. Perhaps more than anyone else he helped to restore the democratic credentials of Germany in the eyes of the world.

**Braun, Wernher von** (1912–1977), after studies at the Technical University, Berlin–Charlottenburg, he joined the weapons' development office of the army in 1932. For the rest of his professional life he worked on rockets, developing the V2 for Hitler and playing a decisive part in putting Americans on the moon in 1969.

**Brecht, Bertolt** (1898–1956), born in Augsburg, his experiences as a medical orderly in the First World War led him into Communism. He gave up medicine in Munich for the theatre in Berlin. He emigrated in 1933, eventually spending the war years in California where he worked on films. He returned to Europe in 1947 settling in East Berlin in 1948. He was offered his own theatre, Berliner Ensemble and honoured by the D D R. Best-known for his *Three Penny Opera* (1928) and *Mother Courage* (1941) his faith was shaken by the workers' rising of 1953.

**von Brentano, Heinrich** (1904–1964), of northern Italian descent he was born in Offenbach and studied law. A co-founder of the C D U in Hesse he was one of the fathers of the Basic Law. He later devised a constitution for a European federal state. In the decisive years 1955–61 he served as West Germany's Foreign Minister, though always under the watchful eye of Adenauer. He had served as Chairman of the C D U/C S U group in the Bundestag, 1949–55.

**Daimler, Gottlieb** (1834–1900), independently of Benz he was co-inventor of the motor car. Founded the company bearing his name.

**Diesel, Rudolf** (1858–1913), born in Paris he developed the diesel engine through Krupp in the 1890s.

**Dieterle, William** (1893–1972) born in Ludwigshafen he worked as an actor in the famous Max Reinhardt theatre in Berlin before turning to the cinema. He became well-known for his film *Geschlecht in Fesseln* (*Sex in Chains*, 1928) in which he took the lead and directed. It dealt, astonishingly, with homosexuality in prison. When the Nazis triumphed Dieterle went to the U S where he was highly successful with films such as: *The Story of Louis Pasteur* (1935); *The Life of Emile Zola* (1937); *Blockade* (1938) one of the few films dealing with the Spanish Civil War; *Juarez* (1939); *The Hunchback of Notre Dame* (1939).

**Dix, Otto** (1891–1969), born into a working class family in Gera, he studied on a scholarship at the Dresden School of Arts and Crafts. In

1914 he volunteered for the army serving in the artillery and war became the dominant theme in his painting up to the 1940s. He was professor at Dresden from 1927 until dismissed by the Nazis for his 'degenerate art'. He remained in Germany despite his precarious position.

**Drexler, Anton** (1884–1942), Bavarian co-founder of the German Workers' Party (later Nazi party) he was a fitter by trade. He lost the party leadership in 1921 to Hitler, later founding his own, unsuccessful party. He died in obscurity in Munich.

**Ebert, Friedrich** (1871–1925), born in Heidelberg he worked as a saddler. He served as member of the Reichstag, 1912–19; co-leader of S P D 1913–19; Chancellor 1918–19; President of Germany 1919–25. As President he suffered the most outrageous personal attacks from right and left.

**Einstein, Albert** (1879–1955), his explanation in 1905 of the photo-electric effect won him the Nobel Prize for physics in 1921. Also in 1905 he published his special theory of relativity. His equation illustrating this theory formed the theoretical basis of the Atom Bomb. Born in Ulm of Jewish parents, Einstein was honoured in Weimar Germany but expelled from the German scientific community by the Nazis. He spent the rest of his life in the U S A becoming a U S citizen. His advice led Roosevelt to order the development of the nuclear bomb.

**Engels, Friedrich** (1820–1895), lived most of his life in Manchester, where he was in business, and London. He supported Marx financially, morally and politically, wrote with Marx *The Communist Manifesto*, and other works. He greatly influenced the S P D.

**Engholm, Björn** (1939–    ), born in Lübeck he trained as a printer before studying politics in Hamburg. He served as Minister of Education and Science 1981–2 in Schmidt's government, having served previously as State Secretary in that ministry. He was a member of the Bundestag 1969–83. He then led the S P D in Schleswig–Holstein, being elected Prime Minister there in 1989. Leader of the S P D since 1991.

**Erhard, Ludwig** (1897–1977), the son of a Fürth shopkeeper he studied economics and sociology after being severely wounded in the 1914–18 war. He then worked in market research (1928–42) being forced to leave because of his refusal to join the Nazi Labour Front. The Americans appointed him Bavarian Economics Minister and, equally briefly, he was professor of economics in Munich. He later had responsibility for preparing the currency reform of 1948 as Director of Economics of the joint U S-British zones (Bizonia), 1948–9. Although he regarded himself more as a Liberal, Adenauer persuaded him to join the C D U. He became known as father of German economic miracle, serving as Minister of Economics of F R G 1949–63. He had bad personal relations with Adenauer who could not avoid appointing him Vice-Chancellor (1957–63), nor prevent him becoming Chancellor, 1963–66. He was pro-American and favoured British entry into the E E C falling out with de Gaulle on these and other matters. The differences with France over the E E C were an important factor in his downfall. He established diplomatic relations with Israel.

**Fallada, Hans** (1893–1947), born in Greifswald he won attention through his socially critical novel *Bauern, Bonzen und Bomben* (*Peasants, Bosses and Bombs*, 1931) and *Kleiner Mann-was nun?* (1932) which Hollywood made into the film *What Now Little Man?* He managed to survive in Nazi Germany.

**Fassbinder, Rainer Werner** (1946–1982), remarkably able and productive actor, theatre and film director of the 'new wave', his films were usually a critical look at Germany in the 1930s, 1940s and 1950s.

**Freisler, Roland** (1893–1945), born in Celle he studied law in Jena. He became a Communist as a P O W in Russia in the First World War but turned to Nazism in 1925. As a leading official of the Ministry of Justice he helped to Nazify the law. As Chairman of the People's Court he presided over the trials of the anti-Hitler July plotters. He was killed in an air raid.

**Fuchs, Anke** (1937–  ). She followed her father, Paul Nevermann, Mayor of Hamburg, into the S P D and after studying law became a trade union official. She served on the executive committee of the I. G. Metall and in the Hamburg parliament, 1971–77. She was State Secretary in the Federal Ministry of Labour, 1977–82 and Minister for Youth, Families and Health in 1982.

**Galen, Clemens August Graf von** (1878–1946). As Catholic bishop of Münster he welcomed Hitler's reoccupation of the Rhineland in 1936 and supported the war in 1939. In 1941 he spoke against the euthanasia programme being the only bishop to do so. This was temporarily suspended. Fearing Catholic opposition the Nazis left him alone. He was promoted to cardinal after the war.

**Genscher, Hans-Dietrich** (1927–  ). The son of a Nation Conservative company lawyer he was born near Halle in what became the D D R.

He attended Friedrich–Nietzsche–Oberschule there before military service. He was briefly a P O W of the Americans. He studied law in Leipzig, his studies being interrupted by illness, and joined the Liberal Democrats. He migrated to Bremen in West Germany in 1952 where he joined the F D P. From 1965 he was a member of the Bundestag and worked hard to bring about the S P D–F D P coalition without disguising his close contact with Helmut Kohl. He served as Minister of Interior of the F R G, 1969–74 and from 1974 Foreign Minister, thus becoming longest serving Foreign Minister in German history. He was one of the key architects of German reunification.

**Goebbels, Joseph** (1897–1945), head of Nazi propaganda from 1929 becoming Minister for Popular Enlightenment and Propaganda in 1933, he was also President of the Reich Chamber of Culture. He remained loyal to Hitler to the end, killing himself and his family in the Hitler bunker in Berlin.

**Göring, Hermann** (1893–1946), commanded Von Richthofen Fighter Squadron in last stages of 1914–18 war, he joined the Nazis in 1922 and wounded in Hitler putsch, 1923. As President of Reichstag from 1932 he was believed to have masterminded the fire of 1933. In 1933 he became Prussian Prime Minister and Minister of Air; 1935: Commander-in-chief of Luftwaffe; 1936: four year plan commissioner; 1940: *Reichsmarschall*. Sentenced to death by the allies, he killed himself.

**Grotewohl, Otto** (1894–1964), member of the Reichstag 1925–33, he became Chairman of Soviet zone S P D in 1945 and led his party into communist-dominated S E D. He served, 1949–64, as head of government of D D R.

**Grass, Günter** (1927–  ), born in Danzig, he served briefly in the Wehrmacht, he studied art in Dusseldorf and Paris and started writing in the 1950s. Best-known for the novel about the Danzig of his childhood, *The Tin Drum*, he became a highly critical, moderate Social Democrat.

**Gropius, Walter** (1883–1969), helped to establish the Bauhaus school of arts and crafts in Dessau in 1919, he was a leading architect in Germany and later in the U S A.

**Hahn, Otto** (1879–1968), won the Nobel Prize for chemistry in 1944 but was better known for his work on splitting the atom. He refused to join the Nazi party but remained in Germany working on nuclear research. Controversy surrounds why he and his colleagues failed to produce an atomic bomb. After 1945 he was elected president of the

Max–Planck–Society. He campaigned against the misuse of nuclear energy.

**Hallstein, Walter** (1901–1982), born in Mainz he was a professor of law at Rostock (1930–41) and then Frankfurt and Main to 1948. He was a close foreign policy adviser to Adenauer in the early years of the Federal Republic. Later he was known as 'Mr Europe' because, after playing a major role in the setting up of the then E E C he served as its President, 1958–67. He was ahead of his time in his views on European integration and resigned after failing to convince de Gaulle. He was a member of the Bundestag 1969–72.

**Hamm-Brücher, Hildegard** (1921–   ). Urged by Theodor Heuss to give up journalism for politics she served in the Bavarian Landtag, as State Secretary in Hesse (1967–69), State Secretary in the Federal Ministry for Education and Science (1969–1972), Chairman of the F D P group in the Bavarian Landtag (1972–76) and Minister of State in the Federal Foreign Ministry (1976–82). She was closely associated with educational reform in favour of the underprivileged and aid to the Third World. She opposed the change of F D P coalition partner from S P D to C D U/C S U in 1982.

**Hauptmann, Gerhart** (1862–1946), the son of a Silesian hotelier he became a sculptor but turned to drama. He won the Nobel Prize for literature in 1912. Perhaps his best known work was *Die Weber* (*The Weavers*, 1892). A romantic socialist in his youth he remained in Nazi Germany and continued to be published.

**Heym, Stefan** (1913–   ), born in Chemnitz of Jewish background he left Germany for the U S A in 1937. There he started his writing career. He served in the U S army but returned to the D D R expressing orthodox SED views for many years. Later he came into conflict with the S E D remaining a Marxist.

**Heinemann, Gustav** (1899–1976), an evangelical Christian, lawyer and member of the board of Krupp in his home town of Essen, he was a founder member of the C D U. There he was mayor until Adenauer appointed him first Minister of Interior of West Germany in 1949. He left the government in 1950 because he disagreed with re-armament, forming his own All-German People's Party (G V P) in 1952. It had no success in the 1953 election and was dissolved in 1956. Heinemann joined the S P D in 1957 and was elected to the Bundestag. He helped to build bridges to church circles. He was elected President of the Federal Republic in 1969 with F D P help.

**Hess, Rudolf** (1894–1987). Officially Deputy to Hitler in the N S D A P he was born in Egypt of German parents. He served as an airforce officer in the 1914–18 war. At Munich University he became influenced by Nazi ideas and took part in the Hitler putsch of 1923. He was imprisoned with Hitler in Landsberg and there acted as his secretary. The two became close and Hess rose rapidly in the N S D A P. He flew to England in 1941 without his leader's knowledge in an apparent attempt to bring peace between Germany and Britain. At Nuremberg he was sentenced to life imprisonment in 1946 and died in Spandau jail. Controversy surrounds his mission and his death.

**Heuss, Theodor** (1884–1963), a journalist and member of the left Liberal German Democratic Party (D D P), he voted in the Reichstag for Hitler's Enabling Act in 1933. He was later banned from writing. In 1945 he was a founding member of the Free Democratic Party and professor of politics in Stuttgart. He served as first President of the F R G, 1949–59.

**von Heyse, Paul** (1830–1914). Born in Berlin he studied there and in Bonn. In 1854 Maximilian II of Bavaria provided him with a pension and he became a leading poet there. He wrote many verse tragedies, novellas, poems and novels. He was also known for his translations of Spanish and Italian songs. His best-known novel was *Kinder der Welt*. His works revealed opposition to state religion and conformism. Translated into 14 languages, his works are little read today. He was awarded the Nobel Prize for Literature in 1910 and ennobled in the same year.

**Himmler, Heinrich** (1900–45). His father was a Bavarian royal tutor and he grew up as a conformist Catholic. A nationalist, he was a cadet at the end of the First World War. He took part in the Hitler putsch, 1923. He was head of the S S, 1929; Munich police chief 1933; chief of German police 1936; Reich Minister of Interior 1943; responsible for organising the 'final solution of the Jewish question' and other similar measures; put in charge of the home army in 1944; expelled from Nazi party and removed from office for attempting peace negotiations, April 1945; committed suicide in British custody.

**Hindemith, Paul** (1895–1963). In the 1920s and 1930s he was regarded as a revolutionary and intellectual innovator having formulated the concept of *Gebrauchsmusik* ('music for use'). He was forced to leave Germany in 1938 but returned in 1951. He turned from his earlier style to neo-classical compositions.

**Hindenburg, Paul von** (1847–1934). Field marshal and commander of German armies on the eastern front, 1915–16, then chief of general staff, 1918, responsible for demobilisation in the west, elected President of the German Republic in 1925, re-elected 1932 and appointed Hitler's Chancellor.

**Hitler, Adolf** (1889–1945), born the son of Alois Hitler (formerly Schicklgruber), an Austrian customs official he only gained German nationality in 1930 yet he was Chancellor of Germany 1933–45, German head of state 1934–45, for his career see p. 35.

**Hochhuth, Rolf** (1931–   ), born near Kassel he made his name with several documentary-style plays. In *Der Stellvertreter* (1963) he attacked Pope Pius XII for his wartime attitude to the Nazis. It was the most successful play performed in West Germany at the time. In *Soldaten* (1967) he alleged there was a plot by Churchill to kill the Polish leader General Sikorski.

**Honecker, Erich** (1912–   ), son of a coalminer from Neukirken/Saar he was sentenced to 10 years for high treason by the Nazis for underground Communist activity in 1935. Chairman of the (Communist) Free German Youth, 1946–55, he was a candidate member of the ruling politburo of the S E D from 1950, full member from 1958 and in that year he became Secretary for Security. In 1971 he replaced Ulbricht as S E D leader becoming head of state in 1976. He was deposed in 1989 and lives in retirement with his wife Margot, formerly Minister of Education.

**Hugenberg, Alfred** (1865–1951), born in Hanover he was chairman of Krupp, 1909–18, before founding the biggest media empire in Germany. His publications and newsreels were misused for nationalist and anti-democratic propaganda. From 1919 to 1945 he was a member of the Reichstag. As chairman of the D N V P (1928–33) he formed an alliance with the Nazis, helping them to power in 1933. He served in Hitler's cabinet until June 1933 when he was forced to resign and dissolve his party. He then gave up politics and survived the Third Reich still a wealthy man.

**Jannings, Emil** (1884–1950), born in Switzerland of an American father and German mother he ran away to sea. After some success in the theatre he turned to film acting in 1916. He soon became a top actor and remained so until 1945. He won an Oscar in Hollywood for his part in the silent film *The Way Of All Flesh*. Back in Germany he starred in *Der blaue Engel* (1930). He was highly regarded by Goebbels and Hitler, playing Bismarck in *Die Entlassung* and the South African leader Krueger in *Ohm Krueger* (1941).

**Jünger, Ernst** (1895–   ), left home in Heidelberg in 1913 to serve briefly in the Foreign Legion. His pharmacist father got him out, but within a year he had joined the German army in which he served with distinction. He studied zoology, philosophy, botany and geology but pursued a career in writing. With his 'technocratic nationalism' and war novels he is believed to have helped pave the way for Nazism. He refused to join the Nazi party, served as an officer, 1940–44, and continued writing after it.

**Kant, Hermann** (1926– ), born in Hamburg he qualified as an electrician. He served in the war, taking part in an anti-fascist school in Polish captivity. He studied in Greifswald and Berlin and became a literary editor. His first novel *Die Aula* (*The Auditorium*, 1965) is his best-known. He joined the S E D in 1949 serving in various functions. He was President of the Writers' Union 1978–89. Kant was widely criticised after 1989 for his association with the S E D, its ideology and practice.

**Käutner, Helmut** (1908–1980), born in Düsseldorf he was a well-known actor, scriptwriter and film director. In the Third Reich he successfully made very popular non-political films such as *Kleider machen Leute* (1940) and *Romanze in Moll* (1942). Some of his work was banned. After the war he stayed in films becoming one of the best-known West German directors. His *Die letzte Brücke* (1954) was a Yugoslav co-production aimed at reconciliation with that state, *Der Hauptmann von Köpenick* was an attack on militarism set in pre-1914 Berlin.

**Keitel, Wilhelm** (1882–1946). Originally an artillery officer Hitler appointed him field marshall and highest ranking soldier. Hitler's closest military adviser, he warned against attacking the Soviet Union. A member of the Nazi party, he implemented the dictator's many notorious orders. He signed the surrender of the German armed forces at the Soviet H Q in Berlin on 9 May 1945. He was found guilty at Nuremburg by the allies and hanged.

**Kelly, Petra** (1947– ), a pioneer of the Green movement, she was elected to the Bundestag in 1983 and again in 1987. A former S P D member she was educated in the U S A (American University, Washington, D C) and worked for the European Commission.

**Kiesinger, Kurt Georg** (1904–1988), born in Württemberg he became a lawyer in Berlin. A Catholic, he joined the Nazi party and headed a department of radio propaganda in the Foreign Ministry. After postwar internment he returned to the law and joined the C D U in 1948 serving in the Bundestag, 1949–58. He was Prime Minister of

Baden-Württemberg, 1958–66, and Chancellor of the F R G, 1966–69. He remained Chairman of the C D U until 1971 and member of the Bundestag until 1976.

**Kohl, Helmut** (1930–   ), born in Ludwigshafen the son of a civil servant in the local tax office. His father had been promoted to officer in the First World War for bravery and was, though Catholic, a supporter of the D N V P. Kohl founded a branch of the youth wing of the C D U in 1947, joining the party in 1948. He worked his way through university (Frankfurt am Main and Heidelberg), studying history and law. In 1958 he gained his doctorate for a study of the development of political parties in the Pfalz after 1945. In 1959 he became the youngest member of the Rhineland–Palatinate parliament, he later (1969–76) served as Prime Minister. His administration founded the Trier/Kaiserslautern University and passed the first nursery law in the Federal Republic. He failed as C D U/C S U Chancellor candidate in 1976 but remained Chairman of the combined party in the Bundestag (1976–82). He had served as deputy Chairman of the C D U and later as Chairman. In 1982 he became the youngest Chancellor of the F R G and first Chancellor of the re-united Germany in October 1990. A Catholic, Kohl married a non-Catholic, Hannelore, from what became the D D R. They have two children.

**Kollwitz, Käthe** (1867–1945). Daughter of a socialist master mason, she was born in Königsberg. She studied art there and in Berlin and Munich. She married a left-wing medical practitioner and lived in Berlin where she taught. Her most famous work was the cycle of paintings, the *Weavers' Revolt* inspired by Hauptmann's *Die Weber*. She opposed the 1914–18 war but lost one of her two sons in it. She was the first woman member of the Prussian Academy of Arts. The Nazis forced her out and banned exhibitions of her work in 1936.

**Krause, Günther** (1953–   ). Born in Rostock he gained his doctorate as a building engineer. A member of the C D U he served as a State Secretary in the last D D R government and headed the East German delegation in the unity negotiations. In 1991 he was appointed Minister of Transport in Kohl's government.

**Krenz, Egon** (1937–   ), held office as the last Communist leader of the D D R briefly in 1989. Trained as a teacher, he headed the youth organisation (F D J) 1974–83, was elected candidate member of the politburo 1976 and full member 1983, he was also S E D Secretary for Security.

**Lafontaine, Oskar** (1943–   ), born in Saarlouis he studied physics before taking up politics. He was mayor of Saarbrücken and later

Prime Minister of the Saar. In 1990 he was S P D Chancellor candidate in the first elections in the reunited Germany.

**Lange, Helene** (1848–1930), a prominent feminist and educational reformer she campaigned for better education for girls and that their education should be under the control of women, not men. She founded the journal *Die Frau* in 1893.

**Leber, Julius** (1891–1945), S P D member of Reichstag, 1924–33, concentration camp inmate, 1933–37. He was executed for his part in the 1944 anti-Hitler plot.

**Lubitsch, Ernst** (1892–1947), born in Berlin he moved to the U S in 1921. He started his career acting in the Max Reinhardt theatre in Berlin and ended it as head of production at Paramount Studios. Among his best-known films are *Ninotchka* (1939) with Greta Garbo and the anti-Nazi *To Be Or Not To Be* (1942).

**Ludendorff, Erich** (1865–1937), with Hindenburg led German forces in 1914–18 war, supported Hitler, taking part in his 1923 putsch.

**Luxemburg, Rosa** (1871–1919), Polish-Jewish socialist, she joined S P D in 1898 and worked as a lecturer at the party school, she opposed revisionism in S P D and took a militant anti-war stand in 1914 for which she was imprisoned. Although she was a critic of Lenin, she helped found the Communist Party of Germany (K P D), she was murdered by right-wing officers in 1919.

**de Maizière, Lothar** (1940–  ), a lawyer and evangelical church official, he was elected Prime Minister of the D D R after the democratic elections of March 1990 and subsequently became a minister in the first government of the re-united Germany. He had been a C D U member when that party was under Communist tutelage. After the C D U of the D D R merged with its West German sister party he was elected Vice-Chairman. He resigned his posts in December 1990 after persistent claims that he had acted as informer for the D D R secret police.

**Mann, Thomas** (1875–1955). He won the Nobel Prize for literature in 1929, a liberal humanist and German patriot world famous for his many novels. He turned his back on Nazi Germany in 1933 and lived in Switzerland and then the U S A. After 1945 he spent his remaining years in Switzerland. His first great work was *Buddenbrooks* (1901), a family chronicle, his last major novel was *Doktor Faustus* (1947) based on the story by Goethe.

**Marx, Karl** (1818–1883), born in Trier of middle class Jewish background his revolutionary theories inspired both the S P D and, later Leninist Communism. He studied history, philosophy and law at Berlin and Bonn and gained his doctorate at Jena. He was forced to seek asylum in London, where he wrote his major works, the *Communist Manifesto* (with Engels) and *Capital* after the failed revolution of 1848.

**Messerschmitt, Willy** (1898–1978), designer of the many planes which carried his name, he set up his company in Augsburg in 1923. He was a pioneer of jet aircraft and played an important part in the revival of German aviation after 1949.

**Mielke, Erich** (1907–  ), a life-long Communist he was involved in building up state security in the Soviet Zone/D D R. He was Minister of State Security, 1957–89, and full member of the politburo, 1976–89.

**Mies van der Rohe, Ludwig** (1886–1969) born in Aachen he followed his father as a stone mason before vocational school and apprenticeship with a Berlin furniture designer. His early architectural work was in the Schinkel tradition. After the 1914–18 war he became a 'revolutionary', designing glass skyscrapers, in 1930 he was appointed Bauhaus director. He left Germany for the U S in 1937, where he had enormous influence and many imitators. He was director of the Illinois Institute of Technology, 1939–59.

**Nernst, Walther Hermann** (1864–1941), established the third law of thermodynamics which dealt with the behaviour of matter at temperatures approaching zero. Awarded Nobel Prize for physics in 1920.

**Niemöller, Martin** (1892–1984), much-decorated U-boat commander of First World War who later studied theology at Muenster becoming an evangelical pastor. A leading member of the *Bekenende Kirche* he spent much of the Nazi years in concentration camps. As a pacifist he opposed re-armament after 1945 and served as a member of the Council of the Evangelical Church and of the presidium of the World Council of Churches.

**Nietzsche, Friedrich** (1844–1900), see chapter 1.

**Ollenhauer, Erich** (1901–1963), Chairman of the S P D 1952–63 he was born in Magdeburg and led the party youth movement in Weimar period. Elected to the S P D executive in 1933 he spent the Hitler years in Prague, Paris and London. He was regarded as a very loyal, old-fashioned functionary rather than a charismatic leader with wide appeal.

**Papen, Franz von** (1879–1969), member of the Centre Party and Prussian parliament he was briefly Chancellor of Germany in 1932.

In Hitler's first government he was Vice-Chancellor, he later served as a diplomat in Vienna and Ankara.

**Paulus, Friedrich** (1890–1957), commanded the ill-fated 6th army at Stalingrad. Hitler promoted him to field marshal hoping he would die rather than surrender but he gave up and later collaborated with the Soviets. He lived in the D D R after the war.

**Planck, Max** (1858–1947), physicist who developed the quantum theory and was awarded the Nobel Prize in 1918.

**Pöhl, Karl Otto** (1929– ), born in Hanover he worked as an economic journalist before serving as a State Secretary in the Finance Ministry under Helmut Schmidt, 1972–77. A Social Democrat he was appointed Deputy Chairman of the Bundesbank in 1977 and Chairman in 1980.

**Porsche, Ferdinand** (1875–1951), originally a plumber, he took evening-class courses in electronics and handicrafts. He soon became the top designer of Daimler sports cars, first in his native Austria and then in Germany. In 1934 Hitler contracted him to design the original Volkswagen.

**Rathenau, Walther** (1867–1922), German–Jewish industrialist, he served as Foreign Minister in 1922 and was murdered by right-wing extremists.

**Rau, Johannes** (1931– ). Born in Wuppertal where he served as mayor he was the son of a parson. He started his political career in the neutralist G V P. Prime Minister of North Rhine-Westphalia, 1978– he stood unsuccessfully as the S P D's Chancellor candidate in 1987.

**Renger, Annemarie** (1919– ), secretary and confidante of S P D leader Kurt Schumacher she served as President of the Bundestag, 1972–76 and Vice-President, 1976– .

**Ribbentrop, Joachim von** (1893–1946), joined the Nazi party in 1932 and became Hitler's foreign policy adviser. He served as Ambassador in London, 1936–38 and Foreign Minister 1938–45. He was convicted at Nuremburg and executed.

**Riefenstahl, Leni** (1902–1987), Berlin dancer and film actress who became widely known as a director of films used by the Nazis for propaganda purposes. She later denied she had been a Nazi.

**Röntgen, Wilhelm Conrad** (1845–1923), he discovered x-rays and in 1901 was awarded the first Nobel Prize for physics.

**Rommel, Erwin** (1891–1944), famous as commander of the Africa

Corps fighting a 'gentlemanly' war against the British (and later Americans as well). The son of a grammar school head he took up soldiering in 1910 and fought in the First World War. He was a tank commander in 1939 and fought in Poland, Belgium and France. He was defeated by the allies in North Africa in 1943 and, after a brief period in Italy, was put in charge of coastal defences in northern France. Hitler had made him a field marshal but later under threat of arrest he took poison. He had been on the fringe of the 1944 bomb plot.

**Rohwedder, Detlev Karsten** (1932–1990), born in Gotha he became a Social Democrat and served as state secretary in the Ministry of Economics before being appointed head of the troubled Hoesch steel firm in 1979. He was appointed to run the *Treuhandanstalt*, the body responsible for disposing of East German Industry in 1930. In 1990 he was killed by terrorists.

**Rosenberg, Alfred** (1893–1946). Hanged by the Allies in 1946 he was a Baltic German who headed the foreign department of the N S D A P. He studied engineering and architecture before leaving Russia in 1917. He protested against the brutal treatment of Soviet prisoners but was also involved in plundering Jewish property.

**Sachs, Nelly** (1891–1970). She won the Nobel Prize for Literature in 1966. Born in Berlin the daughter of a Jewish entrepreneur she escaped the fate of her family, murdered by the Nazis, by emigration to Sweden in 1940. She was the last Jewish German-language poet.

**Schabowski, Günter** (1929–   ), born in Anklam. After completing his grammar school education he went into journalism working for trade union papers. He spent a year at the university of the C P S U in Moscow, 1967–8. He served as editor-in-chief of the S E D paper *Neues Deutschland* before being appointed S E D Secretary for Berlin in 1985. Elected to the Central Committee in 1981 and as candidate member of Politburo (full member 1984). Played a leading role in fall of Honecker and the last phase of the D D R.

**Schacht, Hjalmar** (1877–1970), regarded as Hitler's financial wizard he grew up in the U S A with his German-Danish parents. He gained his doctorate in economics from Berlin and went into banking. He served as President of the Reich Bank, 1923–30 and 1933–39. In 1937 he resigned as Minister of Economics and Commissioner for the War Economy but remained Minister without Portfolio until 1943. He was later briefly arrested by the Nazis.

**Schäuble, Wolfgang** (1942–   ), born in Freiburg, he studied law and economics there and in Hamburg, gaining his doctorate in 1971. He worked briefly as a university lecturer before joining the Baden–Württemberg inspectorate of taxes. Elected to the Bundestag, 1972, he acted as business leader of the C D U/C S U group, 1981–84. He served as Minister for Special Tasks and Head of the Chancellor's Office, 1984–9, and then as Minister of Interior. He played a key role in negotiating German unity.

**Scheel, Walter** (1919–   ), born Solingen, served his time in a savings bank and then as lieutenant in the Luftwaffe 1939–45, winning the Iron Cross twice. An F D P member of the Bundestag 1953–1974, he was Minister for Economic Co-operation 1961–66, Vice-President of the Bundestag 1967–69, Foreign Minister 1969–74, President of the F R G, 1974–79. He played a major role in the development of a new *Ostpolitik* and was a strong supporter of the S P D–F D P coalition.

**Scheidemann, Philipp** (1865–1939), born in Kassel, later a journalist there, he was chairman of the S P D in the Reichstag as the 1914 war started. On 9 November 1918 he proclaimed the Republic from the balcony on the Berlin Castle. He served briefly as Chancellor in 1919. After the Nazis took power he lived in Copenhagen.

**von Schirach, Baldur** (1907–1974), from an old Berlin officers' family, his father left the army to become a theatre director. His mother was American. He joined the Nazi party in 1925 being influenced by Henry Ford's anti-Semitic writing. He was Hitler Youth leader 1931–40 and then governor of Vienna. At Nuremberg he was sentenced to 20 years imprisonment. After his release he renounced his past.

**Schirrmann, Richard** (1874–1961), originator of youth hostels. A school teacher he converted his schoolroom into a dormitory during holidays. The idea took on and led to the establishment of the German Youth Hostels' Association (V D J) in 1913. The International Youth Hostels' Association was founded in 1932 with Schirrmann as its President.

**Schmidt, Helmut** (1918–   ), the son of a schoolteacher he served as an artillery officer in World War II. He spent six months as a British P O W then he studied economics at Hamburg university (1945–9) where he joined the S P D. He worked in the city traffic department before his election to the Bundestag in 1953. He soon was known as a defence expert, he also served as a reserve officer. He was a successful Senator for Interior in Hamburg, 1961–5 after which he returned to the Bundestag as a leading figure in the S P D, becoming Chairman of the parliamentary group in 1966. In 1969 he became Minister of Defence and in 1972 Minister for Economics and Finance. Between

1974–82 he served as Chancellor of the F R G and, with his fluent English, helped to improve the image of West Germany internationally.

**Scholl, Sophie** (1921–1943), a student of biology at Munich University, she participated with her brother Hans in the *Weisse Rose* (White Rose) anti-Nazi resistance group. She was arrested by the Gestapo and executed.

**Schott, Friedrich Otto** (1851–1935), chemist and glass technologist he created the basis for modern, high quality, glass production, founding with Ernst Abbe and Carl Zeiss in 1866 the Jenaer Glaswerk at Jena.

**Schumacher, Kurt** (1895–1952), son of a middle-class West Prussian family, he volunteered for war service in 1914 and was severely wounded, he studied law and politics and took up journalism for the S P D. 1930–33 he served in the Reichstag and then spent ten years in Nazi prisons and camps. He played a key role in setting up the S P D in 1945, becoming its Chairman in 1946. He remained its leader until his death, steering it in a strongly patriotic, anti-Communist direction.

**Schwarzhaupt, Elisabeth** (1901–    ), the daughter of a teacher, she qualified as a teacher herself and then gained a doctorate in law. A member of the moderate Conservative D V P 1919–33, she was prevented by the Nazis from work in the public service. In 1953 she was elected C D U member of the Bundestag and 1961–66 served as the first woman minister (Health) in the F R G.

**Seghers, Anna** (1900–1988), born as Nelly Reiling in Mainz she studied history and philosophy in Cologne and Heidelberg. In 1928 she joined the K P D and spent the Nazi years in France and Mexico. She returned to the Soviet Zone in 1947 and subsequently became a prominent member of the S E D serving on its Central Committee. Her most important novels were: *Das siebte Kreuz* (1942), *Die Rettung* (1943), *Die Toten bleiben jung* (1949).

**Seidel, Ina** (1885–1974), a prominent poet and novelist she was born in Bavaria the daughter of a doctor. Her most famous novel was *Das Wunschkind* (1930) dealing with the stresses of motherhood in Napoleonic Wars. Her *Michaela* (1959) dealt with the situation of intellectuals in the Third Reich.

**Seiters, Rudolf** (1937–    ). A Catholic born in Osnabrück he studied law and politics before entering the local government service. He joined the C D U in 1958 and the Bundestag in 1969. He served as Chairman of the youth wing of the C D U and of the Lower Saxony C D U. Kohl appointed him Minister in charge of the Chancellor's

Office and he came into his own as one of the architects of German unity in 1990.

**Späth, Lothar** (1937– ), C D U Prime Minister of Baden-Württemberg 1978–91, highly popular, widely seen as a future Chancellor. He gained popularity for his efforts to build up his region as a home of high-tech industry.

**Springer, Axel Caesar** (1912–1985), developed the largest media empire in post-war West Germany owning such papers as *Die Welt* and *Bild*. His principles were German re-unification, friendship with Israel, the social market economy and the Basic Law.

**Stauffenberg, Claus Schenk Graf von** (1907–1944), the man who placed the bomb under the table where Hitler was speaking on 20 July 1944, a monarchist he had at first welcomed Hitler's chancellorship. He changed his mind on 9 November 1938, the 'night of broken glass'. His experiences of Nazi policies in the Soviet Union further convinced him of the need to remove Hitler. As a wounded, decorated, colonel and staff officer of the home army he was in a good position to help organise the opposition.

**Steinhoff, Hans** (1882–1945), Bavarian film director and actor, he was responsible for many Nazi propaganda films.

**Stockhausen, Karlheinz** (1928– ), the son of a school teacher he studied music at Cologne University and in Paris. He pioneered electronic music working in the studio of the West German Radio (W D R) in Cologne.

**Stoph, Willi** (1914– ), head of government of the D D R, 1964–73, 1976–89, he also served as Minister of Interior 1952–54; Minister of Defence, 1956–60; head of state, 1973–6. When the Communist regime fell in 1989 he had served in the ruling politburo longer than any other surviving member.

**Stoltenberg, Gerhard** (1928– ), born in Kiel the son of a parson he joined the C D U in 1947. He gained his doctorate in 1954 after studying history and philosophy at Kiel. He was the Chairman of the youth wing of the C D U, 1955–1961; Federal Minister for Scientific Research, 1965–9; Premier of Schleswig-Holstein, 1971–1982; Federal Minister for Finance 1982–9; and Defence Minister since 1989. He also held several party posts, including the deputy Chairmanship of the C D U.

**Strauss, Franz Josef** (1915–1988), son of a butcher, he was a wartime lieutenant in anti-aircraft artillery. A qualified teacher he joined the C S U in his native Bavaria in 1945. He gained a seat in the Bundestag in 1949 and was already Minister for Special Tasks (nuclear power) by 1955. Appointed Defence Minister in 1956 he was forced to resign over the *Spiegel* affair in 1962. He served 1966–69 as Finance Minister and Prime Minister of Bavaria, 1978–88. His limitations were shown when he failed to win the 1980 election as joint C D U/C S U candidate. Popular in Bavaria, he worried the voters outside it.

**Strauss, Richard** (1864–1949), born in Munich the son of a musician he became well-known both as a conductor and innovative composer in the tradition of 'programme music' and successor to Wagner in German opera. With the production of *Salome* (1905) and *Elektra* (1909) he became recognised as a genius in his own right. The Nazis used his reputation by appointing him President of the Reich Chamber of Music in 1933 and Chairman of the Association of Composers. He lost these positions in 1935 because of his dealings with Jewish colleagues but his works continued to be performed.

**Streicher, Julius** (1885–1946), an early Nazi, *Gauleiter* of Franconia and founder of the most rabid anti-Jewish paper *Der Stürmer*. He was condemned at the Nuremburg trials and executed.

**Stresemann, Gustav** (1878–1929). Born in Berlin the son of a beer trader he studied economics there and in Leipzig. He then worked as an industrial interest group official. A National Liberal he supported Germany's war aims in the 1914–18 war. He founded the German People's Party (D V P) in 1918 and served as Chancellor for 103 days in 1923 when he sent troops to deal with the Communists in Saxony and Thuringia and suppress the Hitler Putsch in Munich. As Foreign Minister 1923–9 he had a decisive influence on German foreign policy. Dedicated to reconciliation with France he negotiated the Locarno Treaty and Germany's entry into the League of Nations. He was awarded the Nobel Prize for Peace in 1926.

**Süssmuth, Rita** (1937–   ), professor of education who served as C D U Minister for Youth, Family and Health (Women later added) until her election as President of Bundestag in 1989. This popular C D U politician is regarded as a potential Chancellor.

**Thälmann, Ernst** (1886–1944), transport worker who became leader of the Communist Party of Germany (K P D) in the Weimar Republic. He followed unquestioningly the Stalinist line. He was a member of the Reichstag 1924–33 and a leading member of the Cominterm. He was killed by the Nazis in Buchenwald concentration camp in 1944.

**Töpfer, Professor Klaus** (1938– ), born in Silesia he studied economics gaining his doctorate in 1968. He embarked upon an academic career serving 1978–9 as professor at Hanover University and Director of the Institute for Environmental Research. He joined the C D U in 1972 and was Minister of Environment and Health in the Rhineland-Palatinate, 1985–87 before his appointment as Federal Minister for the Environment, Nature Conservation and Nuclear Safety in 1987.

**Treitschke, Heinrich von** (1834–1896), professor of history and National Liberal member of the Reichstag (1871–1884) he had great influence as an advocate of nationalism and anti-Semitism.

**Ulbricht, Walter** (1893–1973), a carpenter, he joined the K P D in 1919 becoming a professional party worker, he was member of the Reichstag, 1928–33. He spent the Hitler years in Moscow and, unlike many others, survived. He returned to Germany with the Red Army in 1945 and rose rapidly as a man the Soviets trusted. He was leader of the ruling S E D 1950–71, head of state, 1960–73.

**Wagner, Richard** (1813–83), grew up in Leipzig and held a number of musical appointments there before fleeing as a subversive Liberal to Switzerland after the failed revolution of 1848. Ludwig II of Bavaria employed him from 1864. Inspired by old German legends and by Nietzsche he became the greatest German composer of opera.

**Waigel, Theo** (1939– ), a Catholic he gained his Dr Jura in 1967 after studies at Munich and Wuerzburg. He then worked as a lawyer before entering politics. He was Chairman of the youth wing of the C S U, 1971–5, and elected to the Bundestag in 1972, where he served as Chairman of the C S U group from 1982. As Minister of Finance from 1989 he played an important role in the negotiations with the D D R over monetary union.

**Weber, Max** (1864–1920), one of the fathers of sociology he was a professor of commerical law in Berlin and then economics in Freiburg, Heidelberg and Munich.

**Wehner, Herbert** (1906–1990), one of the key architects of the post-1945 S P D. A former Communist he spent the Nazi period in Moscow and then Stockholm where he became a Christian and Social Democrat. He served as Chairman of the S P D parliamentary group 1969–83. From Dresden he worked hard for the restoration of German unity and was Minister for All-German Questions, 1966–69.

**Weizsäcker, Richard von** (1920– ), born in Stuttgart he studied law in Oxford and Grenoble in the 1930s. In the war he served in the infantry being promoted to captain. After 1945 he took up his law studies again, gaining his doctor of law from Goettingen in 1955. He then held positions in insurance and banking. He had married Marianne von Kretschmann, a banker's daughter and through her became head of a private bank. He was also active in the evangelical church becoming a leading lay member. Elected a C D U member of the Bundestag in 1969, he moved to the West Berlin parliament in 1979 being elected mayor in 1981. His election to German president followed in 1984. Thus he became president of the reunited Germany in 1990. His father Ernst von Weizsäcker (1882–1951), a diplomat, was state secretary to the foreign office, 1938–43, and then ambassador to the Vatican. He was sentenced to seven years imprisonment in 1949 for his part in the Nazi state but released as part of a general amnesty in 1950. Richard von Weizsäcker has earned great respect internationally as a man of moderation and reconciliation.

**Wilhelm II** (1859–1941), Kaiser of Germany and King of Prussia, 1888–1918. Promoted sciences and arts but was an autocrat and militarist. After his abdication lived as a country gentleman at Doorn in Holland.

**Wörner, Manfred** (1924–   ), born in Stuttgart, a doctor of international law (Munich University), military flier and C D U executive committee member, he served as Minister of Defence, 1982–8, before his appointment as Secretary General of N A T O.

**Wolf, Christa** (1929–   ), as a refugee from the East she arrived in the Soviet Zone in 1945 studying at Jena and Leipzig, she became a literary editor before turning to writing. A member of the S E D from 1949 she served on its central committee, 1963–67. She gained widespread recognition in both parts of Germany. Her independence brought her into conflict with the S E D. Among her best-known novels are *Der geteilte Himmel* (Divided Sky, 1969), about love in a divided Germany, and *Kinderheitsmuster* (1976) about her childhood in Nazi Germany.

**Zetkin, Clara** (1857–1933) a teacher born in Wiederau (Saxony), she joined the S P D in 1878. She edited the S P D women's journal *Die Gleichheit*, 1895–1917. As an opponent of the 1914–18 war she joined first the U S P D and then the K P D representing it in the Reichstag, 1920–33. She fled to Moscow after the Nazi seizure of power.

**Zeppelin, Ferdinand Graf von** (1838–1917) a Württemberg general and diplomat he played a key role in the development of airships.

**Ziegler, Adolf** (1892–1959), born in Bremen he was Hitler's favourite painter, an early Nazi party member as President of Reich Chamber of Visual Arts played a leading role in banning 'decadent' art.

**Zimmermann, Friedrich** (1925–    ), Secretary General of the C S U 1956–1963, he was a key figure in its success greatly expanding membership. In the Bundestag since 1957, he lead the C S U there, 1976–82. A close associate of Franz Josef Strauss, Kohl found him a tough partner but made him Minister of Interior 1982.

# — Appendix 2: —

## Tables

1 Germany in 1959*

| | | |
|---|---|---|
| Federal Republic of Germany (including West Berlin) | = | 62% of population of 1937 German Reich; 52.7% of land |
| German Democratic Republic (including East Berlin) | = | 24.1% of population of 1937 German Reich; 23% of land |
| Lost eastern territories | = | 13.9% of population of 1937 German Reich; 24.3% of land |

* according to the census of 17 May 1959

## 2 The Federal States (Länder) at unity 1990

| Land | population in millions | seats in Bundesrat | largest party |
|---|---|---|---|
| Baden-Württemberg | 9.46 | 7 | C D U |
| Bavaria | 11.07 | 7 | C S U |
| Berlin | 3.34 | 5 | S P D |
| Brandenburg | 2.61 | 4 | S P D |
| Bremen | 0.66 | 3 | S P D |
| Hamburg | 1.61 | 3 | S P D |
| Hesse | 5.58 | 6 | C D U |
| North-Rhine-Westphalia | 16.9 | 8 | S P D |
| Lower Saxony | 7.0 | 7 | S P D |
| Mecklenburg | 1.95 | 4 | C D U |
| Rhineland-Palatinate | 3.66 | 5 | C D U |
| Saar | 1.05 | 3 | S P D |
| Saxony | 4.84 | 5 | C D U |
| Saxony-Anhalt | 2.92 | 4 | C D U |
| Schleswig-Holstein | 2.57 | 4 | S P D |
| Thuringia | 2.65 | 4 | C D U |

## 3 German Heads of State 1871–1991

### The Rulers of the German Empire

| | |
|---|---|
| Wilhelm I | 1871–1888 |
| Friedrich III | 1888 |
| Wilhelm II | 1888–1918 |

### The Presidents of the Weimar Republic

| | |
|---|---|
| Friedrich Ebert | 1919–1925 |
| Paul von Hindenburg | 1925–1934 |

### The Third Reich

| | |
|---|---|
| Adolf Hitler, Führer | 1934–1945 |
| Admiral Karl Dönitz, President | 1945 |

### The Presidents of the Federal Republic of Germany

| | | |
|---|---|---|
| Theodor Heuss (F D P) | 1st term | 1949–1954 |
| | 2nd term | 1954–1959 |
| Heinrich Lübke (C D U) | 1st term | 1959–1964 |
| | 2nd term | 1964–1969 |
| Gustav Heinemann (S P D) | | 1969–1974 |
| Walter Scheel (F D P) | | 1974–1979 |
| Karl Carstens (C D U) | | 1979–1984 |
| Richard von Weizsäcker (C D U) | | 1984– |

**4** The German Chancellors – a summary of the dates their cabinets took office.

| | Chancellor | Commencement of office |
|---|---|---|
| German Reich | Otto von Bismarck | 18. 1.1871 |
| | Leo von Caprivi | 20. 3.1890 |
| | Chlodwig zu Hohenlohe-Schillingsfürst | 28.10.1894 |
| | Bernhard von Bülow | 17.10.1900 |
| | Theobald von Bethmann Hollweg | 14. 7.1909 |
| | Georg Michaelis | 14. 7.1917 |
| | Georg von Hertling | 01.11.1917 |
| | Max von Baden | 03.10.1918 |
| Weimar Republic | Friedrich Ebert (S P D) | 9.11.1918 |
| | Philipp Scheidemann (S P D) | 13. 2.1919 |
| | Gustav Bauer (S P D) | 21. 6.1919 |
| | Hermann Müller (S P D) | 27. 3.1920 |
| | Konstantin Fehrenbach (Centre) | 21. 6.1920 |
| | Joseph Wirth (Centre) | 10. 5.1921 |
| | Wilhelm Cuno (Independent) | 22.11.1922 |
| | Gustav Stresemann (D V P) | 13. 8.1923 |
| | Wilhelm Marx (Centre) | 30.11.1923 |
| | Hans Luther (Independent) | 15. 1.1925 |
| | Wilhelm Marx (Centre) | 16. 5.1926 |
| | Hermann Müller (S P D) | 28. 6.1928 |
| | Heinrich Brüning (Centre) | 30. 3.1930 |
| | Franz von Papen (Independent) | 1. 6.1932 |
| | Kurt von Schleicher (Independent) | 3.12.1932 |
| Third Reich | Adolf Hitler | 30. 1.1933 |
| Federal Republic of Germany | Konrad Adenauer (C D U) | 15. 9.1949 |
| | Ludwig Erhard (C D U) | 16.10.1963 |
| | Kurt Georg Kiesinger (C D U) | 1.12.1966 |
| | Willy Brandt (S P D) | 21.10.1969 |
| | Helmut Schmidt (S P D) | 16. 5.1974 |
| | Helmut Kohl | 1.10.1982 |

**5** Party and State Leaders of the German Democratic Republic 1949–90

**Co-Chairmen of the Socialist Unity Party (S E D):**
Wilhelm Pieck and Otto Grotewohl                    1946–54

**General Secretary/First Secretary of S E D:**
Walter Ulbricht                                     1950–71
Erich Honecker                                      1971–89
Egon Krenz                                          1989

**Heads of State:**
Wilhelm Pieck (President)                           1949–60
Walter Ulbricht (Chairman, Council of State)        1960–73
Willi Stoph (Chairman, Council of State)            1973–76
Erich Honecker (Chairman, Council of State)         1976–89
Egon Krenz (Chairman, Council of State)             1989*
Manfred Gerlach (Chairman, Council of State)        1989–90**
Sabine Bergmann-Pohl (President, *Volkskammer*)     1990***

**Head of Government with effective power:**
Lothar de Maizière Minister President               1990***

   * 24.10.89 to 6.12.89
  ** 6.12.89 to 5.04.90
*** 5.04.90 to 3.10.90

**6** World Leaders: U S A, Soviet Union, Britain and France

| Presidents of the U S A | | First/General Secretaries of the Soviet Communist Party | |
|---|---|---|---|
| Theodore Roosevelt | 1901–09 | | |
| William H. Taft | 1909–13 | V. I. Lenin | 1917–22 |
| Woodrow Wilson | 1913–21 | J. V. Stalin | 1922–53 |
| Warren G. Harding | 1921–23 | G. Malenkov | 1953 |
| Calvin Coolidge | 1923–29 | N. S. Khruschev | 1953–64 |
| Herbert C. Hoover | 1929–33 | L. Brezhnev | 1964–82 |
| Franklin D. Roosevelt | 1933–45 | Y. Andropov | 1982–84 |
| Harry S. Truman | 1945–53 | K. Chernenko | 1984–5 |
| Dwight D. Eisenhower | 1953–61 | M. Gorbachev | 1985– |
| John F. Kennedy | 1961–63 | | |
| Lyndon B. Johnson | 1963–69 | | |
| Richard M. Nixon | 1969–74 | **British Prime Ministers** | |
| Gerald R. Ford | 1974–77 | | |
| Jimmy Carter | 1977–81 | Marquis of Salisbury | 1900–2 |
| Ronald Reagan | 1981–89 | Arthur Balfour | 1902–5 |
| George Bush | 1989– | Sir H. Campbell-Bannerman | 1905–8 |

*Table 6 continued*

| | | | |
|---|---|---|---|
| H. Asquith | 1908–16 | P. Ramadier | 1947 |
| David Lloyd George | 1916–22 | R. Schuman | 1947 |
| A. Bonar Law | 1922–23 | A. Marie | 1948 |
| Stanley Baldwin | 1923–24 | R. Schuman | 1948 |
| J. Ramsay MacDonald | 1924 | H. Queuille | 1948–49 |
| Stanley Baldwin | 1924–29 | G. Bidault | 1949–50 |
| J. Ramsay MacDonald | 1929–35 | H. Queuille | 1950 |
| Stanley Baldwin | 1935–37 | R. Pleven | 1950–51 |
| Neville Chamberlain | 1937–40 | H. Queuille | 1951 |
| Winston S. Churchill | 1940–45 | R. Pleven | 1951–52 |
| Clement Attlee | 1945–51 | E. Faure | 1952 |
| Winston S. Churchill | 1951–55 | A. Pinay | 1952 |
| Anthony Eden | 1955–57 | R. Mayer | 1953 |
| Harold Macmillan | 1957–63 | J. Laniel | 1953–54 |
| Sir Alec Douglas-Home | 1963–64 | P. Mendes-France | 1954–55 |
| Harold Wilson | 1964–70 | E. Faure | 1955–56 |
| Edward Heath | 1970–74 | G. Mollet | 1956–57 |
| Harold Wilson | 1974–76 | M. Bourges-Maunoury | 1957 |
| James Callaghan | 1976–79 | F. Gaillard | 1957–58 |
| Margaret Thatcher | 1979–90 | P. Pflimlin | 1958 |
| John Major | 1990– | C. de Gaulle | 1958–59 |

**Prime Ministers of the French Fourth Republic 1944–1959**

| | |
|---|---|
| Charles de Gaulle | 1944–46 |
| F. Gouin | 1946 |
| G. Bidault | 1946 |
| L. Blum | 1946–47 |

**Presidents of the French Fifth Republic**

| | |
|---|---|
| Charles de Gaulle | 1959–69 |
| Georges Pompidou | 1969–74 |
| Valery Giscard d'Estaing | 1974–81 |
| Francois Mitterrand | 1981– |

7 The development of the most important parties measured by the results of elections up to 1933, shown as percentages.

| Year of elections for the national parliament | 1871 | 1881 | 1890 | 1903 | 1912 | 1919 | 1920 | 1924 | 1924 | 1928 | 1930 | 1932 | 1932 | 1933 |
|---|---|---|---|---|---|---|---|---|---|---|---|---|---|---|
| | | | | | | | | 4.5 | 7.12 | | | 31.7 | 6.11 | 5.3 |
| Electoral participation | 50.7 | 56.1 | 71.2 | 75.8 | 84.5 | 82.7 | 79.1 | 77.4 | 78.8 | 75.6 | 82.0 | 84.0 | 80.6 | 88.7 |
| Conservatives | 14.1 | 16.3 | 12.4 | 10.0 | 9.2 | | | | | | | | | |
| Free Conservatives | 8.9 | 7.4 | 6.7 | 3.4 | 3.0 | | | | | | | | | |
| German National Peoples' Party | | | | | | 10.3 | 15.1 | 19.5 | 20.5 | 14.2 | 7.0 | 5.9 | 8.8 | 8.0 |
| National Liberals | 30.0 | 14.6 | 16.3 | 13.9 | 13.7 | | | | | | | | | |
| German Peoples' Party | | | | | | 4.4 | 14.0 | 9.2 | 10.1 | 8.7 | 4.5 | 1.2 | 1.8 | 1.1 |
| 'Left' Liberals | 16.0 | 21.1 | 16.0 | 8.3 | 12.3 | | | | | | | | | |
| German Democratic Party | | | | | | 18.6 | 8.4 | 5.7 | 6.3 | 4.9 | 3.8 | 1.0 | 0.9 | 0.9 |
| Centre | 18.6 | 23.2 | 18.6 | 19.7 | 16.4 | 19.7 | 13.6 | 13.4 | 13.6 | 12.1 | 11.8 | 12.5 | 11.7 | 11.2 |
| Bavarian Peoples' Party | | | | | | | 4.2 | 3.2 | 3.7 | 3.1 | 3.0 | 3.2 | 3.1 | 2.7 |
| Social Democrats (S P D) | 3.2 | 6.1 | 19.7 | 31.7 | 34.8 | 37.9 | 21.6 | 20.5 | 26.0 | 29.8 | 24.5 | 21.6 | 20.4 | 18.3 |
| N S D A P | | | | | | | | 6.6 | 3.0 | 2.6 | 18.3 | 37.4 | 33.1 | 43.9 |
| K P D | | | | | | | 2.0 | 12.2 | 9.0 | 10.6 | 13.1 | 14.6 | 16.8 | 12.3 |

**8 Results of the Federal Elections**

| | 1949 | 1953 | 1957 | 1961 | 1965 | 1969 | 1972 | 1976 | 1980 | 1983 | 1987 |
|---|---|---|---|---|---|---|---|---|---|---|---|
| Turnout in % | 78.5 | 86.0 | 87.8 | 87.7 | 86.8 | 86.7 | 91.1 | 90.7 | 88.7 | 89.1 | 84.4 |
| **Number of the above that voted for the parties in %** | | | | | | | | | | | |
| CDU/CSU | 31.0 | 45.2 | 50.2 | 45.3 | 47.6 | 46.1 | 44.9 | 48.6 | 44.5 | 48.8 | 44.3 |
| SPD | 29.2 | 28.8 | 31.8 | 36.2 | 39.3 | 42.7 | 45.8 | 42.6 | 42.9 | 38.2 | 37.0 |
| FDP/DVP | 11.9 | 9.5 | 7.7 | 12.8 | 9.5 | 5.8 | 8.4 | 7.9 | 10.6 | 7.0 | 9.1 |
| The Greens | – | – | – | – | – | – | – | – | 1.5 | 5.6 | 8.3 |
| DP | 4.0 | 3.3 | 3.4 | – | – | – | – | – | – | – | – |
| GDP | – | – | – | 2.8 | – | 0.1 | – | – | – | – | – |
| GB/BHE | – | 5.9 | 4.6 | – | – | – | – | – | – | – | – |
| Centre | 3.1 | 0.8 | 0.3 | – | – | – | – | – | – | – | 0.1 |
| Bavarian Party | 4.2 | 1.7 | 0.5 | – | – | 0.2 | – | – | – | – | 0.1 |
| DRP;NPD | 1.8 | 1.1 | 1.0 | 0.8 | 2.0 | 4.3 | 0.6 | 0.3 | 0.2 | 0.2 | 0.6 |
| KPD;DFU;DKP | 5.7 | 2.2 | – | 1.9 | 1.3 | 0.6 | 0.3 | 0.3 | 0.2 | 0.2 | – |
| Others | 9.1 | 1.5 | 0.5 | 0.2 | 0.3 | 0.2 | 0.1 | 0.3 | 0.1 | 0.1 | 0.6 |
| **No. of seats in the German Federal Parliament** | | | | | | | | | | | |
| CDU/CSU | 139 | 243 | 270 | 242 | 245 | 242 | 225 | 243 | 226 | 244 | 223 |
| SPD | 131 | 151 | 169 | 190 | 202 | 224 | 230 | 214 | 218 | 193 | 186 |
| FDP/DVP | 52 | 48 | 41 | 67 | 49 | 30 | 41 | 39 | 53 | 34 | 46 |
| The Greens | – | – | – | – | – | – | – | – | – | 27 | 42 |
| DP | 17 | 15 | 17 | – | – | – | – | – | – | – | – |
| GB/BHE | – | 27 | – | – | – | – | – | – | – | – | – |
| Centre | 10 | 3 | – | – | – | – | – | – | – | – | – |
| Bavarian Party | 17 | – | – | – | – | – | – | – | – | – | – |
| DRP | 5 | – | – | – | – | – | – | – | – | – | – |
| KPD | 15 | – | – | – | – | – | – | – | – | – | – |
| Others | 16 | – | – | – | – | – | – | – | – | – | – |
| Total | 402 | 487 | 497 | 499 | 496 | 496 | 496 | 496 | 497 | 498 | 497 |
| No. of seats for Berlin | 19 | 22 | 22 | 22 | 22 | 22 | 22 | 22 | 22 | 22 | 22 |

D P = German Party; G B/B H E = German Union of Displaced and Disinherited Persons; D R P = Party of the German Reich; D F U = German Union of Peace.

**9** Election to the first Bundestag of the (united) Federal Republic of Germany 2 December 1990

|  |  | % | seats |
|---|---|---|---|
| total of those entitled to vote | 60,373,753 |  |  |
| turnout | 46,996,733 | 77.8 |  |
| number and % of invalid votes | 552,675 | 1.2 |  |
| number of valid votes | 46,444,058 |  |  |
| C D U | 17,051,128 | 36.7 | 268 |
| S P D | 15,539,977 | 33.5 | 239 |
| F D P | 5,123,936 | 11.0 | 79 |
| C S U | 3,301,239 | 7.1 | 51 |
| The Greens | 1,788,214 | 3.9 | – |
| P D S | 1,129,290 | 2.4 | 17 |
| D S U | 89,340 | 0.2 | – |
| Alliance 90/Greens/Women's movement | 558,552 | 1.2 | 8 |
| Bavarian Party | 31,442 | 0.1 | – |
| Christian League | 39,709 | 0.1 | – |
| Christian Middle | 36,767 | 0.1 | – |
| The Greys (Senior Citizens Protection League) | 386,699 | 0.8 | – |
| The Republicans | 985,557 | 2.1 | – |
| Women's Party | 12,110 | 0.0 | – |
| N P D | 145,895 | 0.3 | – |
| Ecological Democratic Party | 204,813 | 0.4 | – |
| Others (8 parties) | 19,390 |  |  |

**10** Life expectancy

Germany/Federal Republic of Germany
Life expectancy of newborns given in years

|  | 1871/81 | 1901/10 | 1932/34 | 1949/51 | 1970/72 | 1985/87 |
|---|---|---|---|---|---|---|
| Male | 35.6 | 44.8 | 59.9 | 64.6 | 67.4 | 71.8 |
| Female | 38.5 | 48.3 | 62.8 | 68.5 | 73.8 | 78.4 |

**11** Development of the population 1850 – 1940

Germany
Statistics as at mid-year

| YEAR | POPULATION (in 1000) |
|------|------------|
| 1850 | 35 312 |
| 1860 | 37 611 |
| 1870 | 40 805 |
| 1880 | 45 095 |
| 1890 | 49 241 |
| 1900 | 56 046 |
| 1910 | 64 568 |
| 1920 | 61 794 |
| 1930 | 65 084 |
| 1940 | 69 838 |

**12** Population development on the territory of the old (Western) Federal Republic of Germany 1929–88

| YEAR | POPULATION (in 1000) |
|------|------------|
| 1929 | 40 107 |
| 1939 | 43 008 |
| 1949 | 49 198 |
| 1959 | 54 876 |
| 1969 | 60 067 |
| 1979 | 61 382 |
| 1988 | 61 450 |

**13** Population development on the territory of the D D R

| YEAR | POPULATION (in 1000) |
|------|------------|
| 1939 | 16 745 |
| 1949 | 18 793 |
| 1959 | 17 286 |
| 1969 | 17 075 |
| 1979 | 16 740 |
| 1989 | 16 434 |

**14** Churches in West Germany

Protestants

| | members | resignations | conversions | attendances church services |
|---|---|---|---|---|
| 1959 | 26,650,000 | 31,251 | 36,596 | n.a. |
| 1970 | 28,480,000 | 202,833 | 20,990 | 1,410,000** |
| 1980 | 26,104,000 | 119,814 | 30,148 | 1,343,000 |
| 1988 | 25,176,000 | 138,700 | 40,365 | 1,288,000 |

Catholics

| | members | resignations | conversions | attendances church services |
|---|---|---|---|---|
| 1959 | 25,476,000 | 24,014 | 13,951 | 11,876,000** |
| 1970 | 27,195,000 | 69,454 | 5,875* | 10,159,000 |
| 1980 | 26,713,000 | 66,438 | 7,733 | 7,769,000 |
| 1988 | 26,483,000 | 79,562 | 9,145 | 6,115,000 |

\* Figures in this column include those rejoining
\*\* Figures in this column indicate average over the year

**15** Church membership 1987 in per cent

| Protestant | Catholic | Islamic | Other/none |
|---|---|---|---|
| 41.6 | 42.9 | 2.7 | 12.7 |

**16** Social backgrounds of West German Students in Higher Education

| | 1963 | 1973 | 1982 | 1985 | total % of each group in working population 1985 |
|---|---|---|---|---|---|
| civil servant (*Beamter*)* | 33 | 27 | 24 | 24 | 12 |
| white collar | 30 | 34 | 36 | 37 | 30 |
| blue collar | 6 | 12 | 16 | 15 | 45 |
| self employed | 26 | 26 | 21 | 20 | 13 |

\* This includes both humble postal and rail officials as well as top civil servants

**17** Purchasing power in pre-war Germany and post-war West Germany; minutes of work needed by industrial worker to earn:

| | 1kg bread | 1 bottle milk | ½ pound butter | ½ pound coffee | 1 pound pork | 5kWh electricity | 5 Litre petrol |
|---|---|---|---|---|---|---|---|
| 1938 | 30 | 17 | 60 | 100 | 80 | 70 | 150 |
| 1958 | 22 | 11 | 45 | 125 | 74 | 25 | 80 |
| 1988 | 10 | 4 | 7 | 15 | 17 | 5 | 15 |

18 NATO Defence expenditures as % of gross domestic product
Based on constant prices

| Country | Average 1970–1974 | Average 1975–1979 | Average 1980–1984 | Average 1985–1989 | 1985 | 1986 | 1987 | 1988 | 1989e |
|---|---|---|---|---|---|---|---|---|---|
| | (1) | (2) | (3) | (4) | (5) | (6) | (7) | (8) | (9) |
| Belgium | 2.9 | 3.3 | 3.4 | 3.2 | 3.2 | 3.3 | 3.3 | 3.1 | 3.0 |
| Denmark | 2.5 | 2.4 | 2.4 | 2.2 | 2.2 | 2.1 | 2.2 | 2.2 | 2.1 |
| France | 3.9 | 3.8 | 4.1 | 3.9 | 4.0 | 3.9 | 3.9 | 3.8 | 3.7 |
| Germany* | 3.5 | 3.4 | 3.3 | 3.0 | 3.2 | 3.1 | 3.1 | 2.9 | 2.9 |
| Greece | 4.7 | 6.7 | 6.6 | 6.4 | 7.0 | 6.2 | 6.3 | 6.4 | 6.0 |
| Italy | 2.3 | 2.1 | 2.1 | 2.2 | 2.2 | 2.1 | 2.2 | 2.2 | 2.2 |
| Luxembourg | 0.8 | 1.0 | 1.2 | 1.2 | 1.1 | 1.1 | 1.2 | 1.3 | 1.3 |
| Netherlands | 3.5 | 3.2 | 3.3 | 3.3 | 3.3 | 3.3 | 3.3 | 3.2 | 3.2 |
| Norway | 3.6 | 3.0 | 2.9 | 2.9 | 3.0 | 2.8 | 3.0 | 2.9 | 3.0 |
| Portugal | 6.4 | 3.8 | 3.4 | 3.1 | 3.2 | 3.2 | 3.1 | 3.2 | 3.0 |
| Spain | :: | :: | 2.4 | 2.2 | 2.4 | 2.2 | 2.4 | 2.1 | 2.1 |
| Turkey | 2.8 | 4.5 | 4.4 | 3.9 | 4.1 | 4.2 | 3.9 | 3.8 | 3.7 |
| United Kingdom | 5.7 | 5.0 | 5.2 | 4.5 | 5.1 | 4.8 | 4.5 | 4.1 | 4.1 |
| NATO Europe | :: | :: | 3.6 | 3.3 | 3.5 | 3.4 | 3.4 | 3.2 | 3.2 |
| Canada | 2.4 | 2.0 | 2.1 | 2.1 | 2.2 | 2.2 | 2.2 | 2.1 | 2.0 |
| United States | 6.8 | 5.1 | 5.6 | 5.9 | 6.1 | 6.3 | 6.0 | 5.7 | 5.5 |
| North America | 6.4 | 4.9 | 5.3 | 5.6 | 5.7 | 5.9 | 5.7 | 5.4 | 5.2 |
| NATO total | :: | :: | 4.4 | 4.5 | 4.6 | 4.7 | 4.5 | 4.3 | 4.2 |

*These percentages have been calculated without taking into account the expenditures on Berlin if these expenditures were included, the percentages would be as follows:

| | | | |
|---|---|---|---|
| 1970: 3.8 | 1980: 4.1 | 1986: 3.9 | 1988: 3.7 |
| 1975: 4.4 | 1985: 4.0 | 1987: 3.7 | 1989: 3.7 |

**19** The United Germany and the European Community

| | area in 1,000 sq km | % | population (1988) | % | seats in European Parliament |
|---|---|---|---|---|---|
| Germany | 357 | 15.1 | 78,116,000 | 22.9 | 81 |
| Belgium | 31 | 1.3 | 9,883,000 | 2.9 | 24 |
| Denmark | 43 | 1.8 | 5,130,000 | 1.5 | 16 |
| France | 552 | 23.3 | 55,873,000 | 16.4 | 81 |
| Greece | 132 | 5.6 | 9,984,000 | 2.9 | 24 |
| Ireland | 70 | 3.0 | 3,538,000 | 1.0 | 15 |
| Italy | 301 | 12.7 | 57,452,000 | 16.8 | 81 |
| Luxembourg | 3 | 0.1 | 375,000 | 0.1 | 6 |
| Netherlands | 41 | 1.7 | 14,760,000 | 4.3 | 25 |
| Portugal | 92 | 3.9 | 10,287,000 | 3.0 | 24 |
| Spain | 505 | 21.3 | 38,996,000 | 11.4 | 60 |
| U K | 244 | 10.3 | 57,077,000 | 16.7 | 81 |

**20** Germany and U S A

| | |
|---|---|
| Population of united Germany | 78.1 million |
| Populations of California, New York, Illinois, Texas, Vermont and Virginia together | 78.3 million |
| Area of united Germany | 357,000 sq km |
| Area of Illinois and Idaho together | 357,565 sq km |

Life expectancy of newborns

| | Men | Women | |
|---|---|---|---|
| U S A | 71.6 | 78.7 | 1987 |
| West Germany | 72.1 | 78.6 | 1986/88 |

Medical practitioners per 10,000 of population
U S A          22.2 in 1986
West Germany   28.7 in 1988

**21** The Federal Cabinet, 18 January 1991

The following are the members of the cabinet sworn in by President von Weizsäcker, Friday 18 January 1991:

| | | |
|---|---|---|
| Federal Chancellor | **Dr Helmut KOHL** | C D U |
| Foreign Affairs and Deputy Chancellor | **Hans-Dietrich GENSCHER** | F D P |
| Federal Minister for Special Tasks and Head of the Federal Chancellery | **Rudolf SEITERS** | C D U |
| Interior | **Dr Wolfgang SCHÄUBLE** | C D U |
| Justice | **Dr Klaus KINKEL** | F D P |
| Finance | **Dr Theodor WAIGEL** | C S U |
| Economics | **Jürgen MÖLLEMANN** | F D P |
| Food, Agriculture and Forestry | **Ignaz KIECHLE** | C S U |
| Labour and Social Affairs | **Dr Norbert BLÜM** | C D U |
| Defence | **Dr Gerhard STOLTENBERG** | C D U |
| Family Affairs and Senior Citizens | **Frau Hannelore RÖNSCH** | C D U |
| Women and Youth | **Dr Angela MERKEL** | C D U * |
| Health | **Frau Gerda HASSELFELDT** | C S U |
| Transport | **Professor Dr Günther KRAUSE** | C D U * |
| Environment, Nature Conservation and Nuclear Reactor Safety | **Professor Dr Klaus TÖPFER** | C D U |
| Posts and Telecommunications | **Dr Christian SCHWARZ-SCHILLING** | C D U |
| Regional Planning, Housing and Urban Development | Dr Irmgard **ADAM-SCHWAETZER** | F D P |
| Research and Technology | **Dr Heinz RIESENHUBER** | C D U |
| Education and Science | **Professor Dr Rainer ORTLEB** | F D P * |
| Economic Co-operation | **Carl-Dieter SPRANGER** | C S U |

There are 10 C D U Ministers in the Cabinet, four from the C S U and five from the F D P.

\* From the former D D R

# — **Appendix 3:** —

## National flag

The German national flag is the tricolour: three equal horizontal bars of black, red and gold. Black and red were the colours of the old Holy Roman Empire which ended in 1806: in the campaign against Napoleon one particular cavalry corps wore the black and red with gold buttons, a colour combination taken up by the German unity movement in the mid-nineteenth century. Later various German Länder opted to keep their own flags, but the tricolour was revived by the Weimar Republic (1919-1933), done away with by the Nazi regime (1933–45) and once again brought back after the Second World War.

## National Anthem

The national anthem is the *Deutschlandlied*, or 'Song of Germany', third verse of the poem by the nineteenth-century revolutionary Hoffmann von Fallersleben. This is the official English translation:

> Unity and right and freedom
> For the German fatherland;
> Let us all pursue this purpose
> Brotherly, with heart and hand.
> Unity and right and freedom
> Are the pledge of happiness.
> Flourish in this blessing's glory
> Flourish, German fatherland.

Originally the first verse of Hoffmann's poem, which started 'Deutschland über alles', was used, but this has been dropped because it was widely misunderstood abroad. The tune is stolidly royalist, composed by Haydn for the Austrian head of state: 'Gott erhalte Franz den Kaiser' – 'God save Emperor Francis'.

## The Capital

Under Article 2 Para. 1 of the Unification Treaty between the two German states, 'the capital of Germany shall be Berlin. The seat of Parliament and Government shall be decided after the establishment of German unity.'

# — Appendix 4: —

## Chronology 1871–1991

1871 German Empire proclaimed at Versailles after French defeat.
1878 Anti-socialist law introduced.
1879 German-Austrian-Hungary alliance.
1883 First social security law passed.
1884 Founding of German colonial empire.
1888 Wilhelm II becomes emperor.
1890 Bismarck sacked.
1900 German naval law passed.
1904 Anglo-French alliance formed.
1914 Outbreak of First World War.
1916 Battle of Verdun, Battle of Jutland, Battle of the Somme.
1917 U S A enters the war, revolution in Russia.
1918 Armistice followed by abdication of Wilhelm II.
1919 Democratic election to nation parliament. Spartacist rising suppressed.
1922 Mussolini takes power in Italy.
1923 French occupation of Ruhr, left and right revolts.
1925 Hindenburg elected president after death of Ebert.
1929 World economic crisis begins.
1930 Nazis emerge from elections as a majority party.
1933 Hitler appointed Chancellor, heads coalition government, but enabling act gives him dictatorial powers.
1934 Hindenburg dies and Hitler becomes head of state.
1935 Saar returned to Germany, Nazis pass race laws, Anglo-German naval agreement.
1936 German troops reoccupy the Rhineland, Olympic Games held in Berlin, outbreak of civil war in Spain.
1938 Munich agreement, *Anschluss* with Austria, *Reichskristallnacht*.
1939 Prague occupied, Hitler-Stalin pact, Germany attacks Poland, Second World War begins.
1940 German occupation of Denmark, Norway, Netherlands, Luxembourg, Belgium, fall of France, battle of Britain.
1941 Germany attacks Soviet Union, Japan attacks U S A.
1942 Wannsee conference on 'final solution of Jewish question', mass bombing of Germany begins.
1943 Defeat of Germans at Stalingrad, invasion of Italy. Germans defeated Kursk, biggest tank battle of war. Tehran conference.
1944 D-Day landings, bomb plot against Hitler, Soviets reach Germany.
1945 Yalta conference, unconditional surrender of Germany, Potsdam conference, A-bombs on Japan, unconditional surrender of Japan.
1946 S E D set up in Soviet Zone.
1947 U S and British zones merged.
1948 Currency reform in Western zones, Soviet blockade of West Berlin. Communist coup in Czechoslovakia.

1949 Federal Republic of Germany and German Democratic Republic (D D R) set up. Adenauer Federal Chancellor. Communists take power in China, Soviets explode A-bomb. N A T O established.

1950 Outbreak of Korean War.

1951 Setting up of European Coal and Steel Community (forerunner of E E C).

1952 S E D decides on 'building of Socialism' in D D R.

1953 Death of Stalin, rising in D D R against S E D regime.

1955 Sovereignty for Federal Republic and D D R. West Germany joins N A T O. Warsaw Pact established.

1956 20th congress of Soviet Communist Party denounces Stalin, Hungarian revolution crushed by Soviets. Suez campaign.

1957 Saar becomes part of Federal Republic, C D U/C S U gains absolute majority of votes in federal election. Soviets launch satellite in space. Rome Treaty establishes E E C.

1958 Collapse of Fourth French Republic, Fifth Republic inaugurated, headed by de Gaulle.

1959 S P D adopts Bad Godesberg Programme.

1961 Berlin Wall built. Soviets successfully put man in space.

1963 Franco-German Friendship Treaty, Adenauer resigns. Sino-Soviet tension mounts.

1964 Communist China becomes nuclear power. Khruschev ousted from power in Soviet Union.

1967 Six-day Arab-Israeli war.

1968 D D R adopts a new, socialist constitution. Warsaw Pact forces crush 'Prague Spring'.

1969 S P D-F D P coalition replaces C D U/C S U, Willy Brandt becomes Chancellor.

1970 German-Polish Treaty and Soviet-German Treaty agreed.

1971 Four Power Treaty on Berlin signed.

1972 Honecker replaces Ulbricht in D D R. S P D gains its biggest vote in history of Federal Republic.

1973 Basic Treaty between two German states passed Bundestag. Vietnam ceasefire agreed. Yom Kippur War.

1974 Constitution of D D R amended. Brandt resigns as Chancellor.

1976 Helsinki agreements on C S C E signed.

1979 Soviet invasion of Afghanistan. Green Party established.

1980 Solidarity in Poland. Iraq attacks Iran.

1981 Martial law declared in Poland.

1982 Kohl replaces Schmidt as Chancellor.

1985 Mikhail Gorbachev becomes leader of Soviet Union.

1986 Accident at Chernobyl power station in Soviet Union.

1989 Free elections to Polish senate, power sharing agreed in Hungary between Communists and opposition.
Demonstrations and mass emigration force Honecker to resign as D D R leader, replaced by Krenz who also forced to go. Frontiers of D D R, including Berlin Wall opened (9.11).

1990 First free elections in D D R (18 March) won by Alliance for Germany. D-Mark introduced into D D R (1 July), German unity achieved (3 October). First free election in united Germany since 1932 held 2 December with decisive win for C D U/C S U and F D P coalition.

# Bibliography

## Chapter 1

Michael Balfour, *The Kaiser And His Times*, London, 1964

V. R. Berghahn, *Modern Germany*, Cambridge, 1982

William Carr, *A History of Germany 1815–1985*, London, 1987

Gordon A. Craig, *The Politics of the Prussian Army 1640–1945*, Oxford, 1964

T. N. Dupuy, *A Genius For War, The German Army And General Staff 1807–1945*, London, 1977

R. J. Evans, (ed.) *Society and Politics in Wilhelmine Germany*, London, 1980

L. L. Farrar, *Arrogance and Anxiety The Ambivalence of German Power, 1848–1914*, Iowa, 1981

R. H. Fife, *The German Empire Between The Wars*, London 1916

Roger Fletcher, (ed.), *Bernstein to Brandt*, London, 1987

L. Gall, *Bismarck, Vol 1 1815–1871 & Vol 2 1871–1898*, London, 1988

D. Geary, *Karl Kautsky*, Manchester, 1987

D. Geary, *Aspects of German Labour 1871–1933*, London, 1991

S. Haffner, *The Rise and Fall Of Prussia*, London 1980

A. Hall, *Scandal, Sensation and Social Democracy*, Cambridge, 1977

J. Heskett, *Design In Germany 1870–1918*, London, 1986

O. Kirchheimer and F. Neumann (ed.), *Social Democracy and the Rule of Law*, London, 1987

H. W. Koch, *The Origins of the First World War*, London, 1972

A. J. LaVopa, *Prussian Schoolteachers 1763–1848*, Chapel Hill, 1980

W. E. Mosse, *The German-Jewish Economic Elite 1820–1935*, Oxford, 1989

J. N. Retallack, *Notables of the Right*, London, 1988

J. H. Rose, C. H. Herford, E. C. K. Gonner and M. E. Sadler, *Germany in the Nineteenth Century*, Manchester, 1912

G. Roth, *The German Social Democrats in Imperial Germany*, Totowa, N.J., 1963

Eda Sagarra, *A Social History of Germany 1648–1914*, London, 1977

James J. Sheehan, (ed.) *Imperial Germany*, New York, 1976

A. Sommariva and G. Tullio, *German Macroeconomic History 1880–1979*, London, 1986

F. Stern, *The Failure of Illiberalism Essays on the Political Culture of Modern Germany*, New York, 1972

A. J. P. Taylor, *The Course of German History*, London, 1961

A. J. P. Taylor, *War by Time Table*, London 1969

L. C. F. Turner, *Origins of the First World War*, London, 1970

H.-U. Wehler, *The German Empire 1871–1918*, Leamington Spa, 1985

## Chapters 2 – 4

W. T. Angress, *Stillborn Revolution*, London, 1963

A. J. Berlau, *The German Social Democratic Party 1914–21*, Columbia, 1949

J. Caplan, *Government without Administration: State and Civil Service in Weimar and Nazi Germany*, Oxford, 1988

E. H. Carr, *German-Soviet Relations 1919–39*, Baltimore, 1951

W. Carr, *Hitler a Study in Personality and Politics*, London, 1978

F. L. Carsten, *The Reichswehr and Politics, 1919–33*, Oxford, 1966

F. L. Carsten, *Britain and the Weimar Republic*, London, 1984

T. Childers (ed.), *The Formation of the Nazi Constituency 1919–33*, Totowa, N.J., 1986

R. T. Clarke, *The Fall of the German Republic*, London, 1935

R. Coper, *Failure of a Revolution*, Cambridge, 1955

A. Dorpalen, *Hindenburg and the Weimar Republic*, Princeton, 1957

H. L. Dyck, *Weimar Germany and Soviet Russia 1926–33*, London, 1966

E. Eyck, *History of the German Republic* (2 Vols), Oxford, 1962

H. Gatzke, *Stresemann and the Rearmament of Germany*, Baltimore, 1954

P. Gay, *Weimar Culture*, London, 1969

P. and L. Gillman, *'Collar the lot' How Britain Interned and Expelled its Wartime Refugees*, London, 1980

D. J. Goodspeed, *Ludendorff*, London, 1966

H. Gordon, *The Reichswehr and the German Republic*, Princeton, 1957

R. Grunberger, *Germany 1918–45*, London, 1964

S. W. Halperin, *Germany Tried Democracy 1919–33*, London, 1963

P. Hayes, *Industry and Ideology I. G. Farben in the Nazi Era*, Cambridge, 1987

J. Hiden, *Germany and Europe 1919–39*, London, 1977

G. Hirschfeld, (ed.) *The Politics of Genocide*, London, 1986

R. N. Hunt, *German Social Democracy, 1918–33*, London, 1964

R. H. Jarausch, *The Unfree Professions: German Lawyers, Teachers and Engineers, 1900–1950*, Oxford, 1990

K. von Klemperer, *Germany's New Conservatism*, Princeton, 1968

L. Kochan, *The Struggle for Germany 1914–45*, Edinburgh, 1963

J. P. Nettl, *Rosa Luxemburg* (2 Vols), London, 1966

A. Nicholls, *Weimar and the Rise of Hitler*, London, 1980

F. R. Nicosia, *The Third Reich and the Palestine Question*, London, 1985

J. Noakes, *The Nazi Party in Lower Saxony 1921–33*, London, 1971

J. and S. Pool, *Who Financed Hitler?*, New York, 1979

G. Post, *The Civil-Military Fabric of Weimar Foreign Policy*, Princeton, 1973

P. J. Pulzer, *The Rise of Political Anti-Semitism in Germany and Austria*, New York, 1964

A. J. Ryder, *The German Revolution of 1919*, Cambridge, 1967

C. Schorske, *German Social Democracy 1905–17*, Harvard, 1955

P. D. Stachura, *Nazi Youth in the Weimar Republic*, Oxford, 1975

G. Stolper, *The German Economy 1870 to the Present*, New York, 1967

H. A. Turner, *Stresemann and the Politics of the German Republic*, Princeton, 1963

R. G. S. Weber, *The German Student Corps In the Third Reich*, New York, 1986

D. Welch, *Propaganda and the German Cinema, 1933–45*, Oxford, 1983

J. Wheeler-Bennett, *The Nemesis of Power, The German Army in Politics 1918–45*, London, 1967

J. R. C. Wright, *'Above Politics': The Political Attitudes of the German Protestant Church Leadership 1918–33*, Oxford, 1974

## Chapters 5 and 6

W. S. Allen, *The Nazi Seizure of Power*, Chicago, 1965

M. Balfour, *Withstanding Hitler In Germany, 1933–45*, London, 1988

M. Balfour, *Propaganda in War 1939–45*, London, 1979

M. Balfour, and J. Frisby *Helmuth von Moltke: A Leader Against Hitler*, London, 1972

V. R. Berghahn and M. Kitchen (eds), *Germany in the age of Total War*, London, 1981

E. Bethge, *Dietrich Bonhoeffer*, London, 1970

K. D. Bracher, *The German Dictatorship*, London, 1970

E. K. Bramsted, *Goebbels and National Socialist Propaganda*, London, 1965

H.-J. Braun, *The German Economy in the 20th Century*, London, 1990

M. Broszat, *The Hitler State*, London, 1981

H. Bull, (ed.) *The Challenge of the Third Reich*, Oxford, 1986

A. Bullock, *Hitler, a Study in Tyranny*, London, 1952

H. T. Burden, *The Nuremberg Rallies, 1923–39*, London, 1969

R. L. Bytwerk, *Julius Streicher*, New York, 1983

W. Carr, *Arms, Autarky and Aggression, A Study in German Foreign Policy, 1933–39*, London, 1972

W. Carr, *Hitler, A Study in Personality and Politics*, London, 1972

R. Cecil, *The Myth of the Master Race: Alfred Rosenberg and Nazi Ideology*, London, 1972

D. Childs and J. Wharton (eds) *Children In War*, Nottingham, 1990

J. S. Conway, *The Nazi Persecution of the Churches*, London, 1968

A. Dallin, *German Rule in Russia, 1941–44*, London, 1957

H. C. Deutsch, *Hitler and his Generals*, Minneapolis, 1974

H. V. Dicks, *Licensed Mass Murder*, London, 1972

T. Eschenburg, et al *The Road to Dictatorship: Germany, 1918–33*, London, 1970

R. J. Evans, *In Hitler's Shadow*, London, 1969

J. L. Farquharson, *The Plough and the Swastika*, London, 1976

L. Fermi, *Illustrious Immigrants*, Chicago, 1968

J. Fest, *Hitler*, London, 1974

C. FitzGibbon, *20 July*, New York, 1956

G. Fleming, *Hitler and the Final Solution*, Oxford, 1986

P. Fleming, *Invasion 1940*, London, 1957

S. Friedlander, *Pius XII and the Third Reich*, London, 1966

S. Friedlander, *Prelude to Downfall: Hitler and the United States 1939–41*, London, 1967

W. Frischauer, *Himmler, the Evil Genius of the Third Reich*, London

J. F. L. Fuller, *The Second World War*, London, 1948

J. Goebbels, *My Part In Germany's Fight*, London, 1935

R. Goldston, *The Life and Death of the Nazi Germany*, London, 1967

G. P. Gooch, *German Mind and Outlook*, London, 1945

H. Graml (ed.) *The German Resistance to Hitler*, London, 1970

O. J. Hale, *The Captive Press in the Third Reich*, Princeton, 1964

D. Hart-Davis, *Hitler's Games: the 1936 Olympics*, London, 1986

K. Heiden, *Hitler*, London, 1936

K. Hildebrandt, *The Foreign Policy of the Third Reich*, Berkeley, 1973

A. Hillgruber, *Germany and the Two World Wars*, Cambridge, Mass., 1981

G. Hirschfeld (ed.), *Exile in Great Britain*. Leamington Spa, 1984

P. Hoffmann, *German Resistance to Hitler*, Cambridge, Mass., 1988

H. Hohne, *The Order of The Death's Head*, London, 1969

D. Irving, *The Rise and Fall of the Luftwaffe: the Life of Luftwaffe Marshal Erhard Milch*, London, 1973

D. Irving, *The Trail of the Fox: the Life of Field-Marshal Erwin Rommel*, London, 1977

T. L. Jarman, *The Rise and fall of Nazi Germany*, London, 1955

J. Keegan, *The Second World War*, London, 1989

I. Kershaw, *The Nazi Dictatorship*, London, 1985

I. Kershaw, *Popular Opinion and Dissent in the Third Reich: Bavaria 1933–45*, Oxford, 1983

E. Kogon, *The Theory and Practice of Hell*, London, 1950

C. Koonz, *Mother in the Fatherland*, London, 1987

F. Kracauer, *From Caligari to Hitler*, Princeton, 1947

H. Krausnick, *Anatomy of the s s State*, London, 1968

D. Lerner, *The Nazi Elite*, Stanford, 1951

G. Lewy, *The Catholic Church and Nazi Germany*, London, 1964

L. de Long, *The German 5th Column in the Second World War*, London, 1956

R. Manvel and H. Faenkel, *Doctor Goebbels*, London, 1960

R. Manvel and H. Faenkel, *Hermann Goering*, London, 1962

R. Manvel and H. Faenkel, *The July Plot*, London, 1964

R. Manvel and H. Faenkel, *Heinrich Himmler*, London, 1965

R. Manvel and H. Faenkel, *The Canaris Conspiracy*, London, 1969

P. Merkl, *Political Violence under the Swastika*, Princeton, 1975

A. Merson, *Communist Resistance in Nazi Germany*, London, 1986

A. Milward, *The German Economy at War*, London, 1964; *War, Economy and Society, 1939–45*, London, 1977

G. L. Mosse, *The Crisis of German Ideology*, London, 1966

A. Nicholls, and P. Matthias (eds), *German Democracy and the Triumph of Hitler*, London, 1971

J. Noakes and G. Pridham (eds) *Nazism 1919–1945, Vol. 1: The Rise to Power, 1919–1933*, Exeter, 1983

D. Orlow, *The History of the Nazi Party 1919–1945*, 2 Vols, Pittsburg, 1973

R. J. Overy, *Goering the 'Iron Man'*, London, 1983

E. N. Peterson, *The Limits of Hitler's Power*, Princeton, 1964

P. Phillips, *The Tragedy of Nazi Germany*, London, 1969

T. Prittie, *Germans Against Hitler*, London, 1964

R. N. Proctor, *Racial Hygiene Medicine Under The Nazis*, Cambridge Mass., 1988

G. Reitlinger, *The Final Solution*, London, 1953; *The s s, Alibi of a Nation*, London, 1956

N. Rich, *Hitler's War Aims*, 2 Vols, London, 1973

G. Ritter, *The German Resistance*, London, 1958

E. M. Robertson, *Hitler's Pre-War Policy and Military Plans*, London, 1963

H. Rothfels, *The German Opposition to Hitler*, London, 1961

H. Schacht, *Account Settled*, London, 1949

W. Schirer, *Berlin Diary*, London, 1941

W. Schirer, *The Rise and Fall of the Third Reich*, London, 1960

D. Schoenbaum, *Hitler's Social Revolution*, London, 1967

K. P. Schoenhals, *The Free Germany Movement*, New York, 1989

A. Schweitzer, *Big Business in the Third Reich*, London, 1964

R. M. Smelser, *The Sudeten Problem, 1933–38*, London, 1975

M. K. Sorge, *The Other Price of Hitler's War: German Military and Civilian Losses Resulting from World War II*, London, 1986

A. Speer, *Inside the Third Reich*, London, 1970

A. Speer, *Spandau The Secret Diaries*, London, 1976

H. Speidel, *Invasion 1944*, Chicago, 1950

G. H. Stein, *The Waffen s s*, London, 1966

M. Steinert, *Hitler's War and the Germans*, Columbus, 1977

J. P. Stern, *Hitler, the Fuhrer and the People*, London, 1975

J. Stevenson, *Women in Nazi Germany*, London 1975

T. Taylor, *Munich*, New York, 1979

F. Thyssen, *I Paid Hitler*, New York, 1941

M. Toscano, *The Origins of the Pact of Steel*, Baltimore, 1967

H. Trevor-Roper, *The Last Days of Hitler*, London, 1947

H. Trevor-Roper (ed.) *Hitler's Table Talk*, London, 1953

H. Trevor-Roper (ed.) *Hitler's War Directives 1939–45*, London, 1964

R. G. Waite, *Adolf Hitler, the Psychopathic God*, New York, 1977

Sir C. Webster and N. Frankland *The Strategic Air Offensive Against Germany, 1939–45*, London, 1961

A. Werth, *Russia at War*, London, 1964

E. Wiskemann, *The Rome-Berlin Axis*, London, 1966

G. C. Zahn, *German Catholics and Hitler's Wars*, Notre Dame, 1989

A. M. de Zayas, *The Wehrmacht War Crimes Bureau, 1939–1945* Lincoln Nebraska, 1989

Z. A. B. Zeman, *Nazi Propaganda*, London, 1973

## Chapter 7

N. Balabkins, *Germany Under Direct Controls*, New Brunswick, 1964

M. Balfour, *Four Power Control in Germany and Austria, 1945–46*, London, 1956

V. R. Berghahn, *The Americanisation of West German Industry 1945–1973*, Leamington Spa and New York, 1986

L. D. Clay, *Decision in Germany*, New York, 1950

H. Feis, *Churchill, Roosevelt, Stalin*, Princeton, 1957

C. FitzGibbon, *Denazification*, London, 1969

W. Friedmann, *The Allied Military Government of Germany*, London, 1956

J. Gimbel, *The American Occupation of Germany: Politics and the Military 1945–1949*, Stanford, 1968

A. Grosser, *West Germany from Defeat to Re-armament*, London, 1956

A. Hearnden (ed.) *The British in Germany: Education Reconstruction after 1945*, London, 1975

W. Heidemeyer and G. Hindrichs, *Documents on Berlin, 1943–1965*, Munich, 1965

J. Joesten, *Germany What Now?*, Chicago, 1948

H. Krisch, *German Politics under Soviet Occupation*, New York, 1974

W. Leonhard, *Child of the Revolution*, London, 1957

J. S. Martin, *All Honourable Men*, Boston, 1950

D. Middleton, *The Struggle for Germany*, New York, 1950

J. P. Nettl, *The Eastern Zone and Soviet Policy in Germany*, London, 1951

N. Pronay and Keith Wilson *The Political Re-education of Germany and her Allies After World War II*, London, 1985

B. Ruhm von Oppen, *Documents on Germany 1945–55*, London, 1955

G. W. Sandford, *From Hitler to Ulbricht; the communist reconstruction of East Germany, 1945–46*, Princeton, 1983

G. Schaffer, *Russian Zone*, London, 1947

C. C. Schweitzer et al, *Politics and Government in the Federal Republic of Germany, Basic Documents*, Leamington Spa, 1984

B. F. Smith, *Reaching Judgment at Nuremberg*, London, 1977

J. L. Snell, *The Origins of the East-West Dilemma over Germany*, New Orleans, 1959

F. R. Willis, *The French in Germany 1945–1949*, Stanford, 1955

E. Wiskemann, *Germany's Eastern Neighbours*, London, 1956

H. Zink, *The United States in Germany*, Princeton, 1957

## Chapters 8 and 11

K. Adenauer, *Memoirs*, London, 1966–68

R. Augstein, *Konrad Adenauer*, London, 1964

D. L. Bark and D. R. Gress, *A History of West Germany Volume 1 1945–1963*, Oxford, 1969

D. Binder, *The Other German: Willy Brandt's Life and Times*, Washington, DC, 1975

P. M. Blair, *Federalism and Judicial Review in West Germany*, Oxford, 1981

K. Bolling, *Republic In Suspense*, London, 1964

G. Braunthal, *The Federation of German Industry in Politics*, Ithaca, 1965

C. Cate, *The Ides of August The Berlin Wall Crisis 1961*. New York, 1978

D. A. Chambers, *The Social Democratic Party of Germany*, New Haven, 1964

R. Chaput de Saintonge, *Public Administration in Germany*, London, 1961

D. Childs, *From Schumacher to Brandt*, London, 1966

M. Cioc, *Pax Atomica the Nuclear Defense Debate in West Germany During the Adenauer Era*, New York, 1988

E. C. M. Cullingford, *Trade Unions in West Germany*, London, 1976

R. Dahrendorf, *Society and Democracy in Germany*, London, 1968

K. W. Deutsch and L. Edinger, *Germany Rejoins the Powers*, London, 1949

L. Edinger, *Kurt Schumacher*, Oxford, 1965

L. Edinger, *Politics in Germany*, Boston, 1969

L. Erhard, *Prosperity through Competition*, London, 1958

F. Erler, *Democracy in Germany*, Cambridge, Mass, 1965

N. Gelb, *The Berlin Wall*, London, 1986

F. Golay, *The Founding of the Federal Republic of Germany*, Chicago, 1958

W. D. Graf, *The German Left Since 1945*, Cambridge, 1976

A. Grosser, *Germany in Our Time*, London 1971

G. Hallet, *Housing and Land Policies in West Germany and Britain*, London, 1977

W. F. Hanrieder, *West German Foreign Policy 1949–63*, Stanford, 1967

A. Hartley, *Germany East/West*, London, 1968

A. Heidenheimer, *Adenauer and the C D U*, The Hague, 1960

A. Heidenheimer, *The Governments of Germany*, London, 1966

R. Hiscocks, *Democracy in Western Germany*, London, 1957

K. Jaspers, *The Future of Germany*, Chicago, 1967

N. Johnson, *Government in the Federal Republic of Germany*, Oxford, 1973

U. Kitzinger, *German Electoral Politics*, Oxford, 1960

J. L. Knusel, *West German Aid to Developing Nations*, London, 1968

G. Loewenberg, *Parliament in the German Political System*, Ithaca, 1966

P. H. Merkl, *The Origin of the West German Republic*, New York, 1963

P. H. Merkl, *Germany, Yesterday and Tomorrow*, New York, 1965

I. Montague, *Germany's New Nazis*, London, 1967

R. Morgan, *The United States and West Germany 1945–1973*, London, 1973

E. Morris, *Blockade: Berlin and the Cold War*, London, 1973

K. S. Parkes, *Writers and Politics in West Germany*, London, 1986

E. L. Pinney, *Federalism, Bureaucracy and Party Politics in Western Germany*

E. Plischke, *Contemporary Government of Germany*, London, 1964

R. J. C. Preece, Land Elections in the German Federal Republic, London, 1968

T. Prittie, *Divided Germany*, London, 1961

T. Prittie, *Konrad Adenauer*, London, 1972

T. Prittie, *Willy Brandt Portrait of a Statesman*, London, 1974

J. Richardson, *Germany and the Atlantic Alliance*, London, 1966

G. K. Roberts, *West German Politics*, London, 1972

M. Simmons, *Berlin The Dispossessed City*, London, 1988

J. E. Smith, *The Defence of Berlin*, London, 1963

K. Sontheimer, *The Government and Politics of West Germany*, London, 1972

H. Speier, *Germany, Rearmament and Atomic War*, Evanston, 1957

H. Speier, *West German Leadership and Foreign Policy*, Evanston, 1957

H. J. Spiro, *The Politics of German Codetermination*, Cambridge, Mass., 1958

W. Stahl, *The Politics of Post-war Germany*, New York, 1963

F. J. Strauss, *The Grand Design*, London, 1965

K. P. Tauber, *Beyond Eagle and Swastika*,

R. Tilford and R. J. C. Preece, *Federal Germany: The Political and Social Order*, London, 1969

A. and J. Tusa, *The Berlin Blockade*, London, 1988

E. Waldman, *The Goose Step is Verboten: The German Army Today*, New York, 1964

H. C. Wallich, *Mainsprings of the German Economic Revival*, New Haven, 1955

P. Windsor, *German Reunification*, London, 1969

P. Windsor, *City on Leave*, London, 1963

P. Windsor, *Germany and the Management of Detente*, London, 1971

F. A. Vali, *The Quest for a United Germany*, Oxford, 1968

P. Weymar, *Konrad Adenauer*, London, 1957

## Chapters 9 and 10

D. Childs, *East Germany*, London, 1969

J. Dornberg, *The Other Germany*, New York, 1968

T. M. Forster, *The East German Army*, London, 1967

W. Hangen, *The Muted Revolution*, London, 1968

A. M. Hanhardt, *The German Democratic Republic*, Baltimore, 1968

H. A. Holm, *The other Germans: report from an East German town*, London, 1971

L. Hornsby, *Profile of East Germany*, London, 1966

E. von Hornstein, *The Accused: Seven East Germans on Trial*, London, 1965

H. Kohler, *Economic Integration in the Soviet Bloc*, New York, 1965

F. von Nesselrode, *Germany's Other Half*, London, 1963

J. E. Smith, *Germany Beyond the Wall*, Boston, 1968

R. Solberg, *God and Caesar in East Germany*, New York, 1961

C. Stern, *Ulbricht: A Political Biography*, London, 1965

## *Chapter 12*

J. Becker, *Hitler's Children*, London, 1977

K. von Beyme, *The Political System of the Federal Republic of Germany*, London, 1983

M. Balfour, *West Germany: A Contemporary History*, London, 1982

W. Brandt, *People and Politics*, London, 1978

G. Braunthal, *Political Loyalty and Public Service in West Germany*, Amhurst, Mass. 1990

J. Carr, *Helmut Schmidt Helmsman of Germany*, London, 1985

D. P. Conradt, *The German Polity*, New York and London, 1989

E. S. Campbell, *Germany's Past and Europe's Future*, Washington, 1989

D. Childs, *The G D R Moscow's German Ally*, London, 1988

D. Childs and J. Johnson, *West Germany: Politics and Society*, London, 1981

M. Dönhoff, *Foe into Friend: The Makers of the New Germany from Konrad Adenauer to Helmut Schmidt*, London, 1982

K. H. F. Dyson, *Party, State and Bureaucracy in Western Germany*, Beverly Hills, 1977

A. Hearnden, *Education in the Two Germanies*, Westview, 1976

E. Kolinsky, *Parties, Opposition and Society in West Germany*, London, 1984

R. Laird (ed.) *Strangers and Friends: The Franco-German Security Relationship*, London, 1989

G. Langguth, *The Green Factor in German Politics*, Boulder, 1984

H. Lippman, *Honecker and the New Politics of Europe*, London, 1973

P. C. Ludz, *The Changing Party Elite in East Germany*, Cambridge, Mass., 1972

M. McCauley, *Marxism-Leninism in the German Democratic Republic*, London, 1979

M. McCauley, *The German Democratic Republic Since 1945*, London, 1983

C. S. Maier, *The Unmasterable Past: History, Holocaust, and German Identity*, Cambridge, Mass, 1988

A. S. Markovits (ed.), *The Political Economy of West Germany*, New York, 1982

A. S. Markovits (ed.), *The Politics of the West German Trade Unions*, Cambridge, 1986

E. Moreton, *East Germany and the Warsaw Alliance: the Politics of Detente*, Boulder, 1978

S. Padgett and T. Burkett, *Political Parties and Elections in West Germany*, London, 1986

E. Papadakis, *The Green Movement in West Germany*, London, 1984

W. E. Paterson, and Gordon Smith (eds), *The West German Model, Perspectives on a Stable State*, London, 1981

G. Pridham, *Christian Democracy in Western Germany*, London, 1977

T. Prittie, *The Velvet Chancellors*, London, 1979

J. Sandford, *The Mass Media of the German-Speaking Countries*, London, 1976

G. Smith, *Democracy in West Germany*, London, 1979

J. M. Starrels and A. M. Malinckrodt, *Politics in the German Democratic Republic*, New York, 1975

K. Sontheimer and W. Bleek, *Government and Politics of East Germany*, London, 1975

J. Steele, *Socialism with a German Face*, London, 1977

R. Tilford, *The Ostpolitik and Political Change In Germany*, Farnborough, 1975

F. Vogel, *German Business after the Economic Miracle*, London, 1973

I. Wallace (ed.), *East Germany* (World Bibliographical Series Volume 77), Oxford, 1987

G. Wettig, *Community and Conflict in the Socialist Camp*, London, 1975

P. Windsor, *Germany and the Management of Detente*, London, 1971

R. Woods, *Opposition in the G D R under Honecker 1971–85*, London, 1986

## Chapters 13 and 14

D. Abenheim, *Reforging The Iron Cross*, Princeton, 1988

J. Ardagh, *Germany and the Germans*, London, 1987

D. L. Bark and D. R. Gress, *A History of West Germany, Volume 2 Democracy and its Discontents 1963–1988*, Oxford, 1989

H.-G. Betz, 'Post-Modern Anti Modernism: The West German *Republikaner*' in *Politics and Society in Germany, Austria and Switzerland*, Vol 2 No 3, Summer 1990

B. M. Blechman and C. Fisher (eds) *The Silent Partner: West Germany and Arms Control*, Cambridge, Mass., 1988

R. Burns and W. van der Will, *Protest and Democracy in West Germany*, London, 1988

D. Childs, *East Germany to the 1990s: Can it Resist Glasnost?*, London, 1987

D. Childs, *Germany on the Road to Unity*, London, 1990

D. Childs, 'East Germany's First Free Election' *Parliamentary Affairs*, October 1990

D. Childs (ed), *Honecker's Germany*, London, 1985

D. Childs, T. A. Bayliss, M. Rueschemeyer, *East Germany in Comparative Perspective*, London and New York, 1989

C. Clemens, *Reluctant Realists: the C D U/C S U and West German Ostpolitik*, Durham, N.C., 1989

M. Dennis (ed.), *The G D R Approaches the 1990s: The View from Britain*, Bakersfield, C.A., 1988

G. Edwards, *G D R Society and Social Institutions Facts and Figures*, London, 1985

M. D. Hancock, *West Germany: The Politics of Democratic Corporatism*, London, 1989

W. F. Hanrieder, *Germany, America, Europe*, New Haven, 1989

W. Hulsberg, *The German Greens*, London, 1988

I. Jeffries and M. Melzer, *The East German Economy*, London, 1987

H. Kitschelt, *The Logic of Party*

Formation: Ecological Politics in Belgium and West Germany, Ithaca, 1989

K. Koch (ed.), West Germany Today, London, 1989

E. Kolinsky, Women in West Germany, London, 1990

E. Kolinsky (ed.), The Greens in West Germany, Oxford, 1989

H. Krisch, The G D R, Boulder/London, 1985

W. Laqueur, Germany Today: A Personal Report, London, 1985

D. Marsh, The Germans Rich, Bothered and Divided, London, 1989

G. A. Mettox and J. H. Vaughan, Jr, Germany Through American Eyes, Boulder, 1989

F. R. Pfetsch, West Germany: Internal Structure and External Relations, New York, 1988

M. Rueschemeyer and C. Lemke (eds), The Quality of Life in the German Democratic Republic, New York, 1989

G. Smith, W. E. Paterson, P. Merkl (eds), Developments in West German Politics, London, 1989

W. T. Schlauch, 'Defence and Security: the S P D and East-West Relations in the 1980s' in Politics and Society in Germany, Austria and Switzerland, Vol. 3 No 1, Autumn 1990

F. Szabo (ed.), The Bundeswehr and Western Security, London, 1990

J. K. A. Thomaneck and J. Mellis, Politics, Society and Government in German Democratic Republic, Oxford, 1989

T. Wild and P. Jones (eds), De-Industrialisation and New Industrialisation in Britain and Germany, London, 1991

## Publications on Contemporary Germany for the English-speaking reader

Aussenpolitik (Hamburg)

The Economist

German Comments

German Historical Institute Bulletin

German History (Oxford University Press)

German Politics and Society (Harvard University)

German Studies Review (University of Arizona)

The German Tribune (Hamburg)

New German Critique (New York)

Politics and Society in Germany, Austria and Switzerland (Institute of German, Austrian and Swiss Affairs, University of Nottingham)

# General Index

# Index of Persons

Hitler, Adolf: acts against Röhm 66; aims in
   Europe 80, 103; alliance with Hugenberg
   55; appointed Chancellor 60; attacks
   Russia 97; biography 281; bomb plot
   against him 108–9; concludes armistice
   with Pétain 62; decides to invade Norway
   88; declares war on US 100; destroys
   Warsaw 113; Dunkirk decision 91; early
   life 35; exploits Reichstag fire 61; failure
   to withdraw 115; gets dictatorial powers
   64; greeted by Catholics 71; has Dollfuss
   killed 81; issues Directive No. 16 93; kills
   himself 117; launches last Eastern
   offensive 111; Munich Putsch 37; naval
   successes 87; negotiates with Papen 58;
   opposes Young Plan 52; orders raids on